Lecture Notes in Computer Science 4768

Commenced Publication in 1973
Founding and Former Series Editors:
Gerhard Goos, Juris Hartmanis, and Jan van Leeuwen

Lecture Notes in Computer Science

David Doermann   Stefan Jaeger (Eds.)

Arabic and Chinese Handwriting Recognition

SACH 2006 Summit
College Park, MD, USA, September 27-28, 2006
Selected Papers

 Springer

Volume Editors

David Doermann
Stefan Jaeger
University of Maryland
Institute for Advanced Computer Studies
A.V. Williams Building, College Park, MD 20742, USA
E-mail: {doermann, jaeger}@umd.edu

Library of Congress Control Number: 2008923755

CR Subject Classification (1998): I.5, H.2.4

LNCS Sublibrary: SL 6 – Image Processing, Computer Vision, Pattern Recognition, and Graphics

ISSN   0302-9743
ISBN-10   3-540-78198-6 Springer Berlin Heidelberg New York
ISBN-13   978-3-540-78198-1 Springer Berlin Heidelberg New York

Springer is a part of Springer Science+Business Media

springer.com

© Springer-Verlag Berlin Heidelberg 2008
Printed in Germany

Typesetting: Camera-ready by author, data conversion by Scientific Publishing Services, Chennai, India
Printed on acid-free paper   SPIN: 12228713   06/3180   5 4 3 2 1 0

Preface

In the fall of 2006, the University of Maryland, along with various government and industrial sponsors, invited leading researchers from all over the world to a two-day Summit on Arabic and Chinese Handwriting Recognition (SACH 2006). The event acted as a complement to the biennial Symposium on Document Image Understanding Technology (SDIUT), providing a focused glimpse into the state of the art in Arabic and Chinese handwriting recognition. It offered a forum for interaction with prominent researchers at the forefront of the scientific community and provided an opportunity for participants to help explore possible directions of the field. This book is a result of the expansion, peer review, and revision of selected papers presented at this meeting.

Handwriting recognition remains the Holy Grail of document analysis, and Arabic and Chinese scripts embrace many of the most significant challenges. We are pleased to have 16 scientific papers covering the original topics of handwritten Arabic and Chinese, as well as 2 papers covering other handwritten scripts. We asked each author to not only describe the techniques used in addressing the problem, but to attempt to identify the key research challenges and problems that the community faces. The result is an impressive collection of manuscripts that provide various detailed views of the state of research.

In this book, six articles deal directly with Arabic handwriting.

- Cheriet provides an overview of the problems of Arabic recognition and how systems can use natural language processing techniques to correct errors in lexicon-based systems.
- Suen et al. focus on Persian script, providing a historical survey of the language and techniques used in recognition.
- Belaid et al. provide a hybrid approach that attempts to take advantage of both local and global properties of the language.
- Srihari et al. focus on the problem of search, providing an image-based technique for matching words in Arabic documents.
- Abdulkader introduces language models taking advantage of Part of Arabic Words (PAWS) to aid segmentation.

With the increased interest in Arabic recognition, evaluation is of increased interest as well.

- Märgner and El Abed provide a survey of datasets and competitions that have emerged in recent years for Arabic handwriting recognition.

The history of Chinese handwriting recognition research is much longer than the research record for Arabic handwriting recognition.

- Liu provides an extensive survey of the effects of normalization and feature extraction on recognition of Chinese.
- Fujisawa explores techniques for dealing with uncertainty in the Chinese postal automation domain.
- Guo describes an approach to clustering in a coarse-to-fine hierarchical classification system.
- Chang describes techniques for dealing with the large-scale classification problems of Chinese character recognition.
- Nakagawa et al. discuss the challenges and techniques for the online Chinese character recognition problem.

To contrast techniques developed for Chinese and Arabic, several papers have been included that address cross cutting methods applied to other languages.

- Ding et al. apply a segmentation-driven approach to the recognition of both Chinese and Arabic.
- Lopresti et al. focus on word recognition using language models, introducing two new classifiers that are able to adapt for style-specific applications.
- Natarajan describes a complete segmentation-free system that uses classical Hidden Markov Models.

And finally

- Bunke et al. describe a line-level recognition system applied to handwritten English text, and
- Pal et al. describe their work on the recognition of South Indian handwritten scripts.

With this book, we tried our best to provide you with a meaningful overview of the state of the art and research trends. We sincerely hope that the challenges set forth by these authors motivate other researchers to continue to address these difficult problems.

November 2007   Stefan Jaeger
                                                                David Doermann

Table of Contents

Visual Recognition of Arabic Handwriting: Challenges and New
Directions   1
    Mohamed Cheriet

A Review on Persian Script and Recognition Techniques   22
    Sara Izadi, Javad Sadri, Farshid Solimanpour, and Ching Y. Suen

Human Reading Based Strategies for Off-Line Arabic Word
Recognition   36
    Abdel Belaïd and Christophe Choisy

Versatile Search of Scanned Arabic Handwriting   57
    Sargur N. Srihari, Gregory R. Ball, and Harish Srinivasan

A Two-Tier Arabic Offline Handwriting Recognition Based on
Conditional Joining Rules   70
    Ahmad AbdulKader

Databases and Competitions: Strategies to Improve Arabic Recognition
Systems   82
    Volker Märgner and Haikal El Abed

Handwritten Chinese Character Recognition: Effects of Shape
Normalization and Feature Extraction   104
    Cheng-Lin Liu

How to Deal with Uncertainty and Variability: Experience and
Solutions   129
    Hiromichi Fujisawa

An Efficient Candidate Set Size Reduction Method for
Coarse-Classification in Chinese Handwriting Recognition   152
    Feng-Jun Guo, Li-Xin Zhen, Yong Ge, and Yun Zhang

Techniques for Solving the Large-Scale Classification Problem in
Chinese Handwriting Recognition   161
    Fu Chang

Recent Results of Online Japanese Handwriting Recognition and Its
Applications   170
    Masaki Nakagawa, Junko Tokuno, Bilan Zhu, Motoki Onuma,
    Hideto Oda, and Akihito Kitadai

Segmentation-Driven Offline Handwritten Chinese and Arabic Script
Recognition 196
  Xiaoqing Ding and Hailong Liu

Multi-character Field Recognition for Arabic and Chinese
Handwriting... 218
  Daniel Lopresti, George Nagy, Sharad Seth, and Xiaoli Zhang

Multi-lingual Offline Handwriting Recognition Using Hidden Markov
Models: A Script-Independent Approach 231
  Prem Natarajan, Shirin Saleem, Rohit Prasad,
  Ehry MacRostie, and Krishna Subramanian

Handwritten Character Recognition of Popular South Indian Scripts.... 251
  Umapada Pal, Nabin Sharma, Tetsushi Wakabayashi, and
  Fumitaka Kimura

Ensemble Methods to Improve the Performance of an English
Handwritten Text Line Recognizer 265
  Roman Bertolami and Horst Bunke

Author Index 279

Visual Recognition of Arabic Handwriting:
Challenges and New Directions

Mohamed Cheriet

Laboratory for Imagery, Vision and Artificial Intelligence
École de Technologie Supérieure (University of Quebec)
1100 Notre-Dame West, Montreal, Quebec, Canada, H3C 1K3
mohamed.cheriet@etsmtl.ca

Abstract. Automatic recognition of Arabic handwritten text presents a problem
worth solving; it has increasingly more interest, especially in recent years. In
this paper, we address the most frequently encountered problems when dealing
with Arabic handwriting recognition, and we briefly present some lessons
learned from several serious attempts. We show why morphological analysis of
Arabic handwriting could improve the accuracy of Arabic handwriting recognition. In general, Arabic Natural Language Processing could provide some error
handling techniques that could be used effectively to improve the overall accuracy during post-processing. We give a summary of techniques concerning
Arabic handwriting recognition research. We conclude with a case study about
the recognition of Tunisian city names, and place emphasis on visual-based
strategies for Arabic Handwriting Recognition (AHR).

1 Introduction to Arabic Scripts

Arabic, one of the six United Nations official languages, is the mother tongue of more
than 300 million people [1, 14, 21]. Unlike Latin-derived writing, Arabic writing orients
from right-to-left.

Origin. A plausible hypothesis states that the Arabic scripts evolved from the Nabataean
Aramaic scripts. It has been used since the 4th century AD, but the earliest document, an
inscription in Arabic, Syriac and Greek, dates from 512 AD. The Aramaic language has
fewer consonants than Arabic, so during the 7th century new Arabic letters were created
by adding dots to existing letters to avoid ambiguities. Further diacritics indicating short
vowels were introduced, but were only used to ensure the Qur'an was read aloud without
mistakes. Two main types of written Arabic exist:

1. **Classical Arabic** - the language of the Qur'an and classical literature. It is pure
   Arabic and differs from Modern Standard Arabic mainly in style and vocabulary,
   some of which remains undefined, unknown, and implicit.

D.S. Doermann and S. Jaeger (Eds.): SACH 2006, LNCS 4768, pp. 1–21, 2008.
© Springer-Verlag Berlin Heidelberg 2008

2. **Modern Standard Arabic** - the universal language of the Arabic-speaking world understood by all its speakers. In addition to pure Arabic, it includes new foreign arabized words, scientific and technological terms. It is the Academic Language and the language of the vast majority of written material and formal TV shows, lectures, etc. MSA has a clear, well-determined vocabulary as well as explicit, well-established morphological rules and grammar rules.

Historically, the Qur'an was used intensively as a source (or reference) by linguists and grammarians to elicit vocabulary, morphological rules, and grammar. It is worth mentioning the feature of the Qur'an containing most if not all pure Arabic vocabulary, as well as all Arabic morphological and grammatical rules. However, each Arabic speaking country or region also has its own variety of colloquial Arabic. These colloquial varieties of Arabic appear in written form in some poetry, cartoons, and personal letters.

Notable Features of Modern Standard Arabic:

- As illustrated in Table 1, the Arabic alphabet contains 28 letters. Some additional letters appears for writing place names or foreign words containing sounds that do not occur in Standard Arabic, such as /p/ or /g/.

- Words are written in horizontal lines from right to left, and numerals are written from left to right.

- Most letters change form depending on whether they appear at the beginning, middle, or end of a word, or on their own.

- Letters that can be joined are always joined in both handwritten and printed Arabic. The only exceptions to this rule are crossword puzzles and signs in which the scripts is written vertically.

- The long vowels /a:/, /i:/ and /u:/ are represented by the letters 'alif, yā' and wāw, respectively.

- As shown in Figure 1, vowel diacritics, used to mark short vowels and other special symbols, appear only in the Qur'an. They are also used, though with less consistency, in other religious texts, classical poetry, children's textbooks, and by non-native language learners, and, occasionally, in complex texts to avoid ambiguity. Sometimes, the diacritics even have decorative purposes in book titles, letterheads, name places, etc.

As illustrated in Figure 1, the diacritical marks are known as "Tashkeel" (vocalization). Also, illustrated in Table 1, for some letters, dots are also placed either above or below the letter either as single dots or in groups of two or three.

Arabic language. Arabic, a Semitic language, is spoken by approximately 300 million people in 22 countries, including: Afghanistan, Iran, Saudi Arabia, Egypt, and Morocco. There are more then 30 different varieties of colloquial Arabic which include the following languages, according to the degrees of their similarities:

Table 1. Arabic Alphabet in all shapes. a) EF: End of Form b) MF: Middle of Form c) BF: Beginning of Form d) IF: Isolated Form.

Name	EF	MF	BF	IF	Name	EF	MF	BF	IF
DĀD	ض	ض	ض	ض	ALIF	ا			أ
ṬĀ	ط	ط	ط	ط	BĀ	ب	ب	ب	ب
ẒĀ	ظ	ظ	ظ	ظ	TĀ	ت	ت	ت	ت
'AYN	ع	ع	ع	ع	THĀ	ث	ث	ث	ث
GHAYN	غ	غ	غ	غ	JĪM	ج	ج	ج	ج
FĀ	ف	ف	ف	ف	ḤĀ	ح	ح	ح	ح
QĀF	ق	ق	ق	ق	KHĀ	خ	خ	خ	خ
KĀF	ك	ك	ك	ك	DĀL	د			د
LĀM	ل	ل	ل	ل	DHĀL	ذ			ذ
MĪM	م	م	م	م	RĀ	ر			ر
NŪN	ن	ن	ن	ن	ZĀY	ز			ز
HĀ	ه	ه	ه	ه	SĪN	س	س	س	س
WĀW	و			و	SHĪN	ش	ش	ش	ش
YĀ	ي	ي	ي	ي	ṢĀD	ص	ص	ص	ص

FAT-HAH	DAMMAH	KASRAH	SUKOON	SHADDA	MADDAH
ـَ	ـُ	ـِ	ـْ	ـّ	ـٓ

Fig. 1. Diacritics: Arabic marks known as "Tashkeel"

- **Algerian**- spoken by 75 million people in Algeria, Tunisia, Libya and Occidental Sahara.
- **Egyptian** - spoken by 50 million people in Egypt.
- **Moroccan/Maghrebi** - spoken in Morocco by 25 million people.
- **Sudanese** - spoken in Sudan by 25 million people.
- **Saidi** - spoken by 20 million people in Egypt.

- **North Levantine** - spoken in Palestine, Lebanon and Syria by 30 million people.

- **Mesopotamian** - spoken by 55 million people in Iraq, Iran and Syria.

- **Najdi** - spoken in Saudi Arabia, Iraq, Jordan and Syria by 35 million people.

For their utility, effectiveness, and convenience, printed and/or handwritten OCR systems are widely used in many government agencies, commercial departments, research laboratories, and libraries. After thirty years of intensive research, both printed and handwritten OCR products for most scripts (Latin, Hindi, Japanese, Korean, and Chinese) have been developed well and are available in the market.

Research in Arabic handwritten recognition began with early works by Amin [12-13]. Significant work has been done in the Arabic handwritten recognition area and several serious attempts have been undertaken to tackle the Arabic handwriting segmentation and recognition problem [1-5, 12-23].

However, despite the availability of several Arabic printed OCR products in the market, to the our best knowledge, aside from research prototypes developed for the proof of concept, no operationally accurate Arabic handwritten OCR commercial product are available in the market. Thus, an Arabic handwritten OCR system should have significant commercial value. Following the creation of Latin handwriting databases, as in [23], similar Arabic-related efforts have been devoted to the creation of Arabic handwriting databases [4-5] especially useful for training and benchmarking purposes. To date, the degree of success achieved in Arabic handwriting recognition has fallen short of the expected goal.

The rest of the paper is structured as follows: In Section 2, we exhaustively address the most encountered problems when dealing with Arabic handwriting recognition, and briefly present lessons learned from several attempts undertaken in connection with Arabic handwriting. In Section 3, in connection with the important post-processing stage, we show why, where, and how morphological analysis of Arabic characters could improve the accuracy of Arabic handwritten recognition; we also deal with Arabic Natural Language Processing (NLP), and briefly present some techniques that could contribute to improving the accuracy of Arabic handwriting recognition. Section 4 gives a brief summary of ideas and techniques to generate an Arabic lexicon. In Section 5, we present a case study: visual-based recognition strategies for AHR. In Section 6, we conclude and give some perspectives and future trends concerning computational linguistics, natural language processing and soft computing, which constitute promising Arabic handwriting recognition research.

2   Recognition Problems of Arabic Handwriting

It is widely accepted that machine segmentation and recognition of handwritten Arabic scripts presents a difficult problem. Beyond the idealized assumptions, we distinguish among three categories of difficulties. Those that are inherent to the nature and characteristics of the Arabic scripts (i.e. those that are writer independent); those that fall in the responsibility of the writer depending on Arabic writing styles and various calligraphic styles (there are more than a dozen), some are shown in Figure 2. Finally, the third category considers those induced by the quality of the scanned document, particularly for highly degraded historical documents (see Figure 3), used for some applications of real world problems.

Characteristics of the Three Categories of Difficulties for Arabic Recognition:

The first category (writer independent) includes the following characteristics:

- Context-dependency of the Arabic character shape, because each character changes its shape by the location of the characters (e.g., placed before or after other characters). So, the same character appears differently in different words, as it connects smoothly with the other characters placed in front and to the rear (see Table 1 for more details).
- Cursiveness of the Arabic characters, either printed or handwritten.
- Presence of ligatures (see Figure 4).

The second category (writer dependent) includes the following characteristics:

- Every writer has an individual writing style.
- The condition and state of the writer during writing significantly influences handwriting process.

The third category includes the following:

- Ascender and descender of consecutive lines frequently connects.
- Text often is not uniformly spaced.
- Lines may not be straight.
- Handwriting may include interferences
- Characters may touch and there may be broken (sub)words.
- Ink can fade and seep.
- The scanning process can introduce noise from the scanner bed page borders.

Given the complexity, anomalies, and inherent specificities of the Arabic handwriting, approaches and techniques used in other language contexts cannot apply directly to the context of Arabic. These difficulties make Arabic word decomposition (segmentation) in to letters very delicate and not always ensured. So, using the approach of segmentation of words into letters first, followed by recognition of the resulting characters afterwards, does not operate well for Arabic handwritten text. Consequently, many issues in Arabic handwriting still constitute important questions concerning:

- **Segmentation:** Is it mandatory? Which is more productive, to place research efforts on trying to search for novel, more sophisticated, and effective segmentation algorithms of Arabic handwritten characters or to bypass the segmentation process radically (e.g., segmentation-free)?

- **Recognition Paradigms:** Which is the appropriate approach to use for Arabic handwriting? Holistic word-based approach? Local letter-based approach (or analytical)? Or hybrid approach?

- **Recognition Techniques:** Which is the most appropriate technique: algorithm-based? Neural network-based? SVM-based? HMM-based? Symbolic-based? Expert System-based? Fuzzy-based? Possibility-based? Evidence-based? Rough set-based? Syntactic-based? Structural-based? Statistical-based? Hybrid-based?

Fig. 2. Some available Arabic calligraphic styles

- **Post-processing:** Is it more interesting to retain it as an independent stage, or to integrate it in the recognition method. What kind of knowledge is important and how and where it is more appropriate to incorporate?

- **Architecture:** This concerns the handwritten OCR system: Do we need to devise novel architectures or should we reuse and adapt, or extend traditional ones developed for other scripts or for printed Arabic scripts? Which scripts and languages with similarities to Arabic scripts and languages have accurate handwritten OCR systems?

- **Hardware/Software Implementation:** Is it more appropriate to implement the recognition system in terms of software or of a hardware chip? What is the appropriate technology? In both cases, can a compromise be found, that accounts for the environment in which the OCR systems will be deployed and integrated? Is a parallel implementation possible and feasible?

Such questions need in-depth research efforts to provide answers that influence and guide the selection, conception, design, and development of a cost-effective general purpose Arabic handwriting OCR system that satisfies the needs and requirements of users for a large application domain.

However, it seems that, in real world problems, the solution is application-dependent and no unique standard solution exists. All OCR research studies incorporate a mandatory pre-processing and low level segmentation of images to prepare them for segmentation and recognition.

Fig. 3. A sample of highly degraded historical documents

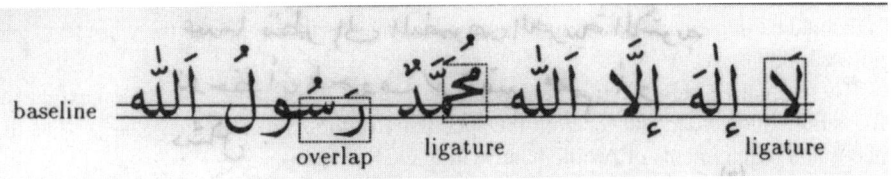

Fig. 4. Baseline, overlap, and ligatures in Arabic

3 Morphological Analysis, Natural Language Processing and Post -Processing

Traditionally, the bulk of the post-processing stage is dedicated to error handling. In this section, we will investigate the contributions and the link of both *Morphological Analysis* and *Natural Language Processing* (NLP) to post-processing, and we will try to place them appropriately in an Arabic recognition system.

Arabic is a highly inflected language1. Some errors passed in the recognition process could be corrected using a post-processing morphological analysis. Most Arabic words are derived morphologically from a list of roots. The root is the bare verb form; in most, its shape can be trilateral or quadrilateral. Most of these roots comprised of three consonants. In Arabic, patterns work as templates, adhering to well-known rules that generate nouns and verbs. Significant work has been done in the Arabic morphological analysis [5]. However, the question still remains as to where in the recognition model would be the appropriate place to use morphology. Morphological analysis could integrate within the recognition method and used effectively to fix lexical errors. It can apply also in post-processing as in traditional recognition approaches. Taking into account the size of the vocabulary, no standard solution will occur for Arabic. Thus, in connection with Arabic handwriting recognition, many questions need answers: Do we need a morphological analyser? A stemmer? Or both?

More questions exist regarding the problem of morphological analysis, for example: which approach should implement the morphological analyser? Symbolic-based (rule-based)? Statistical-based? Or a hybrid approach (rules in conjunction with statistics)?

Which approach provides the best connection with Arabic OCR, root-based? Stem-based? Which technique is the most adequate for Arabic OCR, Automata theory? Exact or approximate matching algorithms? And if we opt for a stemmer, which stemming algorithm is the most appropriate to suit the needs of Arabic OCR? n-grams based? light stemming?

Another possible solution, natural language processing (NLP) could effectively contribute to handling error correction at the Arabic phrase level. Syntax analysis, semantic analysis, and even pragmatic analysis could implement a high-level error handling for errors not caught during recognition. This application would work best in the post-processing stage. Integrating NLP within the recognition module will burden the speed of recognition and hence is not an optimal choice. Too many questions still need addressing, such as: which formalism works best to capture, represent, and handle Arabic language constructs and structures? Conceptual graphs? Semantic networks? Or definite clauses grammars (DCG)? Or another formalism?

Contextual information brings valuable information because it is application-dependent and could be implemented within the pragmatic analyser that to handle the word level and phrase level issues.

To summarize, any solution (morphological analyser, stemmer, NLP, contextual information) should account for both the specificity of the Arabic language, as well as the needs and requirements of Arabic handwriting OCR systems.

---

[1] The class of languages that append inflectional morphemes to words are called inflectional.

4 Lexicon Generation

An Arabic lexicon constitutes the heart of Arabic processing systems for specific applications. Accurate words with grammatical and semantic attributes are essential and highly desirable for OCR systems, as well as for machine translation, text understanding, text summarization, text generation, information retrieval, information extraction, tagging and text mining, etc.

Some questions consider the Lexicon Generation: do we really need a lexicon for recognition purposes? If yes, what are the pertinent attributes to include in connection with Arabic handwriting recognition? How do we build a high quality of lexicon tailored to satisfy the requirement of Arabic OCR? A lexicon may be constructed either manually or automatically. However, manual construction is labor-intensive, time-consuming, and costly. The lexicon size could influence the choice of the recognition paradigm [2].

We propose to generate automatically the Arabic dictionary from an input document-making software, using some Arabic equivalent of the WordNet software, or a computer readable dictionary. However, a semi-automatic approach might constitute a promising solution for the Arabic language.

5 Case Study: Multi-level Arabic Handwritten Word Recognition

To highlight some of the above challenging issues related to Arabic handwriting recognition, we present a case study: Recognition of Tunisian City names, developed by Miled [6-8] during his doctoral research. This application was developed as feasibility study for postal mail automation in Tunisia. We present a strategy for Arabic word recognition by *combining three perceptive levels,* based on *global, analytical and pseudo-analytical approaches*, according to the topological properties of Arabic handwriting. *In the first level (global),* we consider visual indices, which can be generated by diacritics and strokes (tracings) that form the main shapes of the word. Each word is described as a sequence of visual indices, processed by a "global" classifier based on hidden Markov models (HMM). *In the second level*, the word segments into graphemes, then each grapheme transforms into a discrete observation by a vector quantization process. An analytical HMM is developed to manage the observation sequences. At this level, the diacritics are not considered, which allows for a reduction in the number of estimated character models. **The third level**, an intermediate level, relies on the notion of Pseudo-Words or PAWs. It is modeled by HMMs, taking into account the transition probability inter-PAWS. Finally, we combine the three approaches to determine the class of an unknown word. In fact, the global model serves as a filter for the others.

Figure 5 depicts the basic idea of our strategy of the multi-level Arabic handwritten word recognition strategy, exampled (a), as well as the visual perception concept leading to our strategy as shown in (b).

These three levels will create a multi-level Arabic handwritten word recognition strategy. They will be described in detail in the following subsections, followed by our decision strategy and results.

(a)

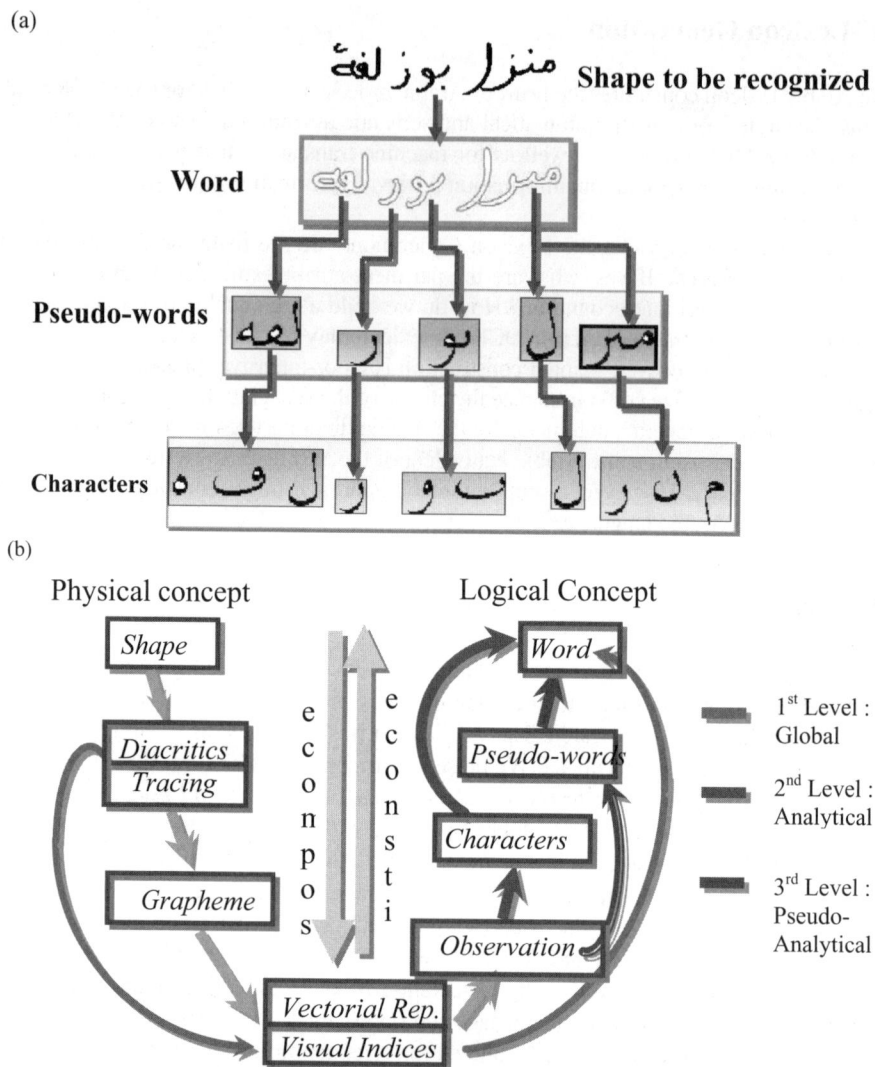

Fig. 5. Multi-level Arabic handwritten word recognition strategy: (a) The three levels; (b) Perceptual concept using top-down and Bottom-up analysis

5.1 1st Perceptive Level: Global

This approach has the goal of describing the word as a global entity by a sequence of visual indices. So, first we detect the information zones in the word. This phase is achieved by the extraction of the image's external contours. These components represent two types of image information: tracings (strokes) and diacritics, as in Figure 6.

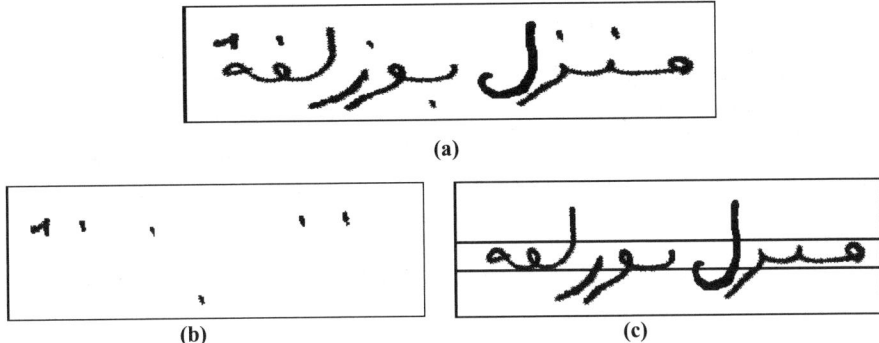

Fig. 6. Detection and separation of information zones of the image: (a) word image; (b) diacritics; (c) baseline and middle zone characters

The global level includes visual indices extraction, followed by Global Markovian Modeling.

(i) Visual Indices Extraction

We define a set of visual indices extracted from the tracing zone and the diacritics. The tracing zone contains the majority of the image information (word). The visual indices from this zone have two types, regularities and singularities [10]. The first type can group indices extracted from the middle zone: (Figure 7) loops, valleys and inter-tracing spacing (noted by "#"); the second includes the prominent features: alefs, ascenders, descenders and tanks [7-9].

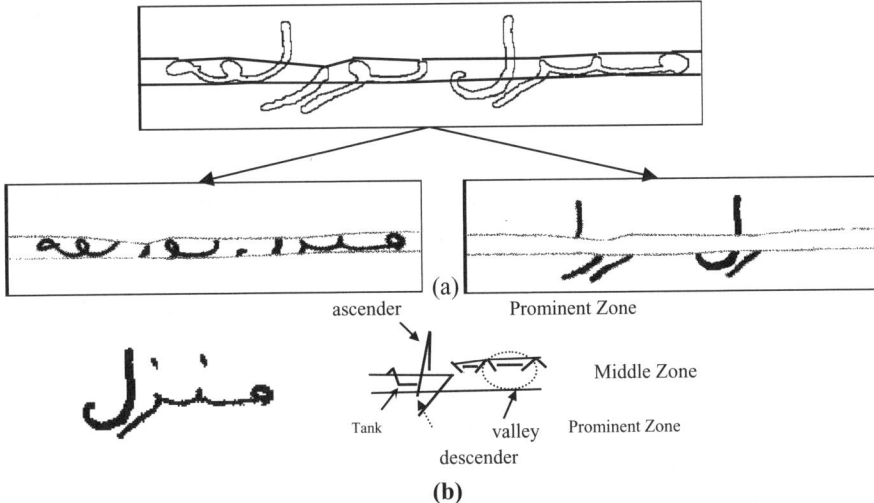

Fig. 7. Some of the Visual Indices extracted from the tracing: (a) middle zone features (left) and ascenders and descenders (right); (b) some prominent features of the word on the left

(ii) *Global Markovian Modeling*

For Global Markovian Modeling, the visual indices described above represent the set of features used in word descriptions. The words are represented by a chronological observation sequence y_1^T (visual indices, Figure 8.). The description direction follows the classical Arabic reading/writing direction, from right to left. The management of this observation sequence is based on Hidden Markov Models (HMMs).

HMMs are soft elastic models widely used in speech and handwriting recognition. This modeling tolerates variability in the writing and adapts perfectly to our type of data. The only problem rests in the relatively large lexicon (232 classes of words), and the few samples for each word class.

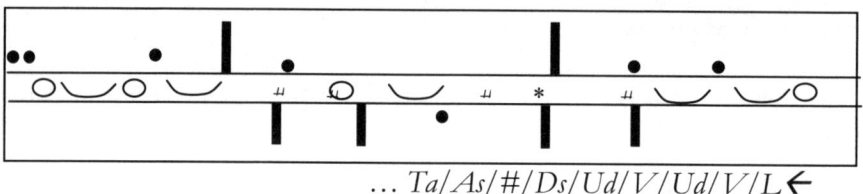

... $Ta/As/\#/Ds/Ud/V/Ud/V/L \leftarrow$

Fig. 8. Representation of the word in Figure 6. (a) as a sequence of visual indices. *As*: ascender; *Ds*: descender; *Ud:* upper-dot ; *L* : loop ; *V* : valley ; *Ta* : tank ; *#*: inter-trace spacing.

In this paper, the "global" HMM, i.e. an HMM for every word class ω_i, is noted as $\lambda_i^G = (A_i, B_i, \Pi_i)$. The models have classical right to left topologies, and they are trained by the *Baum-Welch* algorithm. At this level, we attempt to build a pre-classification module. The global HMM is trained according to the ML criterion, and called the global classifier. For each model λ_i^G of word class ω_i, it computes the associated probability $P(y_1^T / \lambda_i^G)$. The decision rule follows (1):

$$\lambda_k = \arg\max_{\lambda_i}(P(y_1^T / \lambda_i)) \tag{1}$$

Table 2 presents the performance of the global classifier, trained on 4,720 words and tested on 5,900 other words, the lexicon size N = 232 Tunisian city names.

We note the weakness of the recognition rate (τ_{reco}) in the top 1. This classifier filters to reduce the lexicon size. It selects a set of the most probable word classes, noted by Ω_G ,

Table 2. Performance of the global classifier

Ranks	top1	top2	top5	top10
τ_{reco}	58,9%	68,3%	78,2%	86,8%

5.2 2nd Perceptive Level: Analytical

In this section, we present the 2nd perceptual level: an analytical method that is the segmentation of the word tracing to small chunks, known as graphemes, followed by the description of a method called Analytical Markovian modeling.

In cursive Arabic handwriting, a tracing represents a set of characters, or portions of a character (graphemes), attached with links. To describe a word as a sequence of features, we developed a segmentation module to cut strokes into graphemes at this level.

Analytical Markovian Modeling

At this level, each grapheme is represented by a vector of the different measurements, which is used by the classifier to compare an unknown grapheme to known-ones. The decision of the observation given to each grapheme happens with a k-nearest neighbors classifier (k-NN).

The main subject of modeling is the character component. The modeling process is directly link to the segmentation phase, and does not depend on the character as a logical entity but on its shape. Based on this segmentation, we moved from a model per character to a model per family of characters (characters which have the same main body), which reduces the number of models from 30 to 18. The character model is a right-left 3 states model, and considers all possible segments of a character. The states of this model are called μ-states. The transition probabilities between the different states are estimated on the entire database.

The final model fuses the models defined earlier. Its states combine of the μ-states (from character models), encountered while tagging the training set. The associated classifier, for the second level, is also an ML, based on these HMMs for analytical word modeling. This classifier computes, for each model λ_i^A of the class ω_i (with $\omega_i \in \Omega_G$), the associated probability $P(y_1^T / \lambda_i^A)$. The decision rule is as follows (2):

$$\lambda_k = \arg\max_{\lambda_i}(P(y_1^T / \lambda_i)) \qquad (2)$$

Below, we represent words for different experiments using two sets of alphabets, perceptive and fine, and we include some experimental results.

(i) Perceptive Alphabet

Once perceptual features extracted as visual indices clustering is performed on the perceptual alphabet, leading to 18 grapheme classes are labeled from A to R :

1.   A: *alef* shown in Figure 9;

2.   B - D: graphemes with ascenders

3.   E – H : graphemes with both ascenders and descenders

4.   I – M : graphemes with descenders

5.   N – R : graphemes within the middle zone

Fig. 9. An example of a perceptual features

(ii) Fine Alphabet

For the fine alphabet, the word image segments to have fine and accurate character shapes, according to the following steps (Figure 10):

The word image $\Rightarrow$ upper contours extraction $\Rightarrow$ filtering $\Rightarrow$ detection of the Primary Segmentation Points (PSPs) $\Rightarrow$ Selection of the Decisive Segmentation Points (DSPs) $\Rightarrow$ segmentation of the word.

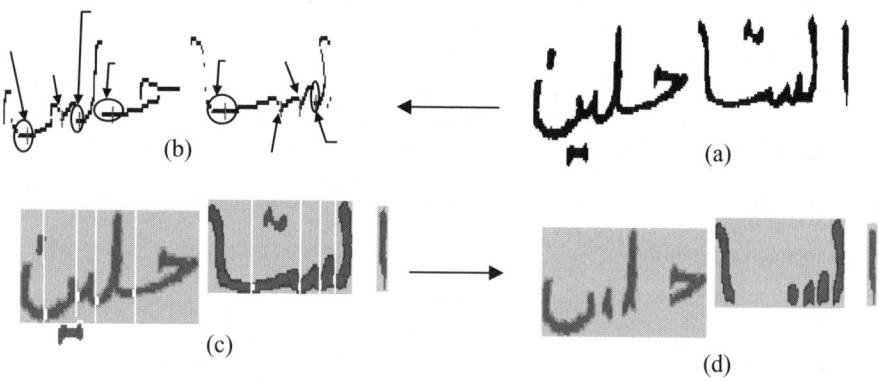

Fig. 10. Sequence of the segmentation process. (a) Original image (b) Primary segmentation points (c) Secondary segmentation points. (d) Segmentation of the word to its fundamental PAWs.

Graphemes Quantization (Statistical features)

At this stage of word preprocessing, graphemes quantization can be defined as:

- Description of each grapheme by a vector of 19 components :
  - 9 structural primitives
  - The first 10 Fourier descriptors
- grapheme labeling → supervised
- infrequent grapheme classes are eliminated

Experimental Results

This section includes the results of two experiments concerning the segmentation of words using perceptive versus fine alphabets, looking to associate graphemes with characters. For each experiment, the training set consists of 4,720 words, and the testing set consists of 5,900 words. The following tables summarize the results for each experiment:

Table 3. 1st Experiment: Perceptive alphabet (18 graphemes)

Ranks	Top1	Top2	Top3	Top5	Top10
Recognition rate	69.68%	79.29%	83.53%	87.56%	91.66%

Table 4. 2nd Experiment: Fine Alphabet

1- Graphemes selection: entropy criterion (50 graphemes)

Ranks	Top1	Top2	Top3	Top5	Top10
Recognition rate	79.54%	86.90%	89.58%	92.24%	94.75%

2- Grapheme selection: Modified K-means (50 graphemes)

Ranks	Top1	Top2	Top3	Top5	Top10
Recognition rate	81.68%	88.12%	90.46%	92.88%	94.92%

The analysis of the main recognition errors (confusions) shows that: word classes with the same handwritten main shapes that can be distinguished by diacritics are the principal cause of confusions. The experimental results show that the fine alphabet outperforms the visual one.

5.3   3rd Perceptive Level: Pseudo-Analytical

As mentioned earlier, the word is a sequence of pseudo-words, to which we apply the multi-level recognition model to extract the specific characteristics of Arabic handwriting.

A pseudo-word is a sequence of characters. The pseudo-word for a PAW model can be viewed as a concatenation of the character models composing the word (see Figure 10). The segmentation phase depends essentially on the set of bi-grams. The segmentation engine behaves in the same way each time it encounters the same bi-gram in a pseudo-word. The parameter of interest is the probability of segmentation by bi-grams. These probabilities can be computed over the entire database.

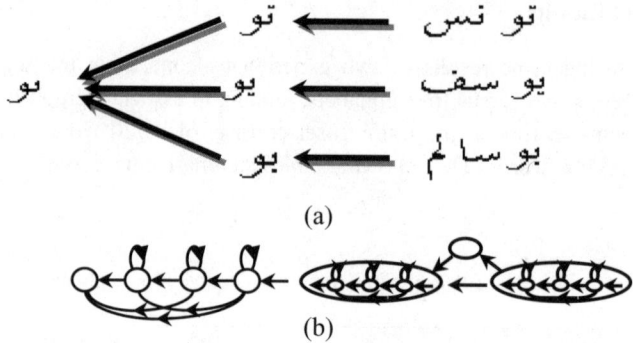

(a)

(b)

Fig. 11. Pseudo-Words or PAWs modelling. (a) the shape in the left is a common PAW (without diacritics) for three different words (on the right). (b) HMM modelling of PAWs.

Experimental Results

This section includes the results of three experiments concerning the segmentation of words using the pseudo-word or PAW concept. For each experiment, the training set consists of 4,720 words, and the testing set consists of 5,900 words. The following tables summarize the results for each experiment:

1st Experiment

Figure 12 shows the experimental results on the same sets of data as above, with a superiority of using strategy **(A):** the modeling of PAWs compared to the strategy in **(B)** the global modeling.

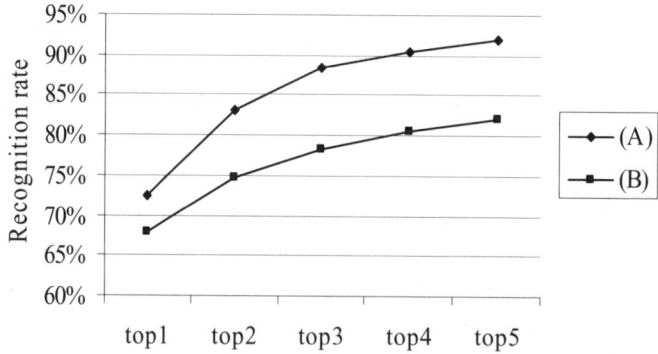

Fig. 12. Performance Comparison on the test set between the Global and Pseudo-Analytical modeling: (A) Pseudo-analytical (B) Global

The following tables summarize the experimental results using different alphabets (perceptive and fine) for sub-word or PAW representation.

Table 5. 2nd Experiment: Perceptive alphabet

1- Graphemes selection: Entropy Criterion (50 graphemes)

Ranks	Top1	Top2	Top3	Top5	Top10
Recognition rates	69.3%	79.6%	85.3%	90.1%	94.7%

2- Modified K-means: unsupervised (50 graphemes)

Ranks	Top1	Top2	Top3	Top5	Top10
Recognition rates	70.8%	79.9%	84.4%	89.5%	93.5%

Table 6. 3rd Experiment: Fine Alphabet (50 graphemes)

Ranks	Top1	Top2	Top3	Top5	Top10
Recognition rates	72.5%	83.0%	87.4%	92.1%	95.8%

The analysis of the main recognition errors shows that: word classes with the same handwritten main shapes that can be distinguished by diacritics are the principal cause of confusion. The experimental results show that the fine alphabet outperforms the visual one as in analytical modeling.

5.4 Decision Strategy and Results

The strategy of recognition of the unknown word has three levels (see Figure 13). Each level is a Maximum Likelihood (ML) classifier, and takes the unknown pattern (noted by x below) as a sequence of observations $y_1^T = (y_1, y_2, ..., y_T)$, presenting visual indices in one level and graphemes in the other.

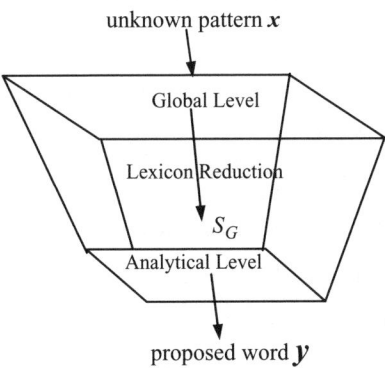

unknown pattern x

Global Level

Lexicon Reduction

S_G

Analytical Level

proposed word y

Fig. 13. Combination of the two level classifiers: x is the unknown word and y is the decision

Below, we summarize the performances of individual classifiers and as a combination of 2 by 2 classifiers:

Table 7. Summary of each perceptual classifier's performance

	top 1	top 5
τ_{reco}_Global 9 VI	58,9%	78,2%
τ_{reco}_Analytical 23 shapes	72,5%	92,0%
τ_{reco}_PseudoAnalytical 23 shapes	81,8%	90,5%

Table 8. 2-2 Classifiers' Combination: Performance

(a) Pseudo-Analytical with Analytical Modeling

	top1	top5
Pseudo-Analytical	72.5%	92.0%
Analytical	81.8%	90.5%
Product of measures	**86.4%**	**94.4%**

(b)   Global with Analytical Modeling

	top1	top5
Global	58.9%	78.2%
Analytical	81.8%	90.5%
Product of measures	**87.2%**	**95.5%**

We use two methods of combination:

In the first method, we considered the two levels of the system as independent. The first level filters the word classes to obtain a set of candidates for the second level, without any other information. The word is assigned to the class ω_k ($y = \omega_k$), for which the model λ_k^A maximizes the emission probability of y_I^T by the second level (the analytical classifier), as follows (3):

$$\lambda_k^A = \arg\max_{\lambda_i^A} P(y_1^T / \lambda_i^A) \; with \; \lambda_i^A \; model \; of \; the \; class \; \omega_i \in \Omega_G \tag{3}$$

The second method employs the stochastically independent assumption of the classifiers, as in Figure 13. The global classifier gives a set of candidates with their maximum likelihoods. A score S_i^{comb} assigns to each candidate $\omega_i \in \Omega_G$, and this score is equal to $P(y_1^T / \lambda_i^G, \lambda_i^A)$. Using the classifiers' independence assumption, we can simplify the computation of the score of each candidate (4):

$$S_i^{comb} \approx P(y_I^T / \lambda_i^G).P(y_I^T / \lambda_i^A) \tag{4}$$

Finally, the word is assigned to the class ω_k ($y = \omega_k$), which maximizes the score after the combination of two classifiers (5):

$$k = \arg\max_i S_i^{comb} \quad with \quad S_i^{comb} \ of \ the \ class \ \omega_i \tag{5}$$

The performances of the first combination method are optimum (85% in top 1) for a size of Ω_G, $N_G = 40$, and they decrease for higher values of N_G. However, the performances of the second combination method are optimal (87% in top 1) for a value of N_G superior to 100 filtered candidates, and they remain relatively constant for higher values of N_G.

Although the results need to be refreshed on the IFN database [4], the proposed approach stresses the complementary role that classifiers play in perceptual level modeling, especially if they are empowered with recent advanced performing methods such as: NN-HMMs, Kernel-based methods (SVMs), and Generative/Discriminative Hybrids. Furthermore, and following the outline of this paper, linguistic information and knowledge domains might be exploited and further incorporated into the recognition engine. For instance, this information can use the a priori probability of city names: a higher probability exists that "Tunis" will occur more frequently than a smaller city name. From this case study, one may possess good clues to tackle other Arabic texts and handwritings.

6 Concluding Remarks

We have addressed the major problems and raised issues that constitute challenges for the effective conception, design and development of Arabic handwritten OCR systems. This study has allowed us to determine, capture, and define "good" functional and non-functional requirements to engineer, in order to build a coherent and versatile implementation of an operational high-adaptability and high-accuracy Arabic Handwritten OCR system. If we develop a viable and generic solution, it will be a building block toward developing operational multilingual OCR systems. In addition to further analysis and understanding of the recognition of Arabic handwriting problems, we will consider a compromised solution with design trade-offs and consideration for due specificity of Arabic scripts and language and increased OCR performance, accuracy, robustness, and adaptability.

The basics of computational linguistics presents an open problem that could benefit accuracy and adaptability without affecting the efficiency of recognition. We believe Arabic computational linguistics will effectively address these challenges. Computational linguistics are crucial to the success of intelligent OCR systems.

Our other purpose was to present the effect of perceptual analysis on designing classifiers and combines them to increase the overall system performance. Visual processing of handwriting will bring greater improvement to this technology, given prior knowledge and knowledge domains. In general, we believe that software architecture of an OCR system, either for printed text or handwritten Arabic or not holds, paramount importance. In particular, we plan to investigate the applicability of soft computing to Arabic handwritten recognition, [2, 25-28]. We propose to explore the possible joint contribution of Arabic computational linguistics, Arabic NLP, and granular soft computing in building novel architectures for Arabic handwritten recognition. Cursive Latin handwriting might also be handled in a similar manner, thus, opening the opportunity for multi-lingual OCR using the same framework. Such hybridization becomes crucial to the success of OCR systems and definitely opens an interesting and highly promising research area.

Acknowledgments. This paper relates to our recently published works [1,2], and more importantly, we are indebted to the team involved, especially for works in [2, 7-9].

References

1. Cheriet, M.: Strategies for Visual Arabic Handwriting Recognition. Issues and Case Study. In: IEEE Int. Conference on Signal Processing and Applications, Sharjah (UAE) (2007) (invited paper)
2. Cheriet, M., Beldjehem, M.: Visual Processing of Arabic Handwriting: Challenges and New Directions. In: Summit on Arabic and Chinese Handwriting (SACH 2006), Washington-DC, pp. 129–136 (2006) (invited paper)
3. Belaid, A., Choisy, C.: Human Reading Based Strategies Off-line Arabic Word Recognition. In: Summit on Arabic and Chinese Handwriting (SACH 2006), Washington-DC, USA, pp. 137–144 (2006) (invited paper)
4. Magner, V., El Abed, H.: Databases and Competitions – Strategies to improve Arabic Recognition Systems. In: Summit on Arabic and Chinese Handwriting (SACH 2006), Washington-DC, pp. 145–153 (2006) (invited paper)
5. Al-Ohali, Y., Cheriet, M., Suen, C.Y.: Databases for Recognition of Handwritten Arabic cheques. Journal of Pattern Recognition 36, 111–121 (2003)
6. Al-Sughaiyer, I.A., Al-Kharashi, I.A.: Arabic Morphological Analysis Techniques. Journal of the American Society for Inf. Sc. and Tech. 55(3), 189–213 (2004)
7. Miled, H.: Stratégies de résolution en reconnaissance de l'écriture semi-cursive: Application aux mots manuscrits arabes. PhD thesis, PSI-La3i UnivRouen, LIVIA ETS, Montreal (1998)
8. Miled, M., Olivier, C., Cheriet, M., Lecourtier, Y.: Coupling observation/letter for a Markovian modeling applied to the recognition of Arabic handwriting. In: Proc. ICDAR, Ulm, Germany, pp. 580–583 (1997)
9. Miled, H., Cheriet, M., Olivier, C.: Multi-level Arabic Handwritten Words Recognition. In: Proc. SSPR/SPR, pp. 944–951 (1998)
10. JSimon, J.C., Baret, O.: Handwriting recognition as an application of regularities and singularities in line pictures. In: Proc. of IWFHR, Montreal, pp. 23–36 (1990)
11. Hani, A., et al.: Deterministic and nondeterministic flow-chart interpretations. JASIS 50(6), 524–529 (1999)
12. Adnan, A., et al.: Handwritten Arabic Character recognition by the IRAC system. In: Proc. Int. Conf. on Pattern Recognition, Miami, pp. 729–731 (1980)
13. Adnan, A., et al.: Recognition of Handwritten Arabic Scripts and Sentences. In: Proc. ICPR, Montreal, (2), pp. 1055–1057 (1984)
14. Al-Badr, B., Mahmoud, S.: Survey and bibliography of Arabic Optical text recognition. Signal Processing 41, 49–77 (1995)
15. Al-Emami, S., Usher, M.: On-line recognition of handwritten Arabic characters. IEEE Trans. PAMI 12(7), 704–710 (1990)
16. Almuallim, H., Yamaguchi, S.: A method for recognition of Arabic cursive handwriting. IEEE Trans. PAMI 9(5), 715–722 (1987)

17. Souici-Meslati, L.L., Sellami, M.: A Hybrid Neuro-Symbolic Approach for Arabic Hand-written Word Recognition. JACII 10(1), 17–25 (2006)
18. Souici-Meslati, L., Farah, N., Sari, T., Sellami, M.: Rule Based Neural Networks Construction for Handwritten Arabic City-Names Recognition. In: Bussler, C.J., Fensel, D. (eds.) AIMSA 2004. LNCS (LNAI), vol. 3192, pp. 331–340. Springer, Heidelberg (2004)
19. Al-sheikh, T.S., El-Taweel, T.S., S.G.: Real-time Arabic handwritten character recognition. Journal of Pattern Recognition 23(12), 1323–1332 (1990)
20. Abuhaiba, S.I., Ahmed, P.: Restoration of temporal information in off-line Arabic handwriting. Journal of Pattern Recognition 26(7), 1009–1017 (1993)
21. Abuhaiba, I.S.I., Mahmoud, S.A., Green, R.J.: Recognition of Handwritten Cursive Arabic Characters. IEEE Trans. PAMI 16(6), 664–672 (1994)
22. Mahmoud, S.A., Abuhaiba, S.I., Green, R.J.: Skeletonization of Arabic characters using clustering based skeletonization algorithm (CBSA). Journal of Pattern Recognition 24(5), 453–464 (1991)
23. Pechwitz, M., Snoussi-Maddouri, S., Margner, V., Ellouze, N., Amiri, H.: IFN/ENIT database of handwritten Arabic words. In: Proc. Colloque Francophone International sur l'Écrit et le Document, Hammamet, pp. 129–136 (2002)
24. Hull, J.J.: A Database for handwritten text recognition research. IEEE Trans. PAMI 16, 550–554 (1994)
25. Zadeh, L.A.: The Roles of Fuzzy Logic and Soft Computing in the Conception, Design, and Development of Intelligent Systems. In: Nwana, H.S., Azarmi, N. (eds.) Software Agents and Soft Computing: Towards Enhancing Machine Intelligence. LNCS, vol. 1198, pp. 183–190. Springer, Heidelberg (1997)
26. Zadeh, L.A.: Soft Computing, Fuzzy Logic and Recognition Technology. In: Proc. IEEE Int. Conf. Fuzzy Systems, Anchorage, AK, pp. 1678–1679 (1998)
27. Zadeh, L.A.: Some Reflections on Soft Computing, Granular Computing and their Roles in the Conception, Design and Utilization of Information/Intelligent Systems. Soft Computing 2, 23–25 (1998)
28. Beldjehem, M., Cheriet, M.: Validation and Verification of Hybrid Min-Max Fuzzy Systems. In: Proc. North American Fuzzy Information Processing (NAFIPS 2006), Montreal, Canada (2006)

A Review on Persian Script and Recognition Techniques

Sara Izadi, Javad Sadri, Farshid Solimanpour, and Ching Y. Suen

Center for Pattern Recognition and Machine Intelligence (CENPARMI)
1455 de Maisonneuve Blvd. West, Suite EV003.403
Montreal, Quebec, Canada, H3G 1M8
{s_izadin,j_sadri,f_solima,suen}@cs.concordia.ca

Abstract. This paper presents the history of the Persian (Farsi) script, as well as the development of different writing styles for the current Persian script. It also addresses the Arabic alphabet adopted and evolved for writing the Persian language as well as different writing styles. This evolution includes further extensions to the Arabic alphabet and altered shapes of some Arabic letters. The differences between current Arabic and Persian handwritings for automated recognition purposes are discussed. A short review on techniques in Persian script recognition is presented, and the shortcomings and challenges in this area are highlighted.

1 Introduction

The current Persian script, also known as Perso-Arabic script, is an important variant form of the Arabic alphabet. Persian and its dialects have official language status in Iran, Afghanistan, and Tajikistan. Persian is also spoken by minorities in Uzbekistan, Turkmenistan, Azerbaijan, Armenia, Georgia, and Southern Russia. Although commonly thought as Persian and Arabic sharing the same alphabet and writing styles, minor yet important differences in their alphabets and their styles of writing differentiate these two scripts. While the necessity exists of having automated script recognition-related applications to serve a large population, this domain has not attracted much attention internationally, remaining the focus of mostly Iranian journals and conferences. Therefore, this paper aims at providing more information about this area of research.

This paper is organized as follows: Section 2 briefly reviews the Persian script history and how the Arabic alphabet replaced the previous Persian alphabet. The creation and the evolution of different writing styles for Arabic and its variants, as well as the relation between those writing styles and the current Persian and Arabic, are given in Section 3. The Persian script had, in turn, branched into other scripts in the neighboring regions, as discussed in Section 4. Characteristics shared among Arabic and other scripts that adopted Arabic are explained in Section 5. More detailed features of the Persian alphabet, digits, and handwriting styles are provided in Section 6. Sections 7-9 review some existing Persian script recognition methods. Finally, Section 10 highlights the challenges with concluding remarks.

D.S. Doermann and S. Jaeger (Eds.): SACH 2006, LNCS 4768, pp. 22–35, 2008.

2   Persian Script Evolution

The Arabic script has been adopted widely for use in many languages including Persian. This section reviews the history of Persian script before and after its adoption of the Arabic alphabet. Throughout three prominent periods, the Persian alphabet evolved [1]. These periods and the transition from one period to another are discussed in this section.

Ancient Persian script was a semi-alphabetic cuneiform script written from left to right. Old Persian script was invented around 525 BC, and consisted of three vowel signs, 33 consonant signs, eight logograms[1], a sign to mark the end of words (word separator), and numeral signs. The consonant signs are syllabic, i.e., they denote a consonant plus a vowel. Figure 1(a) shows some of those signs.

Transformation of the Persian language from the synthetic form of the Old Period to an analytic form of Middle Persian occurred in the third century B.C. Middle Persian or Pahlavi is known mainly from the official inscriptions of the "Sasanian" Empires and Zoroastrian literature. Pahlavi was a complicated writing system read from right to left in horizontal lines. Often, letters formed complicated ligatures. The Pahlavi alphabet and some ligatures are shown in Figure 1(b). In Pahlavi, vowels had multiple pronunciations, and only some vowels were indicated in writing. This explains Pahlavi's complications, despite attempts at improvement made in its later forms.

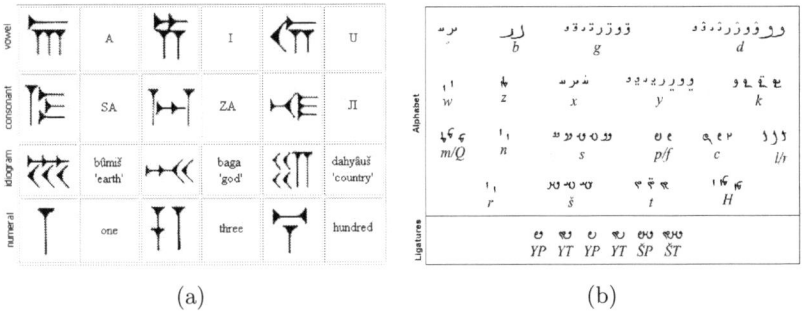

(a)   (b)

Fig. 1. (a) Some symbols of Old Persian script alphabet, (b) Middle Persian alphabet and ligatures

The third period began with the Sassanian dynasty's fall to Arabs in the seventh century. For the next 300 years, Pahlavi script was actively used. Pahlavi was eventually replaced by an alphabet derived from Arabic partially because of the difficulty in reading and writing Pahlavi. The modern Persian alphabet, in use today, is a variation of the Arabic alphabet.

---

[1] Ideograms or logograms are signs that represent a whole word.

3 Development of a Writing System for Modern Persian

While variability of writing styles presents as a major challenge for handwriting recognition systems of all scripts, it holds greater importance for Arabic and its variant forms: as shapes of the letters, proportion of their constructing parts, and their connectivity to other letters can vary. Considering that measurements of geometrical characteristics of handwriting samples, such as curviness or proportions, provide guidance for segmentation or classification in many methodologies, styles can have a large impact on the recognition system functionality.

The styles of Arabic and Persian writing have undergone many changes. The writing styles for the Arabic script in the seventh century were limited to two styles. The first standardization of writing styles occurred in the tenth century. At the same time, six major writing styles were developed that became the basis for developing other writing styles. During this time, more writing styles evolved, and particular writing styles had general appeal for writing Persian and Arabic. A quick review can shed light on why some Persian and Arabic characters do not appear the same, and some connections of the letters of words also differ in today's normal handwriting.

At the start of the Islamic era, people used two types of Arabic scripts: A rounded script called "Naskh", considered unsophisticated, was used for quick writing and secular purposes. The other, a square and angular script called "Kufic" was used to inscribe and copy the Koran. After adopting the Arabic alphabet for Modern Persian writing, Iranian calligraphists, skilled in the rounded Pahlavi script calligraphy, soon set themselves the task of beautifying the new script.

The most outstanding calligraphist of the tenth century (Ibn Muqla, tenth century) distinguished the need for rules of proportion common to any given letter in any script, and systematized the writing of the proliferating variants of cursive Arabic calligraphy. Letters were given precise measurements for their vertical, horizontal, and curved strokes. It is the proto-style for most of today's styles [2]. This system uses the dot as a measuring unit for line proportions, and a circle, with a diameter equal to the Alef's[2] height, as a measuring unit for letter proportions as seen in Figure 2(a).

From the tenth century, calligraphers abandoned the primitive and defective Kufic style, while the Naskh style improved and became one of the legible "six cursive styles"[3] pioneered by IbnMuqla [3]. The famous "six styles" became stable styles in which the height of the alef varied from three to twelve dots[4]. Naskh reached the height of its development in the 12th century and became the style for text, Korans, and ordinary Arabic correspondence. Riq'a, a later style, is popular today for everyday writing in Arabic. Constructed from short strokes and subtle pen motions, Riq'a is easier to write than others styles [8]. The Ta'liq

---

[2] Alef, a straight vertical stroke, is the first letter of the Persian and Arabic alphabets.

[3] The six cursive scripts are: Thuluth, Naskh, Muhaqqaq, Rihani, Riq'a, and Tawqi.

[4] For example, the Alef is five dots high in Naskh. In Thuluth style, the Alef is nine dots high with a crochet or hook of three dots at the top.

Fig. 2. (a) The basic measuring system for Arabic script[4], (b) The letter Ein written in Nasta'liq style on the left and Naskh style on right. The small circle indicates half-point.

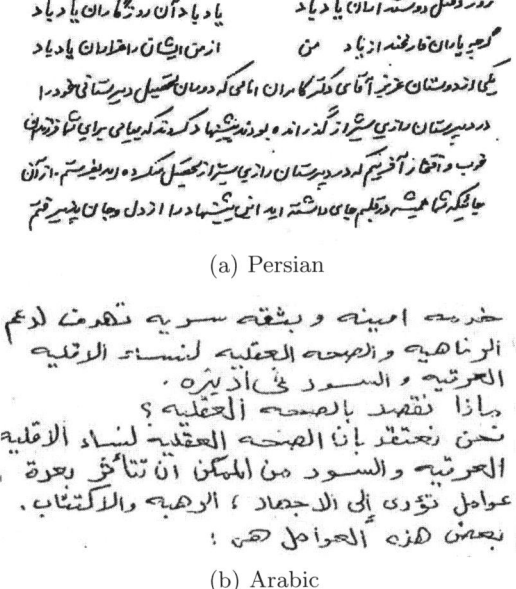

(a) Persian

(b) Arabic

Fig. 3. Samples of normal handwriting in Modern Persian in Nasta'liq style and Arabic

style designed in the tenth century in Iran, addressed the needs of the Persian language. The exaggerated round forms and elongated horizontal strokes that characterized the delicate Ta'liq style were used widely for royal as well as daily correspondence until the 14th century when Ta'liq was replaced by Nasta'liq. Nasta'liq was the predominant style of Persian calligraphy during the 15th and 16th centuries. It has short verticals with no serifs and long horizontal strokes. This unique script must never be written with diacritical vowels [5]. Nasta'liq style has rarely been used for writing Arabic, but has been extremely popular for Persian since its development. "Shekasteh Nasta'liq" succeeds Nasta'liq, and is also currently in use in Iran. Figure 2(b) shows a letter written in Nasta'liq and Naskh and their corresponding measuring dots written by calligraphic pens. The differences in the proportions of the letter's upper curve and the lower curve's tail can be observed. Two samples, written in Persian and Arabic, compare Nasta'liq and Naskh, shown in Figure 3.

4 Modern Persian Script Propagation

The modern Persian script and its most well-known writing style, Nasta'liq, have propagated within many languages having added further extensions to the Persian alphabet. This happened mainly when Persian was the court language of the Mughal empire during their ruling over the Indian subcontinent (1526-1707). The Persian script and Nasta'liq writing style propagated what is now known as Pakistan, India, and Bangladesh, even parts of China, south Asia, and Java. Versions of Nasta'liq serve as the preferred style for writing Pashto and Urdu, the official languages of Afghanistan and Pakistan. In Indian cities with large Urdu-speaking populations, such as Hyderabad and Lakhnaustill, people employ the Nasta'liq style for writing Urdu language. In Table 1, languages written in different forms of the Perso-Arabic script are shown. Among these languages, all the Indian and Turkic ones tended to use the Perso-Arabic script. All of these scripts have rooted from Arabic, therefore have some characteristics in common which are discussed in the following section.

Table 1. Languages that adopted the Perso-Arabic script

Persian	Azari	Uzbek	Sindhi	Kashmiri
Panjabi	Baluchi	Brahui	Urdu	Tajik
Pashto	Dari	Kirghiz	Kurdish	Uyghur

5 Arabic Script and Its Variants' Characteristics

All derived scripts from Arabic are cursive. Therefore, word segmentation is challenging for them. In Arabic script and its variant forms, several letters share the same basic form and differ only by a small complementary part (mostly dots). Letters may take as many as four shapes, depending on their position in the word and the preceding letter in the word. Some letters connect only to the previous letter in the word, creating sub-words if they appear in the middle of the word.

6 Persian Alphabet, Digits, and Writing System

The Persian alphabet has four letters which do not exist in the Arabic alphabet, representing phonemes that Arabic phonology does not have. Some Arabic vowel signs (sukuun, fatHatain, kasratain, Dammatain, hamzat, madda) do not occur in Persian. Two letters omit their dots in Persian. Figure 5 shows some characters, or a combination of character and vowel sign, that never appear

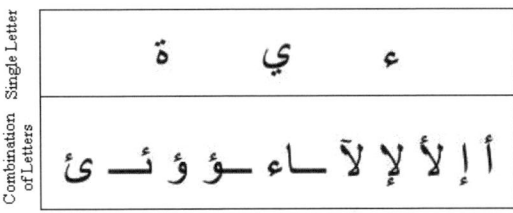

Fig. 4. Combination of letters and vowel signs that exist in Arabic, but not Persian

Isolated	Initial	Medial	Final	Roman	Name	Isolated	Initial	Medial	Final	Roman	Name
ا	ا	ـا	ـا	á	alef	ص	ـصـ	ـصـ	ـص	ş	sád
ب	ـبـ	ـبـ	ـب	b	be	ض	ـضـ	ـضـ	ـض	d	zád
پ	ـپـ	ـپـ	ـپ	p	pe	ط	ط	ـطـ	ـط	ţ	tá
ت	ـتـ	ـتـ	ـت	t	te	ظ	ظ	ـظـ	ـظ	z	zá
ث	ـثـ	ـثـ	ـث	th	se	ع	ـعـ	ـعـ	ـع	'	ayn
ج	ـجـ	ـجـ	ـج	j	jim	غ	ـغـ	ـغـ	ـغ	gh	ghayn
چ	ـچـ	ـچـ	ـچ	ch	che	ف	ـفـ	ـفـ	ـف	f	fe
ح	ـحـ	ـحـ	ـح	h	he	ق	ـقـ	ـقـ	ـق	q	qáf
خ	ـخـ	ـخـ	ـخ	kh	khe	ک	ک	ـکـ	ـک	k	káf
د	د	ـد	ـد	d	dál	گ	گ	ـگـ	ـگ	g	gáf
ذ	ذ	ـذ	ـذ	dh	zál	ل	ـلـ	ـلـ	ـل	l	lám
ر	ر	ـر	ـر	r	re	م	ـمـ	ـمـ	ـم	m	mím
ز	ز	ـز	ـز	z	ze	ن	ـنـ	ـنـ	ـن	n	nún
ژ	ژ	ـژ	ـژ	zh	zhe	و	و	ـو	ـو	v/ú	váv
س	ـسـ	ـسـ	ـس	s	sin	ه	ـهـ	ـهـ	ـه	h	he
ش	ـشـ	ـشـ	ـش	sh	shin	ی	ـیـ	ـیـ	ـی	y/í	ye

Fig. 5. Four different shapes of letters in the Persian alphabet

in Persian. Persian letters and their variant shapes (detached, initial, medial, and final) appear in Figure 5. This characteristic of Persian and Arabic letters increases the effective size of the alphabet from 32 letters to 114. Persian numerals form 13 classes, and Arabic handwritten digits normally form 11 classes [9]. In Nasta'liq style characters rest on an equal line distribution borrowed from the Naskh and curves borrowed from the Ta'liq. The axis of the letters is tilted slightly backwards, as Figure 6 shows. In the Nasta'liq, as in other styles, the letters are proportioned using point-measurement. In Nasta'liq, the same letter is presented in several forms. Not only according to its place in the word, as it is the rule with the Arabic alphabet, but also according to aesthetic alternatives. The alternatives might be used according to the shapes of the

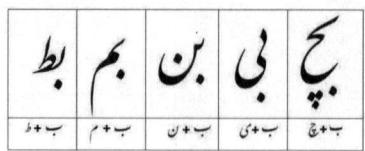

Fig. 6. Letter Ein written in Nasta'liq style [7]

Fig. 7. Combination of two letters written in Nasta'liq style. The first letter is the same in all five examples.

surrounding letters. The most remarkable alternatives happen when certain letters stretch, in which horizontal features lengthen up to 9 or 11 points [7]. Moreover, the shape of the character, even in the fixed position of the word, may change with relation to the next characters, as shown in Figure 6 for a two letter combination. Although the first letter is the same, it does not look the same when connected to different letters.

7   Offline Persian Recognition

Like other scripts, the architecture of Persian script recognition consists of pre-processing, segmentation, recognition, and verification modules. Pre-processing facilitates recognition and may include image processing operations, such as binarization, noise reduction, smoothing, filling, or image transformations such as normalization. Segmentation tries to find connected or touching digits and separates them by introducing segmentation paths. For recognition, a classifier assigns class labels and corresponding confidence values to the segmented digits. Verification is an optional module that approves the decisions made by the recognizer, and it tries to reduce the error rate.

The research in Persian script recognition began in 1980, when a system for machine printed Persian text was developed ([11], [12]). This section briefly reviews some research efforts for offline Persian script recognition.

7.1   Pre-processing and Segmentation

Preprocessing in offline recognition usually includes noise removal, slant/skew correction, size normalization, and contour or skeleton extraction. For word recognition, base line extraction is included in the preprocessing stage. A method for segmentation of handwritten numeral strings in Persian is presented in [10]. Combining foreground and background features and global information from the string image, this method finds segmentation paths to separate the touched digits. In this method, after extracting the skeleton of each connected component, the points of minimum and maximum x coordinate are selected as starting and ending points. The skeleton is then traversed from starting point in clockwise and counter-clockwise directions until both reach the end point. While traversing, at the visited intersection points (points with more than two connected

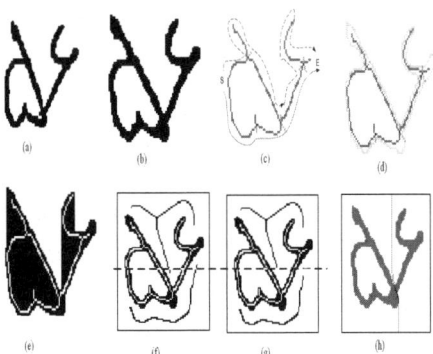

Fig. 8. (a) Original image of touching digits 5 and 6, (b) Pre-processed image , (c) Skeleton traversals from S to E in clockwise: dashed arrows, and counter-clockwise: dotted arrows, direction (d) Mapping of intersection points on the outer contour by bisectors to form foreground-features, (e) Background region, (f) Top/Bottom background skeletons, (g) Top/Bottom-background-skeletons after removing parts that are lower/higher than the middle line, (h) Cutting path for separating 5 and 6.

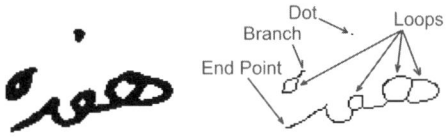

Fig. 9. (a) Original, (b) Structural features shown for the "skeleton" image extracted using the algorithm presented in [13]

branches) foreground feature points are located. Foreground feature points are denoted as the intersection of the bisector of the two branches with the contour of the connected component. In the next step, the skeleton of the background (white pixels) of a connected component is found, and all end points in the background skeleton are extracted (points that have one black neighbor), and they are denoted as background features. The foreground and background feature points are assigned alternatively to construct all possible segmentation paths. The resulting images of those stages are depicted in Figure 7.

8   Feature Extraction

Instead of being handled directly, the samples are usually mapped to the feature space for a summarized, yet comprehensive representation. In other words, by feature extraction, we choose sample information and deliver it to the classifier. Structural features, such as loops, branch-points, endpoints, and dots, are based on the innate aspects of writing. To compute these features, the skeleton of the text image should be extracted, as shown in Figure 7. Methods are categorized using the feature types: structural features, and statistical features. One reason that structural features are more common for the recognition of Persian scripts than Latin scripts is because the primary shapes of many Persian letters are alike, with only the number and locations of their dots differing. Therefore, to differentiate such letters, structural features capture dot information explicitly. Some systems that recognize Persian digits based on structural features are listed in Table 2. Statistical features are numerical measures, computed over the images or regions of the images. Some examples of statistical features include pixel densities, histograms of chain code directions, moments, and Fourier descriptors. Outer profiles, projection histograms, and crossing counts are employed in [14], and [17]. Some systems using statistical features appear with a short description in Table 3.

Table 2. Summary of research that used structural features for Persian script recognition

Research	Pre-Processing	Classifier(s)	Database	Recognition Rate
[14]	Thinning	MLP-NN	Private Persian Digits 4800 Samples 10 Classes	94.44%
[15]	Thinning	SVM & RBF Kernel	Private Persian Chars 3200 Samples 20 Classes	96.92%

9   Persian Online Recognition

In online handwriting recognition, the process of automatic recognition occurs while a person writes. Online handwriting recognition systems deal with handwriting captured by a digitizer. The electronic tablet is a typical capturing device, which contains a pointing device (usually a pen) and a sensing device. Online handwriting recognition can be used with tablet PCs, hand-held computers, personal digital assistants (PDA's), smart phones, etc. There is a comprehensive review of digitizing technology in [23]. The movement of the pen is sensed at equal time or distance intervals. A software application usually records the spatial position and the indications of pen-up/pen-down switching.

Dynamic or temporal information presents the main difference between the online and offline data. It addresses the number and order of strokes. A typical online recognition system consists of the main blocks mentioned in Section 7. Here, the research in online Persian recognition is explained given this general pattern recognition system.

Preprocessing in online handwriting recognition usually includes smoothing, data reduction, normalization and de-hooking. So far, there have been few efforts in segmentation for online Persian script. By thresholding on a change of the angle along the trajectory isolated characters were segmented in [24]. A loop detection method was added in [25] to enhance the result of segmentation.

Table 3. Summary of research that used statistical features for Persian script recognition

Research	Pre-Processing	Feature(s)	Classifier	Database	Recog. Rate
[16]	None	Projection Histogram Outer Profiles Crossing Counts Size	SVM RBF & Polynomial Kernels	Private Persian Digits 9000 Samples	Polynomial: 99.44% RBF: 99.57%
[17]	None	Projection Histogram Outer Profiles Crossing Counts	SVM & RBF Kernel	CENPARMI Persian Digits 8000 Samples	97.32%
[18]	Size-Normalization Thinning	Haar wavelet, 3 resolutions	MLP-NN	Private Persian Digits except "2", "0" 3840 Samples	Digits: 92.33% Characters: 91.81%
[19]	Size & Rotation Normalization	Fractal coding: domain coordinates brightness offset affine transformation		Private Persian Digits except "2", "0" 3840 Samples	Digits: 91.37% Characters: 87.26%
[20]	Thinning	12-Segment template centered by the control point	MLP-NN	Private Persian Digits 730 Samples	97.6%
[21]	Size- Normalization Thinning	Haar wavelet, 3 resolutions	SVM & RBF Kernel	Private Persian Digits: except "2", "0" 3840 Samples Persian Characters: 6080 Samples	MLP & Characters: 92.33% MLP & Digits: 91.81% SVM & Characters: 93.75% SVM & Digits: 92.44%
[22]	Thinning	Coordinate Features	MLP-NN	Private Persian Digits 2430 samples	87%, 85%, 83%, 91% when combined

For the recognition of online Persian script, rule-based classifiers and neural networks (NN) are the mainly used classifiers. A review of these systems is presented in Sections 9.1 and 9.2.

9.1 Rule-Based Recognition Methods

Rule-based recognition has been used vastly in script recognition applications. A recognition rate of 99.6% was reported by T. Al-Sheikh, et al. [26] for their proposed hierarchical rule-based method for online isolated Arabic character recognition. The first level of the hierarchy was based on the number of strokes of the characters, and further division happened by using rule-based classification. Relying on an error-free segmentation, this method cannot handle noisy data or writing variations. A hybrid system using geometrical and structural features and fuzzy techniques was presented by F.Bouslama, et al. [27]. Alimi, et al. [28] minimized error in an online recognition system for isolated Arabic characters in their proposed system. A bank of prototypes was developed for the coded characters, based on directional codes and positional codes. For the recognition of a new pattern, the distance between the pattern and prototype was minimized using dynamic programming. A recognition rate of 96% was reported. Fuzzy set theory was used for both segmentation and classification in [24]. After segmentation, each segment was characterized by four features, described by sets of fuzzy membership functions. A recognition rate of 95% was reported for the isolated characters and some character combinations. In [25], a recognition rate of 75% for the database in [29] was achieved for isolated characters by using fuzzy logic recognition.

Although rule-based classification has succeeded for small numbers of classes, choosing the values of the model parameters for a large number of classes is a challenging task. As the size of symbols grows, correspondingly more rules will be needed, hence the inference slows and does not suit real time applications.

9.2 Neural Network-Based Recognition Methods

Neural networks (NN) can learn complex nonlinear input-output relationships, use sequential training procedures, and adapt themselves to the data. The multi-layer perceptron (MLP) neural network and Self-Organizing Map (SOM/ Kohonen-Network) are the two most widely used NNs in pattern recognition and classification. N. Mezghani, et al. used a Kohonen NN to recognize the basic shape (17 classes were considered) of online isolated Arabic characters [30]. The database they used consisted of 432 samples per class. By combining two separately trained Kohonen maps with a tangent vector and Fourier descriptor features, local and global character descriptions were taken into account in the classification, a recognition rate of 88.38% was achieved. Pruning and filtering the maps, after training, improved the recognition accuracy to 93.54%. The authors in [31] investigated the usefulness of the Kullback-Leibler divergence and the Hellinger distance (as a replacement for the traditionally-used Euclidean distance) in similarity measurements of the feature vectors for training Kohonen maps. The best achieved recognition rate showed an improvement of 0.5% compared to the Euclidean distance by using the Hellinger distance. The Persian isolated characters were also recognized in [32] by using MLP NN. Isolated Persian letters were divided into 12 classes based on the number of dots, shapes, and locations of their diacritics. After recognition of the complementary parts and their locations by two MLP NN's, the character's main shape was analyzed by another NN if further recognition was needed. The reported recognition rate was 93.9% (for 4,144 letters) using the database in [29]. This method assumes that the character's main body is written in the first stroke. This assumption, although valid in most cases, is not always guaranteed.

10   Conclusion

How the Persian language adopted and evolved the Arabic alphabet is discussed in this paper. The characteristics of different writing styles and how they may affect handwriting system recognition, as well as details of Nasta'liq writing style, is presented. A brief review of methods used in offline and online Persian script recognition is provided. Obviously, many challenges still exist in Persian script recognition research. Lack of adequate standard databases and a benchmark for offline and online Persian recognition has made it difficult for researchers to compare their methodologies. Isolated character recognition, while not comprehensive because of different shapes of characters, has been the focus of most of the Persian script recognition research. However, real-world applications have received less attention and word application has remained limited to a small lexicon size. We hope that this motivates more contributions in this challenging area of research .

References

[1] Oktor, P.: Old Persian (2003), (December 8, 2006)
    http://www.fas.harvard.edu/~iranian/OldPersian/index.html
[2] Khatibi, A., Sijelmassi, M.: The Splendor of Islamic Calligraphy, Published by Thames and Hudson (November 2001)
[3] Library of Congress, Global Gateway; Selections of Arabic, Persian, and Ottoman Calligraphy Qur'anic Fragments (2005), (December 8, 2006)
    http://international.loc.gov/intldl/apochtml/apocfragments.html
[4] Salkal Design, Art of Arabic Calligraphy (1997), (December 8, 2006)
    http://sakkal.com/ArabCalligraphyArt5.html
[5] Islamic calligraphy 2004 (December 2006)
    http://www.calligraphyislamic.com/majorStyles.html
[6] Wikipedia, The Free Encyclopedia, Wikimedia Foundation Inc. (2006) (December 8, 2006) http://en.wikipedia.org/wiki/MainPage
[7] Kia'i A., kia.calligraphe (2005) (December 8, 2006):
    http://calligraphiepersane.free.fr/
[8] Zakariya, M.: Zakariya Calligraphy (2002) (December 8, 2006)
    http://www.zakariya.net/history/examples.html
[9] Sadri, J., Suen, C.Y., Bui, T.D.: Application of Support Vector Machines for recognition of handwritten Arabic/Persian digits. In: Proceeding of the Second Conference on Machine Vision and Image Processing and Applications (MVIP), Iran, February 2003, vol. 1, pp. 300–307 (2003)
[10] Sadri, J., Suen, C.Y., Bui, T.D.: Segmentation of Handwritten Numeral Strings in Farsi and English Languages. In: Proceedings of Third Iranian Conference on Machine Vision and Image Processing and Applications (MVIP), Tehran, Iran, February 2005, vol. 1, pp. 305–311 (2005)
[11] Parhami, B., Taraghi, M.: Automatic Recognition of Printed Farsi Texts. In: Proceedings of the Conference on Pattern Recognition, Oxford, England (1980)
[12] Parhami, B., Taraghi, M.: Automatic Recognition of Printed Farsi Texts. Pattern Recognition 14(1-6), 395–403 (1981)

[13] Chen, Y.S., Hsu, W.H.: A New Parallel Thinning Algorithm for Binary Image. In: Proceedings of National Computer Symposium, pp. 295–299 (1985)

[14] Zeyaratban, M., Faez, K., Mozzafari, S., Azvaji, M.: Presenting a New Structural Method Based on Partitioning Thinned Image for Recognition of Handwritten Farsi-Arabic Numerals. In: Proceedings of the Third Conference on Machine Vision, Image Processing and Applications, Farsi, Iran, February 2005, vol. 1, pp. 76–82 (2005)

[15] Dehghan, M., Faez, K.: Farsi Handwritten Character Recognition with Moment Invariants. In: Proceedings of 13th International Conference on Digital Signal Processing, Greece, vol. 2, pp. 507–510 (1997)

[16] Soltanzadeh, H., Rahmati, M.: Recognition of Persian Handwritten Digits Using Image Profiles of Multiple Orientations. Pattern Recognition Letters 25, 1569–1576 (2004)

[17] Solimanpour, F., Sadri, J., Suen, C.Y.: Standard databases for recognition of handwritten digits, numerical strings, legal amounts, letters and dates in Farsi language. In: Proceedings of the 10th Int'l Workshop on Frontiers in Handwriting Recognition, October 2006, pp. 385–389 (2006)

[18] Mowlaei, A., Faez, K., Haghighat, A.T.: Feature Extraction with Wavelet Transform for Recognition of Isolated Handwritten Farsi/Arabic Characters and Numerals. In: Proceedings of 14th International Conference on Digital Signal Processing, vol. 2, July 2002, pp. 923–926 (2002)

[19] Mozaffari, S., Faez, K., Rashidy-Kanan, H.: Recognition of Isolated Handwritten Farsi/Arabic Alphanumeric Using Fractal Codes. In: IEEE Proceedings of Southwest Symposium on Image Analysis and Interpretation, pp. 104–108 (2004)

[20] Harifi, A., Aghagolzadeh, A.: A New Pattern for Handwritten Persian/Arabic Digit Recognition. International Journal of Information Technology 1(4), 293–296 (2004)

[21] Mowlaei, A., Faez, K.: Recognition of Isolated Handwritten Persian/Arabic Characters and Numerals Using Support Vector Machines. In: IEEE Workshop on Neural Networks for Signal Processing, pp. 547–554 (2003)

[22] Nabavi Karizi, S.H., Ebrahimpour, R., Kabir, E.: The Application of Combining Classifiers in Recognition of Farsi Handwritten Digits. In: Proceedings of the Third Conference on Machine Vision, Image Processing and Applications (MVIP 2005). Farsi, vol. 1, pp. 115–119 (2005)

[23] Tappert, C.C., Suen, C.Y., Wakahara, T.: The State of the Art in Online Handwriting Recognition. IEEE Transactions on Pattern Analysis and Machine Intelligence, Farsi 12(8), 787–808 (1990)

[24] Halavati, R., Souraki, S.B., Soleymani, M.: Persian Online Handwriting Recognition Using Fuzzy Modeling. In: International Fuzzy Systems Association World Congress (IFSA) 2005, Beijing, China (July 2005)

[25] Baghshah, M.S.: A Novel Fuzzy Approach to Recognition of Online Persian Handwriting. In: Proceedings of 5th International Conference on Intelligent Systems Design and Applications (ISDA) 2005, September 2005, pp. 268–273 (2005)

[26] Al-Sheikh, T., El-Taweel, S.: Real-time Arabic Handwritten Character Recognition. Pattern recognition 23(12), 1323–1332 (1990)

[27] Bouslama, F., Amin, A.: Pen-based recognition system of Arabic character utilizing structural and fuzzy techniques. In: Second International Conference on Knowledge-Based Intelligent Electronic Systems, pp. 76–85 (1998)

[28] Alimi, A.M., Ghorbel, O.A.: The Analysis of Error in an On-line Recognition System of Arabic Handwritten Character. In: Proceedings of International Conference on Document Analysis and Recognition (ICDAR), August 1995, vol. 2, pp. 890–893 (1995)

[29] Razavi, S.M., Kabir, E.: A Database For Online Persian Handwritten Recognition. In: 6th Conference on Intelligent Systems. In: Farsi, Kerman, Iran (2004)

[30] Mezghani, N., Cheriet, M., Mitiche, A.: Combination of Pruned Kohonen Maps for On-line Arabic Character Recognition. In: International Conference on Document Analysis and Retrieval (ICDAR) 2003, pp. 900–905 (2003)

[31] Mezghani, N., Mitiche, A., Cheriet, M.: A New Representation of Shape and Its Use for Superior Performance in On-line Arabic Character Recognition by an Associative Memory. International Journal on Document Analysis and Recognition (IJDAR) 2005 7(4), 201–210 (2005)

[32] Razavi, S.M., Kabir, E.: Online Persian Isolated Character Recognition. In: The Third Conference on Machine Vision, Image Processing and Applications (MVIP) 2005. In: Farsi, Tehran, Iran, February 2005, vol. 1, pp. 83–89 (2005)

Human Reading Based Strategies for Off-Line Arabic Word Recognition

Abdel Belaïd[1] and Christophe Choisy[2]

[1] LORIA, rue du jardin botanique, 54602 Villers-Lès-Nancy, France
abelaid@loria.fr
[2] ITESOFT Aimargues, Parc d'Andron - Immeuble Le Séquoia, 30470 Aimargues, France
Christophe.Choisy@itesoft.com

Abstract. This paper summarizes techniques proposed for off-line Arabic word recognition. This point of view concerns the human reading favoring an interactive mechanism between global memorization and local verification sim- plifying the recognition of complex scripts such as Arabic. According to this consideration, specific papers are analyzed with comments on strategies.

1 Introduction

Concerning Arabic recognition, the literature proposes several surveys that consider different points of view:

- By stressing the multiplication of the source of information, from a simple classifier to a combination, with simple or hybrid choices of the primitives, as described by Essoukri Ben Amara and Bouslama [1].
- By considering the nature of the script: printed or handwritten, its recognition engines and its applications, like in Lorigo and Govindaraju [2].
- By describing the method nature: symbolic or numeric, as made by Amin [3].

We propose another survey based on the functioning of the human perception spectrum from coarse to fine (i.e. local, analytical or precise). This kind of perception makes it possible to better justify the choice of observations, to order them in classifier cascades, and to propose solutions in case of conflict or problem, and gives sense to the entire chain of recognition.

2 Human Perception of Arabic Writing

Arabic is a calligraphic language. It provides a global rendering of the whole word, and the detail of the letter is often thinned, crushed, sketched so it contributes to the embellishment of the unit (see Figure 1).

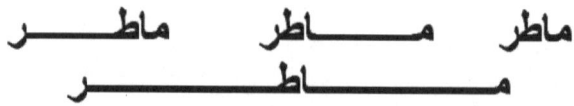

Fig. 1. Same word written with different possible elongations as described in [1]

D.S. Doermann and S. Jaeger (Eds.): SACH 2006, LNCS 4768, pp. 36–56, 2008.
© Springer-Verlag Berlin Heidelberg 2008

Thus, the letter can assume one to four different forms according to its position in the word. The global form becomes the recognized one and the letter passes in the second plan, favoring the total appearance (see Figure 2). Consequently, a bigger alphabet now contains approximately 100 possible forms [1].

Fig. 2. Examples of style fonts of Arabic as described in [4]

However, to facilitate calligraphic reading, diacritics and accents take priority when deciphering letters which have similar base shapes. Second, in order to not force the writer to continue to maintain contact between pen and paper, Arabic offers a decomposition in PAW (Part of Arabic Word), which introduces pauses in the writing that influence the recognition process. The PAWs simplify the script apprehension and simplify the linear recognition. Figure 3 gives an example of Arabic's complexity, with sub-words and diacritic information.

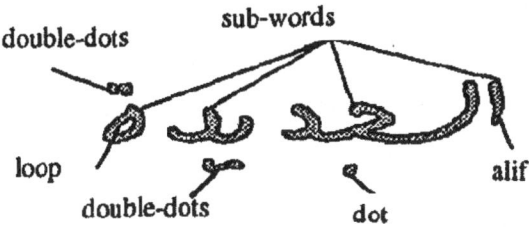

Fig. 3. Arabic writing complexity: example of a handwritten word as shown in [28]

Considering the reading process and the perception of the writing, Arabic reading seems to be more global than syllabic. It is facilitated by separating the word into PAWs, which makes it semi-global.

Some psycho-cognitive experiments proved that when a person reads, the process begins with global vision of the relevant characteristics. The basic experience of reading letter demonstrated the "Word Superiority Effect". To illustrate this phenomenon, McClelland and Rumelhart proposed a reading model [5]. As illustrated in Figure 4, the model operated on three fundamental hypotheses: 1) the perception operates in three different processing levels, each one representing a different abstraction level, 2) the perception implies parallel processing of the visual information, 3) the related processes are interactive, i.e. bottom-up and top-down.

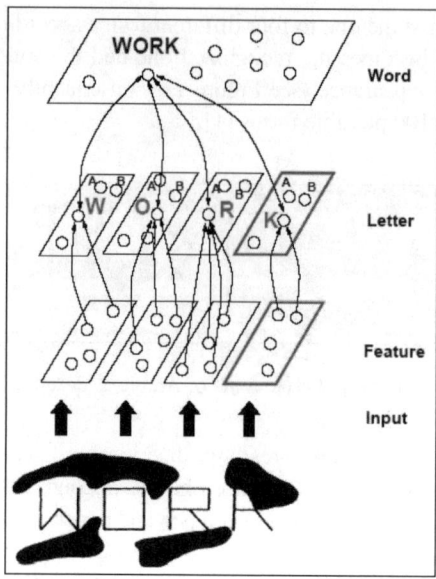

Fig. 4. McClelland and Rumelhart Model

- A person builds a complete image of the environment by accumulating different sources of sensory data. In these various stages of decision-making, he proceeds with a general study of the problem. If this global vision is not sufficient, he seeks more details [6].
- In Arabic writing, the natural "global" pattern is the PAW: words combine PAWs. Furthermore, no clear physical limits occur between words, so words are recognized mainly through different PAW aggregation possibilities, where only one should solve the entire sentence. PAWs could be compared to Latin syllables written separately, which should be gathered correctly to have a meaning.

We can conclude that Arabic writing satisfies the reading principle of McClelland and Rumelhart, as it clearly privileges the "Word Superiority Effects", while adding local perceptual information to facilitate word understanding.

However, the corresponding model must be adapted to consider the PAW intermediate reading level and letter distortions: PAWs introduce an intermediate global level of information, while letter shape variations introduce difficulty to localization and modeling.

3 Computing Perception Levels

All computing methodologies try to simulate a human perception level. Considering human perception of Arabic writing with the particularity of PAW, this leads to a division of the classification methods into four classes:

- Global-based vision classifiers.
- Semi-global-based vision classifiers.
- Local-based vision classifiers.
- Hybrid-level classifiers.

3.1 Global-Based Vision Classifiers

In this holistic approach, the word is regarded as a whole, allowing correlations to the totality of the pattern. This useful or common approach avoids the heavy task of letter localization and recognition use. However, its use remains limited to small vocabularies or use as a pre-classification step, because its complexity grows linearly with the amount of word models.

This category is assimilated to a segmentation-free approach. In fact, it means that if a segmentation method is used, no local interpretation occurs but information gathers at the word level. In such an approach, one should find the best possible interpretation of a word with an observation sequence derived from the word image, without first performing a meaningful segmentation [7].

Several works on Arabic writing derive almost directly from Latin studies. Thus the global approach correctly leads to two questions:

- "Is it possible to adapt classical Latin script approaches correctly to Arabic script?"
- "Is it possible to extract Arabic words as 'simply' as in Latin script?"

Srihari, et al. proposes in [8] a handwritten Arabic word recognition system based on a feature vector similarity measure. The GSC (Gradient, Structural and Concavity) binary features previously used for Latin work in [9] give the best performances. The similarity measure is common to the two languages [9, 41]. A precision of 70% is achieved at a recall of 50% when eight writers were used for training.

The specificity of Arabic writing appears only in a particular part of the work: the word segmentation. Due to the Arabic's nature, the authors cannot directly evaluate the gap between two consecutive PAWs to decide the word limits (see Figure 5). They then use a neural network (NN) on a set of nine features. The authors report the presence of the "Alef" as the first letter of many Arabic words as the most relevant feature [8]. As this hypothesis is not always verified, and due to the natural homogeneous gaps between PAWs, the authors achieve only 60% correct word segmentation.

Al-Badr, et al. consider in [28] that segmenting Arabic words into letters is too difficult a task considering the particular nature of the Arabic script, even when printed text. They propose a segmentation-free approach to recognize words. The key idea involves detecting a set of shape primitives in the analyzed word and arranging them best in the word space. The interpretation of each primitive depends on its context, positions, and the posterior probability maximization, allowing local misrecognition. Word recognition scores vary according to whether words are clean (99.39%), degraded (95.60%) or scanned (73.13%).

This approach is not dedicated specifically to Arabic script. Indeed, the primitive shapes are classical: lines of different lengths and orientations, corners, arcs, curves, etc. The independence of the language has such importance that the authors assume they recognize isolated word. Hence, they elude the important problem of Arabic word segmentation, even though the event was underlined in their paper's introduction.

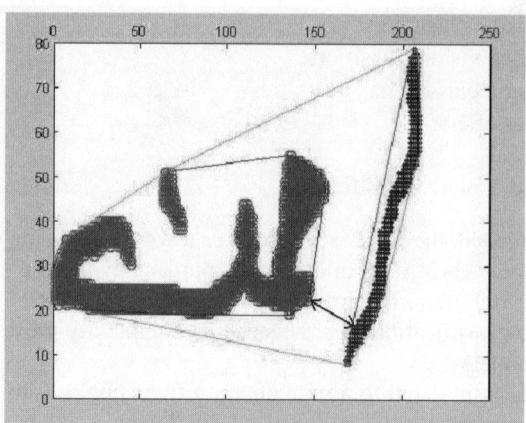

Fig. 5. Gap calculation by Srihari, et al. in [8]

Amin and Mansoor [29] proposed an MLP-based holistic word recognition method for handwritten Arabic words. The MLP input is a global vector composed of six kinds of feature vectors carefully chosen to represent the word globally, such as: number of sub-words (up to five), number of peaks in each sub-word (up to seven), number and position of complementary characters, and curves within each peak with height and width of the peak. Features are dedicated to Arabic word representation, making the system very specific to the language, even though the models are classical. The recognition rate of 98% on different fonts accredits the interest of adapted language specific features.

Here also a question remains: how are the words located in the text? Even though the authors discuss the problem of PAW extraction and their interest in word recognition, they never do explain how they gather several sub-words into a whole word.

Farah, et al. [10] use a battery of three NNs for word recognition, specific features feed each one: statistical, structural, or a mixture. Then, several combination procedures are tested. The NNs used are classical MLPs (Multi Layer Perceptron) with back-propagation algorithm for training. As pixel-based information, statistical features are language-independent: the features define the pixel density in various homogeneous zones of the image. Some structural features are similar to Latin systems: ascenders, descenders, loops, writing baseline. Others remain specific to Arabic writing: presence and number of diacritic dots and their position relative to the baseline. Words, isolated in the database, lead the authors to neglect, in this work, the problem of the location. The tests on 2,400 word images from 100 different writers achieve 94.93% recognition rate, for 0.97% errors and 4.10% of rejection.

Pechwitz and Märgner [19] used semi-continuous Hidden Markov Models (SCHMM) representing characters or shapes, as developed by Huang [20]. For each binary image of a word, the user estimates parameters after a pre-processing phase normalizing the size and the skew of the word. Then, features are collected using a sliding window approach, leading to a language-independent features (see Figure 6). As in Latin script, the middle band of the writing contains the word complexity. For

Arabic writing, it seems better to look at three lines parallel to the baseline at fixed position. The Viterbi algorithm then trains and conducts recognition. In the training phase, a segmental k-means algorithm works. By applying a frame synchronous network Viterbi search algorithm with a tree-structured lexicon representing valid words, the recognition is achieved. The models combine into a word model for each of 946 valid city names. The system obtained 89% word-level recognition rate using the IFN/ENIT database (26,459 images of Tunisian city-names). The words are isolated in the database, thus this work does not deal with the word segmentation problem.

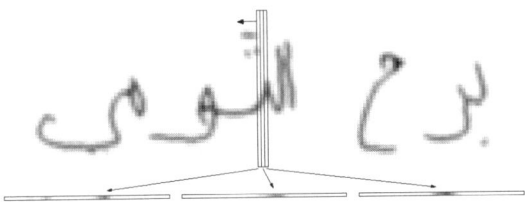

Fig. 6. Feature extraction considered by Pechwitz and Märgner in [19]

Khorsheed and Clocksin propose the use of spectral features for printed Arabic word recognition [33]. As mentioned in several works, the problem of word segmentation is discarded, assuming word images at the input. The originality of this work involves the use of a polar transformation coupled with a Fourier transform that deals with rotation problems (see Figure 7). In a multi-fonts approach, the system obtains 95.4% of good word classification by a simple matching with prototypes using the Euclidian distance on 1,700 samples of different size, angle and translation.

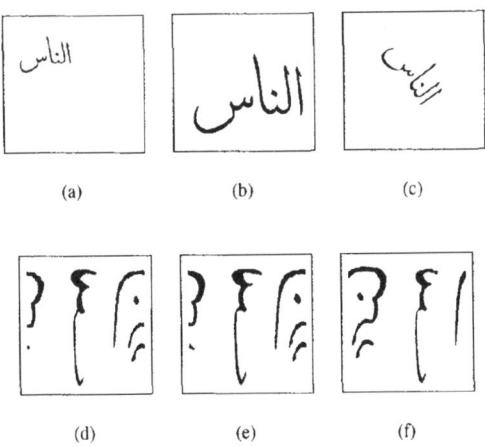

Fig. 7. Polar transform of three images of the same word with different scales and rotation [33]

These works clearly accredit the word superiority principle of McClelland and Rumelhart. Indeed many feature combinations and models perform very well.

But the McClelland and Rumelhart model is not rigorous as it considers two levels: input feature level and word level. This needs less precision than the feature research, but the vocabulary should be limited and each word needs its own modeling.

We note that when the input uses low-level features, it is not necessary to introduce specific information, contrary to the high-level features that need adaptation to the writing nature. We consider extending the McClelland and Rumelhart vision model with another layer, linking the pixel information with high-level features, as the brain works with the input images.

Once looking at these different systems, we can now answer questions asked in the beginning of this section.

The first question concerns the direct reuse of Latin systems on Arabic writing. This question has two answers, one concerns the models and the other looks at the nature of the basic information extracted.

Considering the models, Arabic systems use similar models and measures as Latin ones. We can deduce the adaptation of the models as unnecessary. It is logical because all the classical models perform information without a priori on its nature [8, 10, 19, 28, 29].

Considering the information extraction, all the approaches maintain some classical features used in Latin script. Low-level information based approaches seem able to avoid the addition of specific features as they learn them directly [8, 29, 33]. When high-level features are considered, the particularities of Arabic writing lead some authors to search for more specific features, like diacritic points, elongations, and curves in the beginning or the end of words [10, 29].

The second question concerns Arabic word segmentation (i.e. location in the text) possibilities. The negative answer results from the only work that proposes a segmentation method obtains low segmentation results [8]: other authors deal with segmented words without approaching this problem.

Arabic word segmentation presents more difficulties than Latin writing, for different reasons. The most important one comes from the PAW-level, which introduces a natural segmentation of the writing with similar intra-word and inter-words gaps. This problem is underlined by Al-Badr and Haralick in [28], indicating the justification of Arabic text is not based on inter-word space adjustment but on elongation of some parts of words. Khedher and Abandah confirm this with a statistical study of 262,647 Arabic words in [34], showing an average of 4.3 letters and 2.2 PAWs per word. They conclude the PAW-level defines the real basic block to be processed rather than the word level.

Curiously, several works assume a prior word separation without considering the difficulty of the task. Perhaps it is reminiscent of Latin works, where word segmentation is much easier? We can take such an hypothesis as an explanation of why so few practical, industrial applications to Arabic language exist, despite all these good results.

3.2 Semi-global-Based Vision Classifiers

The particular nature of Arabic writing allows us to describe the language in fewer natural levels: the PAW-level. Indeed, Arabic words are built by a concatenation of several independent written parts that give another natural segmentation level. This natural segmentation allows us to refine the analysis by reducing the basic vocabulary. It explains some approaches that base their work on this level.

By reducing the base vocabulary, it allows the possibility of extending the dictionary. Ben Amara, et al. illustrates this fact in [15] where the PAW-level deals with a moderate vocabulary of city names, usually not treatable with a global word approach. The proposed system used a PHMM (Planar Hidden Markov Model) adapted to the PAW morphology. Hence, a shape vertically decomposes into five horizontal bands, corresponding respectively from top to bottom to the ascenders, the upper diacritic dots, the central writing band, the lower diacritic dots, and the descenders. Each band is associated with a super state which corresponds to an horizontal HMM modeling of the concerned zone (see Figure 8).

Although the PHMM is a classical model used for Latin script [22], its use is clearly dedicated to Arabic writing by the integration of Arabic specificities inside the model. Arabic features directly integrate in the PHMM by adapting the principal HMM to locate the five specific bands of Arabic shapes, while secondary HMMs model the stroke length variations and the diacritic information, aspects that are very specific to Arabic writing. Results are excellent as the authors achieve up to 99.84% recognition for 33,168 samples from a vocabulary of 100 PAWs [31].

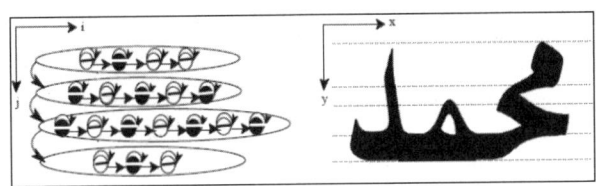

Fig. 8. The PHMM architecture as defined by Ben Amara in [15,31]

Burrow confirms in [17] that Arabic word segmentation is more difficult than for Latin script and proposes to tackle the problem by recognizing the PAWs separately. He hoped this method could cope with the large lexicon of the full database (i.e. IFN/ENIT with 946 different town names from 411 different writers). Interested only in word shape, he considered the tracing approach as detailed in [10, 30] for Latin script. He will in effect be converting an off-line representation into pseudo-on-line representation. Because diacritics are points, their tracing does not make sense; so they are discarded from the PAW images. Then, a PAW transforms in an ordered series of points describing the trace.

Once K-NN classification approach is applied to each PAW, a majority vote is taken on its overall class and repeated for each PAW sample.

First results result in 47% accuracy on PAWs. By refining the scoring system and adding some features, including the number of dots, the author scores at 74% for PAWs on correctly represented classes. Global word recognition, with the addition of word-global features, is studied and improves greatly results, but the input images are supposed to be entire word in this case. No study examines on the possibility of gathering PAW information to find words in a text line.

Concerning the dependence of the language's feature, we can observe that low-level features are able to deal with feature language specificities, as Ben Amara showed (i.e. horizontal run length) by adapting the PHMM model [15, 31]. Structural features proposed by Burrow need to be chosen correctly to reflect language specificities, and their use can highly influence the results [17].

Curiously, few works have concerned the PAW-level. As assessed in the previous section, this level clearly defines the natural global level of Arabic writing. Thus, this section leads to a similar question: Do Latin works influence the tendency to recognize whole words rather than PAWs?

This is correct that in reading Latin, the PAW level does not exist. The McClelland and Rumelhart vision model confirms this, as no intermediate level is given between letters and words. Two solutions exist to adapt this model: the first one extends it by adding a PAW layer between letters and words; the second one decrease the word-level to PAW-level, assuming it is the real global level. The second solution has some advantages, and global approaches would benefit if applied to PAW-level for several reasons:

- Firstly, the PAW vocabulary reduces according to the word vocabulary. Thus, it better manages larger vocabularies.
- Secondly, as PAW-level gives a natural segmentation of a word, the word representation will integrate it in some way. Logically, it works best to divide the representation according to these limits.
- Thirdly, it transforms the word segmentation problem into a PAW gathering problem. Now, the segmentation problem has only empirical solutions, whereas the PAW gathering can use theoretical frameworks as HMM, which can guarantee the optimality of the solution.

We remark that the McClelland and Rumelhart vision model could be extended to a more general approach, where the information gathering could be made recursively through as many levels as necessary. Reinforcing this idea is the fact that "good readers" can recognize word groups rather than isolated words [44]. A level-recursive approach can simulate this fact by gathering information through several higher-abstract structures.

3.3 Local-Based Vision Classifiers

In this vision level, the objective focuses on letters or smaller entities for their interpretation. The process is to gather, bind, and confront these entities to identify the word. Such an analysis level leads to the Sayre dilemma: to find letter limits, a person needs to recognize them, and to recognize requires the ability to localize them. This problem is usually eluded by the use of implicit or explicit segmentation methods.

Fahmy and Al Ali proposed a system with structural features [11]. During a preprocessing phase, slopes and slants are corrected, then some measurements occur, such as stroke width and letter height. The user then normalizes and encodes the word in a canonic form, with a skeleton coding approach used on Latin [21] but adapted to Arabic. The word image divides into several frames, focusing on character parts, and each frame then divides into three segments. Then, classical features like turnings, junctions, and loops, detected from skeletons, become the input of an ANN (Artificial Neural Network). The number of inputs is 35, representing 11 features for each of the three segments of a frame, plus two inputs representing dots. One of these two inputs represents dots above the baseline, while the other input represents dots below the baseline. A recognition rate of 69.7% was obtained on 300 different words from one writer, with a second writing of the 300 words for the training stage.

The system tries to classify the frames: no attempt occurs to gather frames into a complete character. Another point concerns the word segmentation: words are separated at the writing time, eluding the difficult problem of word segmentation.

Trenkle, et al. propose in [32, 39] a printed text recognition system based on an over-segmentation approach (see Figure 9). A full page of text divides into blocks and lines, and each line further breaks into atomic segments, which are part of the character. During recognition, atomic segments group in order to retrieve the whole character according to a Viterbi analysis. Each segment group gives 424 features, obtained from horizontal and vertical projections and an edge-based chain code.

An NN classifies the segment groups: it has 229 outputs according to the 117 regular Arabic character forms, 80 ligature forms, 10 Arabic digits, 20 punctuation characters, and two rejection classes. A set of decision trees also conducts classification. A Viterbi beam search finds the best decoding path for the entire line, given an Arabic text model which is encoded with the rules of Arabic typography. The model combines lexicon-free and lexicon-based approaches, with a vocabulary of 50,000 common Arabic words. A dataset of 722 text images of different qualities is used for the realistic tests: the NN achieves 89.1% recognition, and the set of decision trees obtains 90.7% recognition rate.

This work is complete, as it addresses the problems of printed Arabic text recognition, from page processing and segmentation to text recognition with an ASCII output. The word segmentation problem is elegantly solved by the use of a language model to gather information. We note that the features used are low-level based, so as not to need to integrate Arabic specificities at the character level.

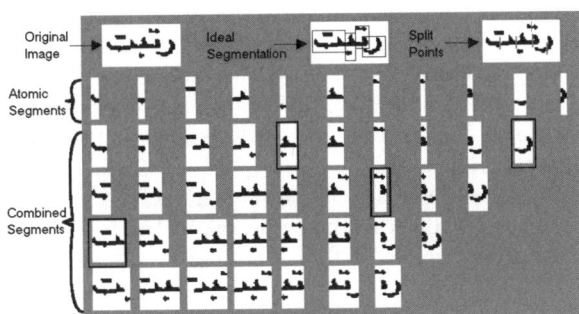

Fig. 9. Over-segmentation applied by Trenkle, et al. in [46, 53]

In Abuhaiba, et al. [14], the authors propose a method for the recognition of free handwritten text. Based on the skeleton representation, the sub-words segment into strokes, that further separated into "tokens". Tokens are single vertices representing dots, loops or sequences of vertices. A "fuzzy sequential machine" identifies the classes. This machine is composed of sets of initial and terminal states. Stroke directions are used for

Fig. 10. Syriac writing: inter-word gaps are larger than intra-word gaps [12]

entering states and as a function for transitioning between states. Tokens are either recognized directly or used to augment the recognizer. This system achieves 55.4% recognition for PAWs, with 17.6% rejection, characters having 51.1% correct answers, with 29.3% of rejection. Employing no lexicon, the PAW vocabulary remains naturally limited. Even given an obsolete computer, the approach needs long calculation time. As assessed by the authors commenting on the relative results, this work proposes new theoretical basis and concepts.

Clocksin and Fernando propose in [12] an analytic system for Syriac manuscripts, a West Semitic language that is less grammatically complex than Arabic. The word segmentation happens more simply in Arabic writing, as the intra-word gaps seem to be clearly smaller than inter-word gaps (see Figure 10), contrary to Arabic writing. The grammatical functions almost appear as word prefixes or suffixes, instead of separate words, so it is not possible to have a global word approach without a huge dictionary. This language construction approaches the Arabic one. Thus, the authors focus on character recognition.

A text page then separates into words using horizontal and vertical projections. Words segment into letters by over-segmenting and removing bad segmentation points with a segmentation approach specially adapted to Syriac writing: approximately 70% of the characters segment correctly. Some features are extracted from character images: different parts of the image and polar transformation. Classification is based on a Support Vector Machine (SVM) considering a "one against one" scheme. As in Arabic, a letter can have different shapes, thus can belong to different classes. The best feature combination gives 91% recognition rate for manuscript letters, and 97% for typeset letters.

As in previous works, this one uses low-level features, and its adaptation to the language specificities occurs through the model learning. The low rate of 70% character segmentation accredits the fact that, as for Latin scripts, a letter segmentation cannot be done correctly.

Miled, et al. [18] propose an analytical approach based on HMMs for the recognition of Tunisian state names. They integrate the notion of PAW in their system. They group letters with the same body but different diacritics to "solve" the problem of diacritic detection and classification. A text line segments into PAWs and isolates letters, then PAWs become graphemes, using their upper contour and heuristic rules in a way similar to approaches for Latin. Each grapheme contains two vectors: the first has topological features corresponding to human perception, like loops, openings, relative size, relative position, etc., the second has moment-like

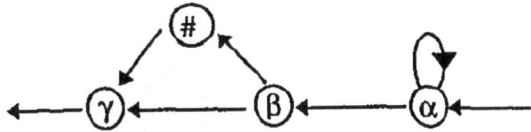

Fig. 11. Word model proposed by Miled, et al. [18]. α, β, and γ stand for characters, and # represents a space.

descriptors (here Fourier descriptors were kept). The grapheme identification uses a K-NN classifier, which obtains 84.90% recognition.

HMM describes word composition. Word models are built by concatenating grapheme states, considering several ways to solve over- and sub-segmentation, and a space state for intra-word gaps (see Figure 11). The approach is "flat": each word has its own HMM representation, and the input sequence is analyzed by all these models. Tests made on isolated word images, has reached 82.52% recognition with a lexicon of 232 words.

This work does not focus the word separation problem, but the HMM approach can solve it at higher representation level. An interesting aspect of this work considers over- and under- segmentation and integrates the intra-word separation as a blank character: All the segmentation problems of Arabic script are then covered.

Fakir, et al. proposes to use the Hough transform for the recognition of printed Arabic characters [38]. A full text page is digitized, noise cleaned, de-skewed and segmented into lines. Then, lines separate into words assuming a bigger gap between words than between PAW. Character segmentation uses the projection profile of the word's middle zone, with a fixed threshold that determines the breaks in the projection profile. A second segmentation applies to extract diacritics.

Features are then extracted using the Hough transform, which applies to the character skeleton to detect strokes (see Figure 12). Thus, a character is represented as a set of strokes. At the recognition step, the set is compared with one reference pattern. A second stage completes the recognition by refining the classification according to the diacritic information. Recognition of 95% is achieved on 300 characters obtained from the segmentation process. The most common confusions occur when thinning brings some different patterns closer.

With no information about the effectiveness of the segmentation itself, 300 words were collected and only 300 letters were used for the test: this supposes that not all the characters were correctly segmented.

Some research closely examines character recognition. They assume that text can be segmented purely into letters. This assumption is unrealistic: the segmentation problem has been presented for some time with Latin script, and many studies have shown it is globally impossible. As it seems more difficult to segment Arabic script, logically this segmentation will not be possible. Sari, et al. confirms the point [40], having proposed a segmentation system dedicated to Arabic writing: they obtain only 86% correct letter segmentation.

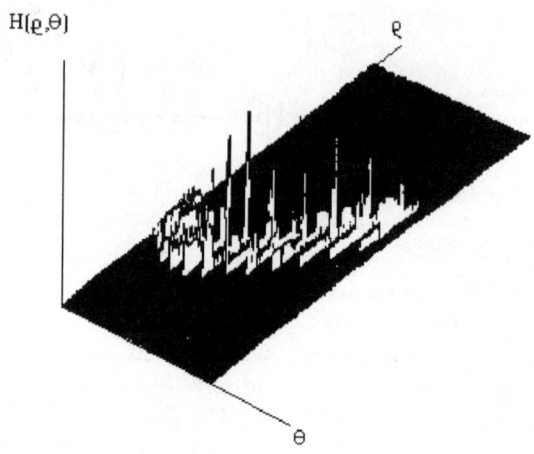

Fig. 12. Array of accumulators' content given by the Hough transform of a character [38]

The value of work based on character recognition reduces to the models and features used that could be integrated into other, more complete works.

Alnsour and Alzoubady proposed in [35] a Neocognitron to classify handwritten characters. The input of this particular NN is composed of structural features: Freeman code chain coordinates of starting and ending points, loops, and primitives such as segments with different orientations, corners and dots. These features allow them to achieve 90% character recognition, with 3.57% rejection. The system assumes a context of handwritten Arabic document recognition software that should be able to segment words directly into letters.

Asiri and Khorsheed propose to use two different NN architectures for handwritten Arabic character recognition [36]. The first architecture has six output nodes and is designed to classify the character into one of the six groups of similar shapes. According to this first solution, a second NN that corresponds to the group will take the final decision. For all NNs, the inputs correspond to a certain number of Haar wavelet transform coefficients. The best results are achieved for 1,024 coefficients and give 88% recognition.

For this work, character samples were collected individually, where writers penned isolated letters into small rectangles.

Cowell and Hussain worked on isolated Arabic printed characters [37]. A character image is normalized by 100x100 pixels, and then a signature is extracted by counting the black pixels in each row and column. This signature is compared to those of a template set, and the modules of the difference for each row and each column is summed: the lower the value, the closer the forms.

The objective aims at a quick matching method: here the signature matching carries 200 comparisons per template, against 10,000 for a direct image matching. No clear result is given, but the confusion matrix supposes a 100% recognition rate.

As previously explained, several approaches give good results, showing that, as for Latin script, the analytic approach can perform very well. Such an approach does present some drawbacks. First is the classical problem of bad segmentation that can lead to over- or under- segmentation; and such errors generally lead to misclassification. Moreover, the segmentation process has to be adapted to Arabic script, to account for its specificities like vertical ligatures: thus Latin segmentation methods cannot be used efficiently without adaptation.

Other problems lie in the approach itself, possibly exacerbated by the language. Thus one problem lies in the observation independence hypothesis. As letters or segments are recognized independently, any error perturbs the whole recognition process. In fact, the McClelland and Rumelhart word superiority effect is not taken into account because the word is not considered as a whole, rather as a sum of small parts.

Another problem lies with the inadequacy between segmentation and models. Indeed, the segmentation is based on structural information totally independent of the model nature. Thus, the modeling is biased at the source by forcing the model to align on non-optimal limits. This may be solved in two ways:

− The use of higher level features presents the first solution: as the image is interpreted, the distortions are implicitly removed. The drawback occurs when any bad interpretation of the image allows the lost of a huge quantity of information, often leading to a misclassification.
− The second way uses implicit segmentation: the models can "choose" their best limits. Unfortunately all the models cannot be used in such an approach without increasing the calculation time exponentially.

We note that in Arabic script, the notion of letter limits varies greatly, as horizontal stroke elongations frequently occur in letters and letter ligatures. This accredits the point of view of Choisy [42] that proposed not to search any letter limits: thus, the model can focus on pertinent letter information without making difficult separation decisions on the fuzzy ligature parts. This proposal fits the McClelland and Rumelhart model, where precise information position is not important, only its presence in an approximate location.

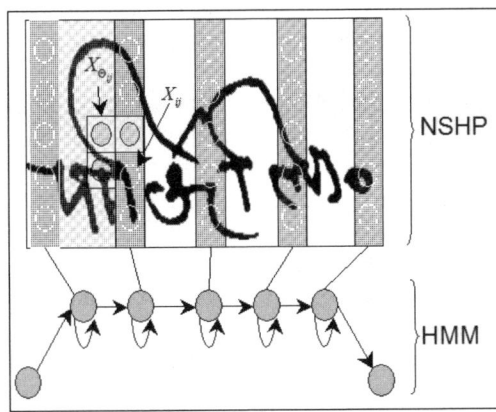

Fig. 13. The NSHP-HMM system applied on Bangla script

The recognition process basically uses a combination of a random field (Non Symmetric Half Plane), drawing its observation directly in the image, and a HMM, taking into account the column observations in the image, hence tackling the problem of length word variations. Figure 13 shows the aspect of this system applied in our Laboratory on Bangla script that presents some calligraphic similarities to Arabic.

3.4 Hybrid-Level Classifiers

By combining different strategies, it is possible to come nearer to principle of reading: the analysis must be global for a good synthesis of information, while being based on local information suitable to make this information emerge [16, 23]. Such a combination better approaches how a person reads, which is to first analyze global word shapes, then searches for local information only to discriminate ambiguous cases.

As local-based approaches gather local information up to words, they could be hybrid ones. An important difference exists between the two approaches: hybrid approaches attempt a multi-level analysis of the writing, while local-based approaches use only the gathering of local information. Hybrid approaches aim to combine different levels of features and interpretation, leading to systems closer to the McClelland and Rumelhart proposal.

Souici, et al. [24] propose a neuro–symbolic hybridization, considering that people rarely, if ever, learn purely from theory or examples. A hybrid system that effectively combines symbolic knowledge with an empirical learning algorithm might be similar to student who is taught using a combination of theoretical information and examples. The neural and symbolic approaches complement each other, so their integration presents an interesting issue.

For that purpose, they defined a neuro-symbolic classifier for the recognition of handwritten Arabic words. First, structural features are extracted from the words contained in the vocabulary. Then, a symbolic knowledge base that reflects a classification of words according to their features is built. Finally, a translation algorithm (from rules to NN) determines the NN architecture and initializes its connections with specific rather than random values, as is the case in classical NNs. This construction approach provides the network with theoretical knowledge and reduces the training stage, which remains necessary because of the variety of styles and writing conditions. The recognition rate varies from 83.55% (4.75% substitution) given by the rule-based approach, 85.5% (14.5% substitution) given by the NN, to 93% (7% substitution) given by the combination.

A similar approach has been applied to handwritten Arabic city-names recognition [43]. The Knowledge Based Artificial NN (KBANN) generated using translation rules compares to a classical MLP. The MLP obtains 80% on 55 vocabulary words, and the KBANN performs 92%. The MLP has a less complex architecture than the KBANN, but has a few more neurons.

The hybrid aspect of these works resides in the NN creations: based on a multi-level word description that considers different levels of rules to classify the word according to its number of PAWs, its features, and its diacritic information. Thus, the network implicitly looks at different perception levels.

Maddouri, et al. proposed a combination of global and local models based on a Transparent NN (TNN) [23]. This model stems from the model proposed by McClelland and Rumelhart for global reading and adapted by Côté [25] for Latin recognition. The TNN is composed of several layers, in which each is associated to a decomposition level of the word. As Coté's TNN had three layers corresponding to features, letters, and words, Maddouri extended it to account for the Arabic PAW-level. Hence, the first level corresponds to features, the second to letters, the third to PAWs, and the fourth to words. In each level, the NN cells represents a conceptual value: primitive, letter, PAW, or word (see Figure 14). Training was operated manually by fixing the weights for the cell connections. These weights are determined statistically, with each word assigned to the various decompositions in the three conceptual levels.

The recognition process operates during several perceptive cycles, propagating hypotheses from a feature level to word level, looking for their association to the composition levels of the word and retro-propagating information from the word level to refine, or to extract the features. More precisely, in propagation movement, the global model proposes a list of structural features characterizing the presence of some letters in the word. Then, it proposes a list of possible letters, PAWs, and words containing these characteristics. In the back-propagation movement, the activated words and PAWs emit some hypotheses on which letters could be present. These hypotheses research the corresponding features, or directly to the letter if it has no robust feature. In this last case, a correspondence between the letter image and the corresponding printed one is performed by a local-based model using the correspondence of their Fourier descriptors, playing the role of a letter shape normalizer.

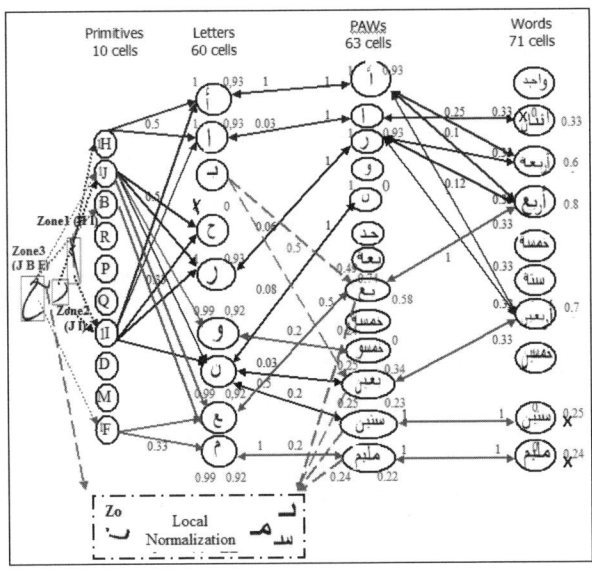

Fig. 14. The TNN approach as defined by Maddouri in [23] on the word "Arbaa"

This principle applies to PAW and word recognition, PAW recognition being made by removing the word layer. The handwritten database contains 2,100 images of the 70 word vocabulary of Arabic literal amounts, containing 63 different PAWs. Using only global features, similar to a simple propagation, PAW recognition rate is 68.42%, and word recognition rate is 90%. The addition of local features in the next perceptive cycles reaches a score of 95% for PAWs and 97% for words.

The value of this approach involves the progressive analysis, according to the discriminative need of the dictionary: thus, for very distinct shapes, a simple propagation may be sufficient. For words with similar shapes, more precise information is needed to discriminate them. The "drawback" comes from the information locali- zation, that becomes increasingly difficult with the information precision, but this "problem" is inherent to the spirit of such an approach.

This work comes close to the McClelland and Rumelhart approach. The word superiority effect increases as word recognition performs better than PAW recognition: word shape features are thus sufficient to achieve correct results. The analysis refining principle is clearly efficient, as shown in the improvement of the score.

As few hybrid approaches exist for Arabic writing, we need to examine interesting work on other languages.

Pinales and Lecolinet in [26] proposed a system, both analytical and global, that emphasizes the role of high-level contextual information (see Figure 15). This model uses a top-down recognition scheme called backward matching and a bottom-up feature extraction process, which operates competitively. This approach has some similarities with the TNN proposed by Côté and Maddouri, as words "retro-propagate" their information to resolve ambiguities and complete missing letters. First results are very encouraging, showing such an approach is pertinent.

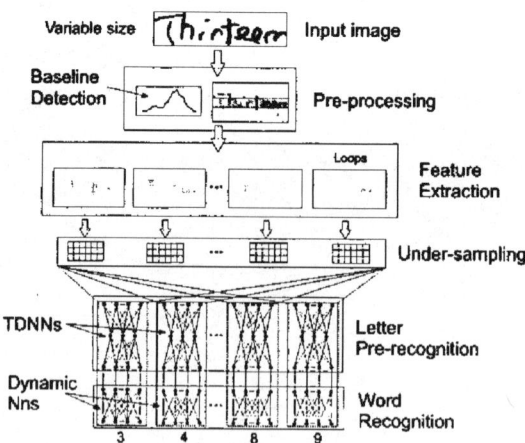

Fig. 15. Pinales and Lecolinet Neural Networks combination architecture [26]

Choisy has introduced another work on Latin script [16]. The approach proposes to use the elasticity property of the NSHP (Non Symmetric Half Plane) to normalize word images in a non-linear way. NSHP delineates focus pixel features based on learned ones, giving an implicit state-based normalization. The normalized images then are analyzed by a classical NN. Results show the efficiency of this approach. The drawback of this approach occurs with the compression of information: even though, contrary to the SDNN, the NN input performs a true adaptation to the image, normalization is a source of information loss.

Results show that hybrid approaches are very efficient. Corroborating the McClelland and Rumelhart approach, the multi-level analysis refines the analysis with more flexibility than other approaches. In particular, the question arises of whether to use information focalization rather than segmenting, which could be an important point in hybrid approaches.

We can conclude that even if the McClelland and Rumelhart model is not proven to be the correct simulation of human reading, their approach still leads to efficient reading systems. This is very interesting because it links the psychology works and the formal representations by computers. We still remark that the proposed model is clearly oriented toward Latin script. For Arabic script, it seems necessary to extend the model with a PAW-level. Thus the McClelland and Rumelhart principle is validated, but the corresponding model should be adapted to the language considered.

4 Conclusion

Several conclusions can be drawn by considering all the research reported in this paper regarding reading Arabic without neglecting the language characteristics.

The first is that low-level features are language independent. Once extracted (similarly for all the scripts), the training process can arrange their proximity to the language studied. At the opposite, high-level features are language-dependent and need to develop specific extraction methods to retrieve all information. Obviously, a combination of these features should perform better, each feature level comple- menting the drawback of the other.

In another point, PAW level proves very important for Arabic script modeling: contrarily to Latin script, the basic entity is not the word. Global approaches should be based on PAW. Analytical ones gain by integrating this information level. A first effect reduces the vocabulary complexity by gathering the information on an intermediate level.

Considering the reading approaches, hybrid ones seem very promising. They efficiently combine different perceptive levels, allowing discrimination of words without a complete description. In comparison with global approaches, the addition of local information allows it to extend the vocabulary with less confusion. Compared to local approaches, hybrid ones avoid the full-segmentation problems and are less disturbed by information loss.

Another conclusion stemmed from the works themselves. In particular, two points arose as problems: segmentation in words and in letters.

The letter segmentation problem was raised a while ago for Latin scripts. Several works examine this case, and it is now commonly accepted that this problem has no solution. As Arabic writing is often described as more complex than Latin, it seems obvious that a letter segmentation cannot be effective. This leads to the question: why are many works based on such a hypothesis? It seems that the experiences gained on Latin languages are not transposed completely too Arabic writing.

Concerning word segmentation (i.e. location in the text), the problem hid in the works on Latin script, in which word separation can be considered as a problem solved in many cases. For Arabic writing, several works accredit the difficulty of this task. As a word analysis is interesting to show the power of reading approaches, there a gap exists between their modeling and their extraction. We think the extraction will increase by gathering PAWs through a mathematical formalism, such as HMM.

Globally, we observe few researches that try to take into account the whole problem of Arabic script. Thus the word segmentation problem is mainly eluded, the PAW-level global recognition was the object of very few works, and several segmentation-based approaches made the irrelevant hypothesis of pure letter segmentation.

Some other problems, like elongations and vertical ligatures, are often cited in Arabic script description, but are taken into account less often in the work itself.

It seems that the main experience brought from Latin works concerns the models and the features, but not problems encountered and processes followed to solve them. In fact, many specific problems were raised, but many works consisted of another set of models, features, methods, from Latin works.

References

[1] Essoukri, N., Amara, B., Bouslama, F.: Classification of Arabic script using multiple sources of information: State of the art and perspectives. Int. Journal on Document Anal. and Recognition (IJDAR) 5, 195–212 (2003)
[2] Lorigo, L.M., Govindaraju, V.: Offline Arabic Handwriting Recognition: A survey. IEEE Trans. on Pat. Anal. and Mach. Int (PAMI) 28(5), 712–724 (2006)
[3] Amin, A.: Off-line Arabic Character Recognition: the state of the art. Pattern Recognition 31(5), 517–530 (1998)
[4] http://www.islamicart.com/main/calligraphy/styles/kufi.htm
[5] McClelland, J.L., Rumelhart, D.E.: An interactive activation model of context effects. Letter perception in Psychological Review 88, 375–407 (1981)
[6] McClelland, J.L., Rumelhart, D.E.: Distributed memory and the representation of general and specific information. Journal of Experimental Psychology: General, 159–188 (1985)
[7] Steinherz, T., Rivlin, E., Intrator, N.: Off-line cursive script word recognition: a survey. Int. Journal on Document Anal. and Recognition (IJDAR) 2, 90–110 (1999)
[8] Srihari, S., Srinivasan, H., Babu, P., Bhole, C.: Handwritten Arabic Word Spotting using the CEDARABIC Document Analysis System. In: Symposium on Document Image Understanding Technology, Maryland, November 2-4 (2005)
[9] Tomai, C.I., Zhang, B., Srihari, S.N.: Discriminatory Power of Handwritten Words for Writer Recognition. In: Proceedings of the 17th International Conference on Pattern Recognition, vol. 2, pp. 638–641 (August 2004)
[10] Farah, N., Khadir, M.T., Sellami, M.: Artificial neural network fusion: Application to Arabic words recognition. In: ESANN 2005, Proceedings - European Symposium on Artificial Neural Networks, Bruges, Belgium, April 27–29 (2005)

[11] Fahmy, M.M.M., Al Ali, S.: Automatic Recognition of Handwritten Arabic Characters Using Their Geometrical Features. Studies in Informatics and Control J. 10 (2001)

[12] Clocksin, W.F., Fernando, P.P.J.: Towards Automatic Transcription of Syriac Handwriting. In: Proc. Int'l Conf. Image Analysis and Processing, pp. 664–669 (2003)

[13] Almuallim, H., Yamagochi, S.: A method of recognition of Arabic cursive handwriting. Pattern Recognition 9(5), 715–722 (1987)

[14] Abuhaiba, I.S.I., Holt, M.J.J., Datta, S.: Recognition of Off-Line Cursive Handwriting. Computer Vision and Image Understanding 71, 19–38 (1998)

[15] Ben Amara, N., Belaid, A.: Printed PAW recognition based on planar hidden Markov models. In: Proceedings of the 13th International Conference on Pattern Recognition, August 25–29, vol. 2, pp. 220–224 (1996)

[16] Choisy, C., Belaïd, A.: Coupling of a local vision by Markov field and a global vision by Neural Network for the recognition of handwritten words. In: ICDAR 2003, Edinburgh, August 3–6, pp. 849–953 (2003)

[17] Burrow, P.: Arabic Handwriting Recognition. Report of Master of Science School of Informatics, University of Edinburgh (2004)

[18] Miled, H., Olivier, C., Cheriet, M., Lecourtier, Y.: Coupling observation/letter for a Markovian modelisation applied to the recognition of Arabic Handwriting. In: Proc. of ICDAR 1997, Ulm, Germany, pp. 580–583 (1997)

[19] Pechwitz, M., Maergner, V.: HMM Based Approach for Handwritten Arabic Word Recognition Using the IFN/ENIT- Database. In: 7th ICDAR, vol. 2, pp. 890–894 (2003)

[20] Huang, X.D., Lee, K.F., Hon, H.: On Semi-continuous Hidden Markov Modeling. In: Proc. of the IEEE Int. Conf. Acoust., Speech, Signal Processing, pp. 689–692 (April 1990)

[21] Senior, A.W., Robinson, A.J.: An Off-Line Cursive Handwriting Recognition System. PAMI 20(3), 308–321 (1998)

[22] Bippus, R.: One-Dimensional and Pseudo 2-Dimensional HMMs for the Recognition of German Literal Amounts. In: ICDAR 1997, Ulm, Germany, vol. 2, pp. 487–490 (August 1997)

[23] Maddouri, S.S., Amiri, H., Belaïd, A., Choisy, C.: Combination of Local and Global Vision Modeling for Arabic Handwritten Words Recognition. In: 8th IWHFR, pp. 128–132 (2002)

[24] Souici, L., Sellami, M.: A hybrid approach for Arabic literal amounts recognition. AJSE, Arabian Journal for Science and Engineering 29(2B), 177–194 (2004)

[25] Côté, M., Lecolinet, E., Cheriet, M., Suen, C.Y.: Building a perception based model for reading cursive script. ICDAR II, 898–901 (1995)

[26] Ruiz-Pinnales, J., Lecolinet, E.: A new perceptive system for the recognition of cursive handwriting. In: ICPR, vol. III, pp. 53–56 (2002)

[27] Zhang, B., Srihari, S.N.: Binary vector dissimilarity measures for handwriting identification. In: Proceedings of the SPIE, Document Recognition and Retrieval, pp. 155–166 (2003)

[28] Al-Badr, B., Haralick, R.M.: A segmentation-free approach to text recognition with application to Arabic text. Int. Journal on Document Anal. and Recognition (IJDAR) 1, 147–166 (1998)

[29] Amin, A., Mansoor, W.: Recognition of Printed Arabic Text using Neural Networks. In: ICDAR 1997, vol. II, pp. 612–615 (1997)

[30] Nishida, H.: An approach to integration of off-line and on-line recognition of handwriting. Pattern Recognition Letters 16(11), 1213–1219 (1995)

[31] Miled, H., Ben Amara, N.E.: Planar Markov Modeling for arabic Writing Recognition: Advancement State. In: ICDAR 2001, Seattle, vol. I, pp. 69–73 (2001)

[32] Trenkle, J., Gillies, A., Erlandson, E., Schlosser, S., Cavin, S.: Advances in Arabic Text Recognition. In: Proceedings of the Symposium on Document Image Understanding Technology, Columbia, Maryland (2001)

[33] Khorsheed, M.S., Clocksin, W.F.: Spectral features for Arabic word recognition. In: ICASSP 2000, vol. 6, pp. 3574–3577 (2000)

[34] Khedher, M.Z., Abandah, G.: Arabic Character Recognition using Approximate Stroke Sequence, Arabic Language Resources and Evaluation Status and Prospects. In: LREC 2002, Las Palmas de Gran Canaria (June 2002)

[35] Alnsour, A.J., Alzoubady, L.M.: Arabic Handwritten Character Recognized by Neocognitron Artificial Neural Network. University of Sharjah Journal of Pure and Applied Sciences 3(2) (June 2006)

[36] Asiri, A., Khorsheed, M.S.: Automatic Processing of Handwritten Arabic Forms Using Neural Networks. Transactions on Engineering, Computing and Technology 7 (August 2005)

[37] Cowell, J., Hussain, F.: A fast recognition system for isolated Arabic character recognition. In: IEEE Information Visualization IV2002 conference, London (July 2002)

[38] Fakir, M., Hassani, M.M., Sodeyama, C.: On the recognition of Arabic characters using Hough transform technique. Malaysian Journal of Computer Science 13(2) (2000)

[39] Gillies, A., Erlandson, E., Trenkle, S.S.: Arabic Text Recognition System. In: Proceedings of the Symposium on Document Image Understanding Technology, Annapolis, Maryland (1999)

[40] Sari, T., Souici, L., Sellami, M.: Off-line Handwritten Arabic Character Segmentation Algorithm: ACSA. In: Proceedings of the Eighth International Workshop on Frontiers in Handwriting Recognition (IWFHR 2002), Niagara-on-the-Lake, Canada, p. 452 (2002)

[41] Jelodar, M.S., Fadaeieslam, M.J., Mozayani, N., Fazeli, M.: A Persian OCR System using Morphological Operators. In: The Second World Enformatika Conference, WEC 2005, Istanbul, Turkey, pp. 137–140 (February 2005)

[42] Choisy, C., Belaid, A.: Cross-learning in analytic word recognition without segmentation. Int. Journal on Document Anal. and Recognition, IJDAR 4(4), 281–289 (2002)

[43] Souici, L., Farah, N., Sari, T., Sellami, M.: Rule Based Neural Networks Construction for Handwritten Arabic City-Names Recognition. In: Bussler, C.J., Fensel, D. (eds.) AIMSA 2004. LNCS (LNAI), vol. 3192, pp. 331–340. Springer, Heidelberg (2004)

[44] http://home.ican.net/~galandor/littera/syn_cor1.htm

Versatile Search of Scanned Arabic Handwriting

Sargur N. Srihari, Gregory R. Ball, and Harish Srinivasan

Center of Excellence for Document Analysis and Recognition (CEDAR)
University at Buffalo, State University of New York
Amherst, New York 14228
{srihari,grball,hs32}@cedar.buffalo.edu

Abstract. Searching handwritten documents is a relatively unexplored frontier for documents in any language. Traditional approaches use either image-based or text-based techniques. This paper describes a framework for versatile search where the query can be either text or image, and the retrieval method fuses text and image retrieval methods. A UNICODE and an image query are maintained throughout the search, with the results being combined by a neural network. Preliminary results show positive results that can be further improved by refining the component pieces of the framework (text transcription and image search).

1 Introduction

While searching electronic text is now a ubiquitous operation, the searching of scanned printed documents, such as books, is still emerging. The searching of scanned handwritten and mixed documents is a virtually unexplored area.

Much current interest surrounds processing handwritten Arabic language documents. One unsolved problem involves developing a reliable method, given some query, to search for a subset among the many such documents, similar to searching printed documents. The challenge comes from the unique structural features of Arabic script and the relative infancy of the handwriting processing field.

Content-based information retrieval (CBIR) is a broad topic in information retrieval and data mining [1]. The distinct areas of CBIR include text retrieval and image retrieval. Correspondingly, two approaches exist to search scanned documents. One approach uses direct image retrieval (word spotting with prototype images). Another converts the document to an electronic textual representation (ASCII for English and UNICODE for Arabic) and searches it with text information retrieval methods used routinely on English-based documents. Both approaches can succeed under ideal circumstances, which are difficult to achieve with current handwriting recognition technology. Image-based searches do not always return correct results. Arabic handwriting recognition technology does not allow full transcriptions of unconstrained documents. By exploiting the strengths of both methods, combining the methods, we achieve better performance than either gives separately.

We describe a framework for versatile search of Arabic handwritten documents. By versatile search, we mean versatility in both the query and the search

D.S. Doermann and S. Jaeger (Eds.): SACH 2006, LNCS 4768, pp. 57–69, 2008.

strategy, combining content-based image retrieval and text-based information retrieval. Both the original scanned image and the (partial) transcription are maintained at all stages. Searches proceed in parallel directions on both document representations. Any query also splits into both an image and a UNICODE representation, which act on the corresponding document instance. The results from the parallel searches combine into a single ranking of candidate documents.

2   Related Work

Searching scanned, printed documents in English has had significant success. Taghva, et al showed [2] that information retrieval performance continues to be high even given imperfect OCR performance. Russell, et al [3] note this can, at least in part, be attributed to redundancy and the fact that, while OCR performance may commit some errors, it performs very well for English. They go on to discuss the use of handwritten and typed queries.

A system for directly searching scanned, handwritten English was discussed in [4]. This system, known as CEDAR-FOX, was developed for forensic document analysis applications [5],[6]. Searching scanned Arabic handwriting within a system known as CEDARABIC, based on CEDAR-FOX, was first reported in [7]. Both systems are designed to be interactive for use by a human document examiner and have many pre-processing operations such as line and word segmentation, rule-line removal, image enhancement, etc.

3   Queries and Searches

The query can take several forms: (i) a UNICODE string of Arabic text (for example, entered on an Arabic keyboard) specifying a word or words the user wants to appear in the handwritten document, (ii) an English word or words corresponding to an idea that should appear in the Arabic document, or (iii) an image of an Arabic word or words. Documents should be returned that also have a representation of this Arabic word.

Word spotting algorithms begin with an image query; either a full word or component prototype characters. The engine searches the document directly, with only minor pre-processing steps, such as noise removal, etc. We take two approaches for word spotting: holistic word shape and character shape. In the word shape based method, features are extracted from prototype word images. This prototype either can be provided with the query, or can be found in a library of images based on a keyword. We then compare the features of a candidate word to the prototype words, choosing the best match. The character shape based method splits a candidate word into sequences of candidate component characters. Each sequence matches to prototypes of the characters in the query word. The sequence of candidate characters with the maximum similarity to the prototypes receives the highest score for that word, with the score acting as a confidence measure. The word shape method performs well given many prototype images. If none are available, the character-based method is the only available approach. In situations where both methods may apply, their rankings combine.

To partially transcribe documents, we use several approaches of word recognition. A baseline, simple method performs a variation of character recognition and tries to deduce a word directly. Arabic has an advantage over other languages, such as English, because of the presence of subwords that are predictably distinct. In a second method, we compare the candidate characters against those suggested by a lexicon of words, choosing the candidate representation with the best score. Given larger lexicons generally result in poorer performance, we limit the lexicon size when using such a method.

4 Framework

Figure 1 gives an overview of the versatile search framework. A key point: both image and text queries are maintained against image and text versions of the document throughout the searching process, with their results being combined with a neural network.

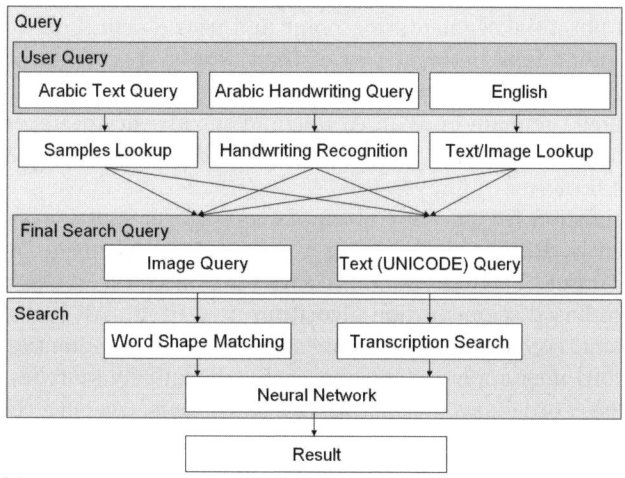

Fig. 1. Versatile Search Framework

A critical common preprocessing step necessary for both methods involves segmenting a page into lines, and sometimes a line into words. Figure 2 shows the CEDARABIC representation of a segmented document.

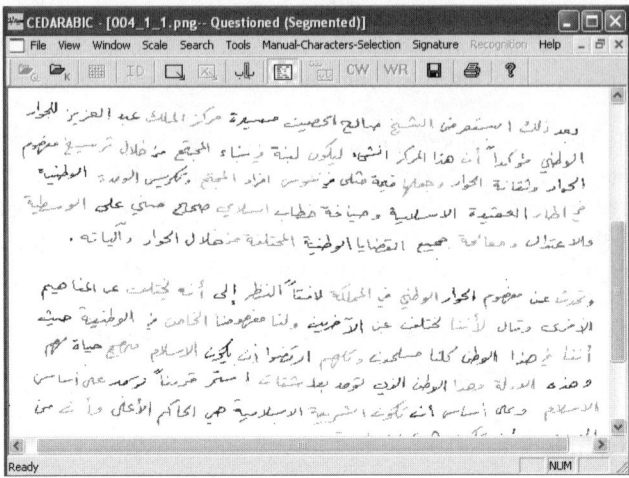

Fig. 2. Segmented Document

5   Segmentation Algorithms

Automatic word segmentation, as presented in [8], takes several features on either side of a potential segmentation point and uses a neural network to decide whether the point falls between two distinct words. The tasks of segmenting Arabic script and segmenting Latin script differ in the presence of multiple dots above and below the main body in Arabic and the absence of upper case letters at the beginning of sentences in Arabic. The method presented had an overall correctness of 60%.

The segmentation free method attempts to perform spotting and segmentation concurrently. Rather than having a candidate word image, an entire line image acts as input. The line splits into segments based on an algorithm similar to the ligature-based segmentation algorithm used in [9]. All realistic combinations of adjacent, connected components are considered as potential areas where the desired word may appear. This approach exhaustively searches a line, looking for a given word image, while, at the same time, keeping the number of evaluations manageable by considering only a small subset of potential regions in the image.

5.1   Automatic Word Segmentation

The process of automatic word segmentation begins by obtaining the set of connected components for each line in the document image. The interior contours or loops in a component are ignored for the purpose of word segmentation, as they provide no information for this purpose. The connected components group into clusters, merging minor components such as dots above and below a major component.

Also particular to Arabic, many words start with the Arabic character "Alef". The presence of an "Alef" strongly indicates the possibility of a word gap between the pair of clusters. The height and width of the component define two parameters used to check if the component is the character "Alef". Every pair of adjacent clusters are candidates for word gaps.

Nine features are extracted for these pairs of clusters and a neural network determines if the gap between the pair is a word gap. The features are: (i) width of the first cluster, (ii) width of second cluster, (iii) difference between the bounding box of the two clusters, (iv) flag set to 1 or 0 depending on the presence or absence of the Arabic character "Alef" in the first cluster, (v) the same flag for the second cluster, (vi) number of components in the first cluster, (vii) number of components in the second cluster, (viii) minimum distance between the convex hulls enclosing the two clusters, and (ix) the ratio between the sum of the areas enclosed by the convex hulls of the individual clusters to the total area inside the convex hull enclosing the clusters together. The minimum distance between convex hulls is calculated by sampling points on the convex hull for each connected component and calculating the minimum distance of all such pairs.

A neural network was trained using these nine features with a feature vector labeled as to whether it is a word gap. This is similar to the neural network approach used for English postal addresses [10], but with different features.

Automated Word Segmentation Performance. The overall performance was found to be 60%. In [8], the authors noted that a more complex set of features is expected to yield a higher level of performance.

5.2   Segmentation-Free Line Processing

The segmentation-free algorithm processes the words on a per line basis rather than relying on pre-segmented words. The algorithm can be viewed as a sequence of steps. First, the image is processed into component lines, then checkpoints are generated for a given line. The line is scanned with a sliding window, generating candidate words and scoring them, as well as filtering nearly equivalent candidates.

Candidate Segmentation Algorithm. The algorithm used on the line to generate checkpoints is essentially the same as the one used to generate candidate character segmentation points in candidate words in the spotting step. It operates via a combination of ligatures and concavity features on an encoded contour of the components of the line image. Average stroke width estimates are used to determine the features.

Ligatures, as noted in [9] present strong candidates for segmentation points in cursive scripts. Ligatures are extracted in a similar way, as in [9]; if the distance between y-coordinates of the upper half and lower half of the outer contour for a x-coordinate is less than or equal to the average stroke width, then the x-coordinate is marked as a ligature element. Concavity features in upper contour and convexities in the lower contour also generate candidate segmentation points, which are especially useful for distinct characters which touch (as opposed to being connected). A ligature will cause any overlapped concavity features to be ignored. For a given x-coordinate, if a concavity and convexity overlap, a segmentation point is added for that x-coordinate.

While the character-based method described in [9] uses this segmentation method to split a word into candidate characters, the segmentation-free line processing method uses it to split the line, to generate candidate word regions on the line. Arabic has predictable regions of white space in a word based on the presence of non-connective characters. Therefore, the number of connected components in a word is predictable as well.

Line Scanning. The method utilizes a sliding window. The scan's direction is unimportant because all realistic combinations of connected components will be considered.

Each character class c in Arabic associates with a minimum and a maximum durational length ($minlen(c)$ and $maxlen(c)$ respectively). These lengths are result from segmenting a representative dataset of characters with the same segmentation algorithm, and taking the minimum and maximum values for each character. Given the nature of the Arabic character set, the upper bound for all characters is five, not four as in [9].

The search algorithm will scan for candidate words consisting of a range of segments. For a given search word W consisting of n characters, c_0 to $c_{n-1} \in W$, the minimum number of segments $minlen(W)$ considered is $\sum_{i=0}^{n-1} minlen(c_i)$ and the maximum considered length $maxlen(W)$ is $\sum_{i=0}^{n-1} maxlen(c_i)$.

The scanning algorithm considers each segment s on a line generated by the segmentation algorithm. For a given segment s_i, if $i = 0$ or if $s_i.left > s_{i-1}.right$ (i.e., horizontal space appears to the left of the segment), it is considered a valid start point. Similarly, for a given segment s_i, if $i = max(s)$ or if $s_i.right < s_{i+1}.left$ (i.e., horizontal space appears to the right of the segment), it is considered a valid endpoint. The algorithm considers candidate words as ranges of segments starting with some valid start point s_i, ending with a valid endpoint s_j, such that $minlen(W) \leq j - i + 1 \leq maxlen(W)$.

While this tends to result in more candidate words, it does not result in a dramatic decrease in performance given each Arabic word is broken only into a few pieces, separated by white space.

Filtering. Often, a candidate word influences neighboring candidate words' scores. Neighboring candidate words are those words with overlapping segments. Often, a high scoring word will also have high scores for neighboring candidates. One issue arises when the high scoring word is, in fact, an incorrect match. In this case, the incorrect choice and several of its neighboring candidates may receive similarly good scores, pushing the rank of the actual word lower in the list. Another issue occurs when the target word appears multiple times in a document. The best matching words' neighboring candidates can depress the second occurrence's rank. Various ways of dealing with the overlap meet with different degrees of success.

The approach taken in the current implementation of our algorithm maintains the candidate word that has the highest score of the overlapping words.

6 Image-Based Word Shape Matching

The word segmentation is an indexing step that occurs before using word shape matching for word retrieval. A two-step approach performs the search: (1) prototype selection: the query (English text) obtains a set of handwritten samples of that word from a known set of writers (the prototypes), and (2) word matching: the prototypes locate each occurrence of those words in the indexed document database. The entire set of test word images is ranked where the ranking criterion is the mean similarity score between prototype words and the candidate word, based on global word shape features.

6.1 Prototype Selection

Prototypes, which are handwritten samples of a word, are obtained from an indexed (segmented) set of documents. These indexed documents contain the groundtruth (English equivalent) for every word image. Such an indexing can be done with a transcript mapping approach, as described in [11]. Synonymous words, if present in the truth, also help obtain the prototypes. Hence, queries such as "country" will result in prototypes that have been truthed as "country" or "nation," etc. A dynamic programming Edit Distance algorithm matches the query text with the indexed word image's truth. Those with distance as zero are automatically selected as prototypes, while others can be selected manually.

6.2 Word-Matching

The word-matching algorithm uses a set of 1,024 binary features for the word images. These binary features are compared using the correlation similarity measure described below to obtain a similarity value between 0 and 1. This similarity score represents the extent of the match between two word images. The smaller the score, the better the match. For word spotting, every word image in the test set of documents is compared with every selected prototype, determining a distribution of similarity values. The distribution of similarity values is replaced by its arithmetic mean. Every word ranks in accordance with this final mean score.

Similarity Measure. The method of measuring the similarity or distance between two binary vectors is essential. The correlation distance performed best for GSC binary features [12], which is defined for two binary vectors X and Y, as in equation 1

$$d(X,Y) = \frac{1}{2}\left(1 - \frac{s_{11}s_{00} - s_{10}s_{01}}{[(s_{10} + s_{11})(s_{01} + s_{00})(s_{11} + s_{01})(s_{00} + s_{10})]^{\frac{1}{2}}}\right) \quad (1)$$

where s_{ij} represents the number of corresponding bits of X and Y that have values i and j.

7 Lexicon-Based Matching

This approach uses the Arabic sequences of characters for words in the lexicon to select sets of prototype images representing the characters forming them. A pre-processing step is a line and word segmentation process, as described in [8]. The candidate word image first splits into a sequence of segments, with an ideal result of individual characters in the candidate word being separated. The segmentation algorithm uses "oversegmented" words attempting to avoid placing more than a single character into a segment. Segments are then rejoined and features extracted, which are, in turn, compared to features of prototype images of the characters. Further issues of under-segmentation unique to Arabic are resolved using compound character classes. A score that represents the match between the lexicon and the candidate word image is then computed. The score relates to the individual character recognition scores for each of the combined segments of the word image.

7.1 Character Dataset

Unlike the method presented in [8], this method depends on character images rather than word images to form a basis for comparison. In this method, the image essentially divides into component characters, and each character is matched for similarity, in contrast to the latter's method of matching an entire word shape. The number of characters in Arabic is rather small compared with the number of potential words, and a library of component characters can easily be incorporated directly into the system. This eliminates the indexing phase of [8].

Such a character database was not readily available, so a new character image dataset was derived from the existing Arabic document dataset produced from the CEDARABIC [7] project. The original dataset consisted of a collection of handwritten documents produced from a variety of authors, described in Section 9.1. The scanned words were individualized and groundtruth in the form of raw ASCII descriptions of the Arabic characters was assigned. The derived dataset consists of images of single Arabic characters and character combinations. Approximately 2,000 images of characters and character combinations in other configurations were created by allowing the ligature based segmentation algorithm to create candidate supersegments of the truthed words. The best candidate supersegments were manually matching to the corresponding character or character combination when the segmentation was successful. Both left to right and right to left versions of the writings were tested by flipping the image along the vertical axis. The original right to left images produced slightly better results (left to right versions occasionally seemed more prone to undersegmenting the words). The 2,000 images represent a small fraction of potential images from this dataset. Work on extending this dataset continues.

7.2 Features

Word Model Recognizer (WMR) features for each of the character images were extracted and incorporated into the recognition engine of CEDARABIC. As described in [13], the WMR feature set consists of 74 features. Two are global features – aspect and stroke ratio of the entire character. The remaining 72 are local features. Each character image is divided into nine subimages. The distribution of the eight directional slopes for each sub-image form this set (8 directional slopes × 9 subimages = 72 features). $F_{l_{i,j}} = s_{i,j}/N_i S_j$, $i = 1, 2, ..., 9$, $j = 0, 1, ..., 7$, where $s_{i,j}$ = number of components with slope j from subimage i, where N_i = number of components from subimage i, and $S_j = max(s_{i,j}/N_i)$. These features are the basis of comparison for the character images derived from the segmentation of words to be recognized. To date, this appears to be the first application of WMR features to Arabic recognition.

To obtain preliminary results, the base shape of a letter was mapped to all derivations of that letter. For example, the base shape of the character *beh* mapped to *beh, teh,* and *theh.* The initial and medial forms of *beh* also mapped to the initial and medial forms of *noon* and *yeh.* If separately truthed versions were available, specifying explicit membership to, for example, *teh,* such characters were included only in *teh*'s set of features.

8 Image Processing and Segmentation

Image processing happens via a method similar, in part, to that described in [14]. First, a chain code representation of the binary image's contours is generated. Noise removal, slant correction, and smoothing occurs. Segmentation is performed via a combination of ligatures and concavity features on an encoded contour of the image's components. Average stroke width is estimated and used to determine the features. The number of segmentation points is kept to a minimum, but, unlike in [14], the maximum number of segmentation points per character is five. WMR features are extracted from segments.

As previously mentioned, this method aims to oversegment words in the hope of eliminating under-segmentation altogether. Under-segmentation in ligature-based segmentation of Arabic text, however, continues to be problematic given the presence of character combinations and vertically separated characters. For example, some writing styles do not mark certain letters with much clarity – especially initial characters, for example, initial *yeh*'s. The ligature-based segmentation proceeds horizontally, seeking breaking points at various positions along the x-axis, so the vertical "stacking" of characters cannot be solved by simply increasing the sensitivity of the segmentation. To solve these issues, character classes were defined corresponding to the common character and vertically occurring combinations.

8.1 Preprocessing Lexicon

An Arabic word is specified as a sequence of the approximately 28 base letters. To aid recognition, a simple algorithm maps the given text to the correct variation of each character. For example, "Alef|Lam|Teh|Qaf|Alef maksura|" maps to "Alef$_i$|Lam$_i$|Teh$_m$|Qaf$_m$|Alef maksura$_f$|," where "i" means the letter is in the initial position, "m" means the letter is in the medial position, "f" means the letter is in the final position, and "s" means the letter is separate. Additional post-processing steps to the Arabic lexicon combine adjacent individual characters in appropriate positions into character combination classes. For example, "$Lam_i|Meem_m|$" is mapped to "$Lammeem_i$."

The new mapping system for the approximately 150 new character classes was incorporated into the character recognition model of CEDARABIC, replacing the support for English letters carried over from CEDARFOX.

8.2   Word Recognition

The objective aims to find the best match between the lexicon and the image. In contrast to [14], up to five adjacent segments are compared to the character classes dictated as possibilities by a given lexicon entry. In the first phase of the match, the minimum Euclidean distance between the WMR features of candidate super-segments and the prototype character images is computed. In the second phase, a global optimum path is obtained using dynamic programming based on the saved minimum distances obtained in the first matching phase. The lexicon is ranked, the entries with the lowest total scores being the closest matches.

Testing proceeded on the same 10 authors' documents, as in [8]. Recognition was attempted on approximately 180 words written by each of the 10 authors (for a total of approximately 1,800 words). Recognition was attempted in two runs, one with a lexicon size of 20 words and one with 100. The lexicon was generated from other words among the 180 being recognized. All the authors wrote the same words for the documents. The words and the lexicons in the tests were the same for all authors.

8.3   Word Spotting

Word spotting proceeds in a similar fashion to word recognition. For word spotting, the lexicon consists only of the word being spotted. A score against this lexicon entry is generated for each candidate word in the document. The candidate words rank according to score, the words with the best scores are most likely to be the spotted word.

From the documents written by the authors, 32 words were chosen at random and "spotted," in a similar fashion to the experiments performed in [8]. Note that the recall for word spotting, when utilizing the expanded Arabic character classes, comes to nearly 80% for a precision of 50, which represents a significant improvement over other methods (using simply the Arabic letters individually and the image based method described in [8]).

9   Results

9.1   Document Image Database

For evaluating the results of our methods, we used a document collection prepared from 10 different writers, each contributing 10 different full page documents in handwritten Arabic. Each document contains approximately $150 - 200$ words each, with a total of $20,000$ word images in the database. The documents were scanned at a resolution of 300 dots per inch, which gives optimal performance of the system.

For each of the 10 handwritten documents, a complete set of truth, comprising of the alphabet sequence, meaning, and the pronunciation in that document, was also given. The scanned handwritten documents' word images were mapped with the corresponding truth information.

9.2   Experiments

To test the combined method, 32 queries were issued on 13,631 records. The neural network was trained on 300 such queries, 150 positive and 150 negative query matches. All remaining records were used for testing. The combined score comes to a score between -1 and 1. A negative score indicates a mismatch, and a positive score a match. A 91% raw classification accuracy was observed.

Using five writers for providing prototypes and the other five for testing, using manually segmented documents, 55% precision is obtained at 50% recall for the word shape method alone. The character-based method achieves 75% precision at the same recall rate. The combined method is consistently better, resulting in about 80% precision. A comparison graph, with the word shape method using five writers, is shown in Figure 3. One search result from CEDARABIC is shown in Fig. 4.

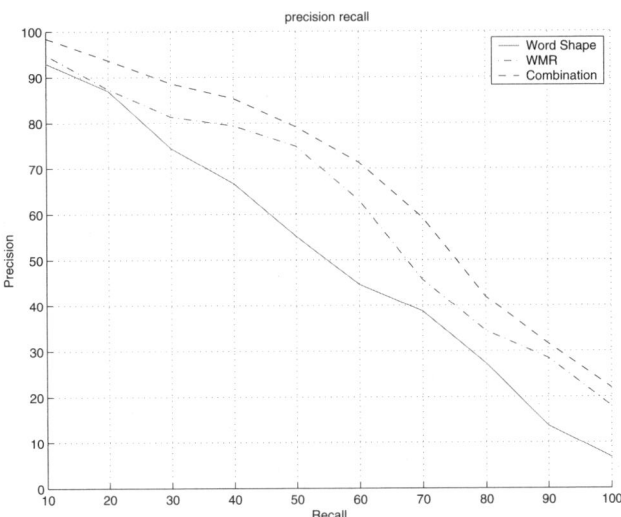

Fig. 3. Precision-recall comparison of word-shape, character-shape and combination approaches

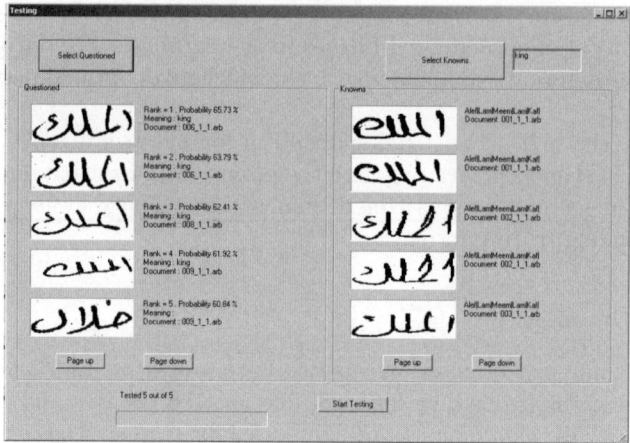

Fig. 4. Word Spotting Testing Results

10   Conclusion and Future Directions

Processing image and text based queries in parallel can result in higher performance than either alone. The versatile search framework presented can apply to many document search problems. The example presented illustrates a word spotting application, but other document search strategies may experience similar performance increases. For example, a partially transcribed document could be represented as a "bag of words," with a term/document matrix. From there, latent semantic analysis TF-IDF (term frequency-inverse document frequency) weights can perform traditional searches, with image search augmenting less than perfect transcription techniques. Furthermore, "plugging in" improved image or text-based search algorithms can help increase overall performance. For our experiments, we used the neural network to weight the two incoming scores. However, features extracted from the images may improve neural network performance.

References

1. Hand, D., Mannila, H., Smyth, P.: Principles of Data Mining. MIT Press, Cambridge (2001)
2. Taghva, K., Borsack, J., Condit, A.: Results of applying probabilistic IR to OCR text. In: Research and Development in Information Retrieval, pp. 202–211 (1994)
3. Russell, G., Perrone, M., Chee, Y.M., Ziq, A.: Handwritten Document Retrieval. In: Proc. Eighth International Workshop on Frontiers in Handwriting Recognition, Niagara-on-the-lake, Ontario, pp. 233–238 (2002)
4. Srihari, S.N., Huang, C., Srinivasan, H.: A search engine for handwritten documents. In: Document Recognition and Retrieval XII: Proceedings SPIE, San Jose, CA, pp. 66–75 (2005)

5. Srihari, S.N., Zhang, B., Tomai, C., Lee, S., Shi, Z., Shin, Y.C.: A search engine for handwritten documents. In: Proc. Symposium on Document Image Understanding Technology (SDIUT 2005), Greenbelt, MD, pp. 67–75 (2003)
6. Srihari, S.N., Shi, Z.: Forensic handwritten document retrieval system. In: Proc. Document Image Analysis for Libraries (DIAL), Palo Alto, CA, pp. 188–194. IEEE Computer Society, Los Alamitos (2004)
7. Srihari, S.N., Srinivasan, H., Babu, P., Bhole, C.: Handwritten Arabic word spotting using the CEDARABIC document analysis system. In: Proc. Symposium on Document Image Understanding Technology (SDIUT 2005), College Park, MD, pp. 123–132 (2005)
8. Srihari, S.N., Srinivasan, H., Babu, P., Bhole, C.: Spotting words in handwritten Arabic documents. In: Document Recognition and Retrieval XIII: Proceedings SPIE, San Jose, CA, pp. 606702-1– 606702-12 (2006)
9. Kim, G., Govindaraju, V.: A lexicon driven approach to handwritten word recognition for real-time applications. IEEE Transactions on Pattern Analysis and Machine Intelligence 19(4), 366–379 (1997)
10. Kim, G., Govindaraju, V., Srihari, S.N.: A segmentation and recognition strategy for handwritten phrases. In: International Conference on Pattern Recognition. ICPR-13, pp. 510–514 (1996)
11. Huang, C., Srihari, S.N.: Mapping transcripts to handwritten text. In: Proc. Tenth International Workshop on Frontiers in Handwriting Recognition (IWFHR), La Boule, France, IEEE Computer Society, Los Alamitos (2006)
12. Zhang, B., Srihari, S.N.: Binary vector dissimilarity measures for handwriting identification. In: Proceedings of the SPIE, Document Recognition and Retrieval, pp. 155–166 (2003)
13. Srihari, S.N., Tomai, C.I., Zhang, B., Lee, S.: Individuality of numerals. In: Proc. Seventh International Conference on Document Analysis and Recognition (ICDAR), Edinburgh, UK, p. 1096. IEEE Computer Society, Los Alamitos (2003)
14. Kim, G.: Recognition of offline handwritten words and extension to phrase recognition. Doctoral Dissertation, State University of New York at Buffalo (1997)

A Two-Tier Arabic Offline Handwriting Recognition Based on Conditional Joining Rules

Ahmad AbdulKader

Google Inc.
Google Inc. 1600 Amphitheatre Parkway Mountain View, CA 94043
ahmadab@google.com

Abstract. In this paper we present a novel approach for the recognition of off-line Arabic handwritten text motivated by the Arabic letters' conditional joining rules. A lexicon of Arabic words can be expressed in terms of a new alphabet of PAWs (Part of Arabic Word). PAWs can be expressed in terms of letters. The recognition problem is decomposed into two problems to solve simultaneously. To find the best matching word for an input image, a Two-Tier Beam search is performed. In Tier One, the search is constrained by a letter to PAW lexicon. In Tier Two, the search is constrained by a PAW to word lexicon. The searches are driven by a PAW recognizer.

Experiments conducted on the standard IFN/ENIT database [6] of handwritten Tunisian town names show word error rates of about 11%. This result compares to the results of the commonly used HMM based approaches.

1 Introduction

The recognition of handwritten text in images, commonly known as offline handwriting recognition, still presents a challenging task. Significant work remains before large scale commercially viable systems can be built. This is truer for Arabic (and other non-Latin scripts in general) than Latin scripts, because less research effort has been put into solving the problem.

Most research in Arabic offline recognition has been directed to numeral and single character recognition [1]. Few examples exist that address the offline recognition of Arabic words problem [5]. The availability of standard publicly available databases of handwritten Arabic text images like IFN/INIT database has encouraged more research [5] [9].

For Latin scripts, HMM (Hidden Markov Model) based approaches have dominated the space of offline cursive word recognition [10] [1]. In a typical setup, a lexicon constrains the output of the recognizer. An HMM is then built for every word in the lexicon, and the corresponding likelihood (probability of data being generated by the model) is computed. The most likely interpretation is then postulated as the correct one.

In the few reported approaches to Arabic recognition, they used methods very similar to the ones used for Latin [5]. Some attempts tried to modify the preprocessing and feature extraction phases to accommodate the different nature of the Arabic script.

D.S. Doermann and S. Jaeger (Eds.): SACH 2006, LNCS 4768, pp. 70–81, 2008.

However, the author is unaware of any attempts, to this date, to exploit the unique properties of Arabic script for recognition purposes or to build systems inspired by the distinct nature of the Arabic handwriting.

In this work, we present an approach that exploits a key (yet often ignored) property of the Arabic writing script in building a recognition system. This property is basically the set of conditional joining rules that govern how Arabic letters connect in cursive writing. In Section 2, we show how this property leads to the emergence of PAWs and how our approach exploits these to build a two-tier recognition system. In Section 3, we describe our recognition system in details. Section 4 reports the experimental results conducted on the publicly available IFN/ENIT database of handwritten Tunisian town names and how these compare to the results reported using alternative approaches.

A system built based on the approach described in this paper was submitted as an entry to the ICDAR05 Arabic word recognition competition [7]. The system was evaluated as the second best system on a blind test set and the best system on the non-blind test set. Further developments to the system were also done after the competition. The author provides remarks on the competition and the effect of the inconsistency between the training and test set distribution.

2   Exploiting the Arabic Writing System

Arabic (*arabī*) is the fourth or fifth most widely-spoken language in the world. It is spoken by close to 300 million people mostly living in North Africa and South West Asia, and is the largest member of the Semitic branch of the Afro-Asiatic language family [11].

Arabic script has a distinct writing system that differs significantly from the commonly known Latin or Han-based writing systems. Below, a brief history describes the writing system and how one of its unique properties has been exploited to build an offline word recognition system.

2.1   The Arabic Writing System

The Arabic script evolved from the Nabataean Aramaic script. It has been used since the 4th century A.D., but the earliest document, an inscription in Arabic, Syriac, and Greek, dates from 512 A.D. The Aramaic language has fewer consonants than Arabic, so, during the 7th century, new Arabic letters were created by adding dots to existing letters to avoid ambiguities. Further diacritics indicating short vowels were introduced, but in general are used only to ensure text (like the Qur'an) is read aloud without mistakes [12].

The Arabic alphabet is written from right to left and is composed of 28 basic letters. Adaptations of the script for other languages, such as Persian and Urdu, have additional letters. No difference exists between written and printed letters; the writing is UNICASE (i.e. the concept of upper and lower case letters does not exist).

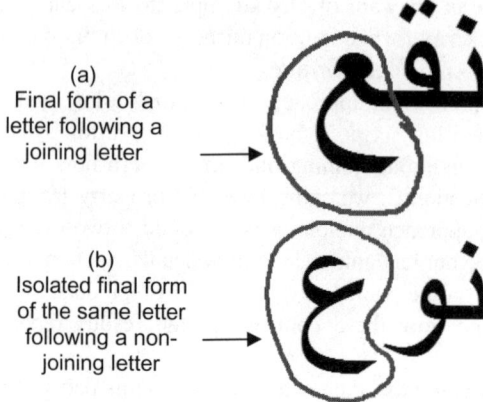

(a)
Final form of a
letter following a
joining letter

(b)
Isolated final form
of the same letter
following a non-
joining letter

Fig. 1. An illustration of the conditional joining property in Arabic script

The Arabic script is cursive, and all primary letters have conditional forms for their glyphs, depending if used at the beginning, middle, or end of a word. Up to four distinct forms (initial, medial, final, or isolated) of a letter might be exhibited [4].

However, only six letters (و ز ر ذ د ا) have either an isolated or a final form and do not have initial or medial forms. If followed by another letter, these six letters do not join with it, and so the next letter can only have its initial or isolated form despite not being the initial letter of a word. This rule applies to numerals and non-Arabic letters as well. This property is often referred to as ***conditional joining***. Figure 1 shows an illustration of this property.

The conditional joining property leads to the emergence of PAWs (Part of Arabic Word). A PAW is a sequence of Arabic letters joined together with no exceptions. Given an Arabic word, it can be deterministically segmented into one or more PAWs.

It is worth noting that an Arabic writer must strictly abide by the conditional joining rule. Otherwise, the handwriting may be deemed unreadable. However, due to sloppiness in writing or image acquisition conditions, PAWs may be physically connected in an image. We empirically estimate that this happens in less than 5% of the overall PAW population. In Section 3.4, we will explain our approach for handling these cases.

2.2 A Two-Tier Approach

Given the conditional joining property of the Arabic writing script, words can be seen as being composed of a sequence of PAWs. In other words, PAWs can be considered an alternative alphabet. The unique number of PAWs constituting a word lexicon grows sub-linearly with the number of words in the lexicon. Figure 2 shows how the number of unique PAWs increases with the size of an Arabic lexicon.

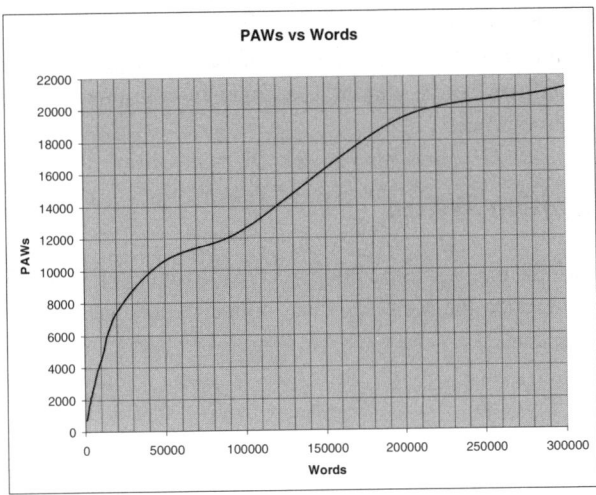

Fig. 2. The number of unique PAWs in a lexicon grows sub-linearly with the number of words

A lexicon of Arabic words can then be decomposed into two lexica. The first is a PAW to letter lexicon, which lists all the unique PAWs and their spelling in terms of the letter alphabet. The second is a word to PAW lexicon that lists all the unique words and their spelling in terms of the PAW alphabet.

Consequently, the problem of finding the best matching lexicon entry to an image can be decomposed into two intertwined problems to solve simultaneously. The first problem lies in finding the best possible mapping from characters to PAWs, constrained by the first lexicon. The second problem is finding the best possible mapping from PAWs to words, constrained by the second lexicon.

This two-tier approach has a number of useful properties. In one property, lexicons constrain the outputs of the recognition process, so a number of character recognition errors can be remedied in the PAW recognition phase. Figure 3 shows an example of this type of potential recognition error. It is unlikely, in this example, that the second letter "ص" would have been proposed by a character recognizer given the poor condition of the handwriting.

Fig. 3. An example image of the لصغر PAW can be confused with لعخر, which is a valid lexicon PAW

In another property, PAWs ultimately have their own prior probability distribution that can be utilized by the PAW recognizer to favor more frequently occurring PAWs. These prior probabilities can be viewed as a linguistic n-gram character model, which drives the recognition process.

3 The Recognition System

A block diagram of the two-tier recognition system is shown in Figure 4. In the following sections, we will describe the pre-processing, normalization, segmentation, recognition, and search steps in detail.

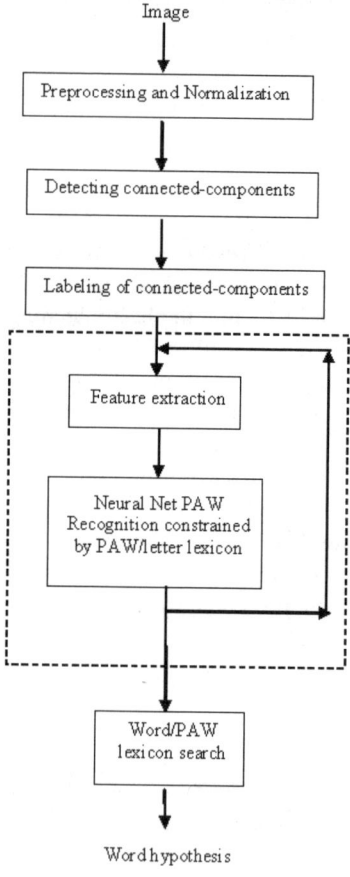

Fig. 4. A block diagram of the recognition system

3.1 Preprocessing, Normalization and Segmentation

The images in the IFN/ENIT database already passed through the basic processing of image binarization, cropping, word segmentation, and noise reduction; so we have skipped these phases in our experiments. The first step of processing detects connected-components. Connected-components whose width and height are below a certain threshold (which is not a critical choice) are obtained. This threshold has been determined empirically throughout the experiments. This step acts as an additional noise reduction step. Connected-components are then sorted from right to left, based on their right-most point. This allows the search algorithm to sequence through the connected-components in an order close to the writing order.

Connected-components are then labeled as 'primary' and 'secondary'. This labeling is performed by detecting relative horizontal overlaps between connected-components and applying safe thresholds on connected-component sizes. Each secondary connected-component must be associated to a primary one. No secondary component can exist alone. Figure 5 shows the grouped connected-components in an image of a word. Each group of connected components contains one primary and one or more secondary connected components.

In 5(a), each connected-component group corresponds to exactly one PAW. We have empirically determined that this case represents 65% of the overall population of words. Figure 5(b) shows how the two connected component groups correspond to one PAW (i.e. the over-segmentation case). Over-segmentation represents 30% of the word population. Figure 5(c) shows how the purple connected component-group is actually

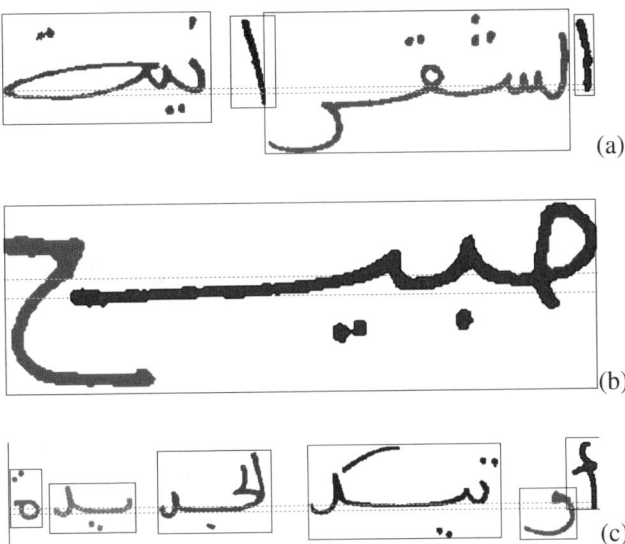

Fig. 5. Three examples of grouped connected-components. (a) The connected-component group is an actual PAW. (b) The PAW was split into two connected-component groups. (c) The PAWs joined into one connected-component group (purple color).

two touching PAWs. This case is not inherently handled by the proposed approach. It constitutes 5% of the cases. We will explain in Section 3.4 how it was handled. As such, a fundamental assumption of the following steps of the system is that PAWs can only occur on connected-component group boundaries.

3.2 The PAW Recognizer

The IFN/ENIT database has a lexicon of 946 Tunisian town names, with 762 unique PAWs in this word lexicon. Although the training database may not necessarily contain at least one sample of each valid word, it appears that at least one sample is present of every valid PAW.

Because the relatively low number of unique PAWs, it was decided to use a Neural Network based classifier to recognize PAWs. As the size of the word lexicon increases along with the number of valid PAWs, it might be impractical to use a Neural Network classifier directly for recognizing PAWs.

In our experiments, we build two Neural Net PAW classifiers. The first classifier is a convolutional Neural Network. Convolution Neural Networks [8] have been reported to attain the best accuracy in offline handwritten digits. In this type of networks, the input image is scaled to fit a fixed size grid while maintaining its aspect ratio. Since the number of letters in a PAW can vary from 1 to 8, the grid aspect ratio must be wide enough to accommodate the widest possible PAW while still maintaining its distinctness. The second classifier is based on features extracted from the directional codes of the connected-components constituting the PAW. Each of these two classifiers has 762 outputs and trained with sets that reflect the prior distributions of PAWs in the word lexicon.

PAWs can exist at the start, middle and final position in a word, and a PAW can constitute an entire word. We'll refer to this as the isolated position. Figure 6 shows example PAWs at each of the four possible positions.

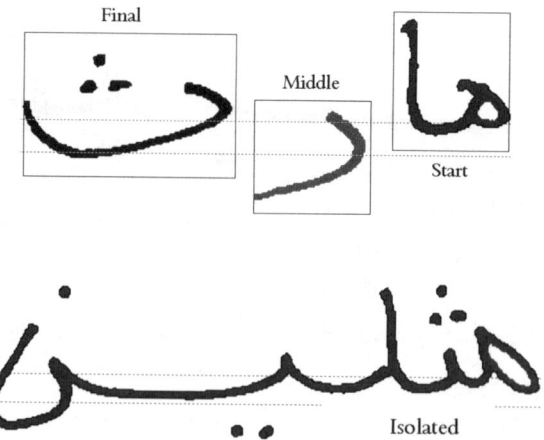

Fig. 6. PAWs at start, middle, and final positions in the word

Each unique PAW does not necessarily exist at all possible positions within a word: start, middle, final, isolated, so it was determined that building a separate classifier for each possible position improves PAW recognition accuracy significantly.

3.3 Beam Search

As mentioned above, the word lexicon can be decomposed into two lexica: letter to PAW lexicon and a PAW to word lexicon. The letter to PAW lexicon constrains the output of the PAW recognizer as mentioned above. The PAW to word recognizer constrains the search for the best matching word.

Beam search is an algorithm that extends the well known best-first search algorithm. Like a best-first search, it uses a heuristic function to evaluate the promise of each node it examines. Beam search, however, only unfolds the first m most promising nodes at each depth, where m is a fixed number, the "beam width". It is commonly used in speech recognition [2].

The Beam search finds the best matching word to an image, using the output of PAW recognizer as a search heuristic. The search algorithm sequences through the connected-components groups and considers either starting a new PAW or adding the group to the existing PAW. The search retains the list of possible PAWs, with their corresponding posterior probabilities produced by the PAW recognizer. Different connected-component group to PAW mappings remain in a lattice of possible segmentations. After sequencing through all the groups, the best possible segmentation is evaluated and chosen as the winning hypothesis.

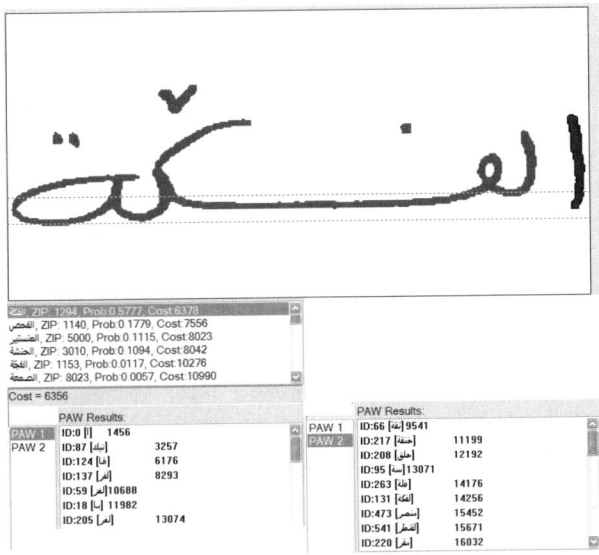

Fig. 7. An recognition example showing the word recognition results in the top list and the PAW recognition results in the lower list boxes

For practical reasons and to ensure that the segmentation possibilities in the lattice do not explode, two heuristics apply. First, the maximum number of connected-component groups per PAW is capped at four. This number has been determined empirically based on the training data. Second, at every step in the lattice, segmentation possibilities with a probability lower than the most probable segmentation, determined by a certain threshold, are pruned. This means that, theoretically, the Beam search may not produce the most probable segmentation. However, this rarely happens in practice.

Figure 7 shows an example image, the final recognition results, and the PAW recognition results of the two connected-component groups. Note that, although the second PAW was misrecognized, the overall word was correctly recognized.

3.4 Handling Exceptions

As noted earlier, the under-segmentation case was empirically determined to constitute approximately 5% of the words. To handle the under-segmentation problem, where more than one PAW becomes segmented as one connected-component group, a final step was added to the process. The final step triggers if the probability of the winning segmentation path in the lattice is lower than a certain threshold. This was found to be strong evidence that under-segmentation had occurred. When triggered, a Viterbi search is performed on the individual PAW recognition results of the connected-component groups. In this search, the edit distance between the each of the PAW to Word lexicon and the recognition results are computed. Both PAW insertions and deletions are allowed, with a penalty associated with each.

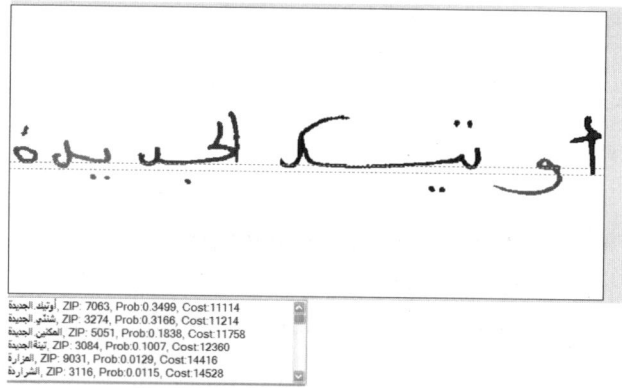

Fig. 8. A recognition example of an under-segmented image. The Viterbi search that is triggered when the best Beam result is lower than a certain threshold produced the correct answer.

4 Experiments

4.1 The Data Set

Experiments were conducted on the publicly available IFN/ENIT database [6]. The database is split into four sets A, B, C, and D. The four sets contain 26,459 images of segmented Tunisian town names handwritten by 411 unique writers, with 115,585 PAWs. The ground truth information is available. Unique word labels number 946, and they are 762 for each image.

Sets A, B, and C were used for training and validation. Set D was used for evaluation. Set D has 6,735 words handwritten by 104 unique writers, none of which contributed any words in sets A, B or C.

In a widely agreed upon rule of thumb in building recognition systems, recognizers are evaluated on a distribution similar to the training set. The four sets have roughly the same writer demographics, word distribution and, consequently, PAW distribution, so our experiments upheld this rule.

4.2 The Training Process

One problem encountered during implementing the recognition system was obtaining data to train the PAW recognizer. As such, the database has word-level ground truth information, but not PAW-level ground truth information. To solve this problem, we followed a bootstrapping technique similar to the bootstrapping from incomplete data in the well-known Expectation-Maximization *EM* setting [3].

As mentioned in Section 3.1, our connected-component segmentation and grouping algorithm results in three different types of segmentation. We call for the first type, exact segmentation, where each of the resulting connected-component groups corresponds to one, and exactly one, PAW. Empirically, it was determined that exact segmentation cases constitute 65% of the total word population.

The number and the identity of the PAWs that constitute the sample's word label can be computed for each training sample. To bootstrap the training process, a conjecture is made that for every sample in the training set where the number of connected-component groups is equal to the number of label PAWs, the identity of a specific PAW corresponds to the ground truth label of the connected-component group at the same position. This conjecture holds almost all the time. Rare cases exist where PAW over-segmentation and under-segmentation occur an equal number of times in a word, which results in breaking the *exact segmentation conjecture*.

As a first step, the PAW recognizers are trained on all the samples that satisfy the *exact segmentation conjecture*, which is 65% of the training data. In subsequent steps, by using the ground truth word label and its corresponding PAWs, the PAW recognizer trained in the previous step segments connected-component groups into PAWs. This happens by running the same algorithm described in Section 3 with only one entry in the word lexicon: the ground truth. This could work only for exactly under-segmented and over-segmented words. So, the under-segmented words, which constitute 5% of the training set, are excluded from the training process. The training step is analogous to the maximization step in EM, while the PAW re-segmentation phase is analogous to the expectation step. This sequence (training, re-segmentation) was repeated three times until no significant change in the accuracy of the PAW recognizer occurred.

4.3 PAW Recognition Results

The results of the two individual PAW recognizers and their combined results are shown in Table 1.

Table 1. The error rates of the individual PAW recognizer and the combined PAW recognizer on set D of the IFN/ENIT database

Recognizer	Top 1 Errors	Top 10 Errors
Convolutional Net	40.13%	12.31%
Directional Codes	32.4%	11.77%
Combined Classifier	19.98%	8.9%

4.4 Word Recognition Results

Table 2 shows the error rates for the overall word recognizer, as measured on set D of the IFN/INIT database. It also gives the results broken down by the type of segmentation encountered in the image.

Table 2. The error rates of overall word recognizer

Data subset	Top 1 Errors	Top 10 Errors
All data	11.06%	4.99%
Exact Segmentation	7.11%	1.67%
Over-Segmented	13.33%	4.39%
Under-Segmented	36.03%	36.03%

5   Conclusion

In this paper we have presented a novel approach to the recognition of lexicon-constrained Arabic handwritten words. The approach exploits the conditional joining of letter properties in Arabic writing to decompose the problem into two problems to solve simultaneously. Using a Neural Network based PAW recognizer; a two-tier Beam search finds the best matching word to the input image. Word error rates of around 11% were achieved on the publicly available IFN/ENIT database. These results compare favorably to the results reported on the same set using an alternative HMM based approach [5].

5.1   The ICDAR05 Competition

The same results were also reported as part of the ICDAR05 Arabic handwritten word recognition competition report. A system that implements the presented approach ranked as the second best entry on the blind-test (whose results are not reported here since the author has no access to it) and the best entry on the non-blind test set (set D).

It is worth noting that the blind set had a different distribution of words than all published sets A, B, C, and D of the database. This, in turn, resulted in an unexpected PAW prior distribution. This may explain why the error rate reported on the blind reported set significantly higher than the non-blind set. The author holds the opinion that the competing recognizers should have been evaluated on a distribution similar to the training set.

Acknowledgment

The author would like to thank the developers of the IFN/INIT database for making it possible to evaluate different Arabic handwritten word recognition systems in an objective manner and increasing interest in Arabic handwriting recognition.

References

[1] Vinciarelli, A., Luettin, J.: Off-Line Cursive Script Recognition Based on Continuous Density HMM. In: International Workshop on Frontiers in Handwriting Recognition, IWFHR 2000 (2000)

[2] Al-Badr, B., Mohmond, S.A.: Survey and bibliography of Arabic optical text recognition. Signal Processing 41, 49–77 (1995)

[3] Ney, H., Mergel, D., Noll, A., Paesler., A.: Data driven search organization for continuous speech recognition. IEEE Transactions on Signal Processing 40(2), 272–281 (1992)

[4] Bilmes, J.A.: A gentle tutorial of the EM algorithm and its applications to parameter estimation for Gaussian mixture and hidden Markov models, Technical Report TR-97-021, International Computer Science Institute, Berkeley, California (1998)

[5] Versteegh, K.: The Arabic Language. Edinburgh University Press (1997)

[6] Pechwitz, M., Maergner, V.: HMM based approach for hand- written Arabic word recognition using the IFN/ENIT database. In: Proc. 7th Int. Conf. on Document Analysis and Recognition, Edinburgh, Scotland (2003)

[7] Pechwitz, M., Maddouri, S.S., Maergner, V., Ellouze, N., Amiri, H.: IFN/ENIT - database of handwritten Arabic words. In: Proc. of CIFED, pp. 129–136 (2002)

[8] Margner, V., Pechwitz, M., Abed, H.E.: ICDAR 2005 Arabic handwriting recognition competition. In: Eighth International Conference on Document Analysis and Recognition. Proceeding, vol. 1, pp. 70–74 (2005)

[9] Simard, P., Steinkraus, D., Platt, J.C.: Best Practices for Convolutional Neural Networks Applied to Visual Document Analysis. In: ICDAR 2003, pp. 958–962 (2003)

[10] Haraty, R.A., El-Zabadani, H.M.: Hawwaz: An Offline Arabic Handwriting Recognition System. International Journal of Computers and Applications (2005)

[11] Steinherz, T., Rivlin, E., Intrator, N.: Off-Line Cursive Script Word Recognition A Survey. International Journal on Document Analysis and Recognition 2, 90–110 (1999)

[12] Wikipedia: Arabic Language, http://en.wikipedia.org/wiki/Arabic

[13] Omniglot: Writing System and Languages of the World, http://www.omniglot.com/writing/arabic.htm

Databases and Competitions: Strategies to Improve Arabic Recognition Systems

Volker Märgner and Haikal El Abed

Technical University Braunschweig,
Institute for Communications Technology (IfN),
Schleinitzstrasse 22, 38106 Braunschweig,
Germany
{v.maergner,elabed}@tu-bs.de

Abstract. The great success and high recognition rates of both OCR systems and recognition systems for handwritten words are unconceivable without the availability of huge datasets of real world data. This chapter gives a short survey of datasets used for recognition with special focus on their application. The main part of this chapter deals with Arabic handwriting, datasets for recognition systems, and their availability. A description of different datasets and their usability is given, and the results of a competition are presented. Finally, a strategy for the development of Arabic handwriting recognition systems based on datasets and competitions is presented.

1 Introduction

Machines are still far from being able to read as humans can. Nevertheless, automatic reading of printed text has reached a high level in many languages and applications, e.g. address reading and check reading. Powerful computers allow the execution of efficient recognition algorithms without special hardware. A gap still to be filled, however, for languages that do not use Latin characters. One such language is Arabic, spoken by more than 230 million people as the official language in 25 countries.

We will not go into details of Arabic writing style, but refer the reader unfamiliar with Arabic to [1] and [2]. The cursive style of even printed Arabic makes the segmentation into characters difficult, and the extensive use of diacritics demands special methods of feature extraction and normalization. Therefore, systems developed for Latin character-based OCR cannot be adapted easily to Arabic.

To date most successful methods for OCR and cursive script recognition are statistical methods, e.g. approaches based on Neural Nets (NN) or Hidden Markov Models (HMM). Like all methods based on statistical approaches, they require a huge amount of data to adapt their parameters to the intended application.

D.S. Doermann and S. Jaeger (Eds.): SACH 2006, LNCS 4768, pp. 82–103, 2008.

Another crucial aspect for recognition system development is the discussion and competition of different approaches. Only the testing of different methods on identical datasets allows for informative comparison. Furthermore, objective quality measuring methods are necessary for ranking the systems. This also constitutes a high motivation for developing advanced methods.

This chapter gives a survey of datasets, competitions, and evaluation tools necessary to improve recognition systems, in general, and Arabic handwritten text recognition in particular. The chapter is organized as follows: In Section 2 a short survey of existing datasets, competitions and evaluation tools for non-Arabic text is given. This section focuses on those parts of non-Arabic recognition systems that can be used to train Arabic text recognition. Even though many elements of recognition systems are unique and independent of the language, some language dependent special properties exist which are discussed in this section. Section 3 describes the state of the art of existing datasets of Arabic handwritten words in some detail, followed by Section 4, which presents systems, methods, and results of the first competition of Arabic handwriting recognition. Section 5 discusses several aspects important for the further development of Arabic handwriting recognition, as summarized in Section 6.

2   Datasets for Text Recognition

The first approaches for automatic character recognition were developed in the beginning of the 1930s, using simple pattern matching methods on selective characters. Special, easy-to-read fonts were designed for the automatic reading on bank forms. In the 1960s, mail sorting machines could read printed text on envelopes. A veritable leap forward happend in the 1990s, when huge datasets became available to the research community [3], allowing the development of statistical methods for OCR systems. Another reason for the progress in the 1990s were annual competitions of OCR accuracy, such as the workshops at the Information Science Research Institute (ISRI), University of Nevada (e.g. [4]). Along with these developments came as a third important aspect, the development of methods for measuring and comparing the quality of recognition systems (National Institute of Standards and Technology (NIST) [3] and ISRI [4]).

This work was highly successful. Powerful OCR systems were realized and useful methods developed. However, it became clear that collecting and labelling data is not only an important task but also an expensive one. Commercial companies tend to exploit their own advantage rather than accelerate development by encouraging competition, making independent funding crucial.

Fortunately, just as OCR development attracted independent support, public funding also became available for the development of handwritten character and word recognition systems. Driven by the need of check reading and postal sorting machines, real world data were made available, e.g., by CEDAR [5]. NIST made available not only data for system development, but also recognition software as a benchmark for future methods. Thus, it was possible to develop and test parts of recognition systems separately, such as a character recognizer or a word-to-character segmentation method. By not having to develop entirely new systems every time, researchers could focus on a particular aspect, significantly facilitating development.

2.1 Synthetic and Artificial Data

The expense of collecting and preparing data for building and optimizing OCR systems resulted in various cost-cutting efforts. One idea was to avoid scanning and labeling of printed text by generating synthetic data [6]. While this approach provides cheap datasets for testing and developing statistical recognition methods, it is clear that a system developed with synthetic data must be retrained before being employed in a real world environment. Concerning handwriting, the development of specially designed forms for collecting artificial data made data preparation for training and testing quicker and cheaper. However, many research groups used this method to build small datasets of their own, resulting in recognition tests performed on these diverse datasets being incompatible with results of other research groups, who used different datasets.

2.2 Competitions

Testing recognition systems with large identical datasets is crucial for performance evaluation. Another challenge comes from their complexity, because they consist of many specialized parts solving very diverse tasks. The recognition rate is a convenient measure for comparing different systems, but it is a global parameter hardly significant for system component development. To improve the overall system quality, it is essential to know the effectiveness of its modules.

The development of meaningful aspects of system evaluation methods was an important part of the aforementioned annual OCR tests at ISRI. The goal of these tests not only publicized the state-of-the-art of page reading systems, but also provided information for improvement through competition and objective assessment. While much has been achieved concerning the evaluation problem (e.g. [7]), the availability of tools and data remains an issue for research, as discussed in the paper [8], published in 2005. For example, it is not enough to measure the quality, based on the symbol output of the recognizer, only by considering the word accuracy. The quality of zoning and the segmentation into words or characters represent an important feature of a recognition system, and should be evaluated too [9]. A more general concept for evaluating system modules separately is presented in [10].

2.3 Requirements on Arabic Datasets

Text recognition for Arabic printed or handwritten words faces the same challenges, to a large degree, as text recognition for Latin character based languages. Given the fundamental differences of the characters and the writing style, some additional features must be considered. In addition to the difference in writing direction, line by line from right to left, the connection of the printed characters differs greatly between Arabic and e.g. English. It is interesting to note that the Arabic set of 28 characters results in 100 different character shapes because most characters can appear in four different shapes depending on the position of the character in a word (isolated, beginning, middle, and end), but capital letters are not known. This numbers approximately twice the amount of the English character set, given the 52 different character shapes of English, including capital letters.

The connectedness of the Arabic printed characters necessitates a more complex segmentation of a word into characters. Moreover, points and other diacritic marks, which are positioned above or below the main character shape, are parts of the characters.

These characteristics of Arabic require a special structure of the dataset designed for training and testing Arabic recognition systems. In addition to these characteristics of printed Arabic, Arabic handwriting has even more differences, which increases the difficulty of the construction of a dataset and recognition process. Fig. 1 gives an example of a handwritten address, written with Latin and Arabic letters. An apparent difference can be seen, with less regularity in the text written with Arabic compared to the text written in Latin characters. Table 1 shows examples of handwritten Arabic words with marked characteristics.

These examples show fundamental differences in the writing of Arabic words compared to English. As writing styles of English differ around the world, the writing style of Arabic also differs from country to country. A critical point is that the way of using ligatures differs particularly.

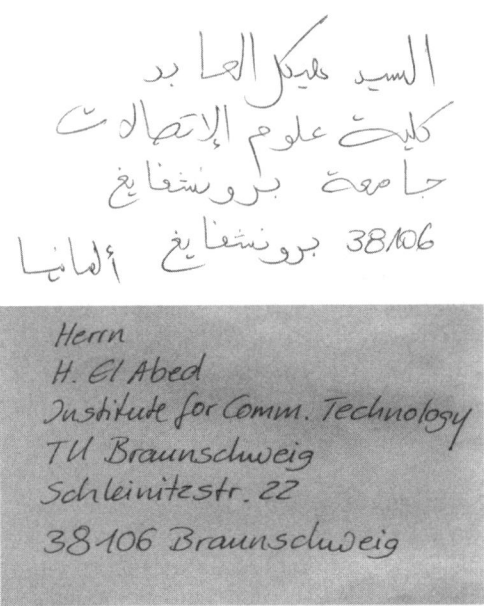

Fig. 1. Example of a handwritten address written in Latin and in Arabic

Table 1. Examples of some typical features of Arabic handwritten words

Example	Description
قـمـتَ	Consecutive letters within a word are typically joined together by a baseline stroke
الشّاطُور	Characters are often stretched through lengthen the connecting line
صلبَةٍ(لا)	Ligatures replace particular character pairs or even triples
ضٍ(لا)	Diacritical mark "Chadda" is used to indicate short vowels or as special form of a character
طـصـالي كـبيرة	The baseline is needed for the recognition, but sometimes difficult to find

Datasets with Arabic text or words must consider these characteristic features. As a result, special labels are assigned, and the amount of differently shaped characters is considered in the incorporation of different words by different writers into the datasets.

3 Datasets of Arabic Text

As noted in Section 2, datasets of typical printed or handwritten words yield the most important part in a recognition system design. Papers on Arabic printed or handwritten word recognition have been published for many years. The first paper on Arabic OCR dates to 1975, the first Arabic OCR system was made available in the 1990s. However, only three papers comparing OCR systems have been published to date, and the newest one is seven years old [11]. To overcome the problem of the lack of large datasets for developing Arabic OCR systems, and to motivate the research on statistical methods, a system for synthetic generation of Arabic datasets was developed according to the approach of English OCR [12]. This allows for fast and simple generation of large datasets.

The situation is no better for Arabic handwritten word recognition. For many years the work published about Arabic handwriting recognition has used small, private datasets, which makes a comparison of methods essentially impossible. Another disadvantage lies in the fact that these private datasets are often too small for reasonable statistical methods. Only a few datasets have been published. Recently, an overview about the state of the art of Arabic offline handwriting recognition was given [1].

In the following, datasets of Arabic words or text are discussed. It must be mentioned that databases presented in papers and used for experiments are often not publicly available. The current availability of the following datasets is mentioned in each section.

3.1   ERIM Arabic Document Database

The Environmental Research Institute of Michigan (ERIM) created a database of machine-printed Arabic documents. These images, extracted from typewritten and typeset Arabic books and magazines, contain a wide variety of fonts and ligatures with quality ranging from poor to good. All images were collected at 300 dpi. This database provides a training and testing set for Arabic text recognition research. The following details are given on the ERIM web site [13].

Database specifications:

- over 750 pages of Arabic text
- all data digitized on 300 dpi flatbed scanner
- grayscale page images available for some pages
- all character information stored as Unicode
- approximately 1,000,000 characters
- truth for characters, as well as ligatures
- over 200 distinct Arabic ligatures
- a wide variety of fonts and data quality
- divided into Training, Statistic, and Test sets
- image format documentation included

Together with the image data, truth files are provided. All this sounds promising, but it was impossible to acquire the database. Apparently the data is unavailable today.

3.2   Al-Isra Database

In a paper at the IEEE Canadian Conference on Electrical and Computer Engineering [14], a database of handwritten Arabic words, numbers, and signatures is described. The data were collected at the Al-Isra University Amman, Jordan. Five hundred randomly selected students contributed handwritten data to the database.

The database consists of:

- 37,000 Arabic words,
- 10,000 digits (Arabian and Indian),
- 2,500 signatures, and
- 500 free-form Arabic sentences,

all saved in grayscale and black and white BMP file formats. The database was announced in 1999, but until now no data has been published on the internet.

3.3   CENPARMI Database

At the IWFHR workshop 2000 in Amsterdam, the Center for Pattern Recognition and Machine Intelligence (CENPARMI) in Montreal presented a database of images from 3,000 checks provided by a banking cooperation [15]. These are images of real, used checks, and the words of the legal amount have been segmented and labeled with an ASCII code sequence for each subword (called PAW = connected **P**art of an **A**rabic **W**ord). Also, the courtesy amount in Indian digits has been segmented and labeled. The data are divided into training and testing sets. The database contains 29,498 subwords, 15,175 digits, and 2,499 legal and courtesy amounts.

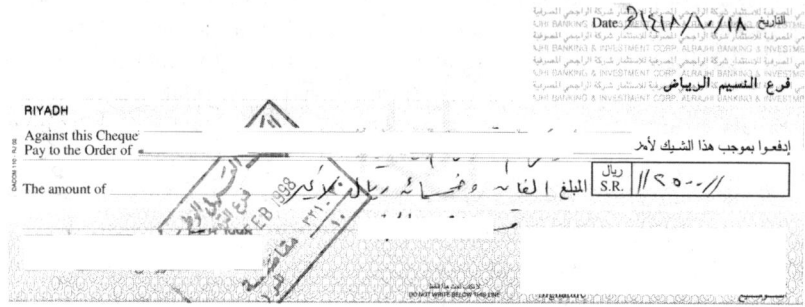

Fig. 2. Example of a check from CENPARMI database

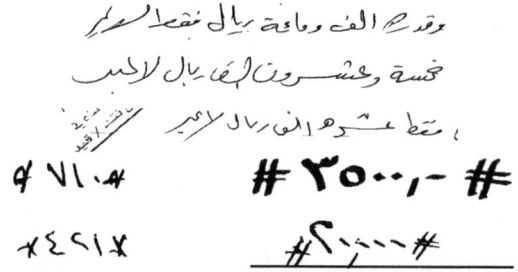

Fig. 3. Examples of legal and courtesy amounts from CENPARMI database

Figures 2 and 3 show examples from the CENPARMI database. The advantage of this database lies in its availability and the real world data that were collected. The disadvantage comes from some subwords being under-represented, so a training of a statistical recognizer becomes severely restricted.

3.4   IFN/ENIT-Database

At the CIFED Conference in 2002, the Institute for Communications Technology (IfN) at Technical University Braunschweig, Germany, and the Ecole Nationale d'Ingeniéurs de Tunis (ENIT), Tunisia, presented a database with handwritten Tunisian town names [16]. This dataset was collected on specially designed forms to make the labeling procedure as simple as possible.

The aim was to collect images of handwritten town names written in a similar quality to town names in an address on a letter. The form was designed to:

- encourage writing without strong constraints,
- collect writing similar to writing on a letter,
- be easy to process automatically, and
- provide additional information about the person who completed it.

A filled example of the devised form appears in Fig. 4. The form consists of three columns and a text block at the bottom. A column on the right hand side of the form lists 12 lines with printed Tunisian town/village names and their respective postcodes, which are automatically selected from the possible 937 names. The sample writers were expected to write the postcode in the left column and the town/village name in the middle column in their individual writing style. Writers had neither a writing line nor a box in which to write, because the processing of the scanned data should be as simple as possible. To provide a light writing guidance, black rectangles were printed on the backside of each page, which mark where to write. In the scanning process, these rectangles can be removed using a simple threshold. Further segmentation operations are unnecessary. The names printed on each form were selected randomly with the condition that each character shape should occur at least 200 times. Therefore, those names with rare character shapes occur more often than names with frequent ones. Each word appears at least three times in the database. A page number provides a form identifier for the subsequent processing. The block at the bottom gives additional information about the age, profession, and identity of the writer. Each writer was asked to complete five forms, with each writing 60 names.

The database (www.ifnenit.com), in version v1.0p2, consists of 26,459 handwritten Arabic names by 411 writers. 937 Tunisian town/ village names are written. Each writer filled some forms with pre-selected town/village names (referred to as "names" in the following) and the corresponding post code. Ground truth was added automatically to the image data and verified manually. Table 2 shows a dataset entry of the IFN/ENIT-database.

This database has an interesting feature in the detailed labeling of the postcode as a label on word level. The character shape sequences, where each character shape depends on its position in the word, receives different labels for each position. Additionally, the position of the baseline is given as straight line. All this information, together with some additional quality measures, have been verified manually several times. The label information allows to train and test recognition systems, either on word or on character level. The given baseline position can be used for the testing of baseline estimation algorithms and the dependency on the baseline accuracy.

Fig. 4. An example of a completed form

Table 3 shows some image examples from the IFN/ENIT-database. Tables 4-6 show important statistics of the IFN/ENIT-database. Table 4 shows the quantities of names, PAWs, and characters subject to the number of words in a name. It can be seen that in most cases the name consists of one word, but some names also appear with four words. The overall number of words in the database is 42,609.

Table 5 presents statistics of the number of PAWs in the names of the database.

Table 6 gives statistics of the age and the profession of the writers who contributed to the database.

Table 2. A data set entry of the IFN/ENIT-database. The symbols M, B, A, E represent the used character shapes (middle, begin, alone, end position in a word.)

Image	قُـرْقَنْـةَ
Ground truth:	
Postcode	3070
Global word	قرقنة
Character shape sequence	ق_B|ر_E|ق_B|ن_M|ت_E|
Baseline y1,y2	77,83
Baseline quality	B1
Quantity of words	1
Quantity of PAWs	2
Quantity of characters	5
Writing quality	W1

Table 3. Examples from the IFN/ENIT-database: A Tunisian village name written by 12 writers

١ ولاد حـفْـوَزَ	أُولاد حقّوزَ	أولا د حنّوز
أ و لا د حـنّـوزَ	حـتّوزَ ١ و د د	أُولاد دفوُنَ
أولاد حـقّـوَزُ	أولا د حـتّو ز	أؤلا د حنُوزَ
أُولا د حـنْـوزَ	أ و لا د حـقّو ز	أؤلادحنوز

3.5 ARABASE Database

In 2005, a relational database for Arabic OCR systems was presented by N. Ben Amara, et al. [17]. The authors claim to have conceived a database to support research for online and offline Arabic handwritten and printed text recognition. All types of images of text phrases, signatures, words, characters, and digits are supposedly included in the database. Also, tools to use the database were announced. To date, only the concept has been presented.

Table 4. Quantity of words, name images, PAWs, and characters in a name

words in a name	names	PAWs	characters
1	12,992	40,555	76,827
2	10,826	54,722	98,828
3	2,599	20,120	36,004
4	42	188	552
Total	26,459	115,585	212,211

Table 5. Frequency of PAWs in a name

Number of PAWs	frequency in %
1	2.99
2	15.35
3	17.60
4	24.84
5	14.67
6	8.24
7	7.32
8	6.04
>8	2.95

Table 6. Age and profession of the writers

age	student	teacher	technician	other	$\sum$
≤ 20	29%	0%	0%	0%	29%
21 - 30	35.6%	4.2%	3.9%	3.9%	47.6%
31 - 40	0.2%	3.4%	4.9%	2.0%	10.5%
> 40	0%	4.1%	5.4%	3.4%	12.9%
$\sum$	64.8%	11.7%	14.2%	9.3%	100%

4   Competitions of Arabic Handwriting

Table 7 presents an overview of the databases of Arabic printed or handwritten words, which were presented in Section 3. Today, only the two bold-printed databases are available for research on Arabic handwriting recognition. Even though more datasets exist, they are not available for public research. It is clear that a considerable lack of databases exists for developing Arabic handwriting recognition systems.

The insights derived from the work done on OCR and handwriting recognition methods and systems for Latin character based languages in the past showed that datasets and competition are the most important prerequisites for developing recognition systems.

Table 7. Databases for Arabic text recognition

Name	Year	Contents	Type	Reference
ERIM	1995	750 pages	printed	[13]
Al-Isra	1999	37,000 words	handwritten	[14]
		10,000 digits		
CENPARMI	2000	2,499 amounts	handwritten	[15]
		2,499 numbers		
IFN/ENIT	2002	26,459 names	handwritten	[16]
ARABASE	2005	?	printed/handw.	[17]

More than 30 research teams today employ the IFN/ENIT-database, published in 2002. This fact motivated the organization of a competition on Arabic handwriting recognition during the ICDAR 2005 conference. The groups working with the IFN/ENIT-database already were especially asked to submit a recognition system.

4.1   ICDAR 2005 Competition

The first competition on Arabic handwriting recognition was based on the IFN/ENIT-database, and the results were presented at the International Conference on Document Analysis and Recognition (ICDAR) 2005. The participating systems were developed using the data of the IFN/ENIT-database and sent to the IfN. All tests were conducted at the IfN, and five groups submitted systems to the competition.

4.1.1 Participating Systems

A short overview of the systems participating in the competition is given in the following.

System ICRA. The system, named ICRA (Intelligent Character Recognition for Arabic), which also means read in Arabic, was developed by Ahmad Abdulkader. Here is a short description of the system:

- The system uses a novel idea inspired by the nature of Arabic writing, based on the concept of the PAW.
- ICRA is a two tier recognizer.
- The 1st tier is a Neural Net based PAW recognizer aided by a PAW lexicon. The PAW lexicon is extracted from the master village names lexicon.
- The 2nd tier is a Neural Net based word recognizer aided by another lexicon. The literals (alphabet) of such a lexicon are actually PAWs and not characters.
- ICRA was trained on sets a, b, and c and tested on set d of the IFN/ENIT-database.
- The main approach of the system was published at IWFHR 2006 conference [18].

System SHOCRAN. The SHOCRAN system (System for Handwritten Optical Character Recognition for Arabic Names), comes from a group of researchers in Egypt. It is declared as a confidential project, so no information about the system is available. The system is trained on all four datasets of the IFN/ENIT-database.

System TH-OCR. The TH-OCR system was developed at the State Key Laboratory of Intelligent Technology and Systems, Department of Electronic Engineering, Tsinghua University, Beijing, China, by Pingping Xiu et al.

Based on previous research work on a multilingual document recognition system for Chinese, Japanese, Korean, English, Tibetan, and Uyghur languages, this research work extended to Arabic OCR. The first step was the development of a printed Arabic document recognition system in 2004 [19]. The system structure of the handwritten Arabic OCR system is similar to that of the printed Arabic OCR system, but the key technologies of handwritten character segmentation and recognition are more complex and sophisticated. The character recognition module uses mainly statistical pattern recognition methods.

System UOB. The UOB system was developed at the University of Balamand, Lebanon by Chafic Mokbel and Ramy El-Hajj in tight collaboration with Laurence Likforman-Sulem from ENST-Paris.

The UOB system is a pure HMM system developed for speech recognition at the origin. It uses a complete toolkit like HTK [http://htk.eng.cam.ac.uk/], which is called HCM. HCM permits the development of large HMM networks, and it integrates language modeling. The properties of the HCM are published in papers in the speech recognition area, e.g. [20]. A paper describing the feature extraction module of the UOB system was presented at ICDAR 2005 [21]. For the UOB system all four datasets were used for training. No confidence measure has been implemented.

System REAM. The next system, REAM (Reconnaissance de l'Ecriture Arabe Manuscrite), comes from a group at the Laboratoire des Systmes et de Traiment du Signal-ENIT, Tunisia. The authors of the system are Sameh Masmoudi Touj, et al.

The system uses a hybrid planar Markov Model to adapt to horizontal and vertical variations of the handwritten word. The approach is presented in a journal paper [22]. The principal idea of this approach involves the partitioning of handwritten words into five logical horizontal bands which correspond to typical Arabic parts of words like upper and lower diacritics, ascenders, descenders, and median zone. This segmentation uses knowledge about the typical Arabic writing style in a sophisticated way. Based on features of the median zone, vertical segmentation points are detected. In the next step, a different technique of feature extraction is adopted for each type of segment. Finally, the recognition is realized using the concept of PHMM.

Table 8. Recognition results in % with IFN/ENIT-database dataset d

System	1	1-5	1-10
ICRA	88.95	94.22	95.01
SHOCRAN	100	100	100
TH-OCR	30.13	41.95	46.59
UOB	85.00	91.88	93.56
REAM*	89.06	99.15	99.62
ARAB-IFN	87.94	91.42	95.62

* System did not run on all data. It is tested on a reduced set of 1000 names only.

4.1.2 Tests

The performance of the five Arabic handwriting recognition systems were evaluated in two steps. In the first step, the dataset d of the IFN/ENIT-database was used. In the second step, the new and, unknown to all participants, dataset e was used.

Results. The systems were first compared on the basis of dataset d of the IFN/ENIT-database. Table 8 shows the results of the five systems in the competition, and we added the results of our system (ARAB-IFN) for comparison, which was presented at ICDAR 2003 [23] and trained on datasets a, b, and c. While some systems used the whole IFN/ENIT-database for training, remarkable differences between the performances of the five systems can be seen. The first column shows the percentage of correctly recognized city names, the second the percentage of correct results within the top five results, and the third column of the top 10 results.

Table 9 shows the recognition results of the systems reached with the new and unknown dataset e. The results of the SHOCRAN system and the REAM system both show a highly reduced recognition rate. The ICRA and UOB systems show a behavior with a slightly reduced recognition rate (comparable with the results of the ARAB-IFN system). The TH-OCR system shows approximately the same result as on the dataset d.

A comparison of the relative error rates of the different systems dependent on the number of PAWs in a name is shown in Fig. 5. It can be seen that, for all systems, the relative error follows generally the frequency of the PAWs in

Table 9. Recognition results in % with the new dataset e

System name	No.	1	1-5	1-10
ICRA	1	65.74	83.95	87.75
SHOCRAN	2	35.70	51.62	51.62
TH-OCR	3	29.62	43.96	50.14
UOB	4	75.93	87.99	90.88
REAM*	5	15.36	18.52	19.86
ARAB-IFN	6	74.69	87.07	89.77

* System did not run on all data. It is tested on a reduced set of 3000 names only.

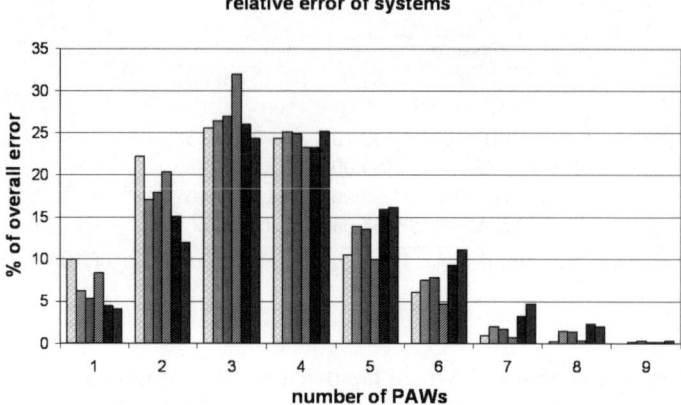

Fig. 5. Relative errors of the systems dependent on the number of PAWs in a name. In each group, the bars are associated with the systems 1-6 from left to right.

System	1	2	3	4	5	6
 بن سعيد القا	3	-	1	1	-	1
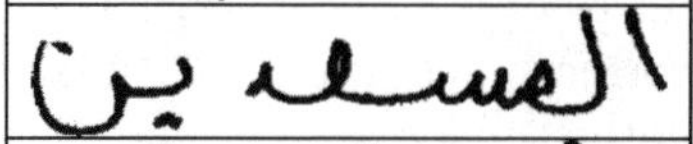 القاسد بن	1	-	-	1	-	1
 أطلسكي بي	2	4	-	4	1	-
 المصديني	1	1	1	1	-	1
 القاسديني	1	1	1	1	1	-
 أكعبيين	1	-	-	3	1	-
 الطاسعدي بن	1	1	1	1	-	1
 لاسعد بن	1	-	1	1	-	1

Fig. 6. Example of a town/village name written by different writers out of dataset *e* and the recognition results (1 first correct, 2 second, ... , - no correct result)

dataset *e* (Table 5). However, some systems show more errors in long words, whereas others in short words. This may depend on the different features and normalizations used.

Fig. 6 shows some examples of a word written by different writers, with the results of the recognition systems. It can be seen that some poorly written words are correctly recognized with some systems, while better written words are still not recognized. At first glance, systems without segmentation show better results on words with connected or broken PAWs than those that segment.

4.2 ICDAR 2007 Competition

We have planned to perform a second competition on the IFN/ENIT-dataset at ICDAR 2007. The dataset for training a system will be upgraded, with the test dataset *e* from the competition ICDAR 2005, to improve training on word level, as the words will be more equally distributed. Additionally, more features of the systems will be measured, e.g., processing time and reject behavior.

5   Steps to Develop Arabic Offline Recognition Systems

The state of the art of Arabic offline handwritten word recognition as presented in the previous sections demonstrates that work remains to be done to achieve Arabic offline handwritten word recognition systems as effective as systems for the recognition of English words.

One important next step to develop Arabic handwritten text recognition systems involves attaining modules equivalent to those needed for Latin-character-based text recognition systems. The results of the first competition of Arabic handwritten word recognition systems showed us that HMM-based recognizers, known to be effective for cursive handwriting recognition, apply well to Arabic handwritten word recognition. It seems clear that Latin character based cursive handwriting has similar features - connected characters, different shape depending on the position in a word - as Arabic handwriting. Yet, the word recognizer is only one part of an offline Arabic handwriting recognition system. A complete system also needs document analysis components, for image preprocessing, document segmentation, text block detection, line segmentation, word segmentation, and baseline estimation. All these processing steps must be done on real world documents, e.g. letters, bank transfer forms, and insurance forms. The competition at ICDAR 2005 was a first step in system development, because it concerned only word recognition performance. A complete system takes as input the paper document and performs all tasks from preprocessing to recognition automatically. Finally, an optimized Arabic text recognition system needs to consider the characteristics of the Arabic language, being its syntax and semantics.

5.1   Characteristics of Databases

The usefulness of a database depends on two main features: the data itself and the structure of the ground truth. The data collection from a selected application should be accomplished first. Before the expensive and time consuming labeling process starts, a data structure for the ground truth and label information must

```
DEMO_001.TIF
DEMO_001.X1 POSTAL_AREA
//MAIN POSTAL AREA
    DEMO_001.X21 REG_NUMBER
    //POSTAL REGISTRATION NUMBER
    DEMO_001:X22 ADDRESSES
    //ADDRESS AREAS
        DEMO_001.X31 TEXTLINES_HW
        //HANDWRITTEN TEXTLINES
            DEMO_001.X41 WORDS_HW
            //HANDWRITTEN WORDS
                DEMO_001.X51 CHARACTER_HW
                //HANDWRITTEN CHARACTERS
        DEMO_001.X32 TEXTLINES_MP
        //MACHINE PRINTED TEXTLINES
    DEMO_001.X23 BARCODE
    //BARCODES
```

Fig. 7. Example of a document hierarchy file

```
BHE:                        /* Begin of Header */
FTY: REC                    /* file type */
PIC: DEMO_001.TIF           /* name of image file */
WUE: 3                      /* number of region */
DES: MAIN POSTAL AREAS      /* region type */
PFN: DEMO_001.X1            /* Name of Parent File */
EHE:                        /* End of Header */
BDA:                        /* Begin of Data */
 .
BDR:                        /* Begin of Data Record */
OID: 3                      /* unique ID of region */
POI: 0                      /* ID of parent region */
OBB: REC 0 0 163 168        /* geom. zone-description */
OBE:                        /* End of Description */
LBL: RECIPIENT_ADDRESS      /* Label of region */
 .                          /* additional information */
EDR:                        /* End of Data Record */
 .
EDA:                        /* End of Data */
EOF:                        /* End of File */
```

Fig. 8. Example of a region description file

be defined. It should be flexible and easy to use. A hierarchical token-based structure, as used in the IFN/ENIT-database, seems to be a good choice, as it is extendable and easy to use [24].

Fig. 9. Example of a gray scale image of a letter

Fig. 10. Another example of a gray scale image of a letter

Fig. 7 shows an example of the hierarchical structure of a document where the names of the files are given, which describe the data of the associated image regions. In the IFN/ENIT-database, the hierarchy consists of only one level.

The format of the region files is line-oriented, with a token of three capital letters at the beginning of each line defining its contents. This format is a byte-stream, easy to read, and OS-independent. Due to the format of the region files, any additional information can be inserted just by adding an appropriate token to the list of possible tokens, without altering the format, as unknown tokens are simply ignored by the corresponding reader. Fig. 8 shows an example of such a file.

Examples of typical real world data, such as addresses written on letters, are shown in Figures 9 and 10. It can be seen that the words in these examples are written more differently than in the form, which was designed for easy labeling, as in the collection of artificial data for the IFN/ENIT-database. The vertical dimensions of the words vary significantly, and the writing lines overlap partially.

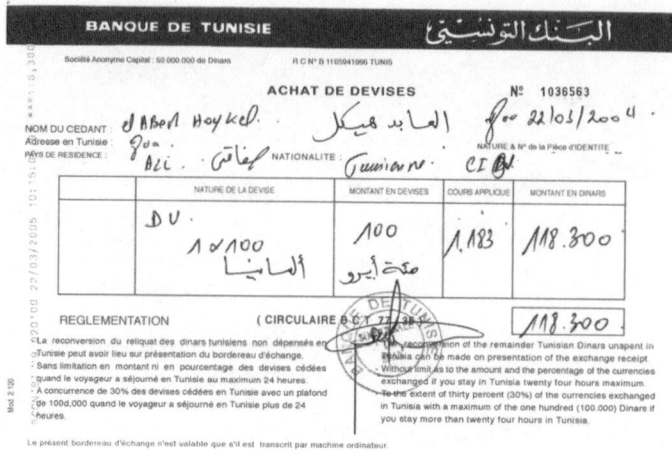

Fig. 11. Example with a section of a filled form with a mixture of handwritten Latin and Arabic characters

These features make segmentation into words and estimation of the baseline of a word difficult tasks.

Therefore, a huge amount of real world data is needed to develop appropriate methods for preprocessing and segmentation. The advantage of a hierarchical database description lies in allowing the usage of parts of the data to test modules of the whole system only.

The address reading application shows that, for the correct interpretation of an address, additional knowledge about the different ways of writing addresses in Arabic is needed. The Arabic writing style, as well as special features, have to be considered, too.

Fig. 11 shows another example of real world data. The form is printed mainly with Latin characters and is filled with words written with Latin and Arabic characters. Here, knowledge about the structure of the form must be available for a successful recognition process.

These few examples of real world data show that using different application aspects are necessary when collecting data for a database.

5.2 Arabic Language Modules

The features of Arabic handwriting must be considered in an Arabic handwriting recognition system along with syntax and semantics to conduct the recognition process. This information can be used implicitly or explicitly during the recognition process to reduce, the lexicon size, and to verify the recognition result on the word or sentence level. Besides using dictionary lookup, letter n-grams (or even word morphology rules) can improve recognition results as well. The use of language modules in recognition systems requires databases that allow the training and testing of such methods.

5.3 Competitions

Competitions organized on the basis of images of real world data are recommended. With the aforementioned hierarchical region description and flexible token-based labeling of the data, a comparison of modules and systems on different levels of complexity becomes possible. Address reading systems, for example, use the image of an envelope as input and deliver name and address of the recipient as output. The test of a single module, e.g., text block location, word segmentation, baseline estimation, and word recognition, is possible if the associated ground truth information is available in the region description.

A crucial aspect of competitions involves the detailed presentation and discussion of different methods to understand which method works better and why. The organization of a workshop to present the results and discuss the different approaches is recommended.

6 Future Work

Considering all the aspects discussed in the previous sections, the next steps to provide better Arabic handwriting recognition systems are obvious. In the following, the necessary steps are listed:

- Selection of interesting fields of application for Arabic handwriting recognition.
- Collection of real world data, perform scanning and labeling of the data to construct a database.
- If real world data are not available: development of a concept to generate an artificial database by selecting people to fill forms. Scanning and labeling may be easier, as the form can be specially designed.
- Organization of a workshop to discuss newest research results and to present a performance evaluation of different systems or modules based on a common dataset, performed by an independent group.
- Formation of new datasets available to research teams immediately. The labels should have the same format for different datasets.
- Development of performance measurements of processing and recognition modules should be considered in the workshops.
- Workshops should be conducted annually, and interdisciplinary contributions encouraged.
- Exchange of methods between handwriting recognition of different languages.

From experience gathered on other languages, these steps should help us reach the goal of developing better Arabic handwriting reading machines. In addition to this short-term objective, we hope to approach a better understanding of the nature of the reading process of humans in general, to reduce the work needed to adapt a system to a new application.

7   Conclusion

In this chapter we have discussed different databases and methods for evaluating recognition modules or systems. Much of the work done on text recognition systems for Latin character based text can adapt to Arabic text recognition. For the time being, the methods used for comparing different systems can be identical to the ones developed for Latin character based OCR systems. Later, special aspects of Arabic writing should be considered. The organization of competitions with the presentation of recognition results and discussions of different approaches form the basis of a successful work on offline Arabic handwriting recognition systems.

References

1. Lorigo, L., Govindaraju, V.: Offline Arabic handwriting recognition: a survey. IEEE Transactions on Pattern Analysis and Machine Intelligence 28(5), 712–724 (2006)
2. Ager, S.: Arabic alphabet, pronunciation and language,
   http://www.omniglot.com/writing/Arabic.htm
3. NIST: NIST special databases and software from the image group,
   www.itl.nist.gov/iaui/vip/databases/defs/
4. Rice, S.V., Jenkins, F.R., Nartker, T.A.: The fifth annual test of OCR accuracy. Technical report, Information Science Research Institute, University of Nevada, Las Vegas (1996)
5. CEDAR: CEDAR database. www.cedar.buffalo.edu/Databases/CDROM1/
6. Kanungo, T., Haralick, R.M.: An automatic closed-loop methodology for generating character groundtruth for scanned documents. IEEE Transactions on Pattern Analysis and Machine Intelligence 21(2), 179–183 (1999)
7. Rice, S.V.: Measuring the Accuracy of Page-Reading Systems. PhD thesis, Department of Computer Science, University of Nevada, Las Vegas (1996)
8. Märgner, V., Pechwitz, M., El Abed, H.: ICDAR 2005 Arabic handwriting recognition competition. In: 8th International Conference on Document Analysis and Recognition (ICDAR), vol. 1, pp. 70–74 (2005)
9. Thulke, M., Märgner, V., Dengel, A.: A general approach to quality evaluation of document segmentation results. In: 3rd IAPR International Workshop on Document Analysis Systems (DAS), vol. 1655, pp. 43–57 (1999)
10. Märgner, V., Karcher, P., Pawlowski, A.K.: On benchmarking of document analysis systems. In: 4th International Conference on Document Analysis and Recognition (ICDAR), vol. 1, pp. 331–336 (1997)
11. Kanungo, T., Marton, G.A., Bulbul, O.: Performance evaluation of two Arabic OCR products. In: SPIE (ed.) Proceedings of AIPR Workshop on Advances in Computer Assisted Recognition, vol. 3584 (1998)
12. Märgner, V., Pechwitz, M.: Synthetic data for Arabic OCR system development. In: 6th International Conference on Document Analysis and Recognition (ICDAR), pp. 1159–1163 (2001)
13. Schlosser, S.G.: ERIM Arabic document database. Environmental Research Institue of Michigan (ERIM),
    http://documents.cfar.umd.edu/resources/database/ERIM_Arabic_DB.html

14. Kharma, N., Ahmed, M., Ward, R.: A new comprehensive database of handwritten Arabic words, numbers, and signatures used for OCR testing. In: IEEE Canadian Conference on Electrical and Computer Engineering, vol. 2, pp. 766–768 (1999)
15. Al-Ohali, Y., Cheriet, M.: Databases for recognition of handwritten Arabic cheques. In: 7th International Workshop on Frontiers in Handwriting Recognition (IWFHR), pp. 601–606 (2000)
16. Pechwitz, M., Maddouri, S.S., Märgner, V., Ellouze, N., Amiri, H.: IFN/ENIT-database of handwritten Arabic words. In: Colloque International Francophone sur l'Ecrit et le Document (CIFED), pp. 127–136 (2002)
17. Ben Amara, N., Mazhoud, O., Bouzrara, N., Ellouze, N.: ARABASE: A relational database for Arabic OCR systems. International Arab Journal of Information Technology 2(4), 259–266 (2005)
18. Abdulkadr, A.: Two-tier approach for Arabic offline handwriting recognition. In: 10th International Workshop on Frontiers in Handwriting Recognition (IWFHR), pp. 161–166 (2006)
19. Jin, J., Wang, H., Ding, X., Peng, L.: Printed Arabic document recognition system. In: SPIE (ed.) Proceedings of the Document Recognition and Retrieval XII, vol. 5676, pp. 48–55 (2004)
20. Mokbel, C., Akl, H.A., Greige, H.: Automatic speech recognition of Arabic digits over telefone network. In: Proc. of RTST (2002)
21. El-Hajj, R., Likforman-Sulem, L., Mokbel, C.: Arabic handwriting recognition using baseline dependant features and hidden markov modeling. In: 8th International Conference on Document Analysis and Recognition (ICDAR), vol. 2, pp. 893–897 (2005)
22. Touj, S., Ben Amara, N., Amiri, H.: Arabic handwritten words recognition based on a planar hidden markov model. International Arab Journal of Information Technology 2(4) (2005)
23. Pechwitz, M., Märgner, V.: HMM based approach for handwritten Arabic word recognition using the IFN/ENIT - database. In: 7th International Conference on Document Analysis and Recognition (ICDAR), pp. 890–894 (2003)
24. Bippus, R., Märgner, V.: Data structures and tools for document database generation: An experimental system. In: 3rd International Conference on Document Analysis and Recognition (ICDAR), vol. 2, pp. 711–714 (1995)
25. Bippus, R.D.: Stochastische Modelle zur off-line Fließschrifterkennung. PhD thesis, Braunschweig Technical University, Institute for Communications Technology (IfN) (1999)
26. Bippus, R., Lehning, M.: Cursive script recognition using semi continuous hidden markov models in combination with simple features. In: IEE European Workshop on Handwriting Analysis and Recognition: A European Perspective, pp. 1–6 (1994)
27. Märgner, V.: SARAT-a system for the recognition of Arabic printed text. In: 11th International Conference on Pattern Recognition (ICPR), Conference B: Pattern Recognition Methodology and Systems, vol. II, pp. 561–564 (1992)
28. Nartker, T.A., Rice, S.V., Lumos, S.E.: Software tools and test data for research and testing of page-reading OCR systems. In: SPIE (ed.), Proceedings of the Document Recognition and Retrieval XII, vol. 5676 (2004)
29. Pechwitz, M.: Automatische Erkennung handgeschriebener arabischer Wörter. PhD thesis, Braunschweig Technical University, Institute for Communications Technology (IfN) (2004)
30. Pechwitz, M., Märgner, V.: Baseline estimation for Arabic handwritten words. In: 8th International Workshop on Frontiers in Handwriting Recognition (IWFHR), pp. 479–484 (2002)

Handwritten Chinese Character Recognition: Effects of Shape Normalization and Feature Extraction

Cheng-Lin Liu

National Laboratory of Pattern Recognition (NLPR),
Institute of Automation, Chinese Academy of Sciences,
P.O. Box 2728, Beijing 100080, P.R. China
liucl@nlpr.ia.ac.cn

Abstract. The technology of handwritten Chinese character recognition (HCCR) has seen significant advances in the last two decades owing to the effectiveness of many techniques, especially those for character shape normalization and feature extraction. This chapter reviews the major methods of normalization and feature extraction and evaluates their performance experimentally. The normalization methods include linear normalization, nonlinear normalization (NLN) based on line density equalization, moment normalization (MN), bi-moment normalization (BMN), modified centroid-boundary alignment (MCBA), and their pseudo-two-dimensional (pseudo 2D) extensions. As to feature extraction, I focus on some effective variations of direction features: chaincode feature, normalization-cooperated chaincode feature (NCCF), and gradient feature. The features are compared with various resolutions of direction and zoning, and are combined with various normalization methods. In experiments, the current methods have shown superior performance on handprinted characters, but are insufficient applied to unconstrained handwriting.

1 Introduction

Since the first work of printed Chinese character recognition (PCCR) was published in 1966 [1], many research efforts have been contributed to both printed and handwritten Chinese character recognition (HCCR). Research on online HCCR began as early as PCCR [2], whereas offline HCCR was started in the late 1970s and has attracted high attention from the 1980s [3]. Many effective methods have been proposed to solve this problem, and the recognition performance has advanced significantly [4,5]. This chapter is mainly concerned with offline HCCR, but most methods of offline recognition apply to online recognition as well [6].

The approaches of HCCR can be grouped roughly into two categories: feature matching (statistical classification) and structure analysis. Based on feature vector representation of character patterns, feature matching approaches

D.S. Doermann and S. Jaeger (Eds.): SACH 2006, LNCS 4768, pp. 104–128, 2008.
© Springer-Verlag Berlin Heidelberg 2008

used to compute a simple distance measure (correlation matching), such as Euclidean or city block distance, between the test pattern and class prototypes. Currently, sophisticated classification techniques [7,8,9], including parametric and non-parametric statistical classifiers, neural networks, support vector machines (SVMs), etc., can yield higher recognition accuracies. Nevertheless, the selection and extraction of features remains an important issue. Structure analysis is an inverse process of character generation: to extract the constituent strokes and compute a structural distance measure between the test pattern and class models. Due to its resembling human cognition and the potential of absorbing large deformation, this approach was pursued intensively in the 1980s and is still advancing [10]. However, due to the difficulty of stroke extraction and structural model building, it is not widely followed.

Statistical approaches have achieved great success in handprinted character recognition and are well commercialized. This is firstly due to the simple implementation of feature extraction based on template matching and classification based on vector computation. Also, effective shape normalization and feature extraction techniques, which improve the separability of patterns of different classes in feature space, have been proposed. Third, current machine learning methods enable classifier training with large set of samples for better discrimination of shapes in different classes.

The methodology of Chinese character recognition has been largely affected by some important techniques: blurring [11], directional pattern matching [12,13,14], nonlinear normalization [15,16], and modified quadratic discriminant function (MQDF) [17]. These techniques, and their variations or improved versions, are still widely followed and adopted in most recognition systems. Blurring is actually a low-pass spatial filtering operation. It was proposed in the 1960s from the viewpoint of human vision and is effective to blur the stroke displacement of characters of the same class. Directional pattern matching, motivated from local receptive fields in vision, predates the current direction histogram features. Nonlinear normalization, which regulates stroke positions as well as image size, significantly outperforms the conventional linear normalization (resizing only). The MQDF is a nonlinear classifier, suitable for high-dimensional features and large numbers of classes. Its variations include the pseudo Bayes classifier [18] and the modified Mahalanobis distance [19].

This chapter reviews the major normalization and feature extraction methods and evaluates their performances in offline HCCR on large databases. The normalization methods include linear normalization (LN), nonlinear normalization (NLN) based on line density equalization [15,16], moment normalization (MN) [20], bi-moment normalization (BMN) [21], modified centroid-boundary alignment (MCBA) [22], as well as the pseudo-two-dimensional (pseudo 2D) extensions of them [23,24]. These methods have been evaluated previously [24], but, in this study, they will be evaluated with better implementation of features.

Though many features have been proposed for character recognition, I focus on the class of direction histogram features, including chaincode direction feature, normalization-cooperated chaincode feature (NCCF) [25], and gradient direction feature. These features have yielded superior performance due to their sensitivity to stroke-direction variance and the insensitivity to stroke-width variance. The gradient direction feature was not examined closely until the success of gradient vector decomposition [26], following a decomposition scheme previously proposed in online character recognition [27]. Alternatively, the direction of gradient was quantized into a number of angular regions [28]. By NCCF, the chaincode direction comes from the original image, instead of the normalized image, but the directional elements are displaced in normalized planes according to normalized coordinates. An improved version of NCCF maps chaincodes into continuous line segments in normalized planes [29].

In the history, some extensions of direction features, such as the peripheral direction contributivity (PDC) [30] and the reciprocal feature field [31], have reported higher accuracy in HCCR when a simple distance metric was used. These features, with very high dimensionality (over 1,000), actually have high redundancy. As background features, they are sensitive to noise and connecting strokes. Extending the line element of direction feature to higher-order feature detectors (e.g., [32,33]) helps discriminate similar characters, but the dimensionality also increases rapidly. The Gabor filter, also motivated from vision research, promises feature extraction in character recognition [34], but is computationally expensive compared to chaincode and gradient features, and, at best, performs comparably with the gradient feature [35].

I evaluate the character shape normalization and direction feature extraction methods on two databases of handwritten characters, ETL9B (Electrotechnical Laboratory, Japan) and CASIA (Institute of Automation, Chinese Academy of Sciences), with 3,036 classes and 3,755 classes, respectively. Recognition accuracies are evaluated using two common classifiers, the minimum distance classifier and modified quadratic discriminant function (MQDF).

This study has a twofold purpose. First, the comparison of major normalization and feature extraction methods can provide guidelines for selecting methods in system development. Second, the results show the degree of performance that the state-of-the-art methods can achieve. I will show in experiments that the current methods can recognize handprinted characters accurately but perform inferiorly on unconstrained handwriting.

In the rest of this chapter, I review major normalization methods in Section 2 and direction feature extraction methods in Section 3. I present experimental results in Section 4, and finally, offer concluding remarks in Section 5.

2   Shape Normalization

Normalization regulates the size, position, and shape of character images, to reduce the shape variation between images of the same class. Denote the input image and the normalized image by $f(x, y)$ and $g(x', y')$, respectively, normalization is implemented by coordinate mapping

$$\begin{cases} x' = x'(x, y), \\ y' = y'(x, y). \end{cases} \tag{1}$$

Most normalization methods use 1D coordinate mapping:

$$\begin{cases} x' = x'(x), \\ y' = y'(x). \end{cases} \tag{2}$$

Under 1D normalization, the pixels in the same row/column in the input image map to the same row/column in the normalized image, hence, the shape restoration capability is limited.

Given coordinate mapping functions (1) or (2), the normalized image $g(x', y')$ is generated by pixel value and coordinate interpolation. In my implementation of 1D normalization, I map the coordinates forward from (binary) input image to normalized image and generate the binary normalized image via coordinate interpolation. For generating the gray-scale normalized image, each pixel is viewed as a square of unit area. By coordinate mapping, the unit square in the input image maps to a rectangle in the normalized plane, and each pixel (unit square) overlapping with the mapped rectangle is assigned a gray level proportional to the overlapping area [29].

In the case of 2D normalization, the mapped shape of a unit square onto the normalized plane is quadrilateral [24]. To compute the overlapping areas of this quadrilateral with the pixels (unit squares) in the normalized plane, I decompose the quadrilateral into trapezoids each exists within a row of unit squares. Each within-row trapezoid is further decomposed into trapezoids within a unit square. After generating the normalized gray-scale image, the binary normalized image is obtained by thresholding the gray-scale image (fixed threshold 0.5).

In my experiments, the normalized image plane is set to a square of edge length L, which is not necessarily fully occupied. To alleviate the distortion of elongated characters, I partially preserve the aspect ratio of the input image. By aspect ratio adaptive normalization (ARAN) [29,36], the aspect ratio R_2 of normalized image is a continuous function of the aspect ratio R_1 of input image:

$$R_2 = \sqrt{\sin(\frac{\pi}{2}R_1)}. \tag{3}$$

R_1 is calculated by

$$R_1 = \begin{cases} W_1/H_1, & \text{if } W_1 < H_1 \\ H_1/W_1, & \text{otherwise} \end{cases} \tag{4}$$

where W_1 and H_1 define the width and height of the input image. The width W_2 and height H_2 of the normalized image similarly relate by the aspect ratio R_2. If the input image vertically elongates, then, in the normalized plane, the vertical dimension is filled (height L) and the horizontal dimension is centered and scaled according to the aspect ratio. Otherwise, the horizontal dimension is filled (width L), and the vertical dimension is centered and scaled. ARAN is depicted in Fig. 1.

The normalization methods depend on the coordinate mapping functions, defined by the 1D and pseudo 2D normalization methods as follows.

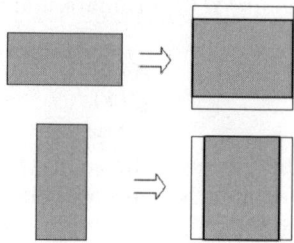

Fig. 1. Aspect ratio adaptive normalization (ARAN). Rectangle with thick line: occupied area of normalized image.

2.1   1D Normalization Methods

Given the sizes of input and normalized images, the coordinate mapping functions of linear normalization (LN) are simply

$$\begin{cases} x' = \frac{W_2}{W_1}x, \\ y' = \frac{H_2}{H_1}y. \end{cases} \tag{5}$$

Both the linear normalization and line-density-based nonlinear normalization (NLN) methods align the physical boundaries (ends of stroke projections) of the input image to the boundaries of the normalized image. The coordinate mapping of NLN is obtained by accumulating the normalized line density projections (line density equalization):

$$\begin{cases} x' = W_2 \sum_{u=0}^{x} h_x(u), \\ y' = H_2 \sum_{v=0}^{y} h_y(v), \end{cases} \tag{6}$$

where $h_x(x)$ and $h_y(y)$ are the normalized line density histograms of x axis and y axis, respectively. They are obtained by normalizing the projections of local line densities into unity sum:

$$\begin{cases} h_x(x) = \frac{p_x(x)}{\sum_x p_x(x)} = \frac{\sum_y d_x(x,y)}{\sum_x \sum_y d_x(x,y)}, \\ h_y(y) = \frac{p_y(y)}{\sum_y p_y(y)} = \frac{\sum_x d_y(x,y)}{\sum_x \sum_y d_y(x,y)}, \end{cases} \tag{7}$$

where $p_x(x)$ and $p_y(y)$ are the line density projections onto x axis and y axis, respectively, and $d_x(x,y)$ and $d_y(x,y)$ are local line density functions.

According to Tsukumo and Tanaka [15], the local line densities d_x and d_y are taken as the reciprocal of horizontal/vertical run-length in the background area or a small constant in the stroke area. While in Yamada, et al. [16], d_x and d_y are calculated considering both background run-length and stroke run-length and are unified to render $d_x(x,y) = d_y(x,y)$. The two methods perform comparably, but Tsukumo and Tanaka's is computationally simpler [5]. By adjusting the density functions of marginal and stroke areas empirically in Tsukumo and Tanaka's method, better performance than Yamada, et al's has been achieved. My experiments employ this improved version of NLN.

The 1D moment normalization (MN) method (a simplified version of Casey's method [20]) aligns the centroid of the input image (x_c, y_c) to the geometric center of the normalized image $(x'_c, y'_c) = (W_2/2, H_2/2)$ and re-bounds the input image according to second-order 1D moments. Let the second-order moments be μ_{20} and μ_{02}, the width and height of the input image are re-set to $\delta_x = 4\sqrt{\mu_{20}}$ and $\delta_y = 4\sqrt{\mu_{02}}$, respectively. The coordinate mapping functions are then given by

$$\begin{cases} x' = \frac{W_2}{\delta_x}(x - x_c) + x'_c, \\ y' = \frac{H_2}{\delta_y}(y - y_c) + y'_c. \end{cases} \tag{8}$$

The bi-moment normalization (BMN) method [21] aligns the centroid of input image as the moment normalization does, but the width and height are treated asymmetrically with respect to the centroid. To do this, the second-order moments are split into two parts at the centroid: μ_x^-, μ_x^+, μ_y^-, and μ_y^+. The boundaries of the input image are re-set to $[x_c - 2\sqrt{\mu_x^-}, x_c + 2\sqrt{\mu_x^+}]$ and $[y_c - 2\sqrt{\mu_y^-}, y_c + 2\sqrt{\mu_y^+}]$. For the x axis, a quadratic function $u(x) = ax^2 + bx + c$ aligns three points $(x_c - 2\sqrt{\mu_x^-}, x_c, x_c + 2\sqrt{\mu_x^+})$ to normalized coordinates $(0, 0.5, 1)$, and similarly, a quadratic function $v(y)$ works for the y axis. Finally, the coordinate functions are

$$\begin{cases} x' = W_2 u(x), \\ y' = H_2 v(y). \end{cases} \tag{9}$$

The quadratic functions can also align the physical boundaries and centroid, i.e., map $(0, x_c, W_1)$ and $(0, y_c, H_1)$ to $(0, 0.5, 1)$. This method is called centroid-boundary alignment (CBA). A modified CBA (MCBA) method [22] also adjusts the stroke density in the central area by combining a sine function with the quadratic functions:

$$\begin{cases} x' = W_2[u(x) + \eta_x \sin(2\pi u(x))], \\ y' = H_2[v(y) + \eta_y \sin(2\pi v(y))]. \end{cases} \tag{10}$$

The amplitudes of sine waves, η_x and η_y, are estimated from the extent of the central area, defined by the centroids of the partial images divided by the global centroid.

2.2   Pseudo 2D Normalization Methods

Horiuchi, et al. proposed a pseudo 2D nonlinear normalization (P2DNLN) method by equalizing the line density functions of each row/column instead of the line density projections [23]. To control the degree of shape deformation, they blurred the line density functions such that the equalization of each row/column depends on its neighboring rows/columns. Though this method promises recognition, it is computationally expensive because of row/column-wise line density blurring.

An efficient pseudo 2D normalization approach, called line density projection interpolation (LDPI), was proposed recently [24]. Instead of line density blurring and row/column-wise equalization, LDPI partitions the 2D line density map into soft strips. 1D coordinate functions are computed from the density projection of each strip and combined into a 2D function. Specifically, let the width and height of the input image be W_1 and H_1, the centroid be (x_c, y_c), the horizontal line density map $d_x(x, y)$ is partitioned into three horizontal strips:

$$d_x^i(x, y) = w^i(y)d_x(x, y), \quad i = 1, 2, 3. \tag{11}$$

$w^i(y)$ $(i = 1, 2, 3)$ are piecewise linear functions:

$$\begin{cases} w^1(y) = w_0 \frac{y_c - y}{y_c}, & y < y_c, \\ w^2(y) = 1 - w^1(y), & y < y_c, \\ w^2(y) = 1 - w^3(y), & y \geq y_c, \\ w^3(y) = w_0 \frac{y - y_c}{H_1 - y_c}, & y \geq y_c, \end{cases} \tag{12}$$

where w_0 controls the weight of the upper/lower part of line density map. A small value of w_0 renders the interpolated 2D coordinate function similar to that of 1D normalization, while a large one may yield excessive deformation. The weight functions with $w_0 = 1$ are depicted in Fig. 2.

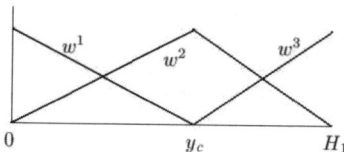

Fig. 2. Weight functions for partitioning line density map into soft strips

The horizontal density functions of three strips project onto the x axis:

$$p_x^i(x) = \sum_y d_x^i(x, y), \quad i = 1, 2, 3. \tag{13}$$

The projections are then normalized to a unity sum and accumulated to give 1D coordinate functions $x'^i(x)$, $i = 1, 2, 3$, which combine to 2D coordinate functions by interpolation:

$$x'(x, y) = \begin{cases} w^1(y)x'^1(x) + w^2(y)x'^2(x), & y < y_c, \\ w^3(y)x'^3(x) + w^2(y)x'^2(x), & y \geq y_c. \end{cases} \tag{14}$$

Similar to the partitioning of horizontal density, the vertical density map $d_y(x, y)$ is partitioned into three vertical strips using weight functions in the x axis. The partitioned density functions $d_y^i(x, y)$, $i = 1, 2, 3$ are similarly equalized and interpolated to generate the 2D coordinate function $y'(x, y)$.

The strategy of LDPI extends to other 1D normalization methods: MN, BMN, and MCBA. The extended versions are called pseudo 2D MN (P2DMN), pseudo 2D BMN (P2DBMN), and pseudo 2D CBA (P2DCBA), respectively. These methods do not rely on the computation of local line density map. Instead, they are directly based on the pixel intensity of a character image. As the soft partitioning of line density map in LDPI, the input character image $f(x, y)$ is softly partitioned into three horizontal strips $f_x^i(x, y)$, $i = 1, 2, 3$, and three vertical strips $f_y^i(x, y)$, $i = 1, 2, 3$. The horizontal strips project onto the x axis:

$$p_x^i(x) = \sum_y f_x^i(x, y), \quad i = 1, 2, 3. \tag{15}$$

For P2DMN, the second order moment is computed from the projection of a strip:

$$\mu_{20}^i = \frac{\sum_x (x - x_c^i)^2 p_x^i(x)}{\sum_x p_x^i(x)}. \tag{16}$$

The width of this strip is re-set to $\delta_x^i = 4\sqrt{\mu_{20}^i}$, which determines the scaling factor of 1D coordinate mapping:

$$x'^i(x) = \frac{W_2}{\delta_x^i}(x - x_c^i) + \frac{W_2}{2}. \tag{17}$$

The 1D coordinate functions of vertical strips are similarly computed from strip projections.

For P2DBMN, the second order moment of a horizontal strip is split into two parts at the centroid of this strip: μ_{20}^{i-} and μ_{20}^{i+}. The bounds of this strip is re-set to $[x_c^i - 2\sqrt{\mu_{20}^{i-}}, x_c^i + 2\sqrt{\mu_{20}^{i+}}]$, which, together with the centroid x_c^i, estimates the quadratic 1D coordinate mapping function $x'^i(x)$. The three 1D coordinate functions of vertical strips are computed similarly.

By P2DCBA, from the vertical projection of each horizontal strip $f_x^i(x, y)$ ($i = 1, 2, 3$), the centroid coordinate x_c^i and two partial centroids x_{c1}^i and x_{c2}^i are computed to estimate the parameters of 1D coordinate mapping function $x'^i(x)$. Similarly, 1D coordinate functions $y'^i(y)$ ($i = 1, 2, 3$) are estimated from the horizontal projections of vertical strips.

More details of pseudo 2D normalization can be found in [24]. Fig. 3 shows some examples of normalization using nine methods (LN, NLN, MN, BMN, MCBA, LDPI, P2DMN, P2DBMN, and P2DCBA). We can see that linear normalization (LN) keeps the original shape (only aspect ratio changed), but NLN can effectively equalize the line intervals. The centroid-based normalization methods (MN, BMN, and MCBA) effectively regulate the overall shape (skewness of gravity, balance of inner/outer stroke density). The pseudo 2D methods make the stroke positions more uniform, and especially, alleviate the imbalance of width/height and position of character parts.

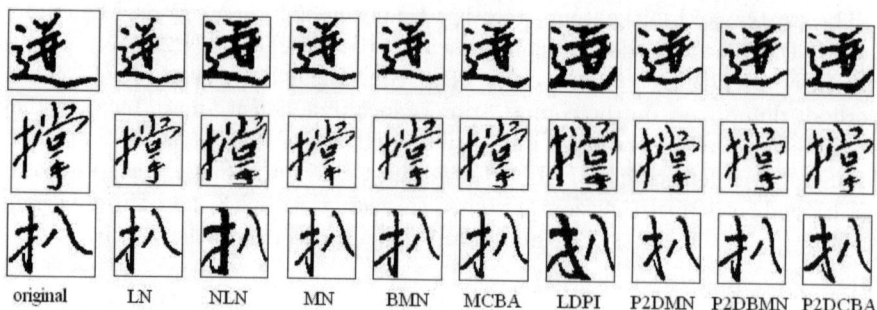

original LN NLN MN BMN MCBA LDPI P2DMN P2DBMN P2DCBA

Fig. 3. Character image normalization by nine methods. The leftmost image is original and the other eight are normalized ones.

3 Direction Feature Extraction

The implementation of direction feature is various depending on the directional element decomposition, the sampling of feature values, the resolution of direction and feature plane, etc. Considering that the stroke segments of Chinese characters can be approximated into four orientations: horizontal, vertical, left-diagonal and right-diagonal, early works used to decompose the stroke (or contour) segments into these four orientations.

Feature extraction from stroke contour has been widely adopted because the contour length is nearly independent of stroke-width variation. The local direction of contour, encoded as a chaincode, actually has eight directions (Fig. 4). Decomposing the contour pixels into eight *directions* instead of four *orientations* (a pair of opposite directions merged into one orientation) significantly improved the recognition accuracy [26]. This is because separating the two sides of a stroke edge can better discriminate the parallel strokes. The direction of a stroke edge can also be measured by the gradient of image intensity, which applies to gray-scale images as well as binary images. The gradient feature has applied to Chinese character recognition in 8-direction [37] and 12-direction [38].

Direction feature extraction is accomplished in three steps: image normalization, directional decomposition, and feature sampling. Conventionally, the

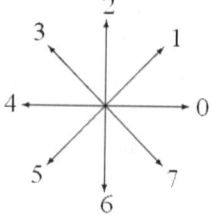

Fig. 4. Eight directions of chaincodes

contour/edge pixels of the normalized image are assigned to a number of direction planes. The normalization-cooperated feature extraction (NCFE) strategy [25], instead, assigns the chaincodes of the original image into direction planes. Though NCFE does not generate the normalized image, the coordinates of pixels in the original image map to a standard plane, and the extracted feature thus depends on the normalization method.

The direction feature is also called direction histogram feature because, at a pixel or a local region in the normalized image, the strength values of N_d directions form a local histogram. Alternatively, I view the strength values of one direction as a directional image (direction plane).

In the following, I first describe the directional decomposition procedures for three types of direction features: chaincode direction feature, normalization-cooperated chaincode feature (NCCF), and gradient direction feature, then address the sampling of direction planes.

3.1   Directional Decomposition

Directional decomposition results in a number of direction planes (the same size as the normalized image), $f_i(x, y)$, $i = 1, \ldots, N_d$. I first describe the procedures for decomposing contour/gradient into eight directions, then extend to 12 and 16 directions.

In binary images, a contour pixel is a black point that has at least one white 4-connected neighbor. The 8-direction chaincodes of contour pixels can be decided by contour tracing, or more simply, by a raster scan [39]. At a black pixel (x, y), denoting the values of 8-connected neighbors counterclockwise as p_k, $0, 1, \ldots, 7$, with the east neighbor being p_0. For $k = 0, 2, 4, 6$, if $p_k = 0$, check p_{k+1}: if $p_{k+1} = 1$ (chaincode $k + 1$), $f_{k+1}(x, y)$ increases by 1; otherwise, if $p_{(k+2)\%8} = 1$ (chaincode $(k + 2)\%8$), $f_{(k+2)\%8}(x, y)$ increases by 1.

For NCCF, I view each chaincode in the original image as a line segment connecting two neighboring pixels, which maps to another line segment in a standard direction plane by coordinate mapping. In the direction plane, each pixel (unit square) crossed by the line segment in the main (x or y) direction is given a unit of direction contribution. To exploit the continuous nature of line segment, the strength of the line direction falling in a pixel is proportional to the length of the line segment falling in the unit square (continuous NCCF [29]). As in Fig. 5, where a line segment mapped from a chaincode covers four unit squares A, B, C, and D. By discrete NCCF, the pixels A and C are assigned a direction unit, whereas by continuous NCCF, all the four pixels are assigned direction strengths proportional to the in-square line segment length.

In gradient direction feature extraction, the gradient vector, computed on the normalized image using the Sobel operator, is decomposed into components in eight chaincode directions. The Sobel operator uses two masks to compute

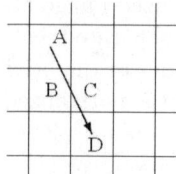

Fig. 5. NCCF on continuous direction plane

-1	0	1
-2	0	2
-1	0	1

1	2	1
0	0	0
-1	-2	-1

Fig. 6. Templates of Sobel gradient operator

the gradient components on two axes. The masks are shown in Fig. 6, and the gradient $\mathbf{g}(x,y) = [g_x, g_y]^T$ at location (x,y) is computed by

$$
\begin{aligned}
g_x(x,y) &= f(x+1,y-1) + 2f(x+1,y) + f(x+1,y+1) \\
&\quad -f(x-1,y-1) - 2f(x-1,y) - f(x-1,y+1), \\
g_y(x,y) &= f(x-1,y+1) + 2f(x,y+1) + f(x+1,y+1) \\
&\quad -f(x-1,y-1) - 2f(x,y-1) - f(x+1,y-1).
\end{aligned}
\tag{18}
$$

The gradient strength and direction can be computed from the vector $[g_x, g_y]^T$. The range of gradient direction can be partitioned into a number (say, 8 or 16) of regions, and each region corresponds to a direction plane. More effectively, the gradient vector is decomposed into components in standard directions, following a strategy previously proposed in online character recognition [27]. In this scheme, if a gradient direction lies between two standard directions, the vector is decomposed into two components, as shown in Fig. 7. The length of each component is assigned to the corresponding direction plane at the pixel (x,y).

Fig. 8 shows the direction planes of three decomposition schemes: NCCF, chaincodes of normalized image, and gradient of normalized image. The direction planes are arranged in order of stroke orientation. We can see that the planes of chaincode directions (third row) are similar to those of gradient directions. The planes of NCCF, describing the local directions of the original image, show some difference. Comparing the original image and the normalized image, the orientation of the right-hand stroke, near left-diagonal orientation, deforms to near vertical. Consequently, the direction planes of the left-diagonal orientation of NCCF are stronger than those of chaincodes and gradients, while the planes of the vertical orientation of NCCF are weaker than those of chaincodes and gradients.

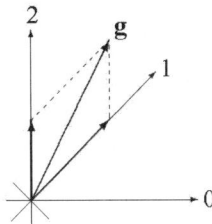

Fig. 7. Decomposition of gradient vector

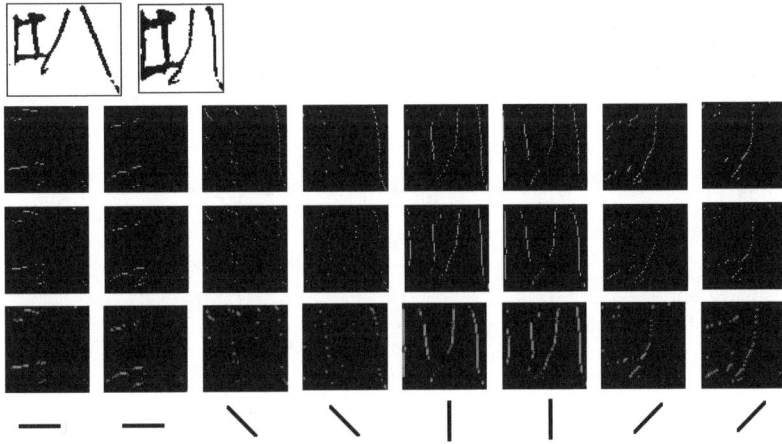

Fig. 8. Original image and normalized image (top row), 8-direction planes of NCCF (second row), chaincode planes of normalized image (third row), and gradient direction planes (bottom row)

3.2 Extension to More Directions

The extension of gradient decomposition into more than eight directions is straightforward: simply setting N_d standard directions with angle interval $360/N_d$ and, typically, with one direction pointing to east, then decompose each gradient vector into two components in standard directions and assign the component lengths to corresponding direction planes. I set N_d to 12 and 16.

To decompose contour pixels into 16 directions, I follow the 16-direction extended chaincodes, which are defined by two consecutive chaincodes. In the weighted direction histogram feature of Kimura et al. [18], 16-direction chaincodes are down-sampled by weighted average to form 8-direction planes.

Again, the 16-direction chaincode of contour pixels can be determined by a raster scan. At a contour pixel (x, y), when its 4-connected neighbor $p_k = 0$ and the counterclockwise successor $p_{k+1} = 1$ or $p_{(k+2)\%2} = 1$, search the neighbors clockwise from p_k until a $p_j = 1$ is found. The two contour pixels, p_{k+1} or $p_{(k+2)\%2}$ and p_j, form a 16-direction chaincode. In Fig. 9, the center pixel has the

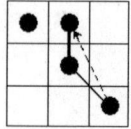

Fig. 9. 16-direction chaincode formed from two 8-direction chaincodes

east neighbor being 0, the north neighbor alone defining the 8-direction chaincode and defining a 16-direction chaincode together with the southeast neighbor. The 16-direction chaincode can be indexed from a table of correspondence between the code and the difference of coordinates of two pixels forming the code, as shown in Fig. 10. Each contour pixel has a unique 16-direction code.

(-2,2)	(-1,2)	(0,2)	(1,2)	(2,2)
6	5	4	3	2
(-2,1)	(-1,1)	(0,1)	(1,1)	(2,1)
7	6	4	2	1
(-2,0)	(-1,0)	(0,0)	(1,0)	(2,0)
8	8		0	0
(-2,-1)	(-1,-1)	(0,-1)	(1,-1)	(2,-1)
9	10	12	14	15
(-2,-2)	(-1,-2)	(0,-2)	(1,-2)	(2,-2)
10	11	12	13	14

Fig. 10. Difference of coordinates and the corresponding 16-direction chaincodes

For decomposing contour pixels into 12 directions, the difference of coordinates corresponding to a 16-direction chaincode appears as a vector (the dashed line in Fig. 9), which is decomposed into components in 12 standard directions as a gradient vector is done. In this sense, the 12-direction code of a contour pixel is not unique. For 12-direction chaincode feature extraction, a contour pixel is assigned to two direction planes, with strength proportional to the component length. For NCCF, the two corresponding direction planes are assigned strengths proportional to the overlapping length of the line segment mapped by coordinate functions, as in Fig. 5.

3.3   Blurring and Sampling

Each direction plane, with the same size as the normalized image, need to be reduced to extract feature values of moderate dimensionality. A simple way is to partition the direction plane into a number of block zones and take the total or average value of each zone as a feature value. Partition of variable-size zones was proposed to overcome the non-uniform distribution of stroke density [13], but is unnecessary for nonlinear or pseudo 2D normalization. Overlapping blocks alleviate the effect of stroke-position variation on the boundary of blocks [40], yet a more effective way involves partitioning the plane into soft zones, which follows the principle of low-pass spatial filtering and sampling [39]. The blurring operation of Iijima [11] implies spatial filtering without down-sampling.

In implementation of blurring, the impulse response function (IRF) of spatial filter is approximated into a weighted window, also called a blurring mask. The IRF is often a Gaussian function:

$$h(x,y) = \frac{1}{2\pi\sigma_x^2} \exp\left(-\frac{x^2 + y^2}{2\sigma_x^2}\right). \tag{19}$$

According to the Sampling Theorem, the variance parameter σ_x relates to the sampling frequency (the reciprocal of sampling interval). On truncating the band-width of Gaussian filter, an empirical formula was given in [39]:

$$\sigma_x = \frac{\sqrt{2}t_x}{\pi}, \tag{20}$$

where t_x is the sampling interval. At a location (x_0, y_0) of image $f(x,y)$, the convolution gives a sampled feature value

$$F(x_0, y_0) = \sum_x \sum_y f(x,y) \cdot h(x - x_0, y - y_0). \tag{21}$$

Fig. 11 shows the blurred images (without down-sampling) of the direction planes in Fig. 8. By blurring, the sparse pixels in direction planes merge into strokes or blobs.

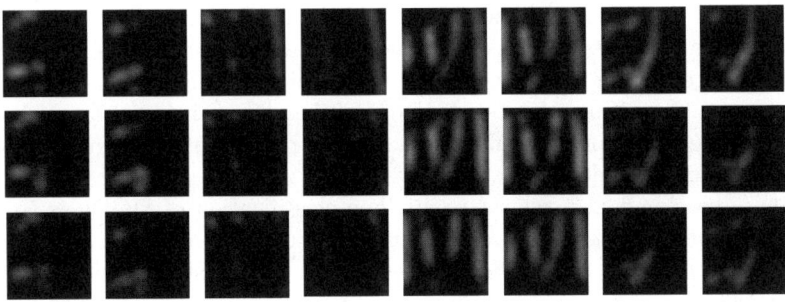

Fig. 11. Blurred images (not down-sampled) of the direction planes in Fig. 8

For ease of implementation, I partition a direction plane into a mesh of equal-size blocks and set the sampling points to the center of each block. Assume to extract $K \times K$ values from a plane, the size of plane is set to $Kt_x \times Kt_x$. From N_d direction planes, the total number of extracted feature values is $N_d \times K^2$.

The extracted feature values are causal variables. Power transformation can make the density function of causal variables closer to Gaussian [7]. This helps improve the classification performance of statistical classifiers. Power transformation is also called variable transformation [41] or Box-Cox transformation [42]. I transform each feature value with power 0.5 without attempt to optimize the transformation functions.

4   Performance Evaluation

I first compare the performance of the normalization and feature extraction methods on two large databases of handprinted characters (constrained writing), then test the performance on a small set of unconstrained handwritten characters.

I use two classifiers: the Euclidean distance to class mean (minimum distance classifier) and the MQDF [17]. For reducing the classifier complexity and improving classification accuracy, the feature vector is transformed to a lower dimensionality by Fisher linear discriminant analysis (FLDA) [7]. I set the reduced dimensionality to 160 for all feature types.

Denote the d-dimensional feature vector (after dimensionality reduction) by $\mathbf{x}$, the MQDF of class ω_i is computed by

$$
\begin{aligned}
g_2(\mathbf{x}, \omega_i) = {} & \sum_{j=1}^{k} \frac{1}{\lambda_{ij}} [(\mathbf{x} - \mu_i)^T \phi_{ij}]^2 \\
& + \frac{1}{\delta_i} \left\{ \|x - \mu_i\|^2 - \sum_{j=1}^{k} [(\mathbf{x} - \mu_i)^T \phi_{ij}]^2 \right\} \\
& + \sum_{j=1}^{k} \log \lambda_{ij} + (d - k) \log \delta_i,
\end{aligned} \tag{22}
$$

where μ_i is the mean vector of class ω_i, λ_{ij} and ϕ_{ij}, $j = 1, \ldots, d$, are the eigenvalues and eigenvectors of the covariance matrix of class ω_i. The eigenvalues are sorted in non-ascending order and the eigenvectors are sorted accordingly. k denotes the number of principal axes, and the minor eigenvalues are replaced with a constant δ_i. I set a class-independent constant δ_i, which is proportional to the average feature variance, with the multiplier selected by a 5-fold holdout validation on the training data set (1/5 of training data is held out for evaluating the candidate values of the multiplier while the remaining 4/5 of data are used for estimating classifier parameters).

In my experiments, k was set to 40. The classification of MQDF is speeded up by selecting 100 candidate classes using a Euclidean distance. The MQDF is then computed on the candidate classes only. Candidate selection is further accelerated by clustering the class means into groups. The input feature vector is first compared to cluster centers, then to the class means contained in a number of nearest clusters. I set the total number of clusters to 220 for the ETL9B database and 250 for the CASIA database.

The MQDF shows promises in classification for HCCR. Even higher performance can be achieved by, e.g., discriminative learning of feature transformation and classifier parameters [37,38]. This chapter, however, does not concern the optimization of classifiers.

4.1   Performance on Handprinted Characters

The normalization and feature extraction methods are evaluated on two databases of handprinted characters. The ETL9B database contains the character images of 3,036 classes (71 hiragana, and 2,965 Kanji characters in the JIS level-1 set), with 200 samples per class. Experiments have widely evaluated this database [18,40,43]. The CASIA database, which was collected by the Institute of Automation, Chinese Academy of Sciences, in the early 1990s, contains the handwritten images of 3,755 Chinese characters (the level-1 set in GB2312-80 standard), with 300 samples per class. Some sample images of the two databases are shown in Fig. 12.

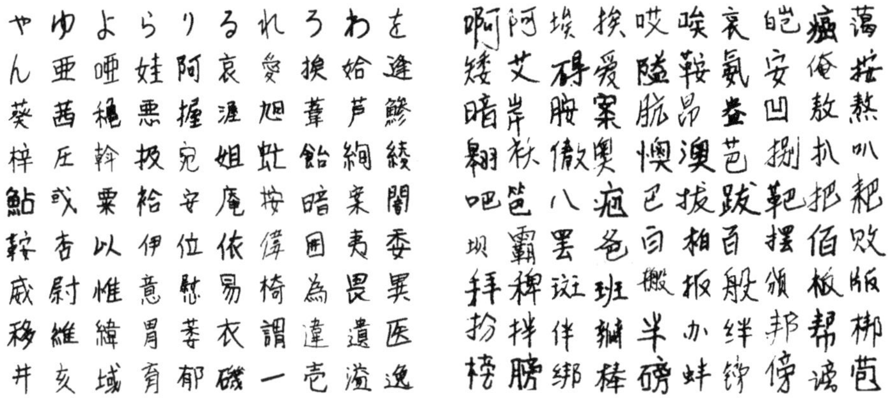

Fig. 12. Some test samples of ETL9B database (left) and CASIA database (right)

In the ETL9B database, I use the first 20 and last 20 samples of each class for testing and the remaining samples for training classifiers. In the CASIA database, I use the first 250 samples of each class for training and the remaining 50 samples per class for testing.

I first compare the performance of three direction features with varying direction resolutions with a common normalization method (Tsukumo and Tanaka's nonlinear normalization (NLN) method with favorable modifications). The direction resolution of features is set to 8, 12, and 16. For each direction resolution, three schemes of sampling mesh are tested. For 8-direction features, the mesh of sampling is set to 7×7 (M1), 8×8 (M2), and 9×9 (M3); for 12-direction, 6×6 (M1), 7×7 (M2), and 8×8 (M3); and for 16-direction, 5×5 (M1), 6×6 (M2), and 7×7 (M3). I control the size of the normalized image (direction planes) as around 64×64, and the dimensionality (before reduction) as less than 800. Table 1 summarizes the settings of the sampling mesh.

On classifier training and testing using different direction resolutions and sampling schemes, the error rates on the test set of ETL9B database are listed in Table 2, and the error rates on the test set of CASIA database are listed in Table 3. In the tables, the chaincode direction feature is denoted by **chn**, NCCF is

Table 1. Settings of sampling mesh for 8-direction, 12-direction, and 16-direction features

Mesh	M1		M2		M3	
	zones	dim	zones	dim	zones	dim
8-dir	7×7	392	8×8	512	9×9	648
12-dir	6×6	432	7×7	588	8×8	768
16-dir	5×5	400	6×6	576	7×7	784

Table 2. Error rates (%) of 8-direction, 12-direction, and 16-direction features on ETL9B database

	Euclidean			MQDF		
chn	M1	M2	M3	M1	M2	M3
8-dir	2.91	2.94	3.02	1.08	1.05	1.09
12-dir	2.43	2.56	2.54	1.02	1.00	**0.97**
16-dir	2.52	**2.40**	2.52	1.20	1.00	1.00
nccf	M1	M2	M3	M1	M2	M3
8-dir	2.61	2.61	2.71	0.93	0.87	0.89
12-dir	2.05	2.06	2.13	0.82	**0.77**	0.78
16-dir	2.05	**2.04**	2.11	0.98	0.85	0.79
grd-g	M1	M2	M3	M1	M2	M3
8-dir	2.59	2.58	2.66	0.93	0.90	0.89
12-dir	2.27	2.30	2.31	0.94	0.86	0.86
16-dir	2.29	**2.19**	2.25	1.08	0.94	**0.85**

Table 3. Error rates (%) of 8-direction, 12-direction, and 16-direction features on CASIA database

	Euclidean			MQDF		
chn	M1	M2	M3	M1	M2	M3
8-dir	5.95	6.07	6.22	2.45	2.37	2.37
12-dir	5.34	5.44	5.53	2.34	2.26	**2.21**
16-dir	5.44	**5.28**	5.37	2.72	2.35	2.29
nccf	M1	M2	M3	M1	M2	M3
8-dir	5.31	5.35	5.49	1.94	1.92	2.00
12-dir	4.44	4.48	4.55	1.86	1.75	**1.73**
16-dir	4.53	**4.42**	4.52	2.17	1.92	1.82
grd-g	M1	M2	M3	M1	M2	M3
8-dir	5.31	5.34	5.41	2.05	2.01	1.97
12-dir	4.94	4.90	4.98	2.09	2.00	**1.95**
16-dir	4.98	4.85	**4.80**	2.42	2.09	1.98

denoted by **nccf**, and the gradient direction feature by **grd-g**. For chaincode feature extraction, the normalized binary image is smoothed using a connectivity-preserving smoothing algorithm [39]. The gradient feature is extracted from a gray-scale normalized image.

We can see that on either database, using either classifier (Euclidean or MQDF), the error rates of 12-direction and 16-direction features are mostly lower than 8-direction features. This indicates that increasing the resolution of direction decomposition is beneficial. The 16-direction feature, however, does not outperform the 12-direction feature. To select a sampling mesh, I focus on the results of 12-direction features. It is noted that by Euclidean distance classification, M1 (6×6) outperforms M2 (7×7) and M3 (8×8), whereas by MQDF, the error rates of M2 and M3 are lower than M1. Considering M2 and M3 perform comparably while M2 has a lower complexity, I take the sampling mesh M2 with 12-direction features for following experiments. The original dimensionality of direction features is now $12 \times 7 \times 7 = 588$.

Table 4. Error rates (%) of various normalization methods on ETL9B database

	Euclidean			MQDF		
Norm.	chn	nccf	grd-g	chn	nccf	grd-g
LN	6.36	5.94	5.97	2.38	2.09	2.11
NLN	2.56	2.06	2.30	1.00	0.77	0.86
MN	2.35	2.07	2.12	0.95	0.83	0.82
BMN	2.33	2.04	2.09	0.92	0.81	0.80
MCBA	2.52	2.19	2.27	1.00	0.84	0.86
LDPI	2.08	1.65	1.90	**0.82**	**0.64**	**0.73**
P2DMN	2.05	1.65	1.84	0.86	0.69	0.74
P2DBMN	**1.97**	**1.60**	**1.78**	0.84	0.69	**0.73**
P2DCBA	2.13	1.81	1.93	0.86	0.72	0.77

By fixing the direction resolution (12-direction) and sampling mesh (7×7), I combine the three types of direction features with nine normalization methods. The weight parameter w_0 of pseudo 2D normalization was set to 0.75 for good recognition performance [24]. The error rates on the test sets of the two databases are listed in Table 4 and Table 5, respectively. Comparing the normalization methods, we can see that pseudo 2D methods are superior to 1D ones, and the linear normalization (LN) is inferior to other 1D normalization methods. To compare the three types of features, I view the error rates of 1D normalization methods and those of pseudo 2D methods separately.

Table 4 and Table 5 demonstrate that with 1D normalization, the NCCF and the gradient feature perform comparably, and both outperform the chaincode feature. Four normalization methods, namely NLN, MN, BMN, and MCBA, perform comparably. With pseudo 2D normalization, the NCCF performs best, and the gradient feature outperforms the chaincode feature. Comparing the pseudo 2D normalization methods, LDPI and P2DBMN outperform P2DMN and P2DCBA (especially on the CASIA database). On both databases, the

Table 5. Error rates (%) of various normalization methods on CASIA database

Norm.	Euclidean			MQDF		
	chn	nccf	grdg	chn	nccf	grd-g
LN	11.38	10.46	10.31	4.11	3.49	3.54
NLN	5.44	4.48	4.90	2.26	1.75	2.00
MN	5.61	4.89	4.90	2.50	2.04	2.06
BMN	5.30	4.54	4.56	2.35	1.93	1.92
MCBA	5.48	4.73	4.83	2.31	1.87	1.96
LDPI	**4.49**	**3.69**	4.21	**1.96**	**1.52**	**1.75**
P2DMN	4.99	3.97	4.33	2.24	1.70	1.91
P2DBMN	4.63	3.71	**4.07**	2.15	1.62	1.76
P2DCBA	4.75	3.95	4.25	2.11	1.68	1.78

NCCF with LDPI normalization yields the best performance, and the NCCF with P2DBMN is competitive.

The gradient feature performs comparably with NCCF with 1D normalization, but is inferior when combined with pseudo 2D normalization. Pseudo 2D normalization, though equalizes the stroke density better than 1D normalization, also deforms the stroke directions remarkably. While the gradient feature describes the deformed stroke directions, NCCF takes the stroke directions of the original image.

4.2 Computation Times

To compare the computational complexity of normalization methods, I profile the processing time in two sub-tasks: coordinate mapping and normalized image generation. The latter is dichotomized into binary image and gray-scale image. Smoothing happens for binary normalized images, but not for gray-scale images.

On the test samples of CASIA database, I measured the CPU times on a Pentium-4-3GHz processor. The average times per sample are shown in Table 6. The processing time of coordinate mapping varies with the normalization

Table 6. Average CPU times (ms) of normalization on CASIA database. Binary normalized images involve smoothing.

	coordinate	binary	grayscale
LN	0.002	0.318	0.133
NLN	0.115	0.331	0.143
MN	0.017	0.321	0.126
BMN	0.024	0.332	0.135
MCBA	0.032	0.336	0.137
LDPI	0.266	1.512	1.282
P2DMN	0.143	1.514	1.236
P2DBMN	0.147	1.536	1.274
P2DCBA	0.156	1.542	1.261

Table 7. Average CPU times (ms) of feature extraction on CASIA database

	direction	blurring
chn	0.121	0.439
nccf	0.458	0.752
grd-g	0.329	1.276

method. The linear normalization (LN) is very fast. NLN is more expensive than other 1D methods, and LDPI is more expensive than the other pseudo 2D methods, because NLN and LDPI involve line density computation. Nevertheless, all these normalization methods are not computationally expensive. Normalized image generation for pseudo 2D normalization methods is time consuming because it involves quadrilateral decomposition. The processing time of a binary normalized image includes a smoothing time of about 0.3ms.

The CPU time of feature extraction is almost independent of the normalization method. It contains two parts: directional decomposition and blurring. For average CPU times of three direction features, see Table 7. The processing time of blurring depends on the sparsity of direction planes (zero pixels are not considered). The direction planes of the chaincode feature are sparse, and those of the gradient feature are densest. The directional decomposition of NCCF takes the most time because it involves line segment decomposition. Gradient direction decomposition is more expensive than chaincode decomposition. Overall, NCCF remains the most computationally efficient because it saves the time of generating the normalized image. The average CPU time of NCCF ranges from 1.21ms to 1.47ms, covering coordinate mapping and feature extraction. For reference, the average classification time of MQDF (with cluster-based candidate selection) for 3,755 classes is 3.63ms, which can be largely reduced by fine implementation though.

4.3   Performance on Unconstrained Handwriting

The accuracies of the best methods on handprinted characters, 99.36% on ETL9B database and 98.48% on CASIA database, are fairly high. To test the performance on unconstrained handwritten characters, I use the classifiers trained from the CASIA database to classify the samples in a small data set, which contains 20 samples for each of 3,755 classes, written by 20 writers without constraint. Some samples of the unconstrained set are shown in Fig. 13.

On the unconstrained set, I evaluate various normalization methods with two good features: NCCF and gradient direction feature. Table 8 lists the error rates. We can see that, as for handprinted characters, the pseudo 2D normalization methods yield lower error rates than their 1D counterparts on unconstrained characters. However, line-density-based nonlinear normalization methods, NLN and LDPI, are evidently inferior to the centroid-based methods. The P2DBMN method performs best, and the P2DCBA method is competitive. Comparing the two types of direction features, the gradient feature outperforms NCCF with 1D normalization methods, but with pseudo 2D normalization, NCCF is superior. Overall, the error rates on unconstrained characters remain high.

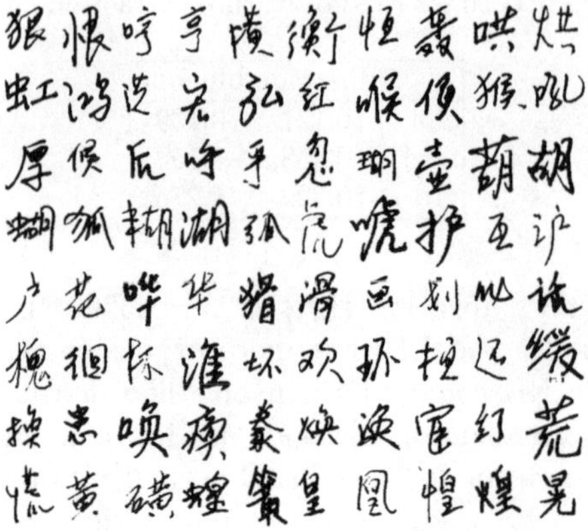

Fig. 13. Samples of unconstrained handwritten characters

Table 8. Error rates (%) on unconstrained handwritten Chinese characters

Norm.	Euclidean		MQDF	
	nccf	grdg	nccf	grd-g
LN	36.04	35.44	21.80	21.46
NLN	26.61	27.04	16.23	16.96
MN	25.63	25.18	16.40	16.09
BMN	25.15	24.53	15.91	15.64
MCBA	25.53	25.06	15.76	15.66
LDPI	24.93	25.60	15.12	15.73
P2DMN	23.48	24.38	14.84	15.37
P2DBMN	**22.75**	**23.35**	**14.27**	**14.64**
P2DCBA	23.80	23.78	14.73	14.79

Fig. 14. Misclassified samples (original image and normalized image) of unconstrained handwritten characters

Fig. 14 shows some misclassified samples by MQDF, with the best normalization-feature combination (P2DBMN and NCCF). Most of the misclassified characters have shapes similar to the assigned class: some are inherently similar (top three rows in Fig. 14), and some others are similar due to cursive writing (fourth and fifth rows). Yet the characters of the bottom row do not seem similar to their assigned classes.

5 Concluding Remarks

I compared various shape normalization and selected feature extraction methods in offline handwritten Chinese character recognition. For direction feature extraction, my results show that 12-direction and 16-direction features outperform the 8-direction feature, and the 12-direction feature has a better tradeoff between accuracy and complexity. The comparison of normalization methods shows that pseudo 2D normalization methods outperform their 1D counterparts. On handprinted characters, a line-density-based method LDPI and a centroid-based method P2DBMN perform best. Comparing three types of direction features, the NCCF and the gradient feature outperform the chaincode feature and compete when 1D normalization is used. With pseudo 2D normalization, the NCCF outperforms the gradient feature. Overall, LDPI or P2DBMN with NCCF form the best normalization-feature combination.

I also tested the performance on a small set of unconstrained handwritten characters, with classifiers trained with handprinted samples. The error rates on unconstrained characters are very high, but the comparison of normalization and feature extraction methods reveals new insights. Though pseudo 2D normalization methods again outperform their 1D counterparts, the line-density-based LDPI method is inferior to the centroid-based methods, and the P2DBMN method performs best. The best normalization-feature combination on unconstrained characters is P2DBMN with NCCF.

Training classifiers with unconstrained handwritten samples will improve the accuracy of unconstrained character recognition. This requires large databases of unconstrained characters. To reduce the error rate (say, to 2% on isolated characters), however, using the current normalization and feature extraction methods and training current classifiers with a large sample set will not suffice. The methods of shape normalization, feature extraction, and classifier design should be re-considered for better recognition of cursively-written characters. Training classifiers discriminatively can improve the accuracy of both handprinted and unconstrained character recognition.

Acknowledgments

This work was supported in part by the Hundred Talents Program of Chinese Academy of Sciences (CAS) and the National Natural Science Foundation of China under grants No.60543004 and No.60121302.

References

1. Casey, R., Nagy, G.: Recognition of printed Chinese characters. IEEE Trans. Electronic Computers 15(1), 91–101 (1966)
2. Stalling, W.: Approaches to Chinese character recognition. Pattern Recognition 8, 87–98 (1976)
3. Mori, S., Yamamoto, K., Yasuda, M.: Research on machine recognition of handprinted characters. IEEE Trans. Pattern Anal. Mach. Intell. 6(4), 386–405 (1984)
4. Hildebrandt, T.H., Liu, W.: Optical recognition of Chinese characters: Advances since 1980. Pattern Recognition 26(2), 205–225 (1993)
5. Umeda, M.: Advances in recognition methods for handwritten Kanji characters. IEICE Trans. Information and Systems E29(5), 401–410 (1996)
6. Liu, C.L., Jaeger, S., Nakagawa, M.: Online recognition of Chinese characters: The state-of-the-art. IEEE Trans. Pattern Anal. Mach. Intell. 26(2), 198–213 (2004)
7. Fukunaga, K.: Introduction to Statistical Pattern Recognition, 2nd edn. Academic Press, London (1990)
8. Duda, R.O., Hart, P.E., Stork, D.G.: Pattern Classification, 2nd edn. Wiley, Chichester (2001)
9. Jain, A.K., Duin, R.P.W., Mao, J.: Statistical pattern recognition: A review. IEEE Trans. Pattern Anal. Mach. Intell. 22(1), 4–37 (2000)
10. Kim, I.J., Kim, J.H.: Statistical character structure modeling and its application to handwritten Chinese character recognition. IEEE Trans. Pattern Anal. Mach. Intell. 25(11), 1422–1436 (2003)
11. Iijima, T., Genchi, H., Mori, K.: A theoretical study of the pattern identification by matching method. In: Proc. First USA-JAPAN Computer Conference, pp. 42–48 (October 1972)
12. Yasuda, M., Fujisawa, H.: An improvement of correlation method for character recognition. Trans. IEICE Japan J62-D(3), 217–224 (1979) (in Japanese)
13. Yamashita, Y., Higuchi, K., Yamada, Y., Haga, Y.: Classification of handprinted Kanji characters by the structured segment matching method. Pattern Recognition Letters 1, 475–479 (1983)
14. Fujisawa, H., Liu, C.L.: Directional pattern matching for character recognition revisited. In: Proc. 7th Int. Conf. Document Analysis and Recognition, Edinburgh, Scotland, pp. 794–798 (2003)
15. Tsukumo, J., Tanaka, H.: Classification of handprinted Chinese characters using non-linear normalization and correlation methods. In: Proc. 9th Int. Conf. Pattern Recognition, Rome, pp. 168–171 (1988)
16. Yamada, H., Yamamoto, H., Saito, T.: A nonlinear normalization method for hanprinted Kanji character recognition—line density equalization. Pattern Recognition 23(9), 1023–1029 (1990)
17. Kimura, F., Takashina, K., Tsuruoka, S., Miyake, Y.: Modified quadratic discriminant functions and the application to Chinese character recognition. IEEE Trans. Pattern Anal. Mach. Intell. 9(1), 149–153 (1987)
18. Kimura, F., Wakabayashi, T., Tsuruoka, S., Miyake, Y.: Improvement of handwritten Japanese character recognition using weighted direction code histogram. Pattern Recognition 30(8), 1329–1337 (1997)
19. Kato, N., Abe, M., Nemoto, Y.: A handwritten character recognition system using modified Mahalanobis distance. Trans. IEICE Japan J79-D-II(1), 45–52 (1996) (in Japanese)

20. Casey, R.G.: Moment normalization of handprinted character. IBM J. Res. Develop 14, 548–557 (1970)
21. Liu, C.L., Sako, H., Fujisawa, H.: Handwritten Chinese character recognition: alternatives to nonlinear normalization. In: Proc. 7th Int. Conf. Document Analysis and Recognition, Edinburgh, Scotland, pp. 524–528 (2003)
22. Liu, C.L., Marukawa, K.: Global shape normalization for handwritten Chinese character recognition: A new method. In: Proc. 9th Int. Workshop on Frontiers of Handwriting Recognition, Tokyo, Japan, pp. 300–305 (2004)
23. Horiuchi, T., Haruki, R., Yamada, H., Yamamoto, K.: Two-dimensional extension of nonlinear normalization method using line density for character recognition. In: Proc. 4th Int. Conf. Document Analysis and Recognition, Ulm, Germany, pp. 511–514 (1997)
24. Liu, C.L., Marukawa, K.: Pseudo two-dimensional shape normalization methods for handwritten Chinese character recognition. Pattern Recognition 38(12), 2242–2255 (2005)
25. Hamanaka, M., Yamada, K., Tsukumo, J.: Normalization-cooperated feature extraction method for handprinted Kanji character recognition. In: Proc. 3rd Int. Workshop on Frontiers of Handwriting Recognition, Buffalo, NY, pp. 343–348 (1993)
26. Liu, C.L., Nakashima, K., Sako, H., Fujisawa, H.: Handwritten digit recognition: Benchmarking of state-of-the-art techniques. Pattern Recognition 36(10), 2271–2285 (2003)
27. Kawamura, A., Yura, K., Hayama, T., Hidai, Y., Minamikawa, T., Tanaka, A., Masuda, S.: On-line recognition of freely handwritten Japanese characters using directional feature densities. In: Proc. 11th Int. Conf. Pattern Recognition. The Hague, vol. 2, pp. 183–186 (1992)
28. Srikantan, G., Lam, S.W., Srihari, S.N.: Gradient-based contour encoder for character recognition. Pattern Recognition 29(7), 1147–1160 (1996)
29. Liu, C.L., Nakashima, K., Sako, H., Fujisawa, H.: Handwritten digit recognition: investigation of normalization and feature extraction techniques. Pattern Recognition 37(2), 265–279 (2004)
30. Hagita, N., Naito, S., Masuda, I.: Handprinted Chinese characters recognition by peripheral direction contributivity feature. Trans. IEICE Japan J66-D(10), 1185–1192 (1983) (in Japanese)
31. Yasuda, M., Yamamoto, K., Yamada, H., Saito, T.: An improved correlation method for handprinted Chinese character recognition in a reciprocal feature field. Trans. IEICE Japan J68-D(3), 353–360 (1985)
32. Teow, L.N., Loe, K.F.: Robust vision-based features and classification schemes for off-line handwritten digit recognition. Pattern Recognition 35(11), 2355–2364 (2002)
33. Shi, M., Fujisawa, Y., Wakabayashi, T., Kimura, F.: Handwritten numeral recognition using gradient and curvature of gray scale image. Pattern Recognition 35(10), 2051–2059 (2002)
34. Wang, X., Ding, X., Liu, C.: Gabor filter-base feature extraction for character recognition. Pattern Recognition 38(3), 369–379 (2005)
35. Liu, C.L., Koga, M., Fujisawa, H.: Gabor feature extraction for character recognition: comparison with gradient feature. In: Proc. 8th Int. Conf. Document Analysis and Recognition, Seoul, Korea, pp. 121–125 (2005)
36. Liu, C.L., Koga, M., Sako, H., Fujisawa, H.: Aspect ratio adaptive normalization for handwritten character recognition. In: Tan, T., Shi, Y., Gao, W. (eds.) ICMI 2000. LNCS, vol. 1948, pp. 418–425. Springer, Heidelberg (2000)

37. Liu, C.L.: High accuracy handwritten Chinese character recognition using quadratic classifiers with discriminative feature extraction. In: Proc. 18th Int. Conf. Pattern Recognition, Hong Kong, vol. 2, pp. 942–945 (2006)
38. Liu, H., Ding, X.: Handwritten character recognition using gradient feature and quadratic classifier with multiple discrimination schemes. In: Proc. 8th Int. Conf. Document Analysis and Recognition, Seoul, Korea, pp. 19–23 (2005)
39. Liu, C.L., Liu, Y.J., Dai, R.W.: Preprocessing and statistical/structural feature extraction for handwritten numeral recognition. In: Downton, A.C., Impedovo, S. (eds.) Progress of Handwriting Recognition, pp. 161–168. World Scientific, Singapore (1997)
40. Guo, J., Sun, N., Nemoto, Y., Kimura, M., Echigo, H., Sato, R.: Recognition of handwritten characters using pattern transformation method with cosine function. Trans. IEICE Japan J76-D-II(4), 835–842 (1993)
41. Wakabayashi, T., Tsuruoka, S., Kimura, F., Miyake, Y.: On the size and variable transformation of feature vector for handwritten character recognition. Trans. IEICE Japan J76-D-II(12), 2495–2503 (1993)
42. Heiden, R.V.D., Gren, F.C.A.: The Box-Cox metric for nearest neighbor classification improvement. Pattern Recognition 30(2), 273–279 (1997)
43. Kato, N., Suzuki, M., Omachi, S., Aso, H., Nemoto, Y.: A handwritten character recognition system using directional element feature and asymmetric Mahalanobis distance. IEEE Trans. Pattern Anal. Mach. Intell. 21(3), 258–262 (1999)

How to Deal with Uncertainty and Variability: Experience and Solutions

Hiromichi Fujisawa

Central Research Laboratory, Hitachi, Ltd.
Tokyo, Japan 185-8601
hiromichi.fujisawa.sb@hitachi.com

Abstract. Uncertainty and variability are two of the most important concepts at the center of pattern recognition. It is especially true when patterns to be recognized are complex in nature and not controlled by any artificial constraints. Handwritten postal address recognition is one such case. This paper presents five principles of dealing with uncertainty and variability, and discusses how to decompose the complex recognition task into manageable sub-tasks. When applicable, block diagrams will clarify the structure of various recognition components. This paper also presents implementation of those principles into real recognition engines. It will demonstrate that high accuracy and robustness of a recognition system, which relates to uncertainty and variability, respectively, can occur only with comprehensive approaches.

1 Introduction

Historically, character recognition was the first concrete subfield of pattern recognition, which was actually studied before the concept of 'pattern recognition' came into existence. Historically, OCRs (Optical Character Readers) read machine-printed characters and handwritten characters in fixed, separate positions on specially designed forms. Today, OCRs have advanced greatly, and can read many types of documents, including business forms, bank checks, mail letter surfaces, book pages, etc.

The capabilities of OCRs have expanded in multiple dimensions. The first dimension is script. Having begun with Arabic numeral characters, recognizable scripts now include Roman alphabets, Japanese syllabic letters, Kanji (Japanese Chinese characters), Chinese characters, Hangul characters, Indian scripts, and Arabic scripts. The second dimension concerns the style of printing and writing. In the case of machine-printed characters, many font faces exist in different sizes. As for handwritten characters, writers were required to 'hand-print' the numerals and upper-case alphabets in a restricted way. Today, advanced OCRs can recognize freely handwritten characters in a limited context such as bank checks and mail pieces. These specialized applications allow OCR algorithms to utilize contextual information to heighten the recognition accuracy to the industry strength.

During these historical technology developments, *uncertainty and variability* have been key issues in technical challenges. Uncertainty refers to the state of something of which we are not sure. In the context of this paper, it is the state of a recognition engine,

D.S. Doermann and S. Jaeger (Eds.): SACH 2006, LNCS 4768, pp. 129–151, 2008.
© Springer-Verlag Berlin Heidelberg 2008

or a recognition component, being uncertain about the input or the output. Therefore, the issue consists of two parts. One concerns how to deal with uncertainty in the input, and the other looks at how to reduce uncertainty in the output. These issues concerning uncertainty are outstanding as recognition tasks become more complex.

Variability presents another key issue. It deals with variations in inputs. If no variations existed, no problems would occur in pattern recognition. Usually, given more variations, recognition performance degrades more, so we try to minimize degradation. Therefore, the issue is *robustness*, and how to make the system more robust.

As a result, modern complex applications require researchers and engineers to think more about uncertainty and variability. This paper presents five design principles and implementation methodologies that lead to higher accuracy and higher robustness. The presentation includes examples from our experience in developing a Japanese postal address recognition system. The technical challenges come mostly from handwritten address recognition.

The following sections are organized as follows. In Section 2, uncertainty and variability in pattern recognition are discussed in some depth and, including how they relate to accuracy and robustness, respectively. Section 3 will describe the problems in Japanese postal address recognition as an example of a complex recognition task. Then, Section 4 will present five design principles to tackle the uncertainty and variability problems, followed by Section 5, which presents implementation methodologies.

2 Uncertainty and Variability

Uncertainty generally exists in input and in output. As mentioned above, a complex recognition task ought to be decomposed into smaller pieces of manageable tasks. So, the whole recognition engine should consist of many components, each of which solves smaller scale pattern recognition problems. It further means that, because each component has an input and an output that holds uncertainty, composition of such unreliable components requires a careful design. The question arises of how to combine recognition components with their uncertain inputs and outputs are uncertain. If they connected in a cascade manner, the accuracy of the final output from 30 such components would be 74 %, even when each component's accuracy was 0.99. Usually, the recognition of one postal address requires more than 30 decisions. Furthermore, to raise each component's accuracy above 0.99 is extremely difficult, presenting the necessity of good design principles, to be discussed in Section 4.

Variability, on the other hand, exists only in the input. However, the variability in uncontrolled inputs, such as in postal addresses, is nonlinear, discontinuous, structural, and unpredictable. To solve the problems of nonlinear, discontinuous, and structural variations requires more than a single highly sophisticated parametric method. Usually, it requires additional logics (or algorithms) and makes the whole recognition engine more complex as a result. The combination of such new logics to other existing parts again presents a technical challenge. This holds especially true for variability not contained in a single character but apparent in a layout of the character lines and surrounding objects. Such spatial variations of printed/handwritten objects are difficult to handle. For example, Japanese mail surfaces have many unrelated, interfering objects, such as advertisements. Recipient addresses are written in several orientations. Finding a recipient address is generally difficult.

Unpredictability of variations, which is a type of uncertainty, influences the developmental methodologies. Concretely speaking, the capture of every (or most of the) variation(s) at a single step is almost impossible, and it is difficult to cope with every problem stemming from variations in a single algorithm. Questions arise of how to cycle the developmental steps, how to organize sample datasets, and how to prioritize the plurality of problems. These questions will be answered in Section 5.

Another discussion about uncertainty and variability involves their relationship to recognition performance. Generally speaking, 'recognition performance' has the following three aspects:

- Accuracy
- Robustness
- Efficiency

Accuracy directly reflects the certainty of recognition outputs. Accuracy is measured as Nc/N or $Nc/(N - Nr)$, where N is the total number of samples, Nc the number of correctly recognized samples, and Nr the number of rejected samples. The latter definition is sometimes referred to as reliability. 'Read rate' (or recognition rate) is sometimes used as a measure of recognition performance, which is defined as Na/N where $Na = N - Nr$. Read rate is used because it can be measured without using ground truth data. Error rate, Ne, is measured as either $Ne = (N - Nc - Nr)/N$ or $Ne = (Na - Nc)/Na$.

Robustness is a concept not discussed much in the context of recognition performance. It has not yet been quantitatively defined, but we think that robustness ought to be a performance measure. Robustness could be defined as a quantity inversely proportional to the read rate's (or accuracy's) degradation against variations. In this paper, instead of defining a single quantity, we try to see it as a read rate curve against variations. Figure 1 shows an example of such read rate profiles of a postal address recognition engine. The horizontal axis shows sample dataset numbers, in which the

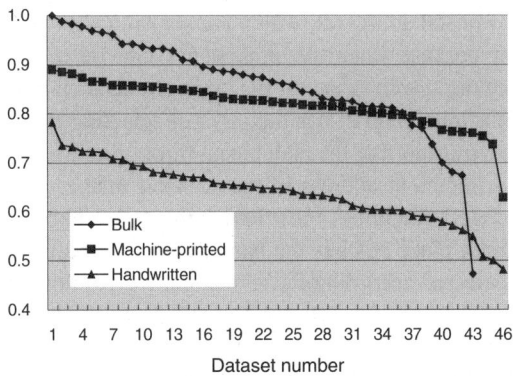

Fig. 1. Read rate profiles

sample datasets have been re-ordered according to their read rates, and the vertical axis shows the read rates.

The mailpiece images forming these datasets were captured from mail sorting machines in separate sessions. Then, due to the varieties of capturing times, each dataset had a different mixture of samples reflecting the operational modes of the post offices. Consequently, some datasets were easier to read than others.

Because the read rate degradation results from variations, we may conclude that the flatter the curve, the more robust the recognition engine. At this moment, we do not have a theoretical background for seeing the robustness characteristics in this manner. However, it is important to note that each dot shows a read rate, which an operator (a customer) of the mail sorting machine could see on the control panel. Therefore, clearly, flattening these curves is a reasonable target for the developers.

The third measure, *efficiency*, as a recognition performance, also presents an important characteristic, representing recognition throughput per unit computation cost. Usually, throughput performance is given as a specification. If latency (recognition time) is not a concern, it is a matter of hardware resources and the cost of the system. We can achieve higher throughput by adding more hardware in parallel. In the case of mail sorting machines, the latency is also important, and therefore, cannot depend only on bigger hardware. Recognition algorithms are constrained by the maximum latency time. In a complex pattern recognition problem, recognition is a search of an optimal interpretation in a huge search space, so the search space ought to be limited optimally while maximizing the read rate.

3 Japanese Postal Address Recognition

3.1 Machine for Reading Postal Addresses

Postal address recognition as an application has contributed to the technology advancement of handwritten character recognition, being technically 'rich' and semantically 'rich.' In other words, it has presented many technical challenges, but the domain is limited to postal addresses, which are semantically well defined. The latter notion is important because linguistic approaches can be introduced with address knowledge to reduce the search space for the optimal interpretation.

A mail sorting machine (Fig. 2) has the tasks of selecting mail pieces individually from the feeder deck, transporting the mail pieces through an image scanner to a sorting bin, recognizing the recipient address in the scanned image, and spraying barcodes representing the recognized address code. Recognition should be accomplished before the corresponding mail piece reaches the barcode printer and the switches that determine which bin is selected according to the recognition result. A large version of the machine has about 400 sorting bins. In the case of the machine shown in Fig. 2, mail pieces run at the speed of 3.4m/s, and maximum latency time for recognition is 3.7s. The throughput is 30,000 to 50,000 mail pieces per hour, depending on the operational

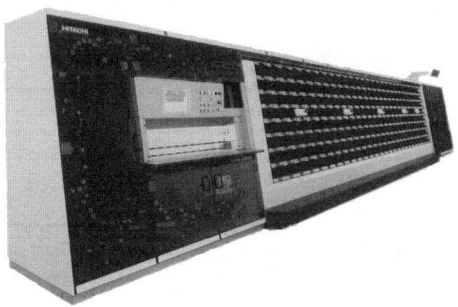

Fig. 2. Mail Sorting Machine (Hitachi)

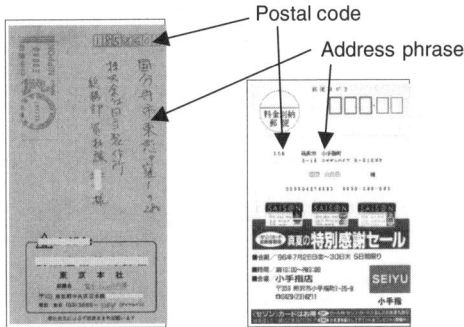

Fig. 3. Mail sample images. (Courtesy of the recipients).

mode. Approximately, average recognition time of 1.5s using 21 computers can attain the maximum throughput.

3.2 Recognition Task

The task of postal address recognition is to identify the character lines of a postal code and an address phrase, then recognize and interpret them. The output, i.e., the recognition result, is an address code that designates a delivery point out of 40 million such points in Japan. The address code has a variable length digit code, which sometimes includes alphabetic information. Its first seven digits equal the postal code, which is written or printed in a separate field. With a few exceptions, a Kanji address phrase corresponds to this postal code. Therefore, a recognition engine can utilize this redundant information to heighten accuracy. The rest of the code has three field numbers, which represents an address point. Sample images of Japanese mail pieces appear in Fig. 3.

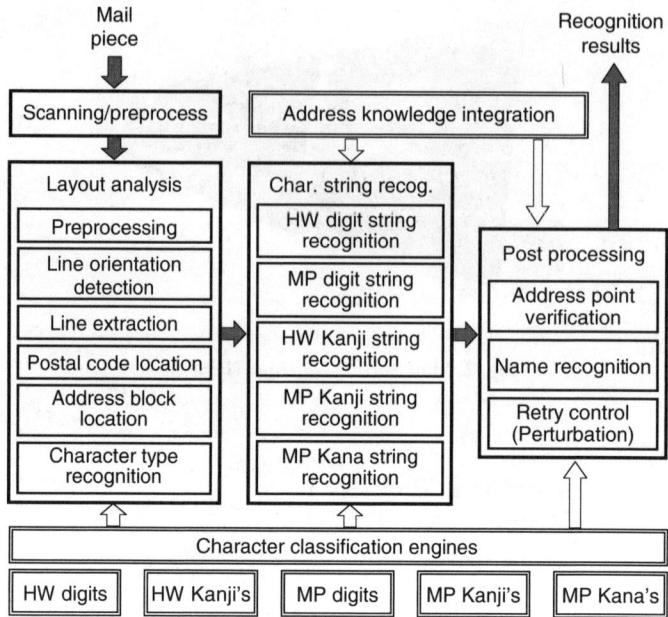

Fig. 4. Recognition components

The recognition task can be decomposed into four steps: (1) image scanning and preprocessing, (2) layout analysis to extract a postal code region and a recipient address block, (3) character string recognition and interpretation, and (4) post processing to verify the recognition result and complete extra recognition tasks. A block diagram for these recognition components is shown in Fig. 4.

As shown in the diagram, each step consists of subcomponents for solving more focused pattern recognition problems. Each subcomponent makes a decision. Therefore, uncertainty and variability carry over to these levels. For example, in layout analysis, the accuracy of line orientation determination from four possible cases of 0°, 90°, 180° and 270° is not 100 percent. This holds true for other subcomponents, and it becomes more difficult when they connect in series. For example, each subcomponent needs to output multiple choices for the next step, when the decision is uncertain.

Some subcomponents connect in a parallel way. It is sometimes necessary to classify an input into one of the cases anticipated and to process it differently. For example, problems in recognizing handwritten character strings and machine-printed character strings are different, so we need to develop separate recognition engines though they are similar in their architectures. Character type recognition for this adaptive treatment is also prone to error; therefore treatment of uncertainty is necessary here too. When the decision appears uncertain, multiple hypotheses are generated. Section 4 will describe the approaches to uncertainty management more closely.

Table 1. Performance Influencing Factors

Components	Performance Influencing Factors
Optical scanning	Low quality printing
	Address written in a dark ink on a dark colored envelope
	Reflecting plastic address window
Binarization and image coding	Low contrast image
	Non-uniform contrast
	Faint/dark printing
	Complex background texture
Address block location	Interfering background such as ads
	Character size variations
	Printing/writing orientations
	Mixture of different orientations
	Irregular address block location
	Interfering sender's address block
	Window shadow
	Non-square handwritten address block
	Irrelevant numbers in an address block
Address line segmentation	Character size variation
	Overlapping handwritten character lines
	Touching handwritten character lines
	Mixing of different writing orientations
	Shadow of plastic window
	Skewed letter images
Character segmentation	Touching characters
	Broken characters
	Non-uniform handwritten character size
	Zero-character-spacing
	Underlines
Character recognition	Multiple scripts
	Low quality character image
	Writing style variations
	Peculiar writing variations
	Writing instrument variations
	Extremely small characters
	Mixture of writing and printing
Character string recognition / Address phrase interpretation	Address expression variations
	Abbreviated address expression
	Incomplete address expression
	Address hidden by a window
	Address hidden by a cancellation stamp
	Extra punctuation
	Wrong address
	Obsolete address

3.3 Technical Difficulties

Technical difficulties can be understood in advance only in an abstract way. In order to attain a target recognition performance, we need to find concrete difficulties for the target recognition engine to meet. We call such factors the *performance influencing factors* (PIFs). These factors are shown in Table 1 for postal address recognition. To solve the problems caused by these factors usually requires additional algorithms in the baseline. Some require totally new methods, and others require modifications of existing algorithms. It is necessary to prioritize the problems by their significance.

Such problems must be solved on a firm basis supported by good design principles, as demonstrated in this paper.

4 Five Design Principles

4.1 Hypothesis-Driven Principle

Resolving input uncertainty must begin with a hypothesis. For example, to locate an address block, we need to have line candidates, which require knowledge of the line orientation. A dilemma occurs, as line orientation relies on line candidates. To solve the dilemma, we can generate hypotheses first and process the input accordingly, then test the results. In this example, we first hypothesize horizontal orientation and extract horizontal line candidates, then try vertical orientation. Then, we can evaluate (or compare) the results to determine the correct hypothesis. At the same time, we achieve the result. We call this a *Hypothesis-Driven* approach.

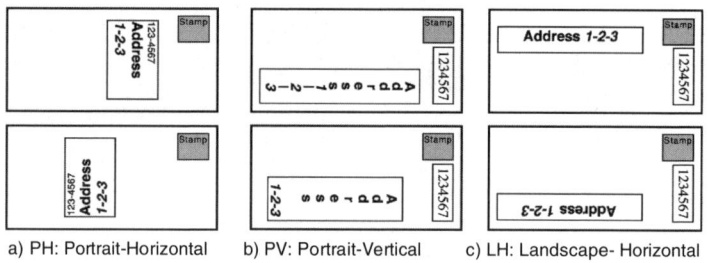

Fig. 5. Six layout types of the address block

In reality, address block location is more complex. In the case of Japanese letter envelopes, six layout types exist for each of the handwritten and machine-printed versions (Fig. 5), with 12 types in total. To cope with this problem, the method we developed hypothesizes the following six types, and evaluates the resulting block candidates based on a Bayesian approach [1]. Note the character orientation is determined later by applying character recognition.

- P-PH: Printed portrait horizontal
- P-PV: Printed portrait vertical
- P-LH: Printed landscape horizontal
- H-PH: Handwritten portrait horizontal
- H-PV: Handwritten portrait vertical
- H-LH: Handwritten landscape horizontal

The evaluation of the hypotheses is based on the confidence value, defined as the *a posteriori* probability of the corresponding hypothesis after observing evidence as in equation (1). Evidence for each hypothesis, H_k, is obtained as a feature vector e_k. The features taken are (a) the averages of the height and width of character lines, (b) the variance of the height and width of character lines, (c) the area of an address block candidate, and (d) the position of the candidate. L in equation (1) is a likelihood ratio of hypothesis H_k to null hypothesis $\overline{H}_k$ and is computed as in equation (2) assuming the statistical independence among the features. The functions, $P(e_{ki} \mid H_k)$ and $P(e_{ki} \mid \overline{H}_k)$, can be learned from the samples.

$$P(H_k \mid e_k) = \frac{\dfrac{P(H_k)}{P(\overline{H}_k)} L(e_k \mid H_k)}{1 + \dfrac{P(H_k)}{P(\overline{H}_k)} L(e_k \mid H_k)} \tag{1}$$

$$L(e_k \mid H_k) = \frac{P(e_k \mid H_k)}{P(e_k \mid \overline{H}_k)} \cong \Pi_{i=1}^{n} \frac{P(e_{ki} \mid H_k)}{P(e_{ki} \mid \overline{H}_k)} \tag{2}$$

A general scheme for this approach can be diagramed as in Fig. 6. In general, hypothesis generation operates by analyzing the input dynamically. However, in the case of address block location, hypotheses are predetermined as described above, so not much is done. Preprocessing may reduce the number of hypotheses. Each process, P_1 to P_n, generates (multiple) candidates of address blocks with the corresponding feature vectors e_k. Hypothesis testing (the evaluation step) computes the aforementioned confidence values and orders the candidates according to those values.

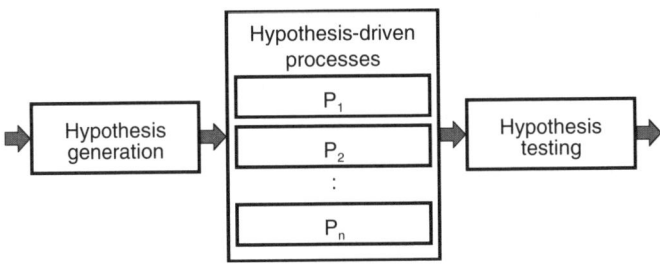

Fig. 6. Hypothesis driven approach

Figure 7 illustrates the address block location process for a simple case. First, based on the size of the input image, the type of the letter is determined to be a postcard rather than an envelope. Then, connected component analysis applies to the binary image, and line candidates are extracted based on the horizontal and vertical hypotheses. In the postcard's case, existence of a message area is hypothesized, and, if true, the message area, which is the lower half, is discarded. The upper half then is analyzed for an address block.

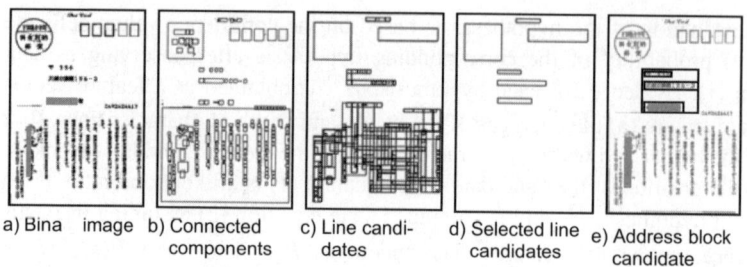

a) Bina   image   b) Connected   c) Line candi-   d) Selected line   e) Address block
                     components   dates   candidates   candidate

Fig. 7. Address block location process

4.2 Deferred Decision/Multiple Hypotheses Principle

The Deferred Decision/Multiple Hypotheses principle is: *"Don't decide when it is uncertain. Leave it to other experts. Give options when it is uncertain."*

Usually, pattern recognition consists of sequential steps of sub-level pattern recognition problems, and sequential decision making can be solved by using dynamic programming for well-defined problems [2]. However, in the case of Japanese postal address recognition, such sub-problems are numerous, as listed below, and also require heuristic approaches.

- Line orientation detection
- Character size (large/small) determination
- Character line formation and extraction
- Address block identification
- Character type (machine-printed/handwritten) identification
- Script (Kanji/Kana) identification
- Character orientation identification
- Character segmentation
- Character classification
- Word recognition
- Phrase interpretation
- Address number recognition
- Building/room number recognition
- Recipient name recognition
- Final decision making (accept/reject/retry)

As discussed before, these steps cannot be connected in a cascade manner, forwarding only the top choice. If the total number of decisions were 30, the accuracy of 0.99 at each step could only produce the total accuracy of 0.74. While attaining the accuracy of 0.99 is extremely difficult, it is possible to attain the cumulative accuracy of 0.99 or higher if we take multiple candidates. Therefore, the Multiple Hypothesis Principle allows the system to propagate multiple hypotheses from component to component. This creates a hierarchical tree of hypotheses to search for an optimum solution.

So, the next question concerns the method of conducting the search. Among the known methods of Hill Climbing Search, Best First Search, Beam Search, and others [3], we basically use Hill Climbing Search (with backtracking), by which we can reach an 'optimum solution' in the shortest time. When the 'optimum solution' is rejected at the final decision step, where it is verified against an address directory, the second best solution is searched. Then, this process repeats while the remaining recognition time affords continuation. As an additional variation to Hill Climbing Search, the Beam Search, used at the later stages, boosts the recognition accuracy. The use of a Beam search at the earlier stages is too costly.

It is also important to control the number of branches (candidates) so the search time will occur within reasonable time bounds. Instead of setting a uniform fixed number for the branching factors, we make branches adaptive by comparing the scores of branches with absolute and relative thresholds. If the scores at a given stage all exist below an absolute threshold, that node is abandoned and backtracked.

The effectiveness of this approach is shown in Fig. 8, where AB stands for address block, MP machine-printed, and HW handwritten.

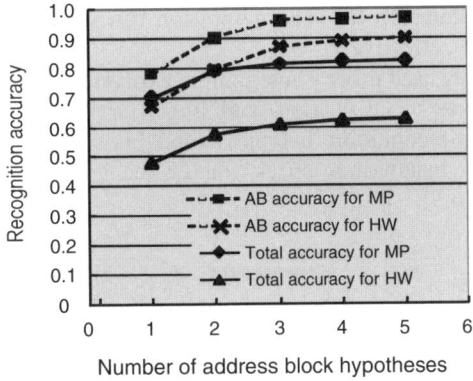

Fig. 8. Relationship between the number of address block candidates and read rate

A general scheme of this approach is illustrated in Fig. 9. The switches are controlled according to the optimum search strategy.

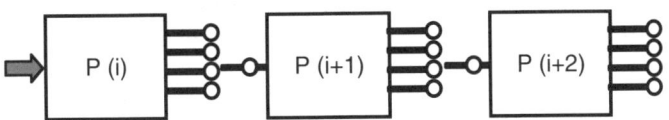

Fig. 9. Multiple hypotheses scheme

4.3 Information Integration Principle

Today, three types of *Information Integration* approaches exist. The first type integrates processes to solve several different problems simultaneously, as a single bigger problem. This principle is equivalent to saying, *"Solve problems by having experts from different fields form a team."* The second type combines different processes to solve one problem, as if, *"Solve a problem by assigning many same-field experts as a team."* The last type seeks more information to heighten the certainty. The following subsections will describe each of these principles more closely.

4.3.1 Process Integration

Historically, segmentation-recognition integration highlights the approach. This technique solves the problem of recognition of touching handwritten digits [4]. The segmentation component performs hypothetical pre-segmentation and generates a network of segmentation hypotheses. Large connected components are considered to be touching digits, and each of them separate into two at the hypothesized points. Uncertainty in touching itself and a touching position is managed by multiple hypotheses.

Recognition-interpretation integration is another two-process integration. If segmentation is reliable, character recognition and linguistic interpretation can integrate into one problem-solving scheme. Handwritten Kanji recognition generates a lattice, which represents character classification candidates, and the lattice is then transformed into a finite state automaton [5]. The automaton can search for valid sequences of characters, i.e., words, effectively.

The most frequently used process integration involves a three-process integration of segmentation, character classification, and linguistic interpretation. The approach, called lexicon-driven recognition, belongs to this class of techniques, and has been successfully used for handwritten check amount recognition and handwritten postal address recognition [6-9].

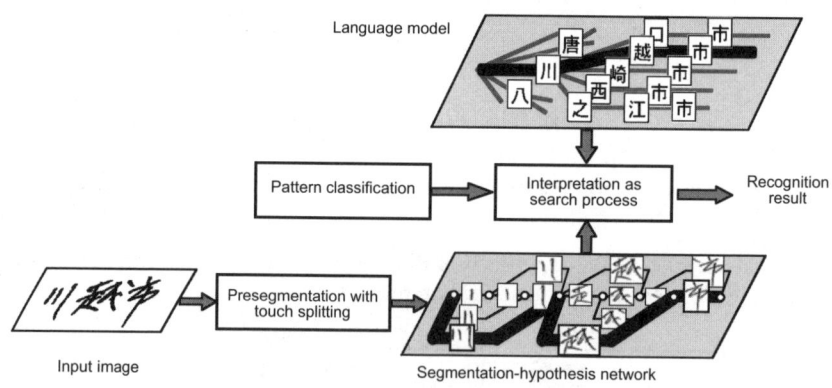

Fig. 10. Segmentation-Recognition-Interpretation Integration

In this approach, linguistic constraints, i.e., linguistic knowledge, solve the segmentation uncertainty and the character classification uncertainty at the same time. Linguistic constraints limit the search space and guide the search in terms of a language model, such as a TRIE structure (Fig. 10) or a Recursive Transition Network representing a context free grammar.

Then, interpretation of the input is conducted, searching for the path in the segmentation hypothesis network that best matches a path in the tree of the language model (TRIE). As the name 'lexicon-driven' suggests, the language model guides the search. Hypothesizing a character class in the language model, the edges from the current node of the segmentation-hypothesis network are evaluated against the hypothesized character class. If a matched edge gives a score greater than a threshold, this character class and the corresponding segmentation edge remain in the search tree, which is a working memory to control the search process. A Beam Search can be used as a search control strategy.

In this way, instead of applying character classification to every pre-segmented pattern in the network, character matching is done only between the hypothesized character class and the patterns on the edges. This efficient search process is quite attractive given the more than 4,000 Kanji character classes in Japan.

A successful application to Japanese handwritten address phrase recognition is reported in [9]. That method recognizes Kanji address phrases and generates a 7-digit code, which corresponds to a postal code. In an experiment on 3,589 actual mail pieces and a lexicon containing 111,349 address phrases, the recognition accuracy was 83.7%, when error was 1.1% by using a Beam Search. The recognition time was about 100ms using a Pentium III/600MHz machine. This method is capable of noise elimination, touching character detection, touching character splitting, and partial matching.

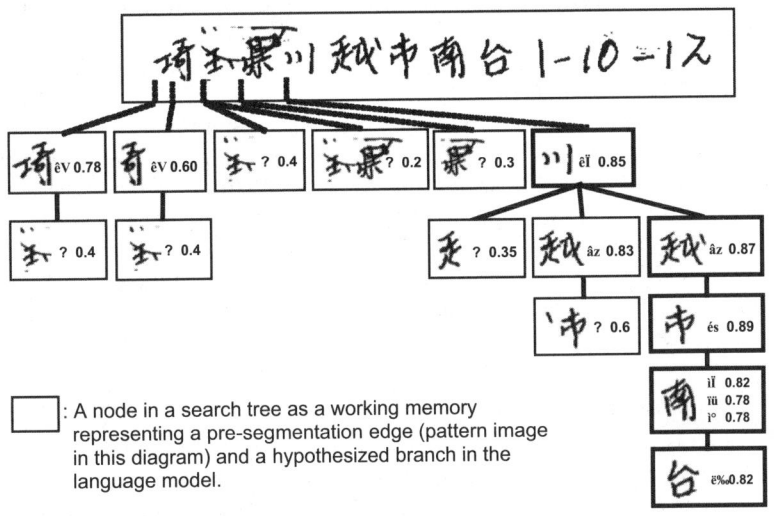

Fig. 11. Adaptive search for an address phrase

This method is also attractive because it can search meaningful patterns (phrases) by ignoring noisy portions and irrelevant character strings. It is similar to 'word spotting' in speech recognition. Figure 11 shows a case where the second and third characters are overlaid with a cancellation stamp. In this example, however, the first three characters represent a prefecture name, which is redundant. After the first five pre-segmented patterns are rejected in the search process, the successful matching process starts with the fourth character (fifth positions from the left) and correctly recognized the city name (4th to 6th characters) and town name (7th to 8th characters). Of course, the language model should have been arranged to include the shortened phrases (without a prefecture name), in addition to the fully expanded phrases (with a prefecture name). In reality, it is important to gather such phrasing variations and to include them into the model.

Regarding the language model, the above example uses a TRIE structure but has a limitation. When word alternatives, word omissions, and subphrase variations occur, a TRIE structure must have subtree repetitions, which sometimes require more memory than is affordable. In such a case, we can use recursive transition network models, i.e., context-free grammar models [10].

4.3.2 Combination-Based Integration

Classifier combination is the second type of Information Integration. It applies the idea of applying multiple independent classifiers to the same input, and then combining the results for better accuracy [11-13]. We expect classifiers to be complementary in their characteristics. Therefore, combining those results can boost the recognition accuracy. Differences in the classifiers can be any combination of recognition schemes (statistical approaches, structural approaches, neural network approaches, etc.), features (structural features, mathematical transformation, Gabor filter, directional feature, etc.), training samples, etc.

Known methods for combination work at the abstract level, the rank level, or the measurement level, depending on the kind of information used [11]. Abstract level combination uses the top candidate of each classifier output to make a final decision. Majority voting and Dempster-Shafer approaches are known for implementation. This type of combination applies to most of the existing classifier engines because it uses only the class labels in the output. Rank level combination uses the ranked lists of candidates from all classifiers to re-rank the results. The third kind, measurement level combination, additionally uses measurements of classifiers to produce a more reliable classification result. Normalized confidence values, computed from the recognition score of each classifier (e.g., distance, probability, etc.), are used to obtain a total score.

4.3.3 Corroboration-Based Integration

Corroboration is the process of finding additional evidence for a higher certainty, or looking for different input information to obtain the same result. One good example is bank check recognition, where a legal amount and a courtesy amount are recognized and combined to get a more reliable result [14]. Another example is postal address recognition. Reading both Japanese 7-digit postal codes and Kanji address phrases, which are almost equivalent to each other, can heighten the read rate and accuracy.

Another example of corroboration in postal address recognition is recognition of a recipient's name (company and/or person's name) to reduce uncertainty in identifying an address point. When address number recognition gives multiple candidate address points due to ambiguity, or when room number recognition fails, we can still use the partial recognition result for address point candidates. Then, by consulting a directory, we can list the candidate recipient's names. By having these candidate names, the recognition engine can try to recognize a recipient's name in the mail piece image. As a matter of fact, recipient's name recognition is necessary in cases such as when the recognized address point is a place with more than one residence or more than one company. This case is not corroboration, however.

The effectiveness of recipient name recognition is shown in Fig. 12 for corroboration cases.

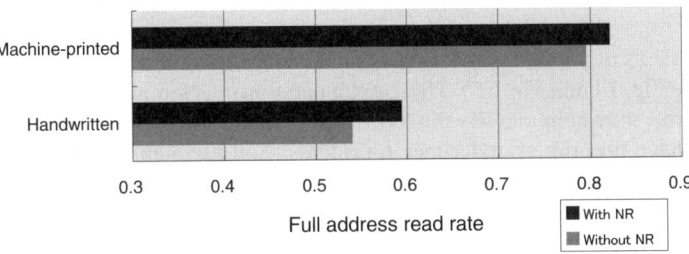

Fig. 12. Effect of name recognition (NR)

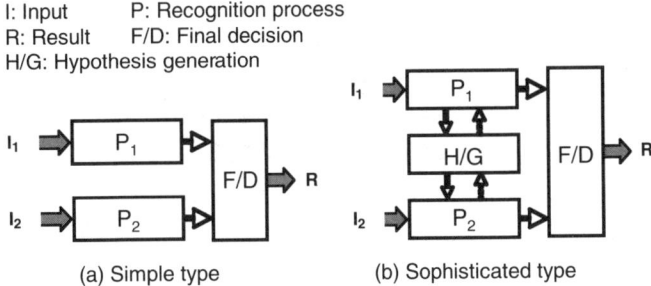

Fig. 13. Corroboration schemes

Corroboration-based information integration can be used in several ways (Fig. 13). One is to reduce the error rate for higher reliability, as for bank check recognition. Another increases the read rate (accept rate) provided that the error rate does not increase, as for postal address recognition. In either case, the final choice of the two objectives is at users' discretion and depends on the optimization criteria given at a higher level.

4.4 Alternative Solutions Principle

The alternative solutions principle states, *"When a problem is difficult, try different approaches as well."*

Many image level problems exist in postal address recognition, including characters that touch each other, underlines that touch characters, window shadow noise, cancellation stamps covering address characters, etc. All of these require special problem solving mechanisms. The Alternative Solutions Principle (which we originally named

Multiple Solution Principle) provides more than one solution to solve the problem. The solutions can be complementary or drastically different from each other.

For touching characters, there may be two different solutions. One attempts to separate a touching pattern [4], and the other designs and trains character classifiers to recognize a touching pattern as a whole; i.e., a *holistic approach*. Training the classifier is applied against a dataset that includes samples of frequently touching character pairs. Touching digit recognition can easily rely on this approach because the number of combinations compares favorably to the number of Kanji classes. The two solutions then merge for a more reliable recognition result.

The problems of window shadow noise and underlines (solid and dotted lines) are of interest (see Fig. 14 and Fig. 15). These extra patterns interfere with recognition, but, at the same time, may help identify the location of address lines. Some Japanese standard envelopes have preprinted underlines for address and recipient's name fields. Therefore, they give a good clue to locate address character lines. The same holds true for window shadows if they form stable contours.

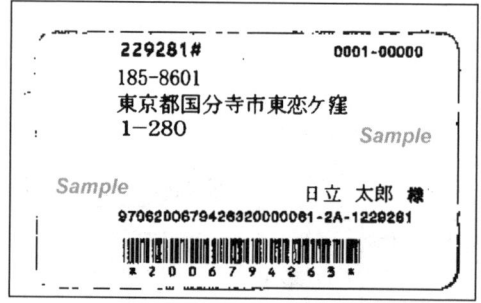

Fig. 14. Window shadow noise

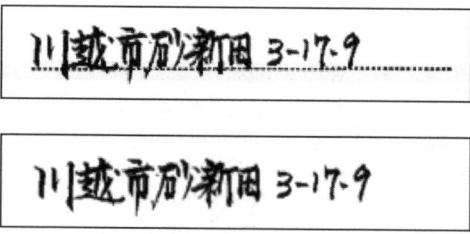

Fig. 15. Dotted underscore

So, the alternative solutions on the one hand attempt to detect such lines, and on the other, attempt to eliminate noisy solid/dotted lines. Elimination of thin, broken, noisy components and recovering a line can be accomplished by applying erosion (thinning) and dilation (thickening) processes, respectively. Separate line extraction algorithms extract stable solid/dotted lines.

These two different solutions, implemented as recognition components, generate two branches in the hypothesis tree, as described in Subsection 4.2. Then, based on the

Hill Climbing strategy, one branch is followed, and, if the final address recognition result stemming from this branch is verified, recognition terminates. Otherwise, the second branch is followed.

4.5 Perturbation Principle

The perturbation principle states, *"When a problem is difficult, try to modify it slightly."*

The perturbation principle applied to character recognition is actually not new. In the 1980s, it was used in commercial OCRs in Japan, where structural character recognition approaches were used for handwritten digit recognition. If an input pattern was unrecognizable due to topological differences, a slight change in images or parameters was introduced for another cycle of recognition.

Recently, the perturbation approach has been studied more systematically [15]. Various transformations are applied to an input image to generate slightly 'perturbed' patterns, assuming these new patterns still belong to the same identity as the original one. The same recognition engine then recognizes these perturbed patterns. The recognition results combine as in a classifier combination. As for transformations, they can be morphological operations, such as dilation and erosion, and/or geometrical transformations, such as rotation, slant (horizontal/vertical), perspective, and shrinking/expanding transformations.

The perturbation approach has been applied successfully in Japanese postal address recognition as well. We have applied a rotational transformation to a rejected input image, which is then placed in the whole recognition process for a second cycle. In practice, due to bounds on recognition time, only one or two cycles of perturbation can occur. However, we can obtain about 10% improvement on average. It is interesting to note that rejection often occurs in the middle of the recognition process, leaving more time to compute. When we did not force limitation on the recognition time and applied more perturbation operations, which include a rotational transformation, re-binarization, and reversing intermediate decisions such as orientation and character type, we could show that 53 % of the rejected handwritten addresses could be correctly recognized, with about 12 % error.

To use this approach widely, two practical issues occur; i.e., additional computational cost and greater chance of errors. For the first issue, in considering the continuous computer performance improvements, the perturbation approach seems to be very promising. To reduce the number of additional errors, a possible solution could involve finding a consistent result in the many recognition results from the different perturbations. The methods used in classifier combination can be borrowed to solve these problems.

5 Implementation Methodologies

5.1 Cycles of Robustness Implementation

In developing pattern recognition systems, a higher-order consideration, or methodology, must exist for improving the recognition performance given unlimited, real samples [16]. It is almost impossible to design the whole recognition system in detail, in advance and build it. Unpredictable problems always await us. Therefore, the developmental process repeats improvements consisting of the steps of acquiring samples, evaluating the performance, analyzing the problems, then solving them:

- Acquire (more) samples and groundtruthing
- Develop a better/additional method and algorithm
- Implement the method and algorithm
- Test and measure performance
- Analyze error and rejection causes
- Identify (additional) PIFs
- Make a plan for the next cycle, including additional sample acquisition and approaches to attack the identified PIFs
- Repeat these steps until the performance becomes satisfactory

The first step of robustness implementation identifies performance influencing factors (PIFs), shown in Table 1. It is to know the 'enemies' or the technical difficulties in reality. The problem is that we can identify such difficulties only after we have a recognition engine or a simulator. Difficulties equal weak points in the methods, algorithms, and the available recognition. To identify them, we simulate experiments on a huge dataset of real samples. A field test of a prototype engine for more than several months is preferred to collect a sufficient number of real samples covering most possible difficult cases. Some problems exist in seasonal changes affecting the incoming mail piece streams. Another factor that requires us to collect a large number of samples comes from the complexity of the system.

In these cycles, additional sample acquisition is a key to making the whole process more efficient and successful. So-called *acceleration datasets,* covering only problematic samples, accelerate the improvement cycles. It is related to *active learning* or *learning with queries*, which is a hot topic in machine learning [17]. By using a rather small number of (problematic) samples, error/rejection cause analysis can be conducted effectively and efficiently.

The cause analysis reveals weaknesses in the existing algorithms, and each problem is classified into one of the PIFs. If a new problem occurs, the list of PIFs extends to include it. It is important to note that each PIF is given a PIF identification code, and every sample in the acceleration datasets associates with one of the PIFs in terms of these codes. In this way, when an improved recognition engine is tested against the acceleration datasets, it is easy to evaluate the effectiveness of the improvement step. More concretely, we can statistically estimate the effect of improvement on the targeted PIFs, and we can prioritize the improvement strategies.

The improvement processes, in terms of refined and/or additional algorithms, naturally make the recognition engine more complex, by introducing more subcomponents. The described design principles alleviate complexity problems and make the improvements more effective.

In an actual project running these cycles, issues exist, such as project management, which includes software and human factors. Some discussions drawn from our experience is located in [18].

5.2 Sample Datasets

Again, the samples that cover the PIFs are the keys for success, but collection of samples is a laborious, repetitive task. Their width and depth vary depending on the progress of the development and on the problems. Development may start with a small number of samples, but difficult problems require more samples.

In general, four kinds of datasets are required:

- Validation datasets
- Training datasets
- Test datasets
- Acceleration datasets

The validation datasets are used for selecting an approach, architecture, and algorithms from their alternatives, while the training datasets tune the parameters of the recognition components. These datasets need to be devised so each recognition component can use them effectively. For example, there should be datasets specially arranged for algorithms of address block location, address line segmentation, character string recognition, etc. In other words, these datasets are the intermediate data.

The test datasets, which should not be used for training, evaluate the recognition performance as a whole. It is recommended for the test samples to remain in multiple datasets. It is not appropriate to mix batches of collections into a huge dataset. Such discipline is not only convenient for experiments, but also essential for evaluating the profile of the recognition performance (Fig. 1). For postal address recognition, mail pieces to be sorted have different characteristics depending on the operational time of the day, week, or month. For example, delivery sequence sorting is done in the early morning, outward dispatch sorting during the day, and bulk mail (business mail) sorting in the afternoon. The same holds true for seasons and areas. Therefore, sample images from different time zones can form separate batches. By doing so, each batch of samples may reveal performance differences, and possibly locate problems seen from the customers' viewpoint.

The acceleration datasets play a major role in robustness implementation. They contain the datasets of "live images" that have been rejected by the recognition engine, where, by definition, *live images* are sample images captured during the system operation. By using these problematic image samples, the cost of groundtruthing, analyzing, and identifying major PIFs can be minimized. This strategy parallels that of active learning, where additional samples are acquired, and most informative samples are selected for additional classifier training [17].

5.3 Basic Tactics for Improvements

In building the recognition engine, control of errors and rejections requires attention. Although error and rejection can be traded against each other, we should note that it is difficult to convert an erroneous answer into a correct one by a single improvement step. Therefore, the basic tactic remains the exterminate errors. To do so, we can set the thresholds high so the errors become rejections. Then, we try to change the rejections into correct answers.

In the following, we discuss the tactics more concretely. To do so, we first classify the final recognition results into the following seven classes:

- C: Correct acceptance
- R1: Rejection due to competing candidates having close scores
- R2: Rejection due to the top candidate having a low score
- R3: Rejection due to an empty candidate list
- E1: Error due to the right candidate being lost in competition
- E2: Error due to the right candidate having a low score
- E3: Error due to the right answer not appearing in the candidate list

When we have E1 or R1, the absolute score values of the top choices are sufficiently high, or at least within a permissible range, but competing (wrong) candidates exist also. In this case, the plan is to change the relative threshold parameters to convert the E1 case into R1, and to train the classifiers further to convert R1 into C. When we have E2 and R2, the plan usually involves re-training the classifiers because we have the right candidate but with a low score. (A 'low score' means the score is less than an absolute threshold.) However, when we have E3 and R3, something went wrong somewhere, possibly in the earlier stages, because no right candidate is given. So, we need to find the 'problems' and convert E3 and R3 at least to R1 or R2. (A rejection by the directory verification is classified as R3.) The 'problems' are usually diverse, coming from PIFs as shown in Table 1. In either case, the threshold values (absolute and relative) should be reviewed to see if they could become rejections.

In the case of 'semantically rich domains' like postal address recognition, we can keep the errors low by consulting with a directory, and we can have many R2 and R3 rejections, instead. To repeat, it is crucial to turn errors into rejections by keeping the right candidate always in the hypotheses. If we succeed, the improvement process may proceed in a positive, straightforward way. So, the tactic reduces the error rate, first, giving more rejections, then raising the correct rate.

5.4 Example Case

In this section, we demonstrate a real example of robustness implementation. It is the development of a Japanese postal address recognition engine used in a Hitachi Mail Sorting Machine (Fig. 2). The data shown here comes from the software simulation experiments in the laboratory.

Read rate profiles of handwritten postal address are shown in Fig. 16 for four software versions, V1 through V4. They are from Oct. 1997, Nov. 1997, Mar. 1998, and Jun. 1999, respectively. The average and the standard deviation of the read rates for the same four versions are also plotted in Fig. 17, where AV and SD represent the average and standard deviation; BK, MP, and HW stand for bulk mail (business mail), machine-printed mail, and handwritten mail, respectively. Robustness, defined as the standard deviation of read rates against a number of sample datasets, as shown in these figures, has not improved much, except for bulk mail (BK).

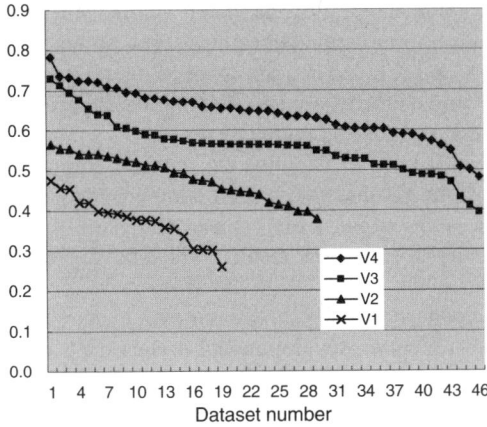

Fig. 16. Read rate profiles for handwritten datasets

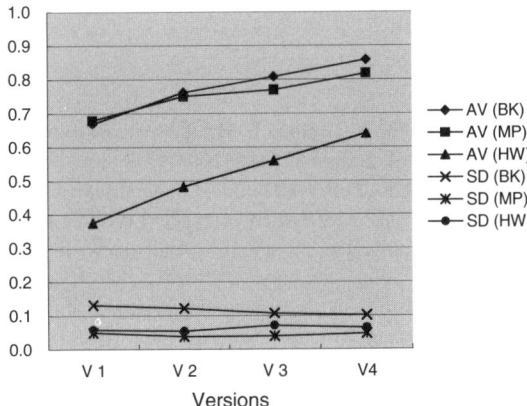

Fig. 17. Read rate improvements

6 Conclusion

This paper has discussed approaches to attacking uncertainty and variability, which present the main themes of pattern recognition. These relate to accuracy and robustness, respectively. We have identified and explained five design principles to tackle these common problems of pattern recognition. These principles are:

- Hypothesis-driven principle
- Deferred decision/Multiple hypotheses principle
- Information integration principle
- Alternative solutions principle
- Perturbation principle

Among these, information integration has been studied intensively in this research community. It includes three approaches: (a) Process integration, (b) Combination-based integration, and (c) Corroboration-based integration. These principles have been explained by relying on the examples from our experience in the development of a Japanese postal address recognition engine.

This paper has shown how to combine recognition components (and subcomponents) to make the whole. As discussed, each component receives an input, which is uncertain, and produces an output, which is also uncertain. Simple combination does not produce satisfactory recognition results. The above principles help solve this combination problem.

Variability in input patterns usually directs our eyes to classifiers, but it should direct us, at a higher level, to a better developmental process of a recognition system. Developing a recognition system with sufficient recognition performance is not a simple process. This paper has discussed these higher-level issues.

In conclusion, comprehensive approaches are mandatory to build an industry strength system. No single solution can be prescribed for high accuracy and high robustness.

References

1. Kagehiro, T., Koga, M., Sako, H., Fujisawa, H.: Address-Block Extraction by Bayesian Rule. In: Proc. ICPR 2004, vol. 2, pp. 582–585 (2004)
2. Fu, K.S., Chien, Y.T., Cardillo, G.P.: A Dynamic Programming Approach to Sequential Pattern Recognition. IEEE Trans. Electronic Computers EC16, 313–326 (1967)
3. Winston, P.H.: Artificial Intelligence, pp. 89–105. Addison-Wesley Publishing Company, Reading (1979)
4. Fujisawa, H., Nakano, Y., Kurino, K.: Segmentation Methods for Character Recognition: From Segmentation to Document Structure Analysis. Proc. IEEE 80(7), 1079–1092 (1992)
5. Marukawa, K., Koga, M., Shima, Y., Fujisawa, H.: An Error Correction Algorithm for Handwritten Chinese Character Address Recognition. In: Proc. 1st ICDAR, Saint-Malo, France, pp. 916–924 (1991)
6. Kimura, F., Sridhar, M., Chen, Z.: Improvements of Lexicon-Directed Algorithm for Recognition of Unconstrained Hand-Written Words. In: Proc. 2nd ICDAR, Tsukuba, Japan, pp. 18–22 (1993)
7. Chen, C.H.: Lexicon-Driven Word Recognition. In: Proc. 3rd ICDAR, Montreal, Canada, pp. 919–922 (1995)
8. Koga, M., Mine, R., Sako, H., Fujisawa, H.: Lexical Search Approach for Char-acter-String Recognition. In: Lee, S.-W., Nakano, Y. (eds.) Document Analysis Systems: Theory and Practice, pp. 115–129. Springer, Heidelberg (1999)
9. Liu, C.-L., Koga, M., Fujisawa, H.: Lexicon-driven Segmentation and Recognition of Handwritten Character Strings for Japanese Address Reading. IEEE Trans. Pattern Analysis and Machine Intelligence 24(11), 425–437 (2002)
10. Ikeda, H., Furukawa, N., Koga, M., Sako, H., Fujisawa, H.: A Context-Free Grammar-Based Language Model for Document Understanding. In: Proc. DAS2000, Rio de Janeiro, Brazil, pp. 135–146 (2000)

11. Suen, C.Y., Nadal, C., Mai, T.A., Legault, R., Lam, L.: Recognition of Totally Uncon-strained Handwritten Numerals Based on the Concept of Multiple Experts. In: Proc. 1st IWFHR, Montreal, Canada, pp. 131–143 (1990)

12. Xu, L., Krzyzak, A., Suen, C.Y.: Methods of Combining Multiple Classifiers and Their Applications to Handwriting Recognition. IEEE Trans. Systems, Man and Cybernet-ics 22(3), 418–435 (1992)

13. Ho, T.K., Hull, J.J., Srihari, S.N.: Decision Combination in Multiple Classifier Systems. IEEE Trans. Pattern Analysis and Machine Intelligence 16(1), 66–75 (1994)

14. Houle, G.F., Aragon, D.B., Smith, R.W., Shridhar, M., Kimura, F.: A Multi-Layered Cor-roboration-Based Check Reader. In: Proc. IAPR Workshop on Document Analysis Systems, Malvern, USA, pp. 495–546 (1996)

15. Ha, T.M., Bunke, H.: Off-Line, Handwritten Numeral Recognition by Perturba-tion. IEEE Trans. Pattern Analysis and Machine Intelligence 19(5), 535–539 (1997)

16. Tang, H., Augustin, E., Suen, C.Y., Baret, O., Cheriet, M.: Spiral Recognition Methodology and Its Application for Recognition of Chinese Bank Checks. In: Proc. 9th IWFHR, Ko-kubunji, Japan, pp. 263–268 (2004)

17. Duda, R.O., Hart, P.E., Stork, D.G.: Pattern Classification, 2nd edn., p. 480. John Wiley & Sons, Chichester (2001)

18. Fujisawa, H., Sako, H.: Balance between Optimistic Planning and Pessimistic Planning in a Mission Critical Project. In: Proc. IEMC2003, Albany, NY, pp. 605–609 (2003)

An Efficient Candidate Set Size Reduction Method for Coarse-Classification in Chinese Handwriting Recognition

Feng-Jun Guo[1], Li-Xin Zhen[1], Yong Ge[1], and Yun Zhang[2]

[1] Motorola Labs, China Research Center, 38F, CITIC Square1168, Nanjing Rd. W.,
Shanghai, P.R.C.
Feng-JunGuo@email.mot.com
[2] Electronic Engineering Department,Shanghai Jiaotong Univ., 800 Dongchuan Rd.,
Shanghai, 200240, P.R.C.
eyunzhang@sjtu.edu.cn

Abstract. In this paper, we introduce an efficient clustering based coarse-classifier for a Chinese handwriting recognition system to accelerate the recognition procedure. We define a candidate-cluster-number for each character. The defined number indicates the within-class diversity of a character in the feature space. Based on the candidate-cluster-number of each character, we use a candidate-refining module to reduce the size of the candidate set of the coarse-classifier. Experiments show that the method effectively reduces the output set size of the coarse-classifier, while keeping the same coverage probability of the candidate set. The method has a low computation-complexity.

1 Introduction

For Chinese character recognition systems, a coarse classifier prunes the search candidates of the fine classifier based on a complex feature. It accelerates the recognition procedure of a system. The coarse classifier technique has been widely used in many practical systems. T.S Lin, et al. presented a coarse-classifier using structure-based features [6]. S.R. Lay, et al. introduced a radical-based coarse-classifier method [7]. Y.Y. Tang provided an overlap clustering based method and proposed a group classifier concept [8], and Y. Yang provided a coarse-classifier method using pivots [11].

A typical coarse classifier method is a clustering based method. In this method, all characters gather into a few clusters. Each cluster covers an amount of characters, which are denoted as member-characters of their own cluster. When a sample inputs into a recognition system, the coarse-classifier selects the first n nearest clusters of the input as candidate-cluster [11]. The system sets the member-characters of these clusters as a candidate set for the following fine-classifier.

In a clustering based Chinese coarse-classifier, in order to achieve the same predefined correct coverage-rate, different characters need different numbers of candidate-clusters, because the within-class diversity of each character is different.

D.S. Doermann and S. Jaeger (Eds.): SACH 2006, LNCS 4768, pp. 152–160, 2008.

In this paper's methodology, we calculate a candidate-cluster-number for each character. The number serves as a measure of the within-class diversity of the character's feature space. Based on such numbers of each character, we reduce the size of the candidate set of the coarse-classifier. The experiments section of this paper shows that the proposed method effectively reduces the size of the coarse-classifier. The computation-consumption of the method is low.

The paper is organized as follows. Section 2 introduces the workflow of a conventional clustering-based coarse-classifier in detail. In Section 3, we describe our candidate-set size reduction method. In Section 4, we provide the experimental result. In Section 5, conclusions are stated.

2   Clustering-Based Coarse-Classifier

The clustering method is a fundamental technique of pattern recognition [1, 2, 3, 4, 5, 9]. In [10], T.Kanungo provided the latest achievement of a K-means cluster method.

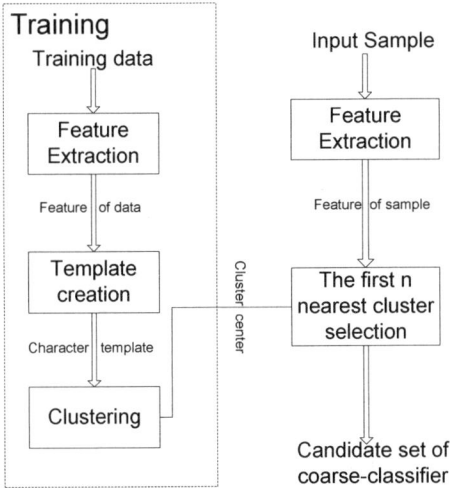

Fig. 1. Workflow of a clustering-based coarse-classifier

Figure 1 shows the workflow of a clustering based coarse-classifier. In the training procedure, firstly, the system calculates one or several templates (cluster center of feature vectors) for each character. Based on these templates, it then creates a small number of clusters, and allocates each template into its nearest cluster. So, a cluster covers the templates of several characters. We name the cluster as the owner-cluster of its covered characters, and denote its covered characters as the element-characters.

When a sample is entered, the coarse-classifier calculates the similarity between its feature and each cluster's center. Then, these similarities are sorted in descending order. Finally, the first n nearest clusters are selected as the candidate-clusters of the input, and the element-characters of these n clusters comprise the candidate set of coarse-classifier.

In the sorted clustering list, we denote $o_{clust}(i)$ as the order-number of the ith cluster for the input sample. Let us call $o_{clust}(i)$ the similarity-order of the ith cluster. The term will be used in the next section.

3   Candidate Set Size Reduction Method

In this section, we describe how to reduce the size of the candidate set by implementing a feature distribution property of characters.

3.1   Feature Distribution Property of the Element-Characters of a Cluster

Let hit_r be a hit-rate of a coarse-classifier. It is a probability that the candidate set of the coarse-classifier contains the ground-truth of the input samples. Equation 1 shows the definition of the hit-rate.

$$hit_r = \frac{C_{cr}}{C_{sum}} \tag{1}$$

where C_{cr} is the counts of samples that are correctly covered by the candidate set of the coarse-classifier, and C_{sum} is the total number of samples in a test set.

As mentioned in Section 2, in the conventional clustering based coarse-classifier method, the system selects a uniform number of candidate-clusters to construct a candidate set. In fact, to obtain a predefined hit-rate, different characters need different numbers of candidate-clusters. Some characters can reach a high hit rate by selecting a small number of nearest clusters. This happens because within-class diversity of each character is different.

Figure 2 provides an intuitive description for within-class diversity of different characters. In Fig. 2, the dash-line ellipses show the boundary of the feature space of characters 1, 2 and 3. The black dots are the templates of each character. Solid-line ellipse and circle represent the boundary of each cluster. The black cross ('+') marks the center of each cluster. In this figure, character 1 is an element-character of cluster A, and its feature space has a small within-class diversity. The features of all samples of character 1 appear very close to the center of the cluster A. So for character 1, we need to select the first 1 nearest cluster as candidate-cluster, and the hit-rate of the coarse-classifier is 100%. For character 3, however, it is an element-character of cluster C, and its feature space has a large within-class diversity. For samples in the lower-left area of character 3, cluster C is the 3rd nearest cluster. So, to achieve a 100% hit-rate, character 3 should select the first 3 nearest clusters as candidate-clusters of the coarse-classifier.

Based on Fig. 2, we draw the following hypothesis. If the within-class diversity of a character's feature is small, the character needs a small number of

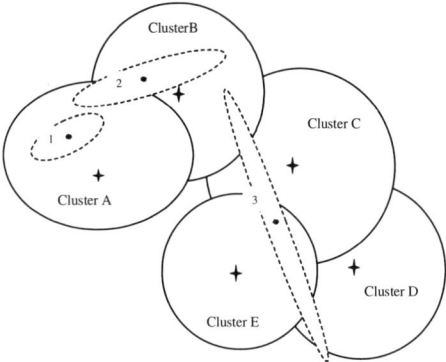

Fig. 2. Cluster and class feature distribution

candidate-clusters to obtain a high hit-rate. Otherwise, it needs a larger number of candidate-clusters to achieve a similar hit-rate.

3.2 Candidate-Set Refining Method Using a Feature Distribution Property

In a large training set, let p_{hit} be a threshold of the hit-rat for each character, and suppose the value of p_{hit} nears 100%. As mentioned in 3.1, to achieve the hit-rate p_{hit}, each character needs a different number of candidate-clusters in the coarse-classifier. Let $ord_{max}(P)$ denote the number of candidate-clusters for a character P, which guarantees that the hit-rate of character P equals p_{hit}. We call $ord_{max}(P)$ the candidate-cluster-number of the character P.

In the data structure of a cluster of the coarse-classifier, we store not only the element-character index of the cluster, but also the candidate-cluster-number of each character. The system uses the candidate-cluster-number of each character to refine the candidate set of the coarse-classifier. Suppose an input is a sample from character P and the owner-cluster of P is the i_{th} cluster. Let $o_{clust}(i)$ be the similarity-order of the i_{th} cluster. Because the value of p_{hit} nears 100%, for training samples of the character P, a very high possibility exists that Eq. 2 holds.

$$o_{clust}(i) \leqslant ord_{max}(P) \qquad (2)$$

Let n be the average number of candidate-clusters of the training set. When a sample is entered, suppose the ith cluster is one of the first n nearest clusters of the sample, and character P is the element-character of the ith cluster. If $o_{clust}(i)$ is larger than $ord_{max}(P)$, the possibility that the input is a sample of character P is very low. Then, we remove the character P from the candidate set of the coarse-classifier. This is a basic method through which we refine the candidate set.

Figure 3 shows the workflow of the candidate-set refining method. When a handwriting sample enters the recognizer, the coarse-classifier extracts the first

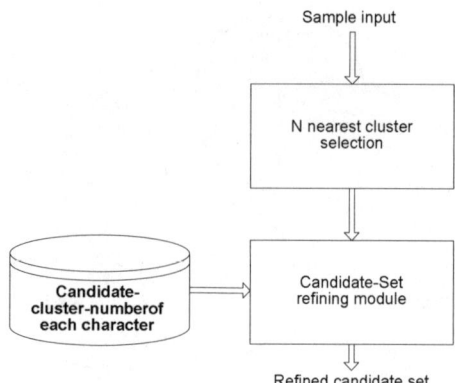

Fig. 3. Workflow of the refining method of candidate set

n nearest clusters, where n is the average number of candidate-clusters. For each element-character of the n nearest clusters, we compare its ord_{max} with the ord_{clust} of its owner-cluster. If the ord_{clust} of its owner-cluster is larger than its ord_{max}, we remove the element-character from the candidate set. Finally, we reduce the size of the candidate set of the coarse-classifier in this way by using a candidate-set refining model.

When the size of a training set increases, the value of the cluster-candidate-number based on the training set can be implemented by an independent test set. Experiments show that the proposed method has a good generalization property.

4   Experiments

The database used in our experiments contains 3755 daily-used handwritten Chinese characters. We separate these samples into a training set and a test set. In the training set, there are 1,169,209 samples. Each class has more than 300 samples written by different people. In the test set, each character has 50 samples. In our experiment, the feature vector of the coarse classifier is a compressed stroke-direction feature with 80 dimensions. The clustering method is based on the LBG algorithm [9].

First, we show the results for the training data. Then, we provide the result for test data. For the independent test set, the result shows the generalization property of the method.

For the clustering based coarse-classifier, clustering is based on the templates of each character. For each character, the number of templates can be set to one or several. The number of templates of each character has an effect on the size of the candidate-set. For the test data, we discuss the results of single-template based clustering and multi-template based clustering, respectively. Furthermore, we discuss how to select the value of p_{hit}.

4.1 Results for the Training Set

Table 1 shows the results of the training set. We list the results for the coarse-classifier applying different total numbers of clusters. Here, the value of p_{hit} is set as 0.996. Let num_{sum} and num_{can} be the total number of clusters and the number of candidate-clusters used in the coarse-classifier, respectively. In this section's tables, the original method stands for the method without a candidate-set refining module. Experimental data in Tab. 1 shows that, for a different total number of clusters, the method reduces the size of the candidate-sets while maintaining the hit-rate.

Table 1. Results of the training set: original method and the method in this paper

Method	num_{sum}	Hit Rate	num_{can}	Candidate set size
Original method	64	99.10%	9	670
	128	99.03%	12	458
	256	99.06%	15	282
	512	99.05%	17	181
Method in this paper	64	99.09%	12	525
	128	99.04%	15	339
	256	99.06%	19	225
	512	99.05%	22	154

4.2 Results for the Test Set

To evaluate the method's generalization property, we test the proposed method using an independent test set. For all experimental data in Section 4.2, the value of p_{hit} is set as 0.996.

Clustering Based on a Single-Template of Each Character. In the experiments in Tab. 2, the clusters of the coarse-classifier use a single-template of each character. The data in Tab. 2 shows, for the single-template case, the proposed method reduces the size of the candidate-set for the test set.

Clustering Based on Multi-Templates of Each Character. In our experiment, for the multi-template case, if several templates of one character fall into the candidate set of a coarse-classifier, the candidate set's size just adds 1 when we calculate its size. Table 3 and 4 use the rule to calculate the size of the candidate set.

Tables 3 and 4 compare the results of the original and proposed method for the multi-template case. For the experiments of Tab. 3, each character has two templates when we conduct clustering. For Tab. 4, the template-number of each character is four. Data in Tab. 3 and 4 show that, in the multi-template case, the proposed method reduces the size of the candidate-set.

Table 2. Results of a test set: clustering based on a single-template of each character

Method	num_{sum}	Hit Rate	num_{can}	Candidate set size
Original method	64	99.14%	9	639
	128	99.04%	12	421
	256	99.04%	15	262
	512	99.05%	18	159
Method in this paper	64	99.14%	12	542
	128	99.04%	15	359
	256	99.04%	19	230
	512	99.05%	23	147

Table 3. Comparison of the results where each character has two templates

Method	num_{sum}	Hit Rate	num_{can}	Candidate set size
Original method	128	99.09%	10	382
	256	99.09%	12	232
Method in this paper	128	99.09%	13	340
	256	99.09%	17	218

Table 4. Comparison of the results where each character has four templates

Method	num_{sum}	Hit Rate	num_{can}	Candidate set size
Original method	128	99.10%	8	357
	256	99.01%	9	204
Method in this paper	128	99.09%	9	319
	256	99.02%	10	189

From the data of Tab. 2, 3 and 4, we can find that by increasing the total cluster number, it weakens the advantage of the proposed method. In the coarse-classifier, however, the number of clusters should not be very large. Otherwise, the coarse-classifier will take much computation time. So, the proposed method in the paper is useful in constructing an efficient coarse-classifier.

4.3 Selection of the Hit-Rate Threshold When Calculating the Candidate-Cluster-Number

In this paper's method, the value of p_{hit} is crucial for the final results. It affects the value of the candidate-cluster number of each character. Figure 4 shows the hit-rates of a test set for different values of p_{hit} in the training procedure. For all

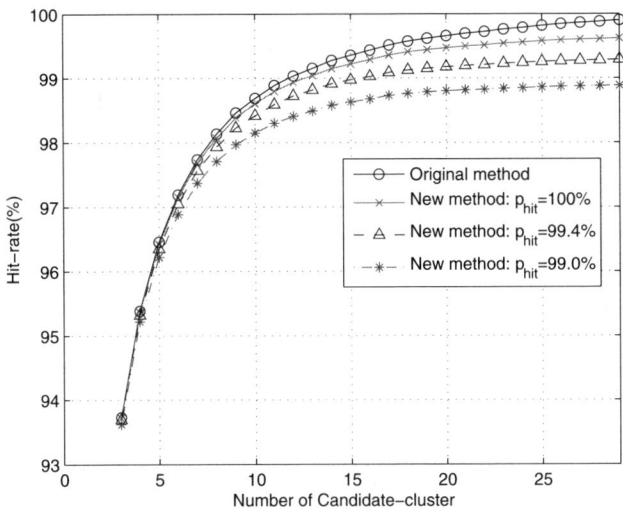

Fig. 4. The upper bound of hit-rate for different p_{hit}

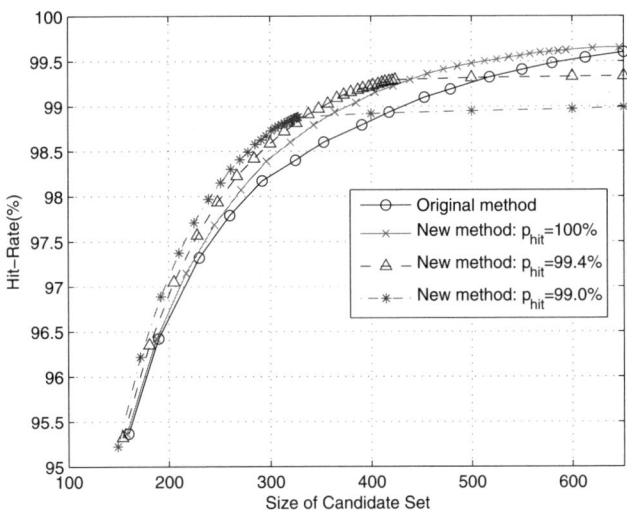

Fig. 5. The relation between hit-rate and the size of candidate-set for different p_{hit}

experiments in Section 4.3, the number of total clusters of the coarse-classifier is 128.

The curves in Fig. 4 show the value of p_{hit} as the upper bound of the hit-rate for the proposed method. If a recognition system requires a high hit-rate, p_{hit} should be set at a high value. Even when p_{hit} is set as 100%, for the test set, the hit-rate of the proposed method degrades compared with the original method. It means that the sample of training data does not cover all the possible boundary-cases of a feature space. So, a large training set is crucial for the proposed method.

Figure 5 shows the relationship between the hit-rate and the candidate-size for different values of p_{hit} in the training procedure. Fig. 5 shows, smaller p_{hit} reduces more element-characters from the candidate-set. When the system uses a small p_{hit}, it can't achieve a high hit-rate because the value of p_{hit} is the upper bound of its hit-rate. So the selection of p_{hit} is a trade-off between the upper bound of the hit-rate and the reduction of the candidate-set.

5   Conclusion

In this paper, we provide an efficient candidate set size reduction method for the coarse-classifier. The method implements the feature distribution information of each character. It defines a candidate-cluster-number of each element-character. Using the number, we refine the selected candidate-clusters to reduce the size of the candidate set. Experiments show the method has a good generalization property. Compared with conventional methods, it adds very little computational consumption and ROM storage size.

References

1. Duda, R.O., Hart, P.E., Stork, D.G.: Pattern Classification. John Wiley & Sons, New York (2001)
2. Bradley, R.S., Fayyad, U.: Refining Initial Points for K-means Clustering. In: Proc. 15th Int'l Conf. Machine Learning Madison, Wisconsin, USA, pp. 91–99 (1999)
3. Lloyd, S.P.: Least Squares Quantization in PCM. IEEE Trans. Information Theory 28, 129–137 (1982)
4. MacQueen, J.: Some Methods for Classification and Analysis of Multivariate Observations. In: Proc. Fifth Berkeley Symp. Math. Statistics and Probability, Berkeley, California, USA, vol. 1, pp. 281–296 (1967)
5. Forgey, E.: Cluster Analysis of Multivariate Data Efficiency vs. Interpretability of Classification. Biometrics 21, 768 (1965)
6. Lin, T.Z., Fan, K.C.: Coarse Classification of On-Line Chinese Characters via Structure Feature-Based Method. Pattern Recognition 27, 1365–1377 (1994)
7. Lay, S.R., Lee, C.H., Cheng, N.J., Tseng, C.C.: On-Line Chinese Character Recognition with Effective Candidate Radical and Candidate Character Selections. Pattern Recognition 29, 1647–1659 (1996)
8. Tang, Y.Y., Tu, L.T., Liu, J., Lee, S.W.: Offline Recognition of Chinese Handwriting by Multifeature and Multilevel Classification. IEEE Trans. PAMI 21, 258–262 (1999)
9. Linde, Y., Buzo, A., Gray, R.M.: An algorithm for vector quantizer design. IEEE Trans. On Comm COM-28(1), 84–95 (1980)
10. Kanungo, T., Mount, D.M., Netanyahu, N.S.: An Efficient k-Means Clustering Algorithm: Analysis and Implementation. IEEE Trans. PAMI 24, 881–982 (2002)
11. Yang, Y., Velek, O., Nakagawa, M.: Accelerating Large Character Set Recognition using Pivots. In: Proc. 7th ICDAR, Edinburgh, Scotland, vol. 4C, pp. 262–267 (2003)

Techniques for Solving the Large-Scale Classification Problem in Chinese Handwriting Recognition

Fu Chang

Institute of Information Science, Academia Sinica, Taipei, Taiwan
fchang@iis.sinica.edu.tw

Abstract. Given the large number of categories, or class types, in the Chinese language, the challenge offered by character recognition involves dealing with such a large-scale problem in both training and testing phases. This paper addresses three techniques, the combination of which has been found to be effective in solving the problem. The techniques are: 1) a prototype learning/matching method that determines the number and location of prototypes in the learning phase, and chooses the candidates for each character in the testing phase; 2) support vector machines (SVM) that post-process the top-ranked candidates obtained during the prototype learning or matching process; and 3) fast feature-vector matching techniques to accelerate prototype matching via decision trees and sub-vector matching. The techniques are applied to Chinese handwritten characters, expressed as feature vectors derived by extraction operations, such as nonlinear normalization, directional feature extraction, and feature blurring.

1 Introduction

The support vector machine (SVM) classification method (Cortes and Vapnik [1]) represents a major development in pattern recognition research because it produces highly accurate results for optical character recognition (Vapnik [2]). In applying SVM to Chinese character recognition (CCR), however, we face a challenge given the large number of class types (at least 3,000) in the Chinese language.

SVM is essentially a method of binary classification, (in which each object is classified as one of two classes). When dealing with a multi-class classification, in which each object is classified as one of m classes, where $m > 2$, the problem must be decomposed into binary classification sub-problems, and the SVM method can be applied to the sub-problems.

Two possible ways exist to decompose the problem: *one-against-others* (Bottou, et al. [3]) and *one-against-one* (Knerr, et al. [4] and Platt [5]). In the former approach, we train m SVM classifiers, each of which classifies a sample (character) as A or not A, where A is one of the m class types. In the latter approach, we train $m(m-1)/2$ class types, each of which classifies a sample as A or B, where A and B are any two class types. The one-against-others approach is computationally costly in terms of CCR training, since it constructs m classifiers, each derived from n training samples, where n is the number of training samples. The one-against-one approach also costs in terms of training, since

D.S. Doermann and S. Jaeger (Eds.): SACH 2006, LNCS 4768, pp. 161–169, 2008.

it constructs $m(m-1)/2$ classifiers; however, each classifier derives from a smaller set of training samples.

To cope with the size of the CCR application, we propose a novel decomposition scheme. First, we use a prototype learning method (Chang, et al. [6] and Chou, et al. [7]) to reduce the number of training samples to a much smaller set of prototypes. We assume that Chinese characters are represented as d-dimensional feature vectors. Therefore, the resultant prototypes are also d-dimensional, and they decompose the feature-vector space into disjoint domains of attraction (DOA)[1], where the DOA of a prototype **p** is defined as the set of feature vectors that find **p** as the nearest prototype.

This decomposition scheme can be useful to SVM. In the training phase, we collect the pairs, referred to as *confusing pairs*, of class types that are the top-k_1 candidates of some training samples. We then construct SVM classifiers for these pairs. In the testing phase, when a test character **x** is given, we collect the top-k_2 candidates of **x** and apply SVM classifiers to the confusing pairs found among the candidates. We then apply a simple voting scheme to re-arrange the involved candidates of **x**.

To reduce the number of CCR candidates further in the testing phase, we can combine of the following methods (Liu, et al. [8]). The first method employs multiple decision trees to determine the candidates collectively for each test character. The second method employs sub-vector matching in a few intermediate steps, using a subset of features in each step. A decision tree then decomposes the feature space into disjoint hyper-rectangles, each of which associates with a number of candidates. Since multiple trees are used, we rely on a voting scheme to decide the candidates for the next step, which uses sub-vectors to further reduce the computational cost of matching test characters with prototypes.

The remainder of the paper is organized as follows. Section 2 contains the learning algorithm for constructing prototypes out of training samples. In Section 3, we describe the post-processing technique that uses SVM in the training and testing phases. Section 4 discusses the methods that accelerates prototype matching, and Section 5 details the experiment results. Finally, in Section 6, we present our conclusions.

2   The Prototype Learning Algorithm

The prototype learning algorithm (PLA) described in this paper is a special version of the adaptive prototype learning (APL) algorithms detailed in Chang, et al. [9]. In fact, the PLA is a simple version of APL, but, unlike general APL, it does not involve any parameters, and thus avoids high computational cost of searching for optimal parameter values. PLA represents a rather fast and reasonable way to decompose the feature vector space so we do not have to spend too much time on the expensive optimization process.

We assume n training samples $(\mathbf{x}_1, y_1), \ldots, (\mathbf{x}_n, y_n)$ drawn independently from the set $R^d \times \Lambda$ according to the same distribution, where $\Lambda = \{1, 2,..., m\}$ is a set of labels or class types. Prototypes also lie in R^d, but they are not necessarily training samples. Moreover, each prototype associates with a label that is also a member of Λ. Two entities (samples or prototypes) are regarded as homogeneous if they have the same

---

[1] They are also called Voronoi cells in the literature.

label, or heterogeneous if their labels are different. When given a set of prototypes, we say that a sample $\mathbf{x}$ is absorbed, if

$$\| \mathbf{x} - \mathbf{q} \| - \| \mathbf{x} - \mathbf{p} \| > 0 , \tag{1}$$

where $\mathbf{p}$ is the nearest homogeneous prototype to $\mathbf{x}$, and $\mathbf{q}$ is the nearest heterogeneous prototype.

The steps of PLA follow:

P1 *Initiation*: For each label y, initiate a y-prototype as the average of all y-samples.
P2 *Absorption Check*: Check whether each sample has been absorbed. If all samples have been absorbed, terminate the process; otherwise, proceed to the next step.
P3 *Prototype Augmentation*: If there are still un-absorbed y-samples, select one and apply the fuzzy c-means (FCM) clustering algorithm to construct clusters, using the selected y-sample and all existing y-prototypes as seeds. Return to P2 to proceed.

Selection of Unabsorbed Samples in P1 and P3: In P1, a y-sample is selected as follows. We let each y-sample cast a vote to its nearest y-sample, and select the one that receives the highest number of votes. In P3, an unabsorbed y-sample is selected as follows. Let $\Psi_y = \{ \mathbf{x}_i : l(\mathbf{x}_i) = y \ \& \ \mathbf{x}_i \text{ is unabsorbed} \}$, where $l(\mathbf{x})$ is the label of an arbitrary $\mathbf{x}$. We let each member of Ψ_y cast a vote for the nearest member in this set. The selected y-sample is the member of Ψ_y that receives the highest number of votes.

Fuzzy c-means in P3: In FCM [9-10], the objective function to be minimized is

$$\sum_{i=1}^{I} \sum_{j=1}^{J} u_{ij}^{\alpha} \| \mathbf{c}_i - \mathbf{x}_j \|^2 , \quad \text{for } \alpha \in (1, \infty) \tag{2}$$

under the constraint

$$\sum_{i=1}^{I} u_{ij} = 1, \quad \text{for } j = 1, 2, ..., J, \tag{3}$$

where u_{ij} is the membership grade of sample $\mathbf{x}_j$ to prototype $\mathbf{c}_i$. Using the Lagrangian method, we can derive the following equations:

$$u_{ij} = \frac{\left(1 / \| \mathbf{c}_i - \mathbf{x}_j \| \right)^{\frac{2}{\alpha-1}}}{\sum_{k=1}^{I} \left(1 / \| \mathbf{c}_k - \mathbf{x}_j \| \right)^{\frac{2}{\alpha-1}}}, \tag{4}$$

$$\mathbf{c}_i = \frac{\sum_{j=1}^{J} u_{ij}^{\alpha} \mathbf{x}_j}{\sum_{j=1}^{J} u_{ij}^{\alpha}}, \tag{5}$$

for $i = 1, 2, ..., I$, and $j = 1, 2, ..., J$ respectively. FCM, a numerical method, finds a locally optimal solution for (4) and (5). Using a set of seeds as the initial solution for $\{ \mathbf{c}_i \}_{i=1}^{I}$, the algorithm computes $\{ u_{ij} \}_{i,j=1}^{I,J}$ and $\{ \mathbf{c}_i \}_{i=1}^{I}$ iteratively. To ensure rapid convergence of FCM, we require the process to stop when the number of iterations reaches 30, or $\sum_{i=1}^{I} \| \mathbf{c}_i^{old} - \mathbf{c}_i^{new} \| = 0$.

The prototypes are thus the cluster centers computed by FCM, which are the weighted sum of all the samples. For this reason, it is possible that the iterative process in steps P1 to P3 could continue to construct new prototypes and never converge [7]. To remedy this problem, we modify P3.

Recall that in P3, we employ FCM to compute a set Λ_y of y-prototypes, using an un-absorbed y-sample $\mathbf{x}$ and existing y-prototypes as seeds. For each $\mathbf{p}$ in Λ_y, let $D_y(\mathbf{p})$ be the set of y-samples for which $\mathbf{p}$ is the nearest y-prototype. If there exists any $\mathbf{p}$ in Λ_y, for which $D_y(\mathbf{p})$ is empty, we declare $\mathbf{x}$ to be a *futile* sample. If a sample is declared *futile* in an iteration, it will not be used as a sample in any subsequent iteration. This modification of P3 ensures the convergence of PLA [9].

3 SVM for Post-processing

When given a set of prototypes, we define the top-k *candidates* of a sample $\mathbf{x}$ as the top-k class types found within the prototypes, which are sorted according to their distances from $\mathbf{x}$. We may have to search for more than k nearest prototypes to obtain the top-k candidates, because two different prototypes could bear the same class type. We then collect the pairs (C_i, C_j), where C_i and C_j are, respectively, the ith and j^{th} candidates of $\mathbf{x}$ for $1 \le i, j \le k$. Note different values of k can be chosen in the training and the testing phases. We assume that k_1 and k_2 candidates are selected in the training testing phases, respectively.

For each confusing pair (C, D), the samples of C and D are labeled, respectively, as 1 and -1. The task of the SVM method is to derive from the C- and D- training samples a *decision function* $f(\mathbf{x})$ in the following form.

$$f(\mathbf{x}) = \sum_{i=1}^{I} y_i \alpha_i K(\mathbf{s}_i, \mathbf{x}) + \beta, \tag{6}$$

where $\mathbf{s}_i$ are support vectors, α_i is the weight of $\mathbf{s}_i$, β is the biased term, y_i is the label of $\mathbf{s}_i$, $i = 1, \ldots, I$, and $K(\cdot, \cdot)$ is a kernel function. The character $\mathbf{x}$ is classified as a C- or D- object, depending on whether $f(\mathbf{x})$ is positive or negative; details are given in [2]. For our application, we adopt the kernel function:

$$K(\mathbf{s}, \mathbf{x}) = (<\mathbf{s}, \mathbf{x}> + 1)^{\delta}, \tag{7}$$

where $<\mathbf{s}, \mathbf{x}>$ is the inner product of $\mathbf{s}$ and $\mathbf{x}$, and δ is the degree of the polynomial kernel function.

In the testing phase, for a character $\mathbf{x}$, we first use the prototype-matching process to find k_2 candidates for $\mathbf{x}$. We then compute the decision functions associated with all confusing pairs found within the top-k_2 candidates of $\mathbf{x}$. If a confusing pair (C, D) is found among the candidates, and $\mathbf{x}$ is classified as a C-type, then C scores one unit. The candidate with the highest score ranks first, the candidate with the second highest score ranks second, and so on. If two candidates receive the same score, their relative positions remain the same. We then rearrange the involved candidates according to their assigned ranks.

Note, three parameters are involved here: δ, k_1 and k_2. To determine their values, we require a set of samples in addition to the set used for training. This new set is called *validation data*. We use the training data to construct SVM classifiers for various values of δ and k_1 and the validation data to compute the accuracy rates of the classifiers under different values of δ and k_1, using k_2 candidates for each test sample. In so doing, we can find the best combination of values for δ, k_1 and k_2.

4 Acceleration of Prototype Learning

Two methods are used to accelerate matching samples with prototypes: multiple trees and sub-vector matching. They have advantages and disadvantages. The tree method, for example, is fast, but has a high risk of excluding the nearest known objects from the candidate list given a short list. In contrast, with the sub-vector matching method, in a lower risk exists of minimizing the candidate list, but the computational cost is high. One way to maximize the benefits of both methods, we combine them as follows. First, we use the tree method to reduce the number of candidates substantially, then apply the sub-vector method to the remaining candidates to find the nearest known object.

4.1 Multiple Trees

Each decision tree is a CART (Breiman, et al. [10]) or a binary C4.5 tree (Quinlan [11]). On each node of the tree, the feature and the split point is chosen to maximize the reduction of impurity [10]. With such a tree structure, we must resolve three issues: 1) how to grow multiple trees, instead of a single tree; 2) how to know when to terminate the tree; and 3) a mechanism to retrieve candidates from the multiple trees.

With regard to the first problem, suppose the training samples are expressed as d-dimensional feature vectors, and we decide to grow t number of trees. We divide each d-dimensional vector into t times e-dimensional sub-vectors so $e \times t \geq d$. If the equality holds, the t sub-vectors will not share any features; otherwise, they will overlap partially. The training samples then split into t sets of sub-vectors and each set is input to a tree. When the tree-growing process has been completed, we store at each leaf the class types of the samples that have reached that leaf.

For the second problem, we do not want to grow a tree to many levels, since the further we go, the smaller the leaves, and the greater the risk of losing critical candidates. Suppose the input samples are e-dimensional vectors, and the total number of training samples is n. One way to limit the growth of the tree is to stop splitting all nodes at level l, where $1 \leq l \leq e$, and count the root level as 1. However, it is unreasonable to require that all paths stop at the same level l, thereby generating leaves of various sizes. Instead, we limit the size of leaves to $u = n / 2^{l-1}$ because, if a tree terminates at level l, the average leaf size of the tree will be u. Therefore, if a node contains less than u samples, we do not split it further. Since the value of u depends on that of l, we write it explicitly as $u(l)$. The optimal value of l is determined in the procedure for solving the third problem, i.e., candidate retrieval.

To retrieve candidates from multiple trees, we first grow t trees, in which the leaf sizes are bounded from above by $u(l)$. We then assume that a training sample is input to these trees and locates on the leaf L_i of tree i, $i = 1, 2, \ldots, t$. For each class type C stored on these leaves, we define its vote count as the number of leaves on which it is stored. We then take the candidate list as the set of C, whose vote count exceeds v, i.e.,

$$Candidate\_List(l, v) = \{C \in \bigcup_{i=1}^{t} L_i : vote\_count(C) \geq v\}. \tag{8}$$

The optimal values of l and v are determined by means of the validation data (cf. Section 3). We first compute the accuracy rate $R_{prototype}$, defined as the proportion of validation samples that match in class type with their nearest prototypes. This represents the accuracy rate we obtain *without* multiple trees. To obtain the accuracy rate *with* multiple trees, we first grow multiple trees that terminate at leaves no larger than $u(l)$. We then input the validation samples into the trees to obtain the accuracy rate $R_{tree}(l, v)$, defined as the proportion of validation samples, whose class types fall within *Candidate_List(l, v)*. We choose l and v such that

$$R_{tree}(l, v) \geq R_{prototype}. \tag{9}$$

The set Θ of (l, v) that satisfies (9) is never empty, since $(1, 1)$ is in Θ. The optimal choice of (l, v) is then the pair in Θ that maintains the minimal size of *Candidate_List(l, v)*.

4.2 Sub-Vector Matching

When we input a test character to the multiple trees, we retrieve from the trees the prototypes with class types that fall within *Candidate_List(l, v)*, for the optimal value of l and v. To avoid wasting time on unlikely candidates, we take the following intermediate steps, each of which performs sub-vector matching.

The first step handles sub-vectors of length d_1, the second step handles sub-vectors of length d_2, and so on, where $d_1 < d_2 < \ldots < d$. At the end of each step, the prototypes whose distance to the unknown object falls below a certain threshold are input to the next step for further processing. In the last step, full-length vectors are matched and the nearest prototypes are output. Two elements must be determined for each step: the feature types included in the sub-vectors and the threshold.

We first sort all feature types by means of their information gain [8, 11]. Then, we employ the features of the top-d_1 ranks in the first step, and the features of the top-d_2 ranks in the second step, and so on.

In the sub-vector matching method, we must determine three elements: the quantity of steps we need to perform, the dimension of the sub-vector used in each step, and the threshold associated with this dimension. Let us assume that the dimension is given, and we want to determine the threshold associated with it. Again, we use validation data for this purpose. We pass the validation samples through full-vector matching as well as sub-vector matching, because we want to set the threshold in such a way that the two matching approaches achieve a comparable performance.

To ensure a robust performance, we associate a threshold with each sample **s** as follows:

$$Threshold(s, \lambda) = \lambda \times Avg\_Dist + (1-\lambda) \times Min\_Dist, \tag{10}$$

where λ is a value between 0 and 1, *Avg_Dist* is the average sub-vector distance between $\mathbf{x}$ and all prototypes, and *Min_Dist* is the minimum sub-vector distance. If $\mathbf{p}$ is a prototype with $\| \mathbf{p} - \mathbf{x} \| < Threshold(\mathbf{s}, \lambda)$, $\mathbf{p}$ is said to be λ-acceptable. We define the *Accuracy_Rate(λ)* as the proportion of validation samples that match in class type with the nearest λ-acceptable prototypes. Let R_{full} be the proportion of validation samples that match in class type with their nearest prototype, with respect to the full-vector distance. The optimal value of λ is then the smallest value for which

$$Accuracy\_Rate(\lambda) \geq R_{full}. \tag{11}$$

We now consider the number of steps to be performed, and the dimension, or the number of features, for each step. We use n_e to denote the number of prototypes passed to the next step if we perform sub-vector matching with dimension e. Suppose the dimension for step i is d_i. We describe what to do for step $i+1$. To perform sub-vector matching at step $i+1$, we need to compute $e \times n_{d_i}$ operations at step $i+1$ and $(d - e) \times n_e$ operations at step $i+2$, assuming that full-vector matching occurs in the second step; therefore, the computational complexity of these two steps is

$$C(e) = e \times n_{d_i} + (d - e) \times n_e. \tag{12}$$

Let $d_{i+1} = \arg\min_{d_i < e \leq d} C(e)$. Two options are available at step $i+1$. Either we perform sub-vector matching with dimension d_{i+1}, or we perform full-vector matching. The complexity of the former is $C(d_{i+1})$, while, latter's is $(d - d_i) \times n_{d_i}$. If

$$C(d_{i+1}) < (d - d_i) \times n_{d_i}, \tag{13}$$

we adopt sub-vector matching with dimension d_{i+1}; otherwise, we adopt full-vector matching. We proceed in this fashion, until dimension d is reached at a certain step.

5   Experiment Results

We evaluated the three techniques by applying them to the ETL9B dataset, which consists of 3,036 Chinese/Hiragana character types. From this dataset, we took 100 samples per character type for training purposes and another 100 samples per character type as validation data. The feature extraction method consisted of three basic techniques (Chang, et al. [12-14]): non-linear normalization (Lee and Park [15] and Yamada, et al. [16]), directional feature extraction ([12], [14]), and feature blurring (Liu, et al. [17]).

If we had to train all one-against-one SVM classifiers for the 3,036 character types out of 303,600 training samples, it would have taken an estimated 32 days using a PC with a Pentium IV 2.4GHz CPU and 2GB RAM. In the testing phase, a fast method like DAGSVM [5], would have required 31.78 seconds to recognize a character and would have stored approximately 1.5×10^8 support vectors in the memory. However, if we use the proposed approach, we need to store only 19,237 prototypes (6.3% of the training samples), and 11,104,041 support vectors (approximately 7% of the support vectors, if all pairs are given as confusing pairs). It is noteworthy that we spent only 61.1 hours training both the prototypes and SVM. The three parameters δ, k_1, and k_2 (cf. Section 3) were found to be 2, 3, and 5, respectively.

By applying multiple trees and sub-vector methods to accelerate the matching of test samples and prototypes, we can recognize 1418.7 characters per second, compared to 57.6 characters per second if a sample had to match all prototypes; thus, the acceleration ratio is 24.6. From the results shown in Table 1, we observe the acceleration methods do not cause any loss in test accuracy.

Table 1. The performance of multiple trees and sub-vector methods

ETL9B (Number of Class Types = 3,036, Number of Prototypes = 19,237)			
	Testing Accuracy	Computing Time(s)	Computing Speed (c/s)
Un-accelerated Matching	93.66%	5,271	57.6
Multiple Trees + Sub-Vector	93.68%	214	1418.7

Using SVM for post-processing boosts the test accuracy rate from 93.68% to 96.59%, but it adds 9,537 seconds to the recognition time so the recognition speed drops from 1418.7 to 31.1characters per second (Table 2).

Table 2. The performance of our proposed methods applied to ETL9B

	Testing Accuracy	Computing Time (s)	Computing Speed (c/s)
Multiple Trees + Sub-Vector	93.68%	214	1418.7
Multiple Trees + Sub-Vector + SVM	96.59%	9,751	31.1

6 Conclusions

We have proposed a combination of three methods to solve the Chinese handwriting recognition problem: prototype learning/matching, SVM, and fast vector matching using multiple trees and sub-vectors. The prototypes and trees provide the means to decompose the feature vector space and help reduce the number of candidates for matching. Sub-vector matching is obviously useful because it avoids wasting time on less likely candidates. By using these techniques in the pre-processing stage, we can exploit the effectiveness of SVM to enhance the test accuracy of the recognition task. The combination of the techniques is not only useful for the current application, but also for many other types of classification problems that involve a large number of class types and training samples.

Acknowledgements. This work was supported in part by the National Science Council, Taiwan, ROC, under Grant: NSC95-2422-H-001-007.

References

1. Cortes, C., Vapnik, V.: Support-vector network. In: Machine Learning, vol. 20, pp. 273–297 (1995)
2. Vapnik, V.: The Nature of Statistical Learning Theory. Springer, New York (1995)
3. Bottou, L., Cortes, C., Denker, J., Drucker, H., Guyon, I., Jackel, L., LeCun, L., Muller, U., Sackinger, E., Simard, P., Vapnik, V.: Comparison of classifier methods: A case study in handwriting digit recognition. In: Proc. Int. Conf. Pattern Recognition., pp. 77–87 (1994)
4. Knerr, S., Personnaz, L., Dreyfus, G.: Single-layer learning revisited: A stepwise procedure for building and training a neural network. In: Fogelman, J. (ed.) Neurocomputing: Algorithms, Architectures and Applications, Springer, New York (1990)
5. Platt, Cristianini, N., Shawe-Taylor, J.: Large margin DAG's for multiclass classification. Advances in Neural Information Processing Systems 12, 547–553 (2000)
6. Chang, F., Lin, C.-C., Chen, C.J.: Applying a Hybrid Method to Handwritten Char-acter Recognition. In: Intern. Conf. Pattern Recognition 2004, Cambridge, vol. 2, pp. 529–532 (2004)
7. Chou, C.H., Lin, C.C., Liu., Y.H., Chang, F.: A Prototype Classification Method and Its Use in A Hybrid Solution for Multiclass Pattern Recognition. Pattern Recogni-tion 39(4), 624–634 (2006)
8. Liu, Y.-H., Lin, C.-C., Lin, W.-H., Chang, F.: Accelerating Feature-Vector Matching Using Multiple-Tree and Sub-Vector Methods. Pattern Recognition 40(9), 2392–2399 (2007)
9. Chang, F., Lin, C.-C., Lu, C.-J.: Adaptive Prototype Learning Algorithms: Theo-retical and Experimental Studies. Journal of Machine Learning Research 7, 2125–2148 (2006)
10. Breiman, L., Friedman, J.H., Olshen, R.A., Stone, C.J.: Classification and Regression Trees. Chapman and Hall, New York (1984)
11. Quinlan, J.R.: Induction of Decision Tree. Machine Learning 1(1), 81–106 (1986)
12. Chang, F., Lin, C.-C., Chen, C.-J.: A hybrid method for multiclass classification and its application to handwritten character recognition. Institute of Information Science, Academia Sinica, Taipei, Taiwan, Tech. Rep. TR-IIS-04-016 (2004)
13. Chang, F., Chou, C.-H., Lin, C.-C., Chen, C.-J.: A prototype classification method and its application to handwritten character recognition. In: IEEE SMC, Hague (2004)
14. Chang, F., Lin, C.-C., Chen, C.-J.: Applying a hybrid method to handwritten character recognition. In: Proc.17th Intern. Conf. Pattern Recognition, pp. 529–532 (2004)
15. Lee, S.-W., Park, J.-S.: Nonlinear shape normalization methods for the recognition of large-set handwritten characters. Pattern Recognition 27(7), 895–902 (1994)
16. Yamada, H., Yamamoto, K., Saito, T.: A nonlinear normalization method for hand-printed Kanji character recognition – line density equalization. Pattern Recognition 23(9), 1023–1029 (1990)
17. Liu, C.-L., Kim, I.-J., Kim, J.H.: High accuracy handwritten Chinese character recognition by improved feature matching method. In: Proc. 4th Intern. Conf. Document Analysis and Recognition, pp. 1033–1037 (1997)

Recent Results of Online Japanese Handwriting Recognition and Its Applications

Masaki Nakagawa, Junko Tokuno, Bilan Zhu, Motoki Onuma,
Hideto Oda, and Akihito Kitadai

Tokyo University of Agriculture and Technology
Naka-cho 2-24-16, Koganei, Tokyo, 184-8588, Japan
nakagawa@cc.tuat.ac.jp

Abstract. This paper discusses online handwriting recognition of Japanese characters, a mixture of ideographic characters (Kanji) of Chinese origin, and the phonetic characters made from them. Most Kanji character patterns are composed of multiple subpatterns, called radicals, which are shared among many (sometimes hundreds of) Kanji character patterns. This is common in Oriental languages of Chinese origin, i.e., Chinese, Korean and Japanese. It is also common that each language has thousands of characters. Given these characteristics, structured character pattern representation (SCPR) composed of subpatterns is effective in terms of the size reduction of a prototype dictionary (a set of prototype patterns) and the robustness to deformation of common subpatterns. In this paper, we show a prototype learning algorithm and HMM-based recognition for SCPR. Then, we combine the SCPR-based online recognizer with a compact offline recognizer employing quadratic discriminant functions. Moreover, we also discuss online handwritten Japanese text recognition and propose character orientation-free and line direction-free handwritten text recognition and segmentation. Finally, as applications of online handwritten Japanese text recognition, we show segmentation of mixed objects of text, formulas, tables and line-drawings, and handwritten text search.

1 Introduction

As PDAs, tablet PCs, and other pen-based or paper-based systems, such as the Anoto [1] and e-pens [2], spread, the demand for improving online handwriting recognition and liberating it from writing constraint is still increasing. In online handwriting recognition, both temporal information of pen tip movement and spatial shape information are available, so it can yield higher recognition accuracy than offline handwriting recognition. Moreover, online handwriting recognition provides good interaction and adaptation capability because the writer can respond to the recognition result to correct misrecognition and rejection.

The research of online handwriting recognition began in the 1960s and has been receiving intensive interest since the 1980s. The comprehensive survey before the 1990s appears in [3][4]. In recent survey papers, Plamondon, et al. mainly

D.S. Doermann and S. Jaeger (Eds.): SACH 2006, LNCS 4768, pp. 170–195, 2008.
© Springer-Verlag Berlin Heidelberg 2008

reviewed the status of western online handwriting recognition [5] while Liu, et al. and Jaeger, et al. reviewed online Chinese and Japanese handwriting recognition [6][7]. In this paper, we mainly discuss online Japanese handwriting recognition, including our recent results.

The Japanese character set consists of various characters: numerals, symbols, Hiragana, Katakana, and Kanji characters of Chinese origin. Hiragana and Katakana are phonetic characters. The former consists of 83 characters, and the latter consists of 86 characters. Kanji characters are idiographic characters. Two classes are defined for the purpose of computer processing: JIS first level and JIS second level (JIS stands for Japanese Industrial Standard). The JIS 1st level set contains 2,965 common characters, which are necessary for reading the newspaper, and the JIS 2nd level set contains 3,390 characters less common and special characters for naming.

Most Kanji character patterns are composed of multiple subpatterns, called radicals, which are shared among many (sometimes hundreds of) Kanji character patterns. This is common in Asian languages of Chinese origin, i.e., Chinese, Korean, and Japanese. Among Kanji character patterns, some patterns are simple, consisting of a single radical, while others are complex with multiple radicals.

In the field of pattern recognition, large volumes of sample patterns are as important as recognition methods. We spent four years compiling two databases of online Japanese handwritten character patterns, named "TUAT Nakagawa Lab. HANDS-kuchibue_d-97-06" (hereafter Kuchibue_d) [8] and "TUAT Nakagawa Lab. HANDS-nakayosi_t-98-09" (hereafter Nakayosi_t) [9]. Kuchibue_d stores 11,962 character patterns from each of 120 people (1,435,440 patterns), and Nakayosi_t stores 10,403 patterns from 163 people each (1,695,689 patterns). Thus, they store more than 3 million patterns in total. About 50 institutions, including more than 10 groups from abroad, use our databases, so we will base our experiments on these databases.

The large number of Japanese character categories affects the classification techniques. In western handwriting recognition, Hidden Markov models (HMM) are successfully applied. However, they are not common in Japanese handwriting recognition because they require huge amount of training data for each character. Therefore, DP-matching comprises the core of many online Japanese handwriting recognizers with several modifications proposed [10]-[12]. These large categories also affect the size of the dictionary (a set of prototype patterns) and the recognition speed, so it has been difficult to use a powerful online recognizer or combine online/offline recognizer to improve the recognition accuracy in a small computer.

The demand to remove writing constraint for online handwriting recognition is increasing steadily as people can write more freely on enlarged surfaces of tablet PCs, electronic whiteboards, and other paper-based handwriting environments. However, segmentation and recognition of online handwritten Japanese text is challenging work, because of the large variation of character size, and people write text horizontally, vertically or even slantwise.

In addressing these problems, we present structured character pattern representation (SCPR)-based online handwriting recognition, which has significant effect for the Japanese character set of the large category size, in Section 2. Section 3 describes the combination of the SCPR-based online recognizer with a compact offline recognizer. Section 4 presents an online handwriting Japanese text recognition method liberated from constraints of line direction and character orientation. Section 5 describes some applications. Section 6 draws conclusions.

2   Character Representation

In this section, we describe a Japanese Kanji character pattern representation, which strongly relates to handwriting recognition.

In the representation for input patterns, the sequence of feature points or line segments in time series are commonly used in online Japanese handwriting recognition [10]-[17] The stroke order and the stroke directions of the input pattern are kept in these sequences. Some recognition methods employ the offline features (e.g. directional features, loops of strokes) extracted from the images of the input patterns [18]-[20]. Employing these representations, instead of the raw data of the input pattern (sampling points by digital pen), reduces the data size and noise.

Early research attempted to extract subpatterns from an input character pattern and recognize the input pattern as the composite of subpatterns, but did not succeed because subpattern extraction was difficult. Instead, many systems employ the pattern structure composed of subpatterns in a prototype representation and expand it to a sequence of feature points, or line segments, when matched with the input pattern. Shape variations or stroke order variations register as multiple alternatives into a subpattern, so they are shared among character patterns that include the subpattern in their shapes. We will see this in more detail in the following sections.

2.1   Structured Character Pattern Representation (SCPR)

Japanese Kanji characters are mostly composed of multiple subpatterns called radicals. SCPR represents a character pattern as a composite of basic subpatterns (primitive, so they are not further decomposed) and structural information of how to combine them (Figure 1) [12].

Here, we present two online handwriting recognition systems. One uses the prototype learning algorithm (PLA) and linear-time elastic matching (LTM) [12][13], and the other system is based on HMM [21]. We call the former system "Sys_LTM" and the latter "Sys_HMM". Both employ the SCPR dictionary in which prototypes of basic subpatterns (BSs) are shared among character categories, as shown in Figure 2.

In the SCPR dictionary of Sys_LTM, all the BS prototypes, as well as the character pattern prototypes, are represented by a square shape with 128 x 128

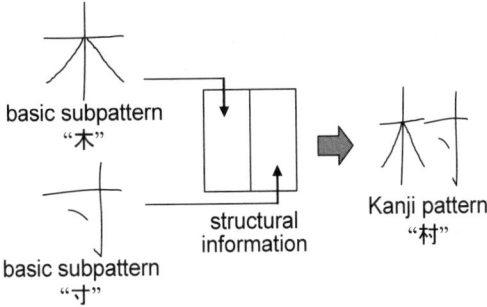

Fig. 1. SCPR

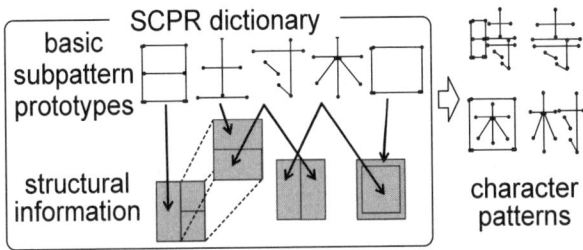

Fig. 2. SCPR dictionary

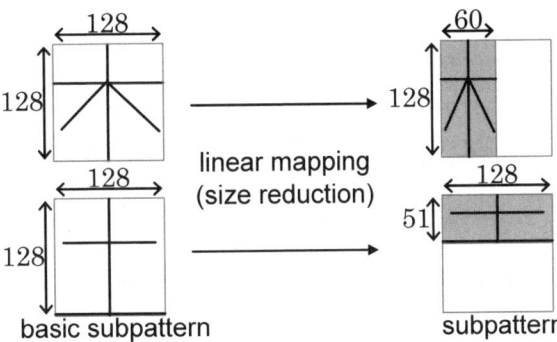

Fig. 3. Size reduction by linear mapping

resolution, and each of them is a sequence of feature points in a time series. When included in prototypes of larger subpattern prototypes or character pattern prototypes, their sizes reduce to bounding boxes in structural information through linear mapping (Figure 3). We call a result of the linear mapping a "mapped BS prototype," even if the mapping is sometimes identical (with no deformation). Hereafter, we refer to this as an MBS prototype.

The SCPR dictionary of Sys_HMM has similar structural information and links to component SCPR-based HMMs in place of BS prototypes.

SCPR provides advantages to the size reduction of the dictionary (a set of prototype patterns) and the robustness against deformation of common radicals.

2.2   Prototype Learning Algorithm (PLA)

No matter the classification method, prototypes greatly influence the performance of classifiers. PLA better approximates discrimination boundaries between different categories in a feature space [22]-[25]. Liu, et al. have shown the advantages of PLA in offline handwritten Kanji character recognition [26].

For online handwriting recognition systems in which prototypes are the sequences of feature points (e.g. Sys_LTM), we have proposed a PLA to improve the BS prototypes by moving their feature points [27]. The base learning method of our PLA is the generalized learning vector quantization (GLVQ) [25]. GLVQ updates the genuine prototype (the closest prototype in the correct class) and the rival prototype (the closest one in different classes) using learning patterns.

Recognition by LTM and PLA. Our PLA uses the correspondences between feature points that are the results of LTM in the process of recognition. In Figure 4, the dash lines show the correspondences. Although general elastic matching methods commonly generate one-to-many or many-to-one correspondences between the feature points, our method of Sys_LTM generates only one-to-one correspondences by discarding the uncertain correspondences.

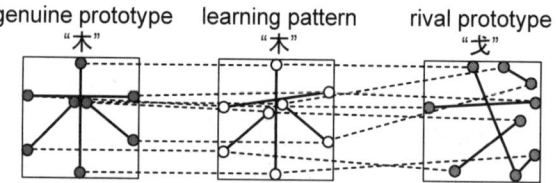

Fig. 4. Correspondences between feature points

SCPR-Based PLA. To improve the prototypes in the SCPR dictionary, we consider each prototype matched with the learning pattern as a composite of MBS prototypes. Figure 5 shows the process of our PLA, improving the feature point v in the BS prototype. Each $u(v)$ is a feature point of the MBS prototype mapped from the feature point v, and each p_l is a feature point in the learning pattern corresponding to $u(v)$. S is the bounding box size of each MBS prototype, and $G(p_l - u(v), S)$ is the function to normalize the displacement $p_l - u(v)$ by the bounding box size. Every displacement between $u(v)$ and p_l is measured and reflected in the feature point v using $G(p_l - u(v), S)$.

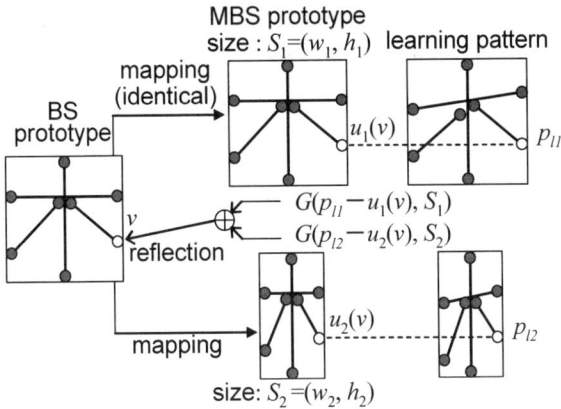

Fig. 5. Displacement reflection

We transform the formulae of GLVQ into (1) and (2) to update the feature points of the BS prototypes.

$$
\begin{cases}
x_i' = x_i + 4\alpha(t)l_k(1-l_k)\dfrac{G(d_j,S_j)G(x_l-x_i,w_i)}{\{G(d_i,S_i)+G(d_j,S_j)\}^2} \\[2mm]
y_i' = y_i + 4\alpha(t)l_k(1-l_k)\dfrac{G(d_j,S_j)G(y_l-y_i,h_i)}{\{G(d_i,S_i)+G(d_j,S_j)\}^2}
\end{cases}
\tag{1}
$$

$$
\begin{cases}
x_j' = x_j - 4\alpha(t)l_k(1-l_k)\dfrac{G(d_i,S_i)G(x_l-x_j,w_j)}{\{G(d_i,S_i)+G(d_j,S_j)\}^2} \\[2mm]
y_j' = y_j - 4\alpha(t)l_k(1-l_k)\dfrac{G(d_i,S_i)G(y_l-y_j,h_j)}{\{G(d_i,S_i)+G(d_j,S_j)\}^2}
\end{cases}
\tag{2}
$$

In the above formulae, (1) and (2), $u(v_i) = (x_{ui}, y_{ui})$ in the genuine prototype maps from $v_i = (x_i, y_i)$ of one BS prototype, while $u(v_j) = (x_{uj}, y_{uj})$ in the rival prototype maps from $v_j = (x_j, y_j)$ of the other BS prototypes. The feature point $p_l = (x_l, y_l)$ in the learning pattern corresponds to $u(v_i)$ and $u(v_j)$. The term $\alpha(t)$ denotes the learning rate. The other parameters l_k, μ_k, d_i, and d_j are defined as follows:

$$
l_k = l_k(\mu_k) = \frac{1}{1+e^{-\zeta\mu_k}}
\tag{3}
$$

$$
\mu_k = \frac{G(d_i,S_i) - G(d_j,S_j)}{G(d_i,S_i) + G(d_j,S_j)}
\tag{4}
$$

$$
d_i = \|p_l - p_i\|
\tag{5}
$$

$$
d_j = \|p_l - p_j\|
\tag{6}
$$

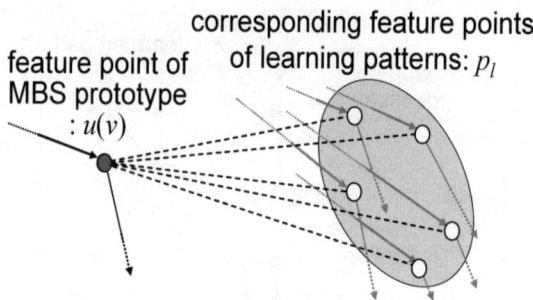

Fig. 6. Distribution of feature points

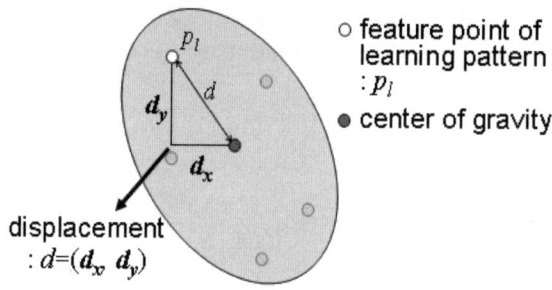

Fig. 7. Distance between the center of gravity and feature points

We obtained the distribution of the feature points in learning patterns corresponding to each feature point in MBS prototypes, as the size of the distribution (the average distance from the center of the distribution to every $l(v)$ in the distribution) shows to what degree each MBS point can move (Figure 6).

To describe the size of distribution, we employed the average distance from the center of the distribution to every $l(v)$ in the distribution (Figure 7).

We employed our database, Nakayosi_t to obtain the distribution. By using the database, we estimated the relations between the bounding box size of MBS prototype $S = (w, h)$ and the distribution size D for vertical and horizontal directions as follows:

$$D_w(w) = 0.0846w + 1.7 \tag{7}$$
$$D_h(h) = 0.0539h + 3.5 \tag{8}$$

The normalization formulae using the relation are as follows.

$$G_w(x_1 - x_2, w) = (x_1 - x_2)\{D_w(128)/D_w(w)\} \tag{9}$$
$$G_h(y_1 - y_2, h) = (y_1 - y_2)\{D_h(128)/D_h(h)\} \tag{10}$$

Evaluation for SCPR-Based PLA. In the experiment, we improved the SCPR dictionary of Sys_LTM to evaluate our PLA. As the set of learning patterns, we employed all the character patterns of the JIS 1*st* level set in Nakayosi_t. We employed another database, Kuchibue_d, for evaluation. In the first step, we generated the averaged BS prototypes by learning patterns. Then, we performed our PLA. Before learning, the recognition rate of Sys_LTM with the dictionary was approximately 84.4% for the data set of evaluation. After learning, the rate improved to 89.1%.

SCPR-Based PLA for Offline Recognition. Now, we describe SCPR and the learning method for offline recognition. In general, offline recognition methods, directional features with four or eight-directional quantization, are extracted from a character pattern divided into an array of cells [20][28]. Therefore, a character (same as a prototype) is represented by a matrix of directional features. In Figure 8, $f_v(i, j)$ is the set of directional features extracted from the cell of the $i - th$ row and $j - th$ column in the character pattern.

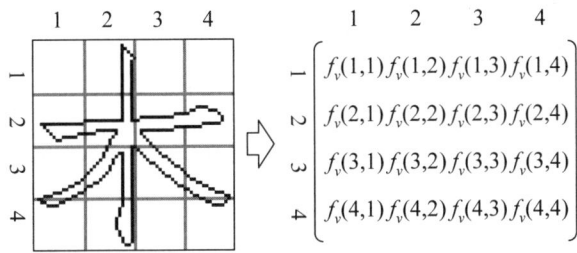

Fig. 8. Matrix of the directional features extracted from the character pattern

When the character C is composed from a set of subpatterns, we can show it as follows:

$$C = \sum_{i=1}^{N_s} A_i S_i \tag{11}$$

(N_s: number of subpatterns, A_i: linear mapping to make a subpattern, S_i: matrix of fv to describe a basic subpattern)

Subpatterns don't overlap each other in Japanese characters, so

$$F_i = A_i^{-1} C \tag{12}$$

Linear mapping transforms the directional features in a basic subpattern. Therefore, when a character pattern is learned and reflected to a subpattern, the directional features again map through inverse mapping with the directions modified. To enable mapping and inverse mapping that may change the directions of segments, the directional features must be extracted and represented finely enough.

For offline character recognition, the dimensions of features often reduce by the K-L transformation:

$$y = \psi^t x \tag{13}$$

In this case, the reduced set of features is difficult to decompose into subpatterns. However, if the reduction is small and ψ is chosen to minimize the mean square error, the original features can be approximated by

$$x \approx \psi y \tag{14}$$

This enables decomposition into subpatterns and reflection to their features. Then, we can realize structural learning for common offline character recognition methods.

2.3 SCPR-Based HMM

The HMM has an ability to model deformations of strokes and variations of sampled feature points, and has been successfully applied to western handwriting recognition [29][30]. For western characters, each character of the alphabet is typically modeled by one HMM and all the words are represented by a sequence of character HMMs. We call this approach "character HMM." However, thousands of characters comprise Asian characters of Chinese origin, so the character HMM leads to a huge amount of memory space and training data [15][32][33][35]. To address this problem, the SCPR-based HMM [31][34] has been proposed.

Recognition by SCPR-Based HMM. The SCPR-based online handwriting recognition system (Sys_HMM) consists of a feature extraction module, a SCPR dictionary mentioned in Section 2.1, SCPR-based HMMs, and a decoder shown in Figure 9. Note that off-stroke information (vector from the pen-up to the next pen-down) is not necessary when we model pen-coordinate features.

In the SCPR-based HMMs, the decoder generates HMMs for each character pattern by connecting one, or more than one, SCPR-based HMMs according to the SCPR dictionary. It then calculates the probability that an input pattern is produced from the HMMs by the Viterbi algorithm. By doing this, we can handle a large number of character patterns with a small number of HMMs.

Modeling of Pen-coordinate Features by SCPR-Based HMM. Though the pen-coordinate feature is no less important than the pen-direction feature, it has not been employed in the SCPR-based HMMs [31][34] because it tends to change when subpatterns are composed into each character pattern. We proposed SCPR-based HMMs that model both the pen-direction and pen-coordinate features.

The basic idea of our approach involves the linear mapping and its inverse mapping, presented in Section 2.1. The BS prototypes reduce to bounding boxes in structural information through a linear mapping when they are included in larger subpatterns or character patterns (Figure 10). Therefore, when a SCPR-based HMM is incorporated into a character pattern by being mapped into the bounding box, we adapt the parameters for pen-coordinate feature according to which character pattern and where incorporated. If each state of SCPR-based HMMs has a Gaussian distribution, the mean vector of the Gaussian distribution, at a state of

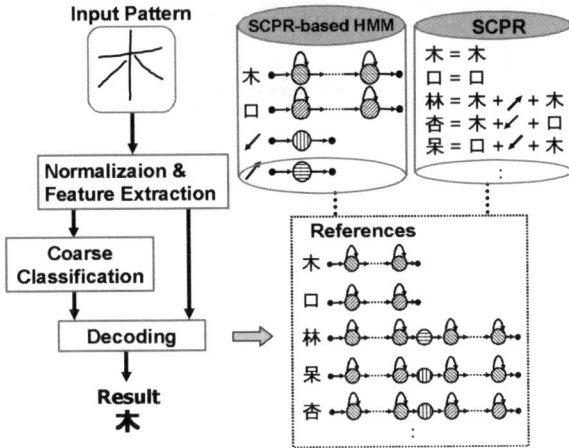

Fig. 9. Recognition by SCPR-based HMM

Character HMM: $\boldsymbol{\mu_i} = (\mu_{ix}, \mu_{iy})$, is adapted by the following equations:

$$\hat{\mu_{ix}} = \mu_{ix} \times \frac{w}{128} + sp_x \qquad (15)$$

$$\hat{\mu_{iy}} = \mu_{iy} \times \frac{h}{128} + sp_y \qquad (16)$$

where μ_{ix} and μ_{iy} denote the mean vectors of the pen-coordinate feature x and y, and (sp_x, sp_y) denotes the top-left corner and $< w, h >$ denotes $< width, height >$ of the bounding box.

In contrast, we apply the inverse of the above mapping when estimating SCPR-based HMMs. A simple idea is to enlarge the size of the bounding box of a mapped basic subpattern in a learning pattern to the normalization size. By applying the inverse mapping, we can exclude character dependency of each subpattern (difference in size and position when it appears in different character patterns) to model pen-coordinate features of the subpattern by SCPR-based HMMs. However, as handwriting usually contains noise due to hand vibration, etc., the inverse mapping may magnify these noises and reflect them into the subpattern. To avoid noise expansion, we employ the displacement normalization mentioned in Section 2.2, instead of inverse mapping each subpattern.

Evaluation for SCPR-Based HMMs. We use only Kanji categories in the JIS 1*st* level set in Kuchibue_d. Patterns from 60 writers were used for training, and those from the remaining 60 writers were used for testing.

First, we evaluated the effect of positional features and directional features upon the latter alone. Table 1 demonstrates the importance of both the directional and positional features. They have increased more than eight points, from 83.6 to 92.3%.

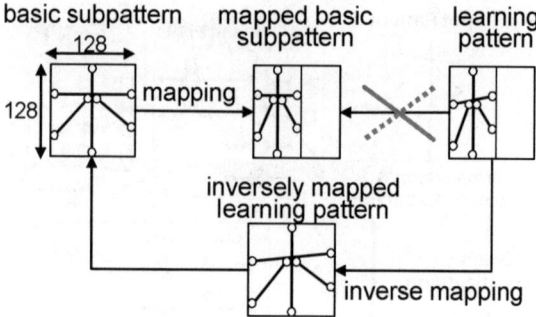

Fig. 10. Mapping and inverse mapping

Table 1. Effect of positional features and directional features

Features	N-best cumulative recognition rate (%)			
	1	-2	-3	-10
directional features	83.6	88.4	90.0	92.7
direct. f + positional f	92.3	95.1	95.9	96.9

Second, we compared the proposed SCPR-based HMMs and the conventional character HMMs with respect to memory size. The former requires 30.68 M bytes, and the latter needs 3.81 M bytes.

3   Classifier Combination

This section describes the combined recognizer, composed of the SCPR-based online recognizer and the offline recognizer. An online handwritten pattern easily converts to an offline pattern by discarding temporal information, so we can apply the offline method. Although the online method is more robust against stroke catenation, running strokes, and deformation of character patterns when compared to the offline method, the offline method is free from stroke-order variation and robust to duplicated strokes when people write two or more times. Therefore, by combining the online method with the offline method, the recognition accuracy improves because they can compensate for their disadvantages. Several attempts have been made to combine the two methods [36][37]. In Japanese character recognition, Tanaka, et al., showed the initial attempt to combine online and offline classifiers [38] while Okamoto, et al., showed the combination in the feature level, i.e., added online features to offline features in an offline recognition scheme [20]. It seems that classifier combination is more flexible than feature combination, as we can employ the most suitable classification method for each set of features.

In this paper, we show succeeding research after [38] to improve recognition accuracy, while increasing recognition speed and reducing memory size. The memory requirements for the offline prototype dictionary are significantly larger than that for the online one. Especially, the dictionary size depends on the number of categories, so the combined recognizer for Japanese characters is difficult for a small computer, such as a PDA. We also propose a compact combined recognizer, composed of the SCPR-based online recognizer and an offline recognizer with a small prototype dictionary.

3.1 Combination Process

To combine the online recognition and the offline recognition, a given online character pattern converts to a bitmap image, then online recognition and offline recognition are processed in parallel. We employ Sys_LTM as mentioned in Section 2.1, as the online recognition method and Modified Quadratic Discriminant Function (MQDF2) [39] as the offline recognition method.

Combination Rule. Various possibilities can combine outputs from multiple classifiers. Kittler, et al. present many combination schemes, such product rule, sum rule, min rule, max rule, median rule, and majority voting [40]. We employ the sum-rule, in which the total score of a combined classifier is the addition of all classifiers. The sum rule is denoted as follows:

$$Assign X \rightarrow C_j \ if$$
$$\sum_{i=1}^{R} P(C_j|fv_i) = \max_{k=1}^{N_{cc}} \sum_{i=1}^{R} P(C_k|fv_i) \tag{17}$$

where N_{cc} denotes the number of character categories, R denotes the number of classifiers, f_v denotes a feature vector extracted from the input pattern X, C_k denotes the prototype and $P(C_k|fv_i)$ denotes the probability that C_k occurs when fv_i is given.

Evaluation Score Normalization. Recognition results, produced by each recognizer, are pairs of a candidate character and an evaluation score that represents similarity or distance. However, each recognizer outputs a different type of evaluation score. The evaluation score of our online recognizer shows similarity. The higher the score, the more likely the candidate is. However, our offline recognizer employs distance. The lower the score, the higher the likelihood is. To combine these recognizers, we apply our likelihood normalization approach [41][42].

3.2 Small Offline Prototype Dictionary

MQDF2 for the offline recognition is given as:

$$g_2(x, \omega_i)$$
$$= \sum_{j=1}^{m} \frac{1}{\lambda_{ij}} [\varphi_{ij}^T (x - \mu_i)]^2$$
$$+ \frac{1}{\delta} \{ \|x - \mu_i\|^2 - \sum_{j=1}^{m} [\varphi_{ij}^T (x - \mu_i)]^2 \}$$
$$+ \sum_{j=1}^{m} \log \lambda_{ij} + (n - m) \log \delta \tag{18}$$

Table 2. Recognition rates of the combined recognizer (%)

Online	Offline		Combined	
	9.7MB	91.8MB	9.7MB	91.8MB
87.2	83.2	86.9	91.4	92.2

where μ is the mean vector, φ is the eigen vector, λ is eigen value, and δ is a modified eigen vector, n is the number of dimension, and m is the number of λ.

While the SCPR dictionary of our online recognizer is only 150KB, the prototype dictionary of the offline recognizer is about 90MB. To reduce the total size of memory, we propose a small prototype dictionary for the offline recognizer by reducing the parameters for MQDF2.

The size of the offline prototype dictionary: S_i is calculated from the size of each parameter $\{s_\mu, s_\varphi, s_\lambda, s_\delta\}$ where s_x denotes the size for the parameter x as follows.

$$S_i = N_{cc} \times \{n \times (s_\mu + m \times s_\varphi) + m \times s_\lambda + s_\delta\} \qquad (19)$$

In this study, we make two extreme sizes of dictionaries. One is 9.7MB whose n is 100 and m is 10. The other is 91.8MB whose n is 256 and m is 40. Each parameter $\{s_\mu, s_\varphi, s_\lambda, s_\delta\}$ requires 16 bits in both the dictionaries. The size of the SCPR dictionary in the online recognizer is 150KB, so the dictionary size of the combined recognizer is almost the same as in the offline recognizer. Hereafter, we call the combined recognizer which employs the 9.7MB dictionary "Sys_9.7MB" and the 91.8MB dictionary "Sys_91.8MB".

3.3 Evaluation of the Combined Recognizer

We trained the online recognizer using Nakayosi_t and the offline recognizer using ETL9B [43] written by 200 participants, each composed of 3,036 character patterns; JEITA-HP [44] written by 580 participants, each composed of 3,306 character patterns; NTT-AT [45] written by 51 participants, each composed of 1,237 character patterns; and Nakayosi_t. We also used Nakayosi_t for normalizing evaluation scores.

The recognition rates appear in Table 2. These rates show no significant difference between the Sys_9.7MB and the Sys_91.8MB, though the correct recognition accuracy of the offline recognizer with 91.8MB dictionary is higher than the offline recognizer with Sys_9.7MB by 3.7 points.

We also compare the processing time of each recognizer on a Pentium IV 3.06 GHz processor with 512MB RAM (Table 3). The Sys_9.7MB outperforms the Sys_91.8MB.

Table 3. Average processing time per character (ms)

Online	Offline		Combined	
	9.7MB	91.8MB	9.7MB	91.8MB
3.32	6.6	18.5	10.6	22.5

Table 4. Recognition rates of the combined recognizer employing bi-gram model (%)

Online	Offline		Combined	
	9.7MB	91.8MB	9.7MB	91.8MB
91.2	97.0 %	97.7	98.6	98.6

Combined Recognizer with Context Postprocessing. We show the recognition accuracy of our combined recognizer with context postprocessing. In this experiment, a character bi-gram model performs as a simple stochastic language model. Given a sequence of character patterns $X = X_1 X_2 \ldots X_i \ldots X_N$, The problem is to find the character string $C = C_1 C_2 \ldots C_i \ldots C_N$ to maximize the probability $P(C|X)$. Using the Bayes rule:

$$P(C|X) = \frac{P(C) \cdot P(X|C)}{P(X)} \tag{20}$$

The term $P(X|C)$ shows the probability of C written as X. The term $P(C)$ shows the context likelihood.

Following the bi-gram model, the probability $P(C)$ is given as:

$$P(C) = P(C_1) \prod_{i=1}^{N-1} P(C_{i+1}|C_i) \tag{21}$$

where N denotes the number of character patterns in a text string, and C_i denotes each character pattern. The uni-gram probability $P(C_1)$ is assumed to be independent from characters. In our study, the character bi-gram language model was trained with the ASAHI newspaper text corpus "CD-HIASK'93".

The recognition results in Table 4 show that the rate of Sys_9.7MB equals the rate of Sys_91.8MB and raises to 98.6%.

4   Online Handwritten Japanese Text Recognition

According to the increasing size of writing surface of pen input devices, demand for online handwritten text recognition is growing. Due to the difference between Japanese and western languages and handwriting, handwritten recognition differs naturally. In this section, we describe some problems of handwritten Japanese text recognition and approaches to tackle those problems.

4.1   Problems

Generally, on large writing surfaces Asian languages of Chinese origin are often written horizontally, vertically, or even diagonally.

Most previous publications and systems assumed only horizontal lines of text [46][47], while we attempted to relinquish any writing constraint from online text input. We proposed a method to recognize mixtures of horizontal, vertical, and slanted lines of text with assuming normal character orientation [48]. Then, we attempted handwriting recognition with characters rotated like in handwritings typical of whiteboards [49].

As mentioned before, Japanese text includes various sizes of character patterns ranging from so-called "half-width" characters like numbers and symbols, Kana characters and Kanji characters of only one radical in the middle, to those consisting of multiple radicals. Moreover, handwriting magnifies even the size variations, as shown in Figure 11. Some characters may be several times longer and/or wider than others.

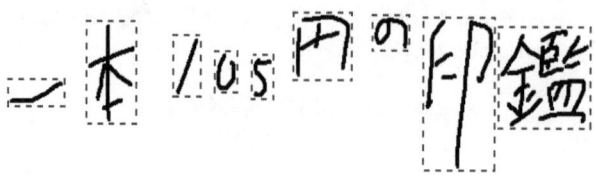

Fig. 11. An example of Japanese handwritten text

Many Japanese characters can be divided into multiple character patterns. For example, the patterns shown in Figure 12(a) can be read as either C_1, a character in itself, or as the two consecutive characters C_2C_3. The correct one is determined by the characters (or strings) preceding and/or following it. In the example of Figure 12(b), the character C_4 follows, which causes the pattern of Figure 12(a) to be read as C_1. In Figure 12(c), the characters C_5C_6 follow, which causes the pattern to be read as two characters C_2C_3. This example shows how the position of character segmentation can differ even for the same handwritten pattern, depending on the context, so it is difficult to segment characters deterministically on the basis of geometrical features alone.

In the next section, we present an enhanced method to recognize online handwriting of arbitrary line directions and character orientations as well as their mixtures.

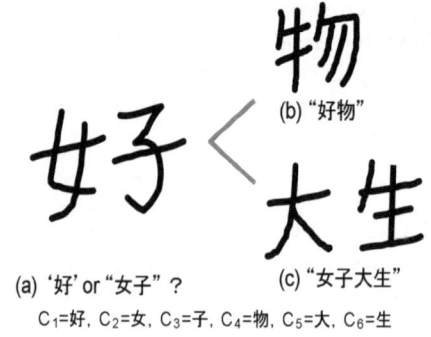

(b) "好物"

(a) '好' or "女子" ?

(c) "女子大生"

C_1=好, C_2=女, C_3=子, C_4=物, C_5=大, C_6=生

Fig. 12. An example of segmentation ambiguity

4.2   Flow of Processing

We first need to define terminology. Character orientation specifies the direction of a character from its top to bottom, while line direction designates the writing direction of a sequence of characters until it changes (Figure 13). A text line is a piece of text separated by new-line or large space, and it is further divided into text line elements at the changing points of line direction. Each text line element has its line direction (Figure 14). The line direction and the character orientation are independent.

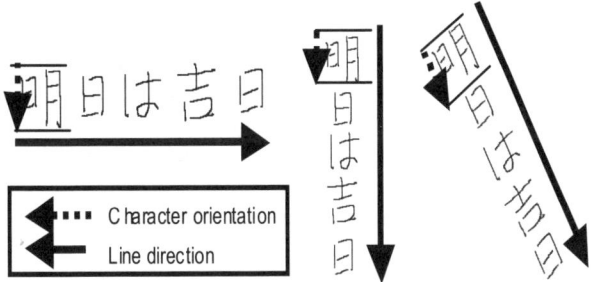

Fig. 13. Line direction and character orientation

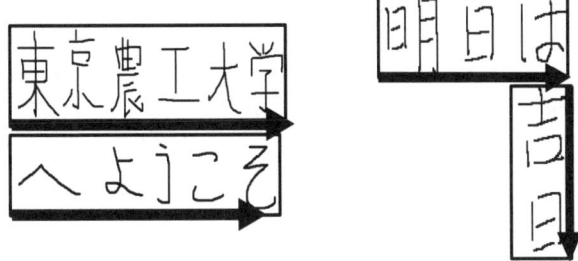

Fig. 14. Text line element and line direction

In the following subsections, we explain the procedure of our online recognition system of handwritten Japanese text, free from character orientation, line direction, and any writing format constraint.

Separation of Handwriting into Text Line Elements. First, we estimate the average character size from all the strokes written on a tablet by measuring the length of the longer side of the bounding box for each stroke, sorting the lengths from all the strokes, and taking the average of the larger 1/3 of them. The estimated average character size decides the threshold for separating written text into text line elements.

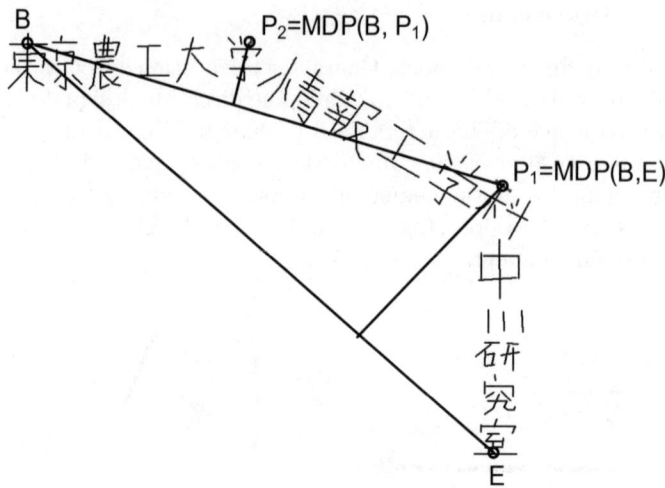

Fig. 15. Detection of directional changing points

Next, we separate freely written text into text lines by a large off-stroke from a previous line to a new line. Then, we separate each text line into text line elements by the changing points of line direction.

To detect the changing points of line direction, we employ a recursive procedure similar to that used to detect corner points [50]. Among a series of coordinates of the centers for the bounding boxes of strokes forming a handwritten text line, it finds the most distant point (MDP) from the straight line connecting the starting, and ending points of the series of coordinates. If the distance is larger than the threshold, then we apply the same procedure to the straight line from the starting point to the MDP, and from the MDP to the ending point, with the result of detecting multiple points of directional change, as shown in Figure 15, with B as the beginning point and E as the ending point. Thus a text line segmented by large space is further segmented into text line elements having different line directions.

Here, it is worth noting that points detected might be within character patterns rather than between characters, as P_1 and P_2 in Figure 15. We will address the problem in a later section, determining the best segmentation points while recognizing handwritten text.

Estimation and Normalization of Character Orientation. When Japanese characters are written, principal pen movement within real strokes remains the same as the character orientation. This happens because Japanese characters, especially Kanji, are composed of downward and rightward strokes. Therefore, if we take the histogram of displacement direction of pen-tip coordinates, we see two peaks, as shown in Figure 16.

Let us assume the intensity of the histogram at the angle θ as $f(\theta)$. Then, take the θ that makes the max value of $f(\theta) \times f(\theta + \pi/2)$ as the character orientation

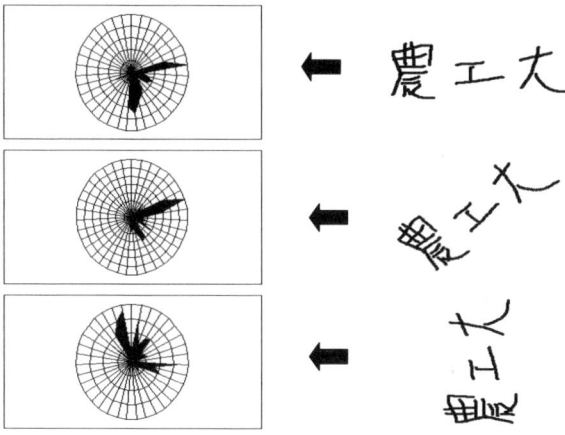

Fig. 16. Two peaks in pen movement direction

for each text line element. To make the peak detection more robust, we take the convolution of $f(\theta)$ and a Gauss function to blur the peak, so it works for slanting characters with rightward strokes and a slightly upward inclination.

After estimating the character orientation, the text line element can be normalized by rotating it.

Hypothetical Segmentation for Each Text Line Element. We hypothetically segment a text line element, after the character orientation normalization, into character patterns using geometric features.

Hypothetical segmentation depends on character orientation and line direction. After normalizing character orientation, it depends on line direction of a text line element, as shown in Figure 17. Note that a segmentation hypothesis often occurs within character patterns, and it differs even for the same character pattern depending on the line direction. The quantization can be finer, but the 4-directional quantization (shown in Figure 17) is adequate and effective to prevent a text line element from being segmented excessively. When the line direction is classified, downward or upward (rightward or leftward), a considerable gap projected on the vertical axis (horizontal axis) or a long off-stroke to the quantized line direction are employed as candidates for segmentation. Strokes or off-strokes to the opposite direction merge their crossing strokes with the result that hypotheses on segmentation can be decreased, which is then effective to accelerate the text recognition and increase the recognition rate.

After the quantization of line direction, we extract multi-dimensional features, such as distance and overlap between adjacent strokes, from each off-stroke and apply the SVM to the extracted features to produce segmentation point candidates [51]. Character size may vary among text line elements, so we estimate the character size again for every text line element. Then, we normalize the extracted multi-dimensional features by the re-estimated character size for each text line element. Each off-stroke is classified into segmentation point, non-segmentation

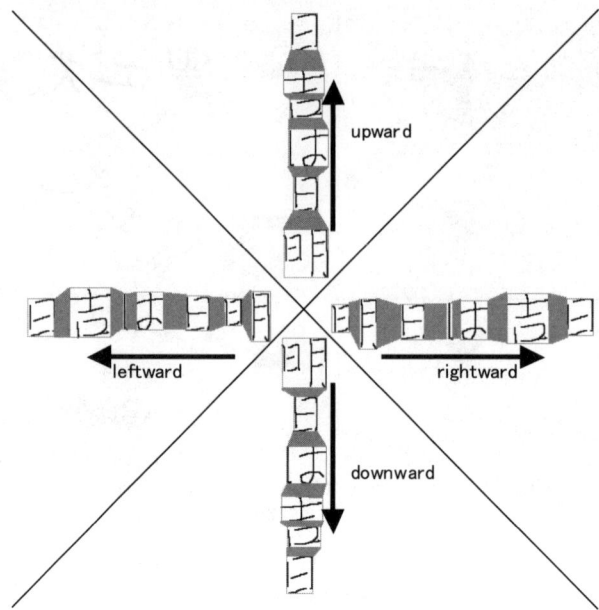

Fig. 17. Quantization of line direction

point, and undecided point, according to the features. A segmentation point should be between two characters, and a non-segmentation point appears within a character pattern. An undecided point is one which cannot be judged as segmented or non-segmented. A segmentation unit bounded by two adjacent segmentation points is assumed to be a character pattern. An undecided point is treated in two ways: as a segmentation point or a non-segmentation point. When treated as a segmentation point, it extracts a segmentation unit.

Construction of Candidate Lattice. A candidate lattice is constructed for each text line, where each arc denotes a segmentation point and each node denotes a character recognition candidate produced by character recognition for each segmentation unit, as shown in Figure 18.

Scores associate with each arc or node following the stochastic model of evaluating the likelihood composed of character segmentation, character recognition, character pattern structure, and context.

The Viterbi search is implemented into the candidate lattice for a handwritten text line and the best segmentation and recognition is determined.

Segmentation of a text line into text line elements by an MDP should not be decisive. Wrong segmentation, within a character pattern, into two text line elements and rotation of the segmented text line elements to normalize character orientation may damage their recognition, as shown in Figure 19. To avoid this problem, we produce multiple alternatives of text line segmentation by choosing the segmentation point among candidates around the MDP. The range of the

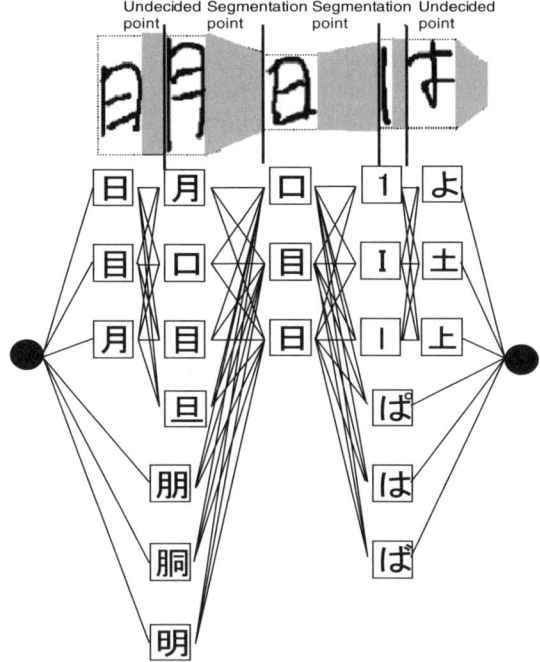

Fig. 18. Candidate lattice

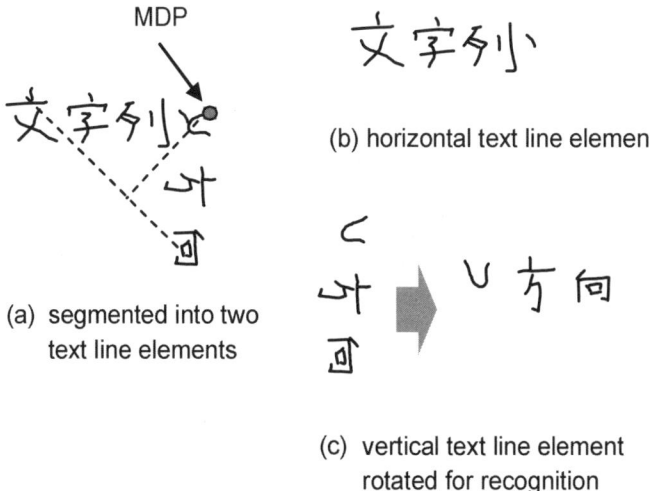

(a) segmented into two
   text line elements

(b) horizontal text line element

(c) vertical text line element
   rotated for recognition

Fig. 19. Problem of segmentation by an MDP

segmentation point's perturbation can be confined within the average character size before or after the MDP. According to each alternative segmentation point, the two text line elements at both sides of the segmentation point are rotated with character orientations normalized when necessary and recognized. Then, the Viterbi search chooses the best segmentation point.

Model of Free Format Recognition. We made a model and recently formalized it for online handwritten Japanese text recognition free from line-direction constraint and writing format constraint, such as character writing boxes or ruled lines [42][52]. The model evaluates the probability of character segmentation, character recognition, character pattern structure, and context. The likelihood of character pattern structure considers the plausible height, width, and inner gaps within a character pattern that appears in Chinese characters composed of multiple subpatterns.

The problem involves finding the character string $C = C_1C_2...C_i...C_N$ to maximize the likelihood $L(C|X)$ that a handwritten text line pattern X is recognized as the character string C. After several steps of approximations and modifications, we arrive at the following formula:

$$L(C|X)$$
$$= \log P(C_1) + \sum_{i=1}^{N-1} \log P(C_{i+1}|C_i)$$
$$+ \sum_{i=1}^{N} (\log P(X_i|St_i, C_i) + \log P(St_i/\bar{C}|C_i))$$
$$+ \sum_{i=1}^{N-1} (\log P(gap_i/\bar{C}|C_i, C_{i+1})) \tag{22}$$

where,

N	: number of characters in C.
$P(C_{i+1}|C_i)$	: probability that a character C_{i+1} follows C_i (bi-gram probability).
$P(X_i|St_i, C_i)$	: probability that a character C_i is written in a structure St_i and represented by the stroke sequence X_i.
$\bar{C}$	: average size of the character sequence C.
$P(St_i/\bar{C}|C_i)$	: probability that a character C_i is written in a structure St_i.
$P(gap_i/\bar{C}|C_i, C_{i+1})$	: probability that an outer gap : gap_i appears between C_i and C_{i+1}.

In the right-hand side of the above equation, the second term considers context likelihood in terms of a bi-gram, the third term relats to character recognition likelihood, the fourth and fifth terms evaluate character pattern structure likelihood and outer gap likelihood, respectively.

5   Application

In this section, we show two types of online handwriting applications: segmentation and recognition of mixed text, formulas, tables, and line-drawings; and handwritten text search.

5.1   Segmentation and Recognition of Mixed Objects

As the writing area of pen input devices grows, users can easily write text, mathematical formulae and figures on the screen. It is one of the most important benefits of pen interfaces that people can write these objects by a single pen without switching the device, mode, or software, and without any writing restriction such as grids or boxes. However, it requires the difficult task to separate online handwritten patterns into Japanese text, figures, and mathematical formulas. We approached this problem earlier [53]. Recently, we take a probabilistic approach to this problem and employed stroke features, stroke crossings, and stroke densities. Moreover, we partially applied segmentation by recognition. Although the current recognizer for formulae is only a prototype, we have achieved about 81% correct segmentation for all the strokes in Kondate_t, the newly prepared database of mixed patterns [54]. Figure 20 shows an example of separating mixed objects. Our new approach is generally better but less effective in distinguishing figures from other components.

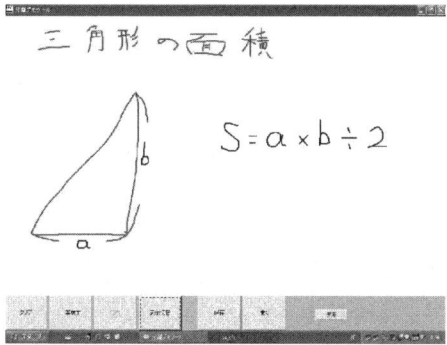

Fig. 20. Separation of handwriting into text, formula and line drawing

5.2   Online Handwritten Text Search

As various pen input devices become popular, online handwritten text will be accumulated. Without a search method, however, accumulated online handwritten text can not be utilized effectively. Search of online handwritten text by employing a pattern matching method without character recognition was reported in [55]. Lopresti, et al. proposed a stroke search method, "Script Search Algorithm," which searches a long handwritten text pattern and finds approximate patterns of a keyword [56]. Also, we have proposed a method for writing-box-free online Japanese handwritten text search, based on the online Japanese handwritten text recognition, mentioned in Section 4 [57]. It searches for a target keyword in the candidate lattice composed of candidate segmentations and candidate characters, as shown in Figure 18, which has been generated beforehand by the background process of online handwriting recognition. Figure 21 shows an example of online handwritten text search. As the performance of recognizer improves, the performance of search upgrades.

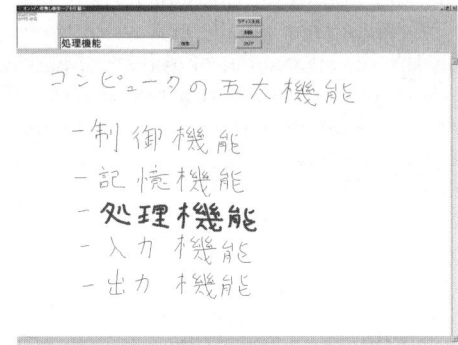

Fig. 21. Searching a keyword from free format handwritten text

6   Conclusion

We presented online handwriting recognition of Japanese characters. Most Kanji character patterns are composed of multiple subpatterns called radicals, and these subpatterns are shared among many character patterns, so we have employed structured character pattern representation (SCPR). SCPR is effective in terms of the size reduction of the prototype dictionary and the robustness to deformation of common subpatterns. Then, we described a prototype learning algorithm and HMM-based recognition for SCPR. We combined the SCPR-based online recognizer with a compact offline recognizer. Moreover, we also presented online handwritten Japanese text recognition free from character orientation and line direction constraints. Finally, we showed some applications of online handwritten Japanese text recognition.

Acknowledgments

This research is being partially supported by Grant-in-Aid for Scientific Research under the contract number (B) 17300031 and the MEXT fund for Promoting Research on Symbiotic Information Technology.

References

1. http://www.anoto.com
2. http://www.e-pen.com
3. Tappert, C.C., et al.: The State of the Art in On-Line Handwriting Recognition. IEEE, Trans. PAMI 12(8), 787–808 (1990)
4. Nakagawa, M.: Non-Keyboard Input of Japanese Text - On-line Recognition of Handwritten Characters as the Most Hopeful Approach. J. Information Processing 13(1), 15–34 (1990)
5. Plamondon, R., et al.: On-Line and Off-Line Handwriting Recognition: a Comprehensive Survey. IEEE Trans. PAMI 22(1), 63–82 (2000)
6. Jaeger, S., et al.: The State of the Art in Japanese On-line Handwriting Recognition Compared to Techniques in Western Handwriting Recognition. IJDAR 6(2), 75–88 (2003)
7. Liu, C.L., et al.: On-Line Recognition of Chinese Characters: the State of the Art. IEEE Trans. PAMI 26(2), 198–213 (2004)
8. Nakagawa, M., et al.: On-line Handwritten Character Pattern Database Sampled in a Sequence of Sentences without any Writing Instructions. In: Proc. 4th ICDAR, pp. 376–381 (1997)
9. Nakagawa, M., et al.: Collection of On-line Handwritten Japanese Character Pattern Databases and Their Analysis. IJDAR 7(1), 69–81 (2004)
10. Shin, J., et al.: Stroke Correspondence Search Method for Stroke-Order and Stroke-Number Free On-Line Character Recognition - Multilayer Cube Search (in Japanese). IEICE Trans J82-D-II(2), 230–239 (1999)
11. Kobayashi, M., et al.: RAV (Reparameterized Angular Variations) Algorithms for Online Handwriting Recognition. IJDAR 3(3), 181–191 (2001)
12. Nakagawa, M., et al.: Robust and Highly Customizable Recognition of On-line Handwritten Japanese Characters. Proc. 13th ICPR 3, 269–273 (1996)
13. Nakagawa, M., et al.: A Linear-Time Elastic Matching for Stroke Number Free Recognition of On-Line Handwritten Characters. In: Proc. 4th IWFHR, pp. 48–56 (1994)
14. Yokota, T., et al.: An On-line Cuneiform Modeled Handwritten Japanese Character Recognition Method Free from Both the Number and Order of Character Strokes (in Japanese). Trans. IPSJ 44(3), 980–990 (2003)
15. Takahashi, K., et al.: A Fast HMM Algorithm for On-Line Handwritten Character Recognition. In: Proc.4th ICDAR, pp. 369–375 (1997)
16. Ishigaki, K., et al.: A Top-down On-line Handwritten Character Recognition Method via the Denotation of Variation. In: Proc. ICCPCOL, pp. 141–145 (1998)
17. Rammer, U., et al.: An Iterative Procedure for the Polygonal Approximation of Plane Closed Curves. CGIP 1, 244–256 (1972)
18. Kawamura, A., et al.: On-line Recognition of Freely Handwritten Japanese Characters Using Directional Feature Densities. Proc. 11th ICPR 2, 183–186 (1992)
19. Hamanaka, M., et al.: On-line Japanese Character Recognition Experiments by an Off-line Method. In: Proc. 2nd ICDAR, pp. 204–207 (1993)
20. Okamoto, M., et al.: On-line Handwritten Character Representation using Directional Features and Direction-Change Features (in Japanese). Journal of IEE Japan 119(3), 358–366 (1999)
21. Tokuno, J., et al.: Pen-Coordinate Information Modeling by SCPR-based HMM for On-line Japanese Handwriting Recognition. In: Proc. 18th ICPR. WED-P-II-1, vol. 3 (2006)

22. Kohonen, T., et al.: Improved Versions of Learning Vector Quantization. Proc. IJCNNI 1, 545–550 (1990)
23. Geva, S., et al.: Adaptive Nearest Neighbor Pattern Recognition. IEEE Trans. NN 2(2), 318–322 (1991)
24. Juang, B.-H., et al.: Discriminative Learning for Minimum Error Classification. IEEE Trans. SP 40(12), 3043–3054 (1992)
25. Sato, A., et al.: A Formulation of Learning Vector Quantization Using a New Misclassification Measure. In: Proc. 14th ICPR, pp. 322–325 (1998)
26. Liu, C.-L., et al.: Evaluation of Prototype Learning Algorithms for Nearest-neighbor Classifier in Application to Handwritten Character Recognition. Pattern Recognition 34, 601–615 (2001)
27. Kitadai, A., et al.: Prototype Learning for Structured Pattern Representation Applied to On-line Recognition of Handwritten Japanese Characters (Published On-line). IJDAR, 1433–2825 (2007)
28. Liu, C.-L., et al.: Preprocessing and Statistical /Structural Feature Extraction for Handwritten Numeral Recognition Process of Handwriting Recognition, pp. 161–168. World Scientific, Singapore (1997)
29. Hu, J., et al.: HMM based On-line Handwriting Recognition. IEEE Trans. PAMI 18(10), 1039–1045 (1996)
30. Starner, T., et al.: On-Line Cursive Handwriting Recognition Using Speech Recognition Methods. Proc. ICASSP 5, 125–128 (1994)
31. Kim, H.-J., et al.: On-line Recognition of Handwritten Chinese Characters based on Hidden Markov Models. Pattern Recognition 30(9), 1489–1499 (1997)
32. Ito, H., et al.: An On-line Handwritten Character Recognition Method based on Hidden Markov Model (in Japanese). Technical Report of IEICE PRMU97-85, 95–100 (1997)
33. Okamoto, D., et al.: An HMM Implementation for On-line Handwriting Recognition Based on Pen-coordinate Feature and Pen-direction Feature. In: Proc. 8th ICDAR, pp. 26–30 (2005)
34. Nakai, M., et al.: Sub-stroke Approach to HMM-based On-line Kanji Handwriting Recognition. In: Proc. 6th ICDAR, pp. 491–495 (2001)
35. Cho, S.-J., et al.: Bayesian Network Modeling of Hangul Characters for On-line Handwriting Recognition. In: Proc. 7th ICDAR, pp. 207–211 (2003)
36. Manke, S., et al.: Combining Bitmaps with Dynamic Writing Information for On-line Handwriting Recognition. Proc. 13th ICPR, 596–598 (1994)
37. Vinciarelli, A., et al.: Combining Online and Offline Handwriting Recognition. In: Proc. 7th ICDAR, pp. 844–848 (2003)
38. Tanaka, H., et al.: Hybrid Pen-Input Character Recognition System Based on Integration of Online-Offline Recognition. In: Proc. 5th ICDAR, pp. 209–212 (1999)
39. Kimura, F., et al.: Modified Quadratic Discriminant Functions and the Application to Chinese Character Recognition. IEEE Trans. PAMI 9(1), 149–153 (1987)
40. Kittler, J., et al.: On Combining Classifiers. IEEE Trans. PAMI 20(3), 222–239 (1998)
41. Velek, O., et al.: A New Warping Technique for Normalizing Likelihood of Multiple Classifiers and its Effectiveness in Combined On-Line/Off-Line Japanese Character Recognition. In: Proc. 8th IWFHR, pp. 177–182 (2002)
42. Nakagawa, M., et al.: A Model of On-line Handwritten Japanese Text Recognition Free from Line Direction and Writing Format Constraints. IEICE Trans E88-D(8), 1815–182 (2005)
43. Saito, T., et al.: On the Data Base ETL9 of Handprinted Characters in JIS Chinese Characters and Its Analysis. Trans. IEICE J68-D(4), 757–764 (1985)

44. Kawatani, T., et al.: Handwritten Kanji Recognition with Determinant Normalized Quadratic Discriminant Function. Proc. 15th ICPR 2, 343–346 (2000)
45. http://www.ntt-at.com/products_e/jwords/
46. Fukushima, T., et al.: On-line Writing-box-free Recognition of Handwritten Japanese Text Considering Character Size Variations. Proc. 15th ICPR 2, 359–363 (2000)
47. Senda, S., et al.: A Maximum-Likelihood Approach to Segmentation-Based Recognition of Unconstrained Handwriting Text. In: Proc. of 6th ICDAR, pp. 184–188 (2001)
48. Inamura, Y., et al.: An On-line Writing-box-free and Writing-direction Free Recognition System for Handwritten Japanese Text (in Japanese). Technical Report of IEICE PRMU100-37, 17–24 (2000)
49. Nakagawa, M., et al.: On-line Handwritten Japanese Text Recognition Free from Constrains on Line Direction and Character Orientation. In: Proc. 7th ICDAR, pp. 519–523 (2003)
50. Senda, S., et al.: Box-free Online Character Recognition Integrating Confidence Values of Segmentation (in Japanese). Technical Report of IEICE PRMU98-138, 17–24 (1998)
51. Zhu, B., et al.: Segmentation of On-Line Handwritten Japanese Text Using SVM for Improving Text Recognition. In: Bunke, H., Spitz, A.L. (eds.) DAS 2006. LNCS, vol. 3872, pp. 208–219. Springer, Heidelberg (2006)
52. Nakagawa, M., et al.: A Formalization of On-line Handwritten Japanese Text Recognition Free from Line Direction Constraint. Proc. 17th ICPR 2, 359–362 (2004)
53. Machii, K., et al.: On-line Text/Drawings Segmentation of Handwritten Patterns. In: Proc. 2nd ICDAR, pp. 710–713 (1993)
54. Mochida, K., et al.: Separating Figures, Mathematical Formulas and Japanese Text from Free Handwriting in Mixed On-Line Documents. IJPRAI 18(7), 1173–1187 (2004)
55. Senda, S., et al.: MemoPad: Software with Functions of Box-free Japanese Character Recognition and Handwritten Query Search (in Japanese). Technical Report of IEICE PRMU99-75, 85–90 (1999)
56. Lopresti, D., et al.: On the Searchability of Electronic Ink. Proc. of 4th IWFHR, 156–165 (1994)
57. Oda, H., et al.: A Search Method for On-line Handwritten Text Employing Writing-box-free Handwriting Recognition. In: Proc. 9th IWFHR, pp. 545–550 (2004)

Segmentation-Driven Offline Handwritten Chinese and Arabic Script Recognition

Xiaoqing Ding and Hailong Liu

Dept. of Electronic Engineering, Tsinghua University,
State Key Laboratory of Intelligent Technology and Systems
100084, Beijing, China
{dxq,lhl}@ocrserv.ee.tsinghua.edu.cn

Abstract. The market of handwriting recognition applications is increasing rapidly due to continuous advancement in OCR technology. This paper summarizes our recent efforts on offline handwritten Chinese script recognition using a segmentation-driven approach. We address two essential problems, namely isolated character recognition and establishment of the probabilistic segmentation model. To improve the isolated character recognition accuracy, we propose a heteroscedastic linear discriminant analysis algorithm to extract more discrimination information from original character features, and implement a minimum classification error learning scheme to optimize classifier parameters. In the segmentation stage, information from three different sources, namely geometric layout, character recognition confidence, and semantic model are integrated into a probabilistic framework to give the best script interpretation. Experimental results on postal address and bank check recognition have demonstrated the effectiveness of our proposed algorithms: A more than 80% correct recognition rate is achieved on 1,000 handwritten Chinese address items, and the recognition reliability of bank checks is largely improved after combining courtesy amount recognition result with legal amount recognition result. Some preliminary research work on Arabic script recognition is also shown.

1 Introduction

Research on handwritten script recognition has received increasing attention in recent years, since it meets with the demands from a wide range of commercial applications, such as automatic postal address reading, bank check processing, recognition of handwritten contents in forms, etc. Different ways exist to categorize handwritten script recognition. Depending on how the handwriting is acquired and converted to digital form, the research field can be distinguished as online and offline script recognition. For online, dynamic time information captured from the writing device increases the recognition accuracy, while for offline scripts, such information is unavailable and the recognition accuracy is usually much lower. According to the language, the scripts to be recognized can be specified as Roman, Asian, Arabic, etc, which can operate differently in recognition strategies, according to respective characteristic.

D.S. Doermann and S. Jaeger (Eds.): SACH 2006, LNCS 4768, pp. 196–217, 2008.

In this paper, we focus our attentions on the problem of offline handwritten Chinese script recognition. Compared with Roman script recognition [1][2][3][4], there has been relatively less research work done in this area. Most published papers concern the segmentation problems [5][6][7][8][9][10], post-processing [11], or specific applications [12][13][14][15][16].

Chinese handwritten script recognition presents a challenging problem for the following reasons:

1) There exists great variety in the styles of handwritten scripts.
2) Accurate segmentation is very difficult to obtain under many situations. The gaps between characters are often small, and sometimes adjacent characters touch or overlap (Fig. 1).
3) Misclassifications of characters often occur, especially with cursive script.
4) The unique feature of Chinese characters poses extra difficulties: The pattern class number is enormous (several thousands), many Chinese characters have very complex structures, and there also exist many similar characters.

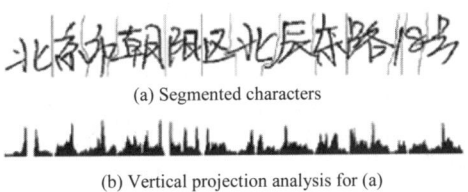

(a) Segmented characters

(b) Vertical projection analysis for (a)

Fig. 1. Typical handwritten Chinese script that touch and overlap

In general, script recognition approaches can divide into two categories, namely holistic approaches and segmentation-driven approaches. The former approaches apply more often to western script processing, where words, instead of single characters, are treated as basic units for recognition. The size of the lexicon (legal vocabulary) that can be handled by holistic approaches is usually limited. When the lexicon size becomes too large, or no extra gaps occur between words, e.g. in the case of Chinese scripts, segmentation-driven approaches are more favorable. In this situation, scripts are first segmented into a sequence of isolated units, either characters or parts of characters (radicals, graphemes), then these units are recognized separately to obtain the final script recognition result. Our work also adapts this segmentation-driven approach is also adopted in our work.

A sequential script recognition scheme appears in Fig.2. After acquiring a script image, it is necessary pre-processing steps such as binarization, noise removal and slant correction. Then, the script image segment into characters and are recognized

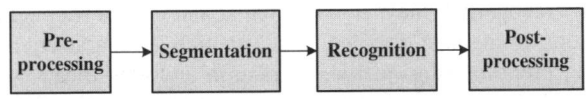

Fig. 2. Sequential script recognition scheme

individually by the isolated character recognition engine. Finally, context based post-processing is called to correct the errors that may occur in the recognition step. Apparently, this sequential structure has an error accumulation problem. Incorrect segmentation will lead directly to recognition errors, which could not be corrected even by post-processing.

To overcome this deficiency, we use a global optimization scheme in our script recognition algorithm. As shown in Fig.3, after an over-segmentation step, a probabilistic segmentation framework is established, which takes into account the information from geometrical layout, isolated character recognition, and contextual constraints. Multiple paths corresponding to different segmentation and recognition results are evaluated, and the best one becomes the final script interpretation. In the procedure, two essential problems should be solved well, i.e. how to design a high performance isolated character recognizer, and how to describe the probabilistic segmentation model.

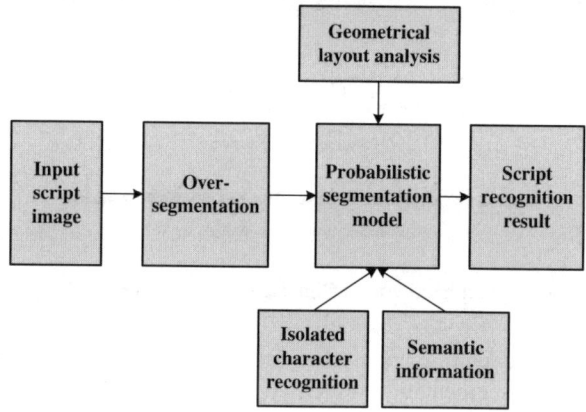

Fig. 3. Flowchart of our proposed Chinese script recognition algorithm

The remainder of the paper is organized as follows: Section 2, discusses the algorithms for isolated character recognition, and Section 3 deals with the over-segmentation procedure. In Section 4, we establish the probabilistic segmentation framework; experimental results on postal address and bank check recognition follow in Section 5. In Section 6, we present our work on Arabic script recognition. Finally, conclusions and future work are summarized in Section 7.

2   Isolated Handwritten Character Recognition

Isolated character recognition plays a fundamental and crucial role in the whole script recognition system. In the past decades, huge amounts of character recognition algorithms, including preprocessing, feature extraction and classification, have been reported [17][18]. In our recognition engine, nonlinear normalization based on line-density equalization [19] first applies to character images to reduce stroke deformation. After that, the high resolution gradient feature is extracted [20][21], and a modified quadratic discriminant function (MQDF) [22] works as the main classifier. To enhance the discriminative ability of the recognition engine, we proposed a novel heteroscedastic linear discriminant analysis (HLDA) method to extract more discriminative information from the original feature vector [23], and apply a minimum classification error (MCE) learning scheme [21] to adjust the MQDF parameters estimated by the maximum likelihood method.

2.1 Heteroscedastic Linear Discriminant Analysis

Dimensionality reduction, or specific feature extraction, is crucial in pattern recognition. It is necessary not only to reduce computational cost, but also to solve the "curse of dimensionality," when the number of training samples is small relative to the feature dimensionality. From the viewpoint of classification, feature extraction should preserve as much class-separability as possible in the lower dimensional space. Of all the supervised feature extraction techniques, linear discriminant analysis (LDA) is probably the most frequently used, which aims at maximizing the between-class scatter S_B while minimizing the within-class scatter S_W. Although LDA is efficient and simple to implement, it has its own deficiencies. LDA implicitly assumes that all the pattern classes are Gaussian distributed and have equal covariance, so it extracts discriminative information only from the difference of class mean, while ignoring the discriminative information in the difference of class covariance. Therefore, when the practical feature data is heteroscedastic, LDA cannot perform optimally. Following Loog's original work [24][25], we have proposed a new HLDA algorithm to generalize LDA to heteroscedastic feature data [23].

For simplicity, we assume the within-class matrix equals to the identity matrix, i.e. $S_W=I$. The between-class scatter matrix S_B can decompose as

$$S_B = \sum_{i=1}^{C-1} \sum_{j=i+1}^{C} p_i p_j S_{Eij}, \tag{1}$$

in which

$$S_{Eij} = (m_i - m_j)(m_i - m_j)^T, \tag{2}$$

C is the pattern class number, p_i and m_i are the prior probability and mean vector of class i, respectively. S_{Eij} is called the Directed Distance Matrix (DDM), associated with class i and j, which as it not only gives the distance between two classes by its eigenvalues but also implies the directions in which the distance could be found by its eigenvectors. Under the homoscedastic Gaussian assumption of LDA, the corresponding S_{Eij} has only one non-zero eigenvalue, which equals the Euclidean distance

$$d_{Eij} = (m_i - m_j)^T (m_i - m_j). \tag{3}$$

S_{Eij} and d_{Eij} is related by $tr(S_{Eij})=d_{Eij}$.

The LDA feature transformation matrix Φ is achieved by maximizing a Fisher criterion, which can be represented by coupling the pairwise-class separability criterion,

$$J_F(\Phi) = tr[(\Phi^T S_W \Phi)^{-1}(\Phi^T S_B \Phi)] = \sum_{i=1}^{C-1} \sum_{j=i+1}^{C} tr[(\Phi^T \Phi)^{-1}(\Phi^T S_{Eij} \Phi)]. \tag{4}$$

Under the homoscedastic assumption, Euclidean distance is sufficient to measure the dissimilarity between two Gaussian distributions. If we went further to consider the heteroscedastic situation, Chernoff distance should replace Euclidean distance:

$$d_{Cij} = (m_i - m_j)\Sigma_{ij}^{-1}(m_i - m_j) + \frac{1}{\alpha(1-\alpha)}\log\frac{|\Sigma_{ij}|}{|\Sigma_i|^\alpha|\Sigma_j|^{1-\alpha}}, \tag{5}$$

where Σ_i and Σ_j are the covariance matrices of class i and j, α is a constant determined by $\alpha = p_i/(p_i + p_j)$, and $\Sigma_{ij} = p_i\Sigma_i + p_j\Sigma_j$. The DDM corresponding to Chernoff distance can be derived as

$$S_{Cij} = \Sigma_{ij}^{-1/2}(m_i - m_j)(m_i - m_j)^T\Sigma_{ij}^{-1/2} + \frac{1}{\alpha(1-\alpha)}\Big(\log\Sigma_{ij} - \alpha\log\Sigma_i - (1-\alpha)\log\Sigma_j\Big), \tag{6}$$

since $tr(S_{Cij}) = d_{Cij}$. Replace S_{Eij} with S_{Cij} in (4), we get the Chernoff criterion

$$J_C(\Phi) = \sum_{i=1}^{C-1}\sum_{j=i+1}^{C} p_i p_j tr[(\Phi^T\Phi)^{-1}(\Phi^T S_{Cij}\Phi)]. \tag{7}$$

Given our overly large number of pattern classes, e.g. in handwritten Chinese character recognition, the pairwise-class calculation scheme can be computationally too expensive. Also, the logarithm items in (6) appear computationally unstable. Therefore, we may discard the logarithm item and use the global mean vector m_0 to avoid pairwise-class calculation, thus (7) simplifies as

$$J_M(\Phi) = \sum_{i=1}^{C} p_i tr[(\Phi^T\Phi)^{-1}(\Phi^T S_{Mi}\Phi)], \tag{8}$$

where

$$S_{Mi} = \Sigma_{i0}^{-1/2}(m_i - m_0)(m_i - m_0)^T\Sigma_{i0}^{-1/2}, \tag{9}$$

and

$$\Sigma_{i0} = p_i\Sigma_i + \frac{1}{C}S_W = p_i\Sigma_i + \frac{1}{C}I. \tag{10}$$

In (8), S_{Mi} corresponds to Mahalanobis distance $d_{Mi} = (m_i - m_0)^T\Sigma_{i0}^{-1}(m_i - m_0)$, as $tr(S_{Mi}) = d_{Mi}$. $J_M(\Phi)$ is the new Mahalanobis criterion that we propose, and the heteroscedastic LDA algorithm based on this criterion is called M-HLDA.

The above discussion works under the assumption that $S_W = I$. If not, we can always perform a whitening transformation $y = S_W^{-1/2}x$ in the original feature space. After getting the optimal transformation Φ in the whitened feature space with the Mahalanobis criterion, we can transform back to the original feature space with an inverse transformation $x = S_W^{1/2}y$. The Mahalanobis criterion in the original feature space can be represented as

$$J_M(\Phi) = \sum_{i=1}^{C} p_i tr[(\Phi^T S_W^{1/2} S_W^{1/2}\Phi)^{-1}(\Phi^T S_W^{1/2} S_{Mi}' S_W^{1/2}\Phi)], \tag{11}$$

where S'_{Mi} is the DDM matrix in the whitened feature space. The M-HLDA solution finally devolves to finding the eigenvectors corresponding to the largest d eigenvalues of matrix $\sum_{i=1}^{C} p_i S_W^{-1} \times (S_W^{1/2} S'_{Mi} S_W^{1/2})$. In this way, we retain the simplicity of LDA solution, and only a generalized eigenvalue problem needs to be solved when calculating the optimal M-HLDA feature transformation matrix.

We have applied the proposed M-HLDA feature extraction algorithm to the HCL2000 handwritten Chinese character database [20], achieving a 10% drop in the misclassification rate over conventional LDA.

2.2 Discriminative Training on Parameters of Modified Quadratic Discriminant Function

In the compressed d-dimensional feature space, the MQDF distance for an unknown pattern x can be derived under the Gaussian distribution assumption:

$$h_i(x) = \frac{1}{\sigma^2}\{\|x - \mu_i\|^2 - \sum_{j=1}^{k}(1 - \frac{\sigma^2}{\lambda_{ij}})[\varphi_{ij}^T(x - \mu_i)]^2\} + \sum_{j=1}^{k}\log\lambda_{ij} + (d-k)\log\sigma^2. \tag{12}$$

$$i = 1, 2...C$$

And, the decision rule is

$$C(x) = \arg\min_i h_i(x). \tag{13}$$

In (12), μ_i and Σ_i denote the mean and covariance of class i, λ_{ij} and φ_{ij} denote the j-th eigenvalue (in descending order) and the corresponding eigenvector of Σ_i, $k(k<d)$ is the number of dominant principal axes, and σ^2 is a constant to compensate for the estimation error on small eigenvalues caused by the lack of training samples.

The parameters of MQDF classifier are estimated by the maximum likelihood (ML) method. ML estimation aims at fitting the assumed probabilistic model, but it is not necessarily optimum in terms of classification accuracy. Therefore, we use a minimum classification error (MCE) training scheme to adjust the MQDF parameters, which is originally proposed by Katagiri and Juang [26][27], and later introduced in the character recognition field to couple with different classifier forms [28][29][30].

To apply MCE training, we first reform the representation of MQDF distance as

$$h_i(x) = \sum_{j=1}^{d}(e^{-\tau_{ij}}\varphi_{ij}^T x - m_{ij})^2 + 2\sum_{j=1}^{d}\tau_{ij} + H, \tag{14}$$

where H is a discrimination irrelevant constant to ensure $h(x)>0$. Meanwhile, some necessary parameter transformations are implemented as

$$\tau_{ij} = \begin{cases} (\log\lambda_{ij})/2 & j \leq k \\ \log\sigma & j > k \end{cases}, \quad m_{ij} = e^{-\tau_{ij}}\varphi_{ij}^T\mu_i. \tag{15}$$

MQDF parameters can be denoted as $\Theta = \{\theta_i\} = \{m_{ij}, \tau_{ij}, \varphi_{ij}\}$ $i = 1, 2...C, j = 1, 2...d$.

Assume that x_n is a training pattern from class m, the misclassification measure on x_n is defined by

$$d(x_n,\Theta) = h_m(x_n,\theta_m) - \bar{h}_m(x_n,\Theta,\eta).\qquad(16)$$

The latter term on the right side of (16) collectively represents the MQDF distances of all the rival classes

$$\bar{h}_m(x_n,\Theta,\eta) = \left(\frac{1}{C-1}\sum_{i=1,i\neq m}^{C} h_i(x_n,\theta_i)^{-\eta}\right)^{-\frac{1}{\eta}}\quad(\eta>0)\qquad(17)$$

Embedding $d(x_n,\Theta)$ into a sigmoid function, we get a continuous loss function $s(x_n,\Theta)$ with respect to Θ,

$$s(x_n,\Theta) = \frac{1}{1+e^{-\gamma d(x_n,\Theta)}}\quad(\gamma>0).\qquad(18)$$

When η and γ approach infinity, $s(x_n,\Theta)$ becomes the simple 0-1 loss. The empirical loss on the entire training set $X=\{x_1, x_2, \dots x_N\}$ summarizes of the individual loss,

$$S(X,\Theta) = \sum_{n=1}^{N} s(x_n,\Theta).\qquad(19)$$

$S(X,\Theta)$ then minimizes using a generalized probability descent (GPD) algorithm[23]. The ML estimation is taken as the initial Θ, and gradually improved estimation can be obtained by an iterative scheme

$$\Theta_{t+1} = \Theta_t - \varepsilon_t \nabla s(x_t,\Theta_t).\qquad(20)$$

According to derivation rules,

$$\frac{\partial s(x_n,\Theta)}{\partial\theta_i} = \frac{\partial s(x_n,\Theta)}{\partial d(x_n,\Theta)}\frac{\partial d(x_n,\Theta)}{\partial h_i(x_n,\theta_i)}\frac{\partial h_i(x_n,\theta_i)}{\partial\theta_i},\qquad(21)$$

the three terms on right side of (21) are calculated as (22), (23), (24), respectively.

$$\frac{\partial s(x,\Theta)}{\partial d(x,\Theta)} = \gamma s(x_n,\Theta)(1-s(x_n,\Theta))\qquad(22)$$

$$\frac{\partial d(x_n,\Theta)}{\partial h_i(x_n,\theta_i)} = \begin{cases}\frac{1}{C-1}\left(\frac{\bar{h}_m(x_n,\Theta,\eta)}{h_i(x_n,\theta_i)}\right)^{\eta+1} & i\neq m\\ -1 & i=m\end{cases}\qquad(23)$$

$$\frac{\partial h_i(x_n,\theta_i)}{\partial m_{ij}} = -2\left(e^{-\tau_{ij}}\varphi_{ij}^T x - m_{ij}\right)$$

$$\frac{\partial h_i(x_n,\theta_i)}{\partial\tau_{ij}} = -2e^{-\tau_{ij}}\varphi_{ij}^T x\left(e^{-\tau_{ij}}\varphi_{ij}^T x - m_{ij}\right)+2\qquad(24)$$

Theoretically the eigenvectors φ_{ij} can also be optimized by the GPD algorithm, but it will take extra effort to retain the orthogonal and normal constraints. Therefore, only m_{ij}

and τ_{ij} are updated in our training procedure, and φ_{ij} is left unchanged. The learning rate ε_t in (20) is set as $\varepsilon_t = \varepsilon_0(1 - t/N)$, the initial learning rate ε_0, as well as the parameters η and γ in the classification loss function are all determined experimentally.

By using MCE training and other discrimination schemes, we have achieved excellent performance on Chinese character recognition [18]. On the ETL9B database, a 99.33% correct rate is achieved on the test set, while on the HCL2000 database a 99.56% correct rate is achieved on the test set.

3 Over-Segmentation

Given the extreme difficulty segmenting scripts into isolated characters without any prior knowledge, we adopt an over-segmentation and merging strategy in our script recognition algorithm.

The goal of over-segmentation aims to cut a script image into a radical sequence. Each extracted radical belongs to only one character, thus correct segmentation can be realized by selecting a proper merge path of radicals. Ordinary segmentation algorithms, such as projection histogram analysis and connected component analysis cannot work well when adjacent characters touch. Therefore, we attempt to extract the elemental units in the Chinese characters, i.e., strokes. Black pixel run-length analysis is implemented on the script image, run-lengths that are close and approximately in the same direction are tracked to form a stroke. Details of the stroke extraction algorithm can be found in [31][32].

Each stroke is contained within a rectangle called a bounding box. According to the extent of overlap between adjacent bounding boxes, we can iteratively merge strokes into radicals. The whole over-segmentation procedure is demonstrated in Fig. 4.

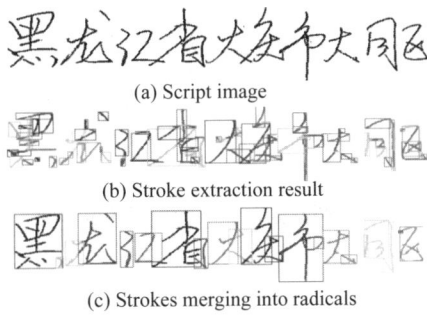

(a) Script image

(b) Stroke extraction result

(c) Strokes merging into radicals

Fig. 4. Over-segmentation procedure

4 Probabilistic Framework for Segmentation Model

After the radical sequence is extracted from the script image, each possible radical merging path then corresponds to a segmentation result, and produces a specific character image sequence. The segmentation then converts to an optimal merging path selection problem. Obviously, the geometrical layout has an important impact on deciding which path should be selected. The isolated character recognition as well as semantic information also influences the segmentation results. Therefore in our work, all these information are integrated in a probabilistic model.

Let E denote a radical sequence $(e_1, e_2,...,e_N)$ given by over-segmentation, S denote a path that merges $(e_1, e_2,...,e_N)$ into a character image sequence $(I_1, I_2,...,I_M)$ $(M \leq N)$, and O denotes an interpretation to recognize $(I_1, I_2,...,I_M)$ as $(c_1, c_2,...,c_M)$.

$$E = (e_1, e_2,..., e_N),$$
$$S = (I_1, I_2,..., I_M),$$
$$O = (c_1, c_2,..., c_M).$$

(25)

After over-segmentation, we must find the optimal segmentation and interpretation (S^*, O^*), given the radical serial E, according to the maximum a posterior (MAP) criterion.

$$(S^*, O^*) = \arg\max_{S,O} P\{S, O \mid E\}.$$

(26)

Following the Bayesian formula,

$$P\{S, O \mid E\} = P\{S \mid E\}P\{O \mid E, S\} = P\{S \mid E\}P\{O \mid S\}.$$

(27)

In the above equation, the item $P(S|E)$ appears as a geometrical layout confidence, and the item $P(O|S)$ appears as a string recognition confidence. We discuss the detailed representation of these two confidences, respectively.

4.1 Geometrical Layout Confidence

The geometrical layout confidence measures the probability of a certain combination of radical series purely using geometrical shape analysis. This confidence does not associate to the character recognition results and semantic information.

In our algorithm, the following three kinds of geometrical feature are evaluated (Fig. 5):

1) Distances between the centers of adjacent character images, which are denoted by d_i, $i=1,2,...M-1$,
2) Widths of each character image, which are denoted by w_i, $i=1,2,...,M$, and
3) Ratios of the height and width of each character image, denoted as $r_i=h_i/w_i$, $i=1,2,...,M$.

Other geometrical features can also be considered [12], but we use only the above three features. Treating these features as random variables and assume they are independently Gaussian distributed, we can estimate the mean and covariance of each feature by the maximum likelihood method on a training set. Given that writing styles of scripts vary significantly, the estimated parameters usually are not stable even with certain normalizations. So we directly compute the mean and variance inside each particular script image, adapting to the writing style, to a certain extent.

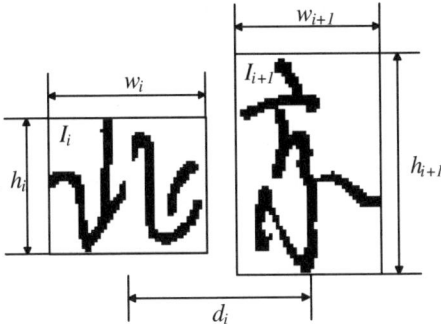

Fig. 5. Geometrical features extracted from the character image sequence

The joint probabilities of distance, width, and ratio variables are calculated respectively as

$$P(d_1, d_2, ... d_{M-1}) = \prod_{i=1}^{M-1} \frac{1}{\sqrt{2\pi}\sigma_d} \exp\{-\frac{(d_i - \mu_d)^2}{2\sigma_d^2}\}, \tag{28}$$

$$P(w_1, w_2, ... w_M) = \prod_{i=1}^{M} \frac{1}{\sqrt{2\pi}\sigma_w} \exp\{-\frac{(w_i - \mu_w)^2}{2\sigma_w^2}\}, \tag{29}$$

$$P(r_1, r_2, ... r_M) = \prod_{i=1}^{M} \frac{1}{\sqrt{2\pi}\sigma_r} \exp\{-\frac{(r_i - \mu_r)^2}{2\sigma_r^2}\}. \tag{30}$$

Thus, the geometrical layout confidence of the radical merging path S could be defined as,

$$P(S \mid E) = P(I_1, ... I_M \mid e_1, ... e_N) \propto P(d_1, d_2, ... d_{M-1}) P(w_1, w_2, ... w_M) P(r_1, r_2, ... r_M). \tag{31}$$

4.2 Character String Recognition Confidence

Having decided the segmentation path S radicals can merge into character images accordingly, and recognized by the isolated character classifier. For each input character image, the classifier outputs K candidates, together with the corresponding distances in increasing order. Misclassification often happens, so the first candidate is not assured to be correct. The next step involves selecting a best character string interpretation from the candidate sets.

In the unconstrained or open vocabulary situation, the N-gram model is often used, which has been introduced to natural language processing for a long time and widely used in speech recognition and OCR post-processing [11].

According to Bayesian rule,

$$P(O \mid S) = P(c_1, ... c_M \mid I_1, ... I_M) = \frac{P(I_1, I_2, ... I_M \mid c_1, c_2, ... c_M) P(c_1, c_2, ... c_M)}{P(I_1, I_2, ... I_M)}. \tag{32}$$

If we consider only the transition probability between two adjacent characters, the N-gram model becomes Bi-gram, thus we have

$$P(c_1, c_2, ... c_M) = P(c_1) \times \prod_{i=1}^{M-1} P(c_{i+1} \mid c_i). \tag{33}$$

The recognition results for different character images are independent, so we can derive

$$P(I_1, I_2, ... I_M \mid c_1, c_2, ... c_M) = \prod_{i=1}^{M} P(I_i \mid c_i) = \prod_{i=1}^{M} \frac{P(I_i)}{P(c_i)} \prod_{i=1}^{M} P(c_i \mid I_i). \tag{34}$$

$P(c_i)$ is a prior probability, which can be assumed equal for each class, $P(I_i)$ can also be treated as a constant under a fixed segmentation path.

$P(c_i|I_i)$ is the confidence for recognizing image I_i as c_i, which can be calculated by the output distances of the isolated character recognizer [33] as follows,

$$P(c_i \mid I_i) = \frac{\exp(-d_{k(c_i)} / \theta)}{\sum\limits_{k=1}^{K} \exp(-d_k / \theta)}, \tag{35}$$

where d_k is the character recognition distance of the kth candidate, and $k(c_i)$ denotes the candidate position of c_i in the classifier outputs. θ is an estimated variance.

4.3 Optimization Method

Taking a logarithm operation on (25),

$$(S^*, O^*) = \arg\max_{S, O} \log P\{S, O \mid E\} = \arg\max_{S, O} \{ \log P\{S \mid E\} + \log P\{O \mid S\} \}. \tag{36}$$

Optimizing the objective function directly could be computationally too expensive, so we exploit a three-step approximate optimization scheme.

1) In the first step, only the first part of the objective function, i.e., the geometrical layout confidence $\log P(S|E)$, is maximized. Using a dynamic programming algorithm, we can get L candidate segmentation paths $S_1, S_2 ... S_L$ ($L=100\sim200$), which have the largest L layout confidences $\log P(S_l|E)$, $l=1,2,...L$. Other segmentation paths are considered unlikely and eliminated.

2) In the second step, the recognition confidence $\log P(O|S)$ is maximized, given a fixed segmentation path S_l.

$$O_l^* = \arg\max_{O} \log P(O \mid S_l), l = 1, 2 ... L. \tag{37}$$

A HMM model formulizes this procedure. Character images $I_1, I_2, ... I_M$ correspond to the observations in the HMM model, while the inherent classes $c_1, c_2, ..., c_M$ correspond to the states in the HMM model. The initial probabilistic distribution of states $\pi = \{\pi_i\}, 1 \le i \le C$, and the transition probabilities between adjacent states $A^1 = \{a^1_{ij}\}, 1 \le i, j \le C$, can both be estimated from the training data. The conditional probability matrix $B = \{P(I|c)\}$, which represents the occurrence of observation image I given state c can be calculated from the isolated character recognizer's outputs.

Neglecting the subscript l in (37), the optimal class interpretation $(c_1^*, c_2^*, \ldots, c_M^*)$, given a character image sequence $(I_1, I_2, \ldots I_M)$, can be found by a Viterbi searching algorithm.

$$
\begin{aligned}
(c_1^*, c_2^*, \ldots c_M^*) &= \arg\max_{c_1, c_2, \ldots c_M} P(c_1, c_2, \ldots c_M \mid I_1, I_2, \ldots I_M) \\
&= \arg\max_{c_1, c_2, \ldots c_M} P(c_1) \times \prod_{i=1}^{M-1} P(c_{i+1} \mid c_i) \prod_{i=1}^{M} P(c_i \mid I_i).
\end{aligned}
\tag{38}
$$

3) Finally, the optimal segmentation path, as well as the class interpretation (S^*, O^*), is obtained by,

$$
(S^*, O^*) = \arg\max_{1 \le l \le L} \left\{ \log P(S_l \mid E) + \log P(O_l^* \mid S_l) \right\}.
\tag{39}
$$

5 Applications

The handwritten Chinese script recognition algorithm discussed above has a wide range of applications. We investigate two typical applications, postal address reading and legal amount recognition on bank check.

5.1 Postal Address Reading

Automatic mail sorting machines have been used in China for years. However, these machines are only recognizes postcodes on the envelope, and postcodes cannot provide detailed address information, and sometimes they are incorrectly written by the mail senders or even missing. Therefore, to provide a higher grade of postal automation and better delivery service, the Chinese address scripts on the envelope should also be recognized.

We extracted address scripts on 946 real envelopes from a Beijing postal office and tested the recognition algorithm on them. The Bi-gram model is trained using a lexicon (reference database) containing over 100,000 Beijing address items. As shown in Table 1, the total address recognition accuracy on character level is 87.2%, with errors originating in two sources, isolated character recognition error (3.1%) and

Table 1. Postal address recognition performance

Address item sample number	946
Total character number	12,891
Segmentation error rate	9.7%
Isolated character recognition error rate	3.1%
Address recognition rate (character level)	87.2%
Address recognition rate (lexicon matching)	>80%

segmentation error (9.7%). For address interpretation, script recognition is not the last step, the lexicon is employed again to match with the recognition result, which can further reduce errors. In our experiment, the matching accuracies of various types of address are all more than 80% [35]. Further research aiming at better utilizing the lexicon in segmentation and recognition procedure continues [40].

Fig. 6 illustrates the selection of segmentation path, as well as the character recognition candidates. The result represented by Fig. 6-a corresponds to a higher probability than all other alternatives, for example, the one represented by Fig. 6-b. Therefore, it is accepted as the final address segmentation and interpretation result.

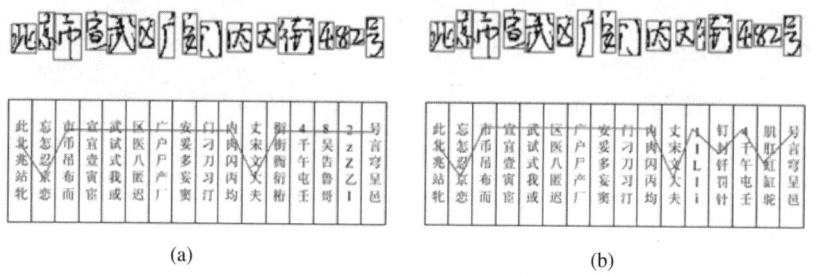

(a)
(b)

Fig. 6. Example of two different segmentation path and candidate selection results. (a) path1 (b) path2

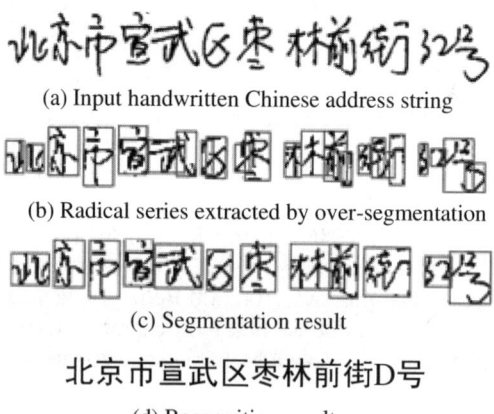

(a) Input handwritten Chinese address string

(b) Radical series extracted by over-segmentation

(c) Segmentation result

北京市宣武区枣林前街D号

(d) Recognition result

Fig. 7. Some errors in address recognition

Some incorrect segmentation and recognition postal address samples appear in Fig.7. The numerals in address scripts often can cause trouble in segmentation, since their geometrical features are quite inconsistent with the surrounding Chinese characters. This problem will be further investigated.

5.2 Legal Amount Reading on Bank Check

On a bank check image, usually two kinds of amount exist: courtesy and legal (Fig. 8). A good check reading system should be able to use their redundancy. We aim to recognize legal amounts using the proposed script recognition algorithm and cross-validate the results with the recognition results of courtesy amounts, thus efficiently reducing the check recognition errors.

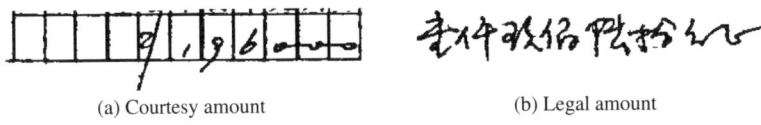

(a) Courtesy amount   (b) Legal amount

Fig. 8. Example of courtesy amount and legal amount on Chinese bank check

Compared with postal address reading, in check reading we need to operate with a much smaller lexicon, which is favorable for recognition. The Chinese characters appearing in legal amounts can be categorized into three types: numerals (e.g. '壹'), units (e.g. '万') and termination tags ('正' or '整'). The transition between these characters should satisfy certain constraints: the amount must start with a numerical character and end with a termination tag, unit characters in one amount item must appear in descending order, etc. The major transition rules between characters in legal amounts can be illustrated by Fig. 9. These constraints can actually help in learning the Bi-gram model, since we cannot acquire a large amount of check samples for training use.

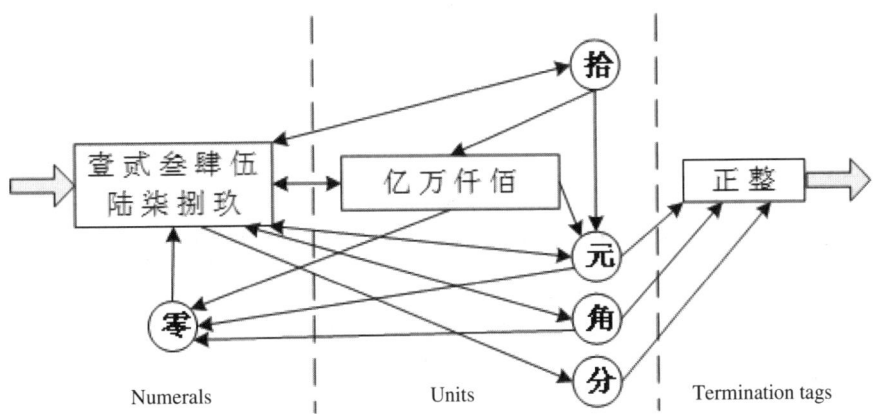

Fig. 9. Transition rules for characters in legal amount

Fig.10 illustrates an example of the candidate selection procedure by an HMM model. The correct legal amount should be '壹万陆仟元正', given the first candidate sequence output by the isolated character recognizer is '壹万陆伍元正', the recognition error is corrected after using the semantic information.

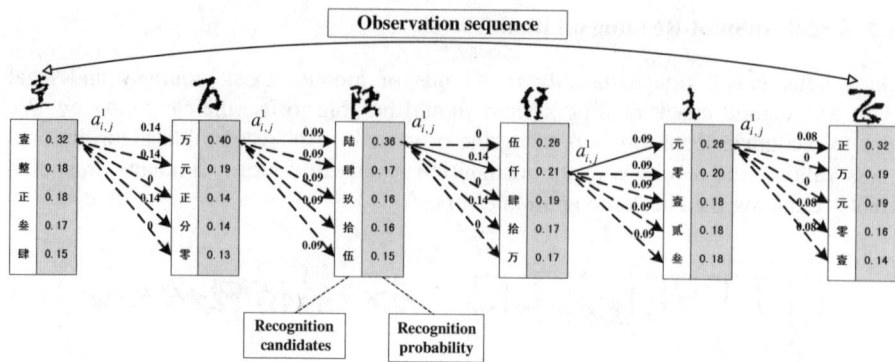

Fig. 10. Candidates selection by an HMM model in legal amount recognition

If the probability of the final selected path appears lower than a pre-defined threshold, we consider the result unreliable and reject it. Usually rejection happens when the scanning quality of check image is too low or when the handwriting is too cursive (Fig. 11).

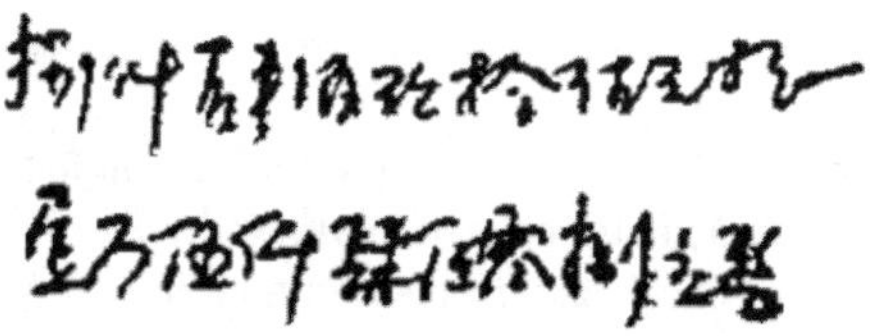

Fig. 11. Examples of rejected legal amount

We collected 2,053 real bank check image samples for our recognition experiments, all of which contain both courtesy and legal amounts. One thousand images are training samples, used for the isolated character recognizer, establishing the semantic model. The other 1,053 sample are used for testing.

Three check amount recognition algorithms are compared, namely a courtesy amount recognition (CAR) method, a legal amount recognition (LAR) method proposed in this paper, and a fusion algorithm utilizing both CAR and LAR results. The performance of the three algorithms is listed in Table 2. It can be observed that, after combing extra legal amount recognition result in CAR, substantially lower rejection and higher recognition rates are achieved with an approximately equal error rate, so the whole recognition reliability of check amounts is largely improved.

Table 2. Check recognition performance comparison of different algorithms

Algorithm	Recognition Rate	Rejection Rate	Error Rate
CAR	45.59%	54.13%	0.28%
LAR	29.06%	70.75%	0.19%
Fusion	66.10%	33.62%	0.28%

6 Arabic Script Recognition

Given the increasing interaction between the western and Arabic cultures, research on Arabic OCR has received increasingly more attention in recent years. Arabic script has its unique characteristics, and is hard to directly implement the same recognition scheme directly as in Chinese script recognition. Several most prominent features closely relevant to Arabic script recognition are listed, as follows:

1) Arabic alphabets have 28 basic characters, most of which have four different forms depending on their positions in a word.

2) Arabic script is very cursive. Characters in a word usually connect along a base-line, which brings crucial challenges to designing the segmentation algorithm (Fig. 12)

3) Many Arabic characters have sub (secondary) parts, positioned either above or below the main parts of characters (Fig. 12). The relative positions between them vary greatly. These 'parts' are named graphemes in Arabic script.

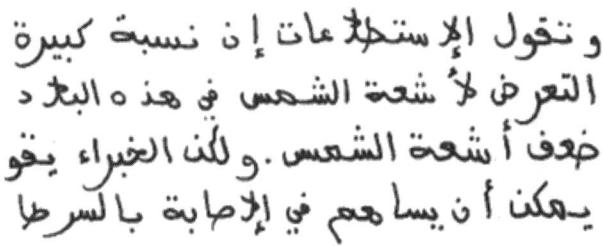

Fig. 12. Typical Arabic script samples

Considering these characteristics, in the recognition procedure of isolated Arabic character, we actually attempt to recognize graphemes instead of the integer characters. The main part of basic Arabic characters consists of 16 forms: ط, ع, ١, ح, د, ر, س, ى, و, ه, ن, م, ل, ل, ة, ب; the upper subparts consist of four forms: • (1-dot), •• (2-dot), •• (3-dot) and ٵ (hazma); and the lower subparts have two forms: • and ••. If the class label of an Arabic character image I is c, and the main part I^c, upper subpart I^u and lower subpart I^d can be labeled by c^c, c^u, and c^d, respectively, thus $I=(I^c, I^u, I^d)$, $c=(c^c, c^u, c^d)$. Notice, in many cases, the subparts can be a null image, i.e. $c^u=\varnothing$ or $c^d=\varnothing$.

For the correct segmentation, we must find the corresponding associations between the sub and main parts. Most past work just attribute the subparts to their nearest main parts [36][37], assuming the correct cutting columns on main parts can also cut subparts correctly. However, this simple strategy may fail when dealing with the script, as shown in Fig. 13. To solve this problem, we proposed a novel 3-queue segmentation model in [38], which considers all the possible combination of subparts and main parts when generating the segmentation path.

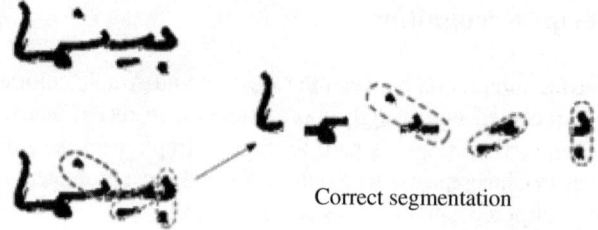

Correct segmentation

Fig. 13. An Arabic script example that subparts cannot associate with its nearest main part

As illustrated in Fig.14, we find the main connected component in the script image (Fig. 14-a), was which the baseline can be extracted by the Hough transform (Fig. 14-b). Then a contour analysis operates on the Arab script, and a series of candidate cutting points found if they satisfy one of the following descriptions:

1) Local bottom points on top contour (Fig. 14-c),
2) Points on top (bottom) contour that have a distance to the contour on the other side smaller than a preset threshold (e.g. average stroke width) (Fig. 14-d),
3) Intersection points of top contour and baseline (Fig. 14-e).

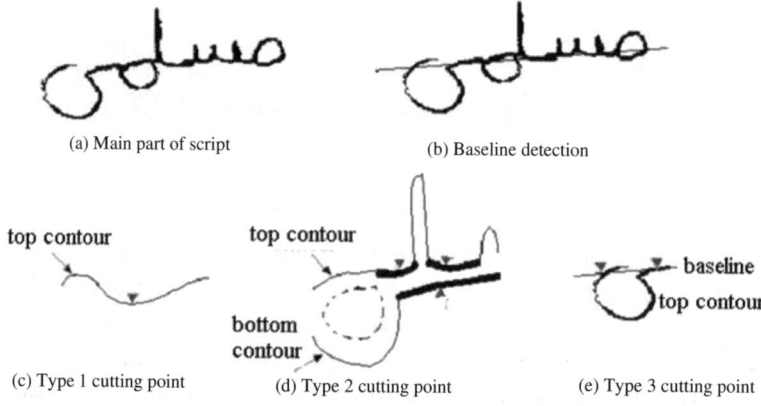

(a) Main part of script

(b) Baseline detection

top contour

top contour

bottom
contour

baseline

top contour

(c) Type 1 cutting point

(d) Type 2 cutting point

(e) Type 3 cutting point

Fig. 14. Candidate cutting point detection on Arabic script

Two adjacent candidate cutting points should have at least a certain distance between them; therefore, some redundant candidate cutting points can be filtered.

According to these candidate cutting points, the main part of Arabic script is over-segmented into a sequence of graphemes, as illustrated in Fig. 15-b. If we further consider the sequence of the upper parts and lower parts, the whole script can be represented by a 3-queue grapheme sequence (Fig. 15-c). Denote the sequences of main parts, upper and lower subparts as $(e_1,e_2,...,e_{Nc})$, $(e_1^u, e_2^u,...e_{Nu}^u)$ and $(e_1^d, e_2^d,...,e_{Nd}^d)$, respectively, all in the left-to-right order. N_c, N_u and N_d are the numbers of graphemes in these three queues.

Assume the 3-queue grapheme sequence should merge into a M character image sequence $(I_1, I_2, \ldots I_M)$ (Fig. 15-c), the corresponding segmentation path can be visualized in a 3-D space (Fig. 15-e). $X = \{x_0, x_1, \ldots x_M\}$ is a sequence of 3-dimensonal integer vectors, which indicates the cutting position. The start position $x_0 = \{0,0,0\}$ and the end position $x_M = \{N_c, N_u, N_d\}$.

The recognition of geometrical layout confidence for Arabic script closely initiates the cases of Chinese script in Section 4.1. However, the semantic information is not used in the probabilistic segmentation model for Arabic script because of the lack of training samples.

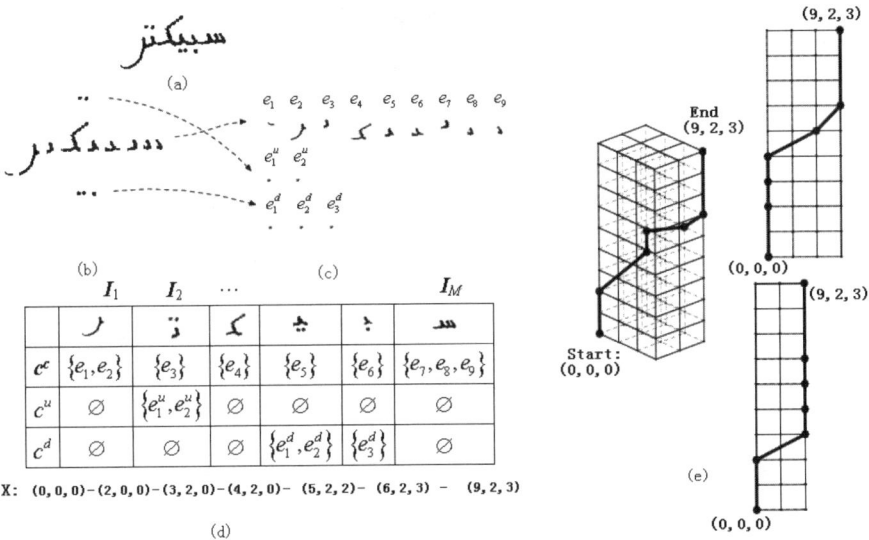

X: (0,0,0)−(2,0,0)−(3,2,0)−(4,2,0)− (5,2,2)− (6,2,3) − (9,2,3)

(d)

Fig. 15. Example of the cutting mechanism of the 3-queue segmentation model. (a)Arabic script (b) Over-segmentation result (c) 3-queue grapheme sequence (d) Characters merged by the graphemes (e) Segmentation path displayed in a 3-D space.

Given a character image sequence $(I_1, I_2, \ldots I_M)$, the optimal class interpretation $(c_1^*, c_2^*, \ldots, c_M^*)$ can be obtained by

$$(c_1^*, c_2^*, \ldots c_M^*) = \arg\max_{c_1, c_2, \ldots c_M} P(c_1, c_2, \ldots c_M \mid I_1, I_2, \ldots I_M) = \arg\max_{c_1, c_2, \ldots c_M} \prod_{i=1}^{M} P(c_i \mid I_i)$$

$$= \arg\max_{(c_i^c, c_i^u, c_i^d)_{i=1..M}} \prod_{i=1}^{M} I(c_i \mid c_i^c, c_i^u, c_i^d) P(c_i^c \mid I_i^c) P(c_i^u \mid I_i^u) P(c_i^d \mid I_i^d). \tag{40}$$

In (40), items $P(c_i^c|I_i^c)$, $P(c_i^u|I_i^u)$ and $P(c_i^d|I_i^d)$ can be calculated from the distance outputs of the isolated grapheme recognizer, given the item $I(c_i|c_i^c, c_i^u, c_i^d)$ is a variable with value {0 or 1} reflecting logical constraint. If graphemes c_i^c, c_i^u, c_i^d can be combined into a legal Arabic character c_i, we set $I(c_i|c_i^c, c_i^u, c_i^d)=1$, otherwise $I(c_i|c_i^c, c_i^u, c_i^d)=0$. Given 16, 5 and 3 kinds of grapheme for main part, upper part and lower part, respectively, the number of possible combination cases is 16×5×3=240.

However, only 28 valid Arabic Alphabet exist, this indicates that logical constraint plays an important role in selecting the optimal segmentation path.

The Arabic script recognition algorithm is evaluated on a handwritten Arabic text database containing 20,000 characters. Half the samples are segmented and labeled manually to train the isolated grapheme recognizer, and the other half remains for testing. These testing samples are divided into five subsets $S_1, S_2,..., S_5$ according to different writing styles, as illustrated in Fig.16, each subset contains approximately 2,000 characters. We compare the recognition performance of our recognition algorithm with another method presented in [39], which uses the same testing data, but simply associates the subparts with the nearest main parts in segmentation. The comparison result is shown in Table 3, the average recognition rate on the test sets using our algorithm is 59.2%, while in [39] attains only a 41.3% recognition rate. This result indicates the virtue of the proposed 3-queue segmentation model.

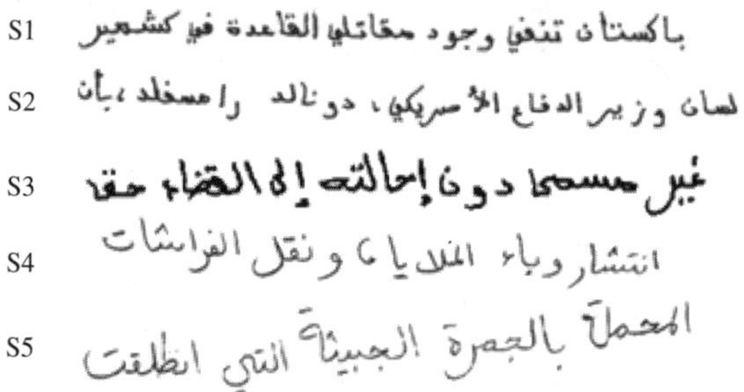

S1   باكستان تنفي وجود معاتلي القاعدة في كشمير

S2   لسان وزير الدفاع الأمريكي، دونالد رامسفلد ،بأن

S3   غير مسمى دون إحالته إلى القضاء حتى

S4   انتشار وباء الملاريا، ونقل الفراشات

S5   المحملة بالجمرة الجبينة التي انطلقت

Fig. 16. Arabic script samples of different writing styles

Table 3. Performance comparison on Arabic script recognition accuracy (%)

	S1	S2	S3	S4	S5	Average
Proposed method	69.0	59.4	57.7	54.9	54.9	59.2
Method in [39]	43.1	44.1	46.5	34.6	38.2	41.3

7 Conclusions and Future Work

In this paper, we present a segmentation-driven offline handwritten script recognition framework. Feature extraction algorithm based on heteroscedastic linear discriminant analysis is proposed, and the classifier optimization method by minimum classification error learning is applied to improve isolated character recognition accuracy. To obtain the optimal segmentation and interpretation of script, a probabilistic framework is established to integrate information from three sources: geometrical layout, character recognition confidence, and semantic model. Experimental results on multiple applications, including Chinese postal address reading, bank check recognition, and Arabic text reading, have demonstrated the effectiveness of our algorithms.

Much work still remains to be done to further improve handwritten script recognition accuracy. The efficient utilization of the domain knowledge in specific applications presents one important concern. Arabic script recognition accuracy remains low and needs major improvements for practical use. Given the lack of Arabic training samples, we have not been able to use semantic information in our Arabic script recognition algorithm, which should be further investigated in the future.

Acknowledgment

The authors would like to thank Qiang Fu, Yan Jiang, Pingping Xiu and Junxia Gu for their valuable contributions to this paper. Financial support by National Natural Science Foundation of China (project 60472002) is gratefully acknowledged. The postal address reading project is also funded by Siemens AG under contract number 20030829 - 24022SI202.

References

1. Senior, A.W., Robinson, A.J.: An off-line cursive handwriting recognition system. IEEE Trans. PAMI 20(3), 309–321 (1998)
2. Arica, N., Yarman, V.F.T.: An overview of character recognition focused on off-line handwriting. IEEE Trans. on Systems, Man, and Cybernetics—Part C: Applications and Reviews 31(2), 216–233 (2001)
3. Koerich, A.L., Sabourin, R., Suen, C.Y.: Large vocabulary off-line handwriting recognition: A survey. Pattern Analysis and Applications 6(2), 97–121 (2003)
4. Bunke, H.: Recognition of cursive Roman handwriting - past, present and future. In: Proc. of 7th International Conference on Document Analysis and Recognition, pp. 448–459 (2003)
5. Casey, R.G., Lecolinet, E.: A survey of methods and strategies in character segmentation. IEEE Trans. PAMI 18(7), 690–706 (1996)
6. Lu, Y., Shridhar, M.: Character segmentation in handwritten words - An overview. Pattern Recognition 29(1), 77–96 (1996)
7. Tseng, L.Y., Chen, R.C.: Segmenting handwritten Chinese characters based on heuristic merging of stroke bounding boxes and dynamic programming. Pattern Recognition Letters 19(8), 963–973 (1998)
8. Tseng, Y.H., Lee, H.J.: Recognition-based handwritten Chinese character segmentation using a probabilistic viterbi algorithm. Pattern Recognition Letters 20(8), 791–806 (1999)
9. Gao, J., Ding, X.Q., Wu, Y.S.: A segmentation algorithm for handwritten Chinese character recognition. In: Proc. of 5th International Conference on Document Analysis and Recognition, pp. 633–636 (1999)
10. Zhao, S.Y., Chi, Z.R., Shi, P.F., Yan, H.: Two-stage segmentation of unconstrained handwritten Chinese characters. Pattern Recognition 36(1), 145–156 (2003)
11. Li, Y.X., Ding, X.Q., Tan, C.L., Liu, C.S.: Contextual post-processing based on the confusion matrix in offline handwritten Chinese script recognition. Pattern Recognition 37(9), 1901–1912 (2004)
12. Xue, J.L., Ding, X.Q.: Location and interpretation of destination addresses on handwritten Chinese envelopes. Pattern Recognition Letters 22(6), 639–656 (2001)

13. Yu, M.L., Kwok, P.C.K., Leung, C.H., et al.: Segmentation and recognition of Chinese bank check amounts. International Journal on Document Analysis and Recognition 3(4), 207–217 (2001)

14. Liu, C.L., Koga, M., Fujisawa, H.: Lexicon-driven segmentation and recognition of handwritten character strings for Japanese address reading. IEEE Trans. PAMI 24(11), 1425–1437 (2002)

15. Lu, Y., Tan, C.L., Shi, P.F., Zhang, K.H.: Segmentation of handwritten Chinese characters from destination addresses of mail pieces. International Journal of Pattern Recognition and Artificial Intelligence 16(1), 85–96 (2002)

16. Tang, H.S., Augustin, E., Suen, C.Y., et al.: Recognition of unconstrained legal amounts handwritten on Chinese bank check. In: Proc. of 17th International Conference on Pattern Recognition, pp. 610–613 (2004)

17. Plamandon, R., Srihari, S.N.: Online and offline handwriting recognition: A comprehensive survey. IEEE Trans. PAMI 22(1), 63–84 (2000)

18. Suen, C.Y., Mori, S., Kim, S.H., Leung, C.H.: Analysis and recognition of Asian scripts - the state of the art. In: Proc. of 7th International Conference on Document Analysis and Recognition, pp. 866–878 (2003)

19. Yamada, H., Yamamoto, K., Saito, T.: A nonlinear normalization method for handprinted Kanji character recognition – line density equalization. Pattern Recognition 23(9), 1023–1029 (1990)

20. Liu, C.L., Nakashima, K., Sako, H., Fujisawa, H.: Handwritten digit recognition: investigation of normalization and feature extraction techniques. Pattern Recognition 37(2), 265–279 (2004)

21. Liu, H.L., Ding, X.Q.: Handwritten character recognition using gradient feature and quadratic classifier with multiple discrimination schemes. In: Proc. of 8th International Conference on Document Analysis and Recognition, pp. 19–25 (2005)

22. Kimura, F., Takashina, K., Tsuruoka, S., Miyake, Y.: Modified quadratic discriminant functions and its application to Chinese character recognition. IEEE Trans. PAMI 9(1), 149–153 (1987)

23. Liu, H.L., Ding, X.Q.: Improve handwritten character recognition performance by Heteroscedastic linear discriminant analysis. In: Proc. of 18th International Conference on Pattern Recognition, vol. 1, pp. 880–883 (2006)

24. Loog, M., Duin, R.P.W., Haeb-Umbach, R.: Multiclass linear dimension reduction by weighted pairwise fisher criteria. IEEE Trans. PAMI 23(7), 762–766 (2001)

25. Loog, M., Duin, R.P.W.: Linear dimensionality reduction via a heteroscedastic extension of LDA: the Chernoff criterion. IEEE Trans. PAMI 26(6), 732–739 (2004)

26. Juang, B.H., Katagiri, S.: Discriminative learning for minimum error classification. IEEE Trans. on Signal Processing 40(12), 3043–3054 (1992)

27. Katagiri, S., Juang, B.H., Lee, C.H.: Pattern recognition using a family of design algorithms based upon the generalized probability descent method. Proceedings of the IEEE 86(11), 2345–2373 (1998)

28. Watanabe, H., Katagiri, S.: Subspace method for minimum error pattern recognition. IEICE Trans. on Information and System E80-D(12), 1095–1104 (1997)

29. Zhang, R., Ding, X.Q., Zhang, J.Y.: Offline handwritten character recognition based on discriminative training of orthogonal Gaussian mixture model. In: Proc. of 6th International Conference on Document Analysis and Recognition, pp. 221–225 (2001)

30. Liu, C.L., Sako, H., Fujisawa, H.: Discriminative learning quadratic discriminant function for handwriting recognition. IEEE Trans. on Neural Networks 15(2), 430–444 (2004)

31. Tseng, L.Y., Chuang, C.T.: An efficient knowledge based stoke extraction method for multi-font Chinese characters. Pattern Recognition 25(12), 1445–1458 (1992)
32. Wang, R., Ding, X.Q., Liu, C.S.: Handwritten Chinese address segmentation and recog- nition based on merging strokes. Journal of Tsinghua Univ (Sci & Tech) 44(4), 498–502 (2004)
33. Liu, C.L., Nakagawa, M.: Precise candidate selection for large character set recognition by confidence evaluation. IEEE Trans. PAMI 22(6), 636–642 (2000)
34. Fu, Q., Ding, X.Q., Liu, C.S., Jiang, Y., Ren, Z.: A Hiddern Markov Model based segmen- tation and recognition algorithm for Chinese handwritten address character strings. In: Proc. of 8th International Conference on Document Analysis and Recognition, pp. 590– 594 (2005)
35. Jiang, Y., Ding, X.Q., Fu, Q., Ren, Z.: Application of Bi-gram driven Chinese handwritten character segmentation for an address reading system. In: 7th International Workshop on Document Analysis Systems, pp. 220–231 (2006)
36. Olivier, C., Miled, H., et al.: Segmentation and coding of Arabic handwritten words. In: Proc. of 13th International Conference on Pattern Recognition, pp. 264–268 (1996)
37. Cheung, A., Bennamoun, M., Bergmann, N.W.: An Arabic optical character recognition system using recognition-based segmentation. Pattern Recognition 34(2), 215–233 (2001)
38. Xiu, P.P., Peng, L.R., Ding, X.Q., Wang, H.: Offline handwritten Arabic character seg- mentation with probabilistic model. In: Proc. of 7th International Workshop on Document Analysis Systems, pp. 402–412 (2006)
39. Jin, J.M., Wang, H., Ding, X.Q., Peng, L.R.: Printed Arabic document recognition system. In: Latecki, L.J., Mount, D.M., Wu, A.Y. (eds.) Vision Geometry XIII. Proceedings of the SPIE 5676, pp. 48–55 (2004)
40. Jiang, Y., Ding, X.Q., Ren, Z.: Substring alignment method for lexicon based handwritten Chinese string recognition and its application to address line recognition. In: Proc. of 18th International Conference on Pattern Recognition, vol. 2, pp. 683–686 (2006)

Multi-character Field Recognition for Arabic and Chinese Handwriting

Daniel Lopresti[1], George Nagy[2], Sharad Seth[3], and Xiaoli Zhang[2]

[1] Lehigh University, Bethlehem, PA 18015, USA
lopresti@cse.lehigh.edu
[2] Rensselaer Polytechnic Institute, Troy, NY 12180, USA
{nagy,zhangxl}@ecse.rpi.edu
[3] University of Nebraska, Lincoln, NE 68588, USA
seth@cse.unl.edu

Abstract. Two methods, Symbolic Indirect Correlation (SIC) and Style Constrained Classification (SCC), are proposed for recognizing handwritten Arabic and Chinese words and phrases. SIC reassembles variable-length segments of an unknown query that match similar segments of labeled reference words. Recognition is based on the correspondence between the order of the feature vectors and of the lexical transcript in both the query and the references. SIC implicitly incorporates language context in the form of letter n-grams. SCC is based on the notion that the style (distortion or noise) of a character is a good predictor of the distortions arising in other characters, even of a different class, from the same source. It is adaptive in the sense that, with a long-enough field, its accuracy converges to that of a style-specific classifier trained on the writer of the unknown query. Neither SIC nor SCC requires the query words to appear among the references.

1 Introduction

From the perspective of character recognition, Arabic and Chinese are situated at the opposite ends of the spectrum. The former has a small alphabet with word-position dependent allographs, is quasi-cursive, and has diacritics, ascenders, and descenders. The latter has an indefinitely large number of classes (of which only the first $\sim 20,000$ have been coded), essentially word-level symbols (many with a radical-based substructure), and fixed-pitch block characters. Arabic strokes can be approximated by arcs of circles, while most Chinese strokes are straight, with a $\sim 1:7$ range in width (like brush strokes), and a flourish at the end. Unlike Arabic, Chinese does not have deliberate loops.

They also exhibit some commonalities. Both have been incorporated in the scripts used by other languages: Arabic in Urdu and Persian, Han in Japanese and Hangul, among many others. Both have traditional roots and forms dating back several thousand years, preserved in a large body of classical manuscripts, and have undergone considerable and diverse modifications in each host language and region of the world. Nevertheless, both scripts have preserved sufficient

D.S. Doermann and S. Jaeger (Eds.): SACH 2006, LNCS 4768, pp. 218–230, 2008.

uniformity to link cultures that can no longer understand each other's speech. Their classical forms are prized and cultivated in calligraphy, which combines visual and language arts. Neither script has upper and lower case.

Industrial-strength Arabic and Chinese OCR products must also be able to recognize Latin characters, "Arabic" (Indian) numerals, and Western punctuation. This introduces additional complexity, more because of the need to handle diverse, intermingled reading orders and output codes than because of the increased number of classes.

Many thousands of papers (the very first of which, coincidentally, is [1]) have been written on Chinese character recognition. By the time of our first survey [2] much of the research was appearing in Chinese and Japanese publications. In our second survey [3], we found little new research in the West. Recent research collaboration with Professor C-L Liu at the Pattern Recognition Laboratory of the Chinese Academy of Science (CASIA), visits with Professor X. Ding at Tsinghua University, and a tour of Hanwang High Technology in Beijing acquainted us with the largest concentrations of character research activity in the world and some of China's thriving OCR industry.

Research on Arabic character recognition (actually Farsi) began in the late sixties. Scattered projects, mainly by speakers of Arabic in the West, increased until the turn of the millennium, when research began to grow exponentially. Nearly one thousand reports have already been published, mostly in English and French. Nevertheless, work on Arabic OCR lags far behind Chinese OCR because of the lack of monolithic government and market support, and of large, publicly available databases. For a recent survey of the state-of-the-art in offline Arabic handwriting recognition, please see [4].

Extrapolating successful methods from Western (including Russian) OCR is insufficient for either Arabic or Chinese because, ideally, every glyph of an entire document must be considered simultaneously before a label is assigned to any one of them. In practice, this notion translates to field classification, where glyphs that are difficult to recognize in isolation (or that cannot be isolated/segmented) are recognized in conjunction with several others.

Given the wide range of different problems exhibited by the two scripts, tackling both simultaneously is a strategy for research that can bring benefits not only to character recognition on other scripts (such as those derived from Sanskrit), but also to the wider field of pattern recognition. It will foster the development of large vocabulary classifiers that span complex character shapes (Chinese) and complex word shapes (Arabic). Below, we outline how we propose to apply field classifiers, which have already proven successful on easier tasks, to Arabic and Chinese documents.

We elaborate on two orthogonal ideas: Symbolic Indirect Correlation (SIC) and Style Constrained Classification (SCC). The former recognizes unknown sequences of features (possibly spanning several characters) by finding and reassembling its constituent subsequences in the feature sequence representation of labeled reference text. The unknown word(s) need not be represented in the reference set, only their lexical constituents (i.e., symbol polygrams). Style-based classification, on the other hand, has been applied to distorted-but-segmented patterns. It maximizes the posterior probability of the field feature vector of same-source words or phrases given the transcript, under the constraint of source or style specific statistical dependence between all the features of the field.

As is customary in many-class problems, a hierarchical approach can be used to reduce the number of candidate classes to which it is necessary to apply the full power of more advanced methods. We believe that top-50 classification with less than 1% error on a lexicon of several thousand Arabic words or Chinese characters is within the state of the art, and that field classification can differentiate similar candidates in this reduced list.

We are not aware of any adequate handwritten test data with full context in either Arabic or Chinese. A proposal for the essential characteristics of such a database was presented at SDIUT05 [5].

2   Arabic Character Recognition

Symbolic Indirect Correlation (SIC) is a general approach for recognizing text that cannot be reliably segmented into characters, as is the case with most offline and online handwriting in non-hieroglyphic scripts.

SIC recognition is based on local matches between unsegmented patterns at both the feature and lexical levels. At the feature level, the unknown pattern is compared to a known (reference) string of features, and the results are captured in the form of a match graph. Another matching process is used to find polygram co-occurrences between the lexical transcripts of the reference string and every class to be recognized. In a second-level matching, the order of feature co-occurrences is compared to the order of polygram co-occurrence in the lexical transcript of each class, and the unknown pattern is given the label of the best matching lexical class.

SIC offers distinct advantages over prevailing approaches. It avoids the usual integrated segmentation-by-recognition loop. Unlike other whole-word recognition methods, SIC does not need feature-level samples of the words to be recognized. Finally, unlike methods based on Hidden Markov Models, it does not require estimation of an enormous number of parameters by a fragile bootstrap process. Furthermore, SIC can compensate for noisy features or inaccurate feature matching by increasing the length of the reference set.

We introduced SIC in [6,7] with a representation based on ordered bipartite graphs and established its advantages through simulations with a significant amount of noise. Later investigations showed that, in the presence of excessive noise, the sub-graph isomorphism based approach to the second-level matching requires an unreasonably large reference set [8,9]. A maximum-likelihood approach [10] avoids this computational bottleneck in the second-level matching. This method seems promising for Arabic recognition, so we describe in some detail how we build candidate solutions to the query; interested readers will find full technical details in [10,11].

The second-level matching assigns the labels of the best-fitting segments in the reference set to each matching segment in the query. The assignment is constrained by the order of the (possibly overlapping) matches. The probability of each candidate solution to the query is computed as follows.

With a large enough reference set, the feature matches between the query and the words in the reference string cover most, if not all, of any query word. Further, a feature match may or may not occur between the query and any given reference word or phrase; the same also holds true for a lexical match (bigrams or higher polygrams) between the pair. Thus, when a candidate solution to the query is built by assigning a polygram to each matched feature segment in the query, one of four possible conditions applies to the assignment with respect to every reference word. The assigned polygram:

1. occurs in the reference word, and there is a segment match (valid match),
2. does not occur in the reference word, but there is a segment match (spurious match),
3. occurs, but there is no segment match (missed match), and
4. does not occur, and there is no segment match (correct reject).

The conditional probabilities of these events can be estimated by matching the reference words against each other. Then, they are used to estimate the likelihood of each candidate solution and the solution with the maximum likelihood is chosen.

While our work on SIC has been restricted to English handwriting, we believe it would apply well to Arabic handwriting because the two languages share many common characteristics. These include linear order of writing, strong baseline, and three well-defined zones (ascender, descender, and median). Other unique features of Arabic writing also argue favorably for SIC:

- Connection of adjacent letters is prescribed by rigorous rules in Arabic. The resulting connected components at the sub-word level (PAWs) may themselves be connected by hasty writers. The segment-free recognition of SIC has been demonstrated to work on cursive English.
- Different shapes of letters at the beginning, middle, and end of a PAW require only that sufficient instances of each kind be included in the reference set.
- Occasionally, Arabic writing breaks from the usual right-to-left order by placing two successive characters one on top of the other. If this happens with some consistency in the writing, a feature-level match of the compound character in the unknown word and the reference string would be correlated in SIC with the corresponding bigram in the second-level matching. Similar considerations apply to the recognition of letters that are sometimes written out of sequence by Arabic writers.

To substantiate these claims, we have recently initiated work on applying SIC to recognize offline handwriting using a sample of images from the database of handwritten Arabic town names [12]. At this point, we have completed only the first-level matching at the feature and lexical levels. The features were adopted from English handwriting with minor variations; we expect substantial improvement with feature sets specifically developed for Arabic writing, such as the one reported in [13].

In our preliminary explorations, we selected a reference set of eight town names (numbered 2, 7, 8, 29, 45, 48, 51, and 52), transcribed by writer ae07. We chose four other town names (numbered 1, 3, 14, and 42) by the same writer as query words. The latter had good bigram coverage by the reference set. We used the Smith-Waterman algorithm [14] to find the local alignments (matches) for feature-level matching. The algorithm uses a flexible cost function that allows for mismatches, insertions, and deletions and finds the optimal sequence of such steps needed to match the two subsequences. For a given cost function, it finds the strongest matches starting at every position of the query string against the reference string. False matches abound at shorter segments, hence match-score thresholds are set to minimize the likelihood of a false match. Empirically, this is found to filter out most of the matches corresponding to unigrams and character fragments. The same algorithm was adapted to lexical matching of the transcripts of the query and reference strings.

Two examples of the lexical and feature match graphs, shown in Figs. 1-4, convey a sense of how the SIC approach might apply to Arabic handwriting recognition. The same query, ae07_014, is matched with the reference ae07_002 in Figs. 1-2 and with the reference ae07_045 in Figs. 3-4.

In Figs. 1 and 3, we show the distance matrices constructed using the Smith-Waterman algorithm, with the lexical comparison depicted on the left side of the figure (part (a)) and the signal comparison depicted on the right side of the figure (part (b)). Figs. 2 and 4, on the other hand, present the induced match graphs, with part (a) showing the lexical match graph and part (b) showing the feature match graph. The strength of a match is shown as a positive-integer weight on the corresponding edge in the graph; it indicates the extent of the matching segments. For visualization purposes, the match strength is also denoted by the thickness of edges in the figures. Typically, the lexical matching is conducted for exact bigram and higher-order n-gram matches and results in one or two matches. The feature matching often yields many more edges for the same pair of words, even for a threshold value that is high enough to minimize single-character matches. In these examples, we have chosen to show only the top-three candidate edges in each case.

Fig. 2(a) shows that only one lexical match exists in this particular example: the bigram (aaA laB) at position 5 in the query word matches with the same bigram at position 5 in the reference word, where the positions are counted from right-to-left in accordance with the Arabic writing convention. In Fig. 2(b), this lexical match is correctly identified by the strongest match, of strength 370, in the feature graph. However, the feature graph also includes two spurious edges, of strength 365 and 360, respectively, that do not have corresponding edges in the lexical graph.

In the second example, Fig. 4(a) shows two lexical matches: a 4-gram at the beginning of the query word matching at position 5 in the reference word and a

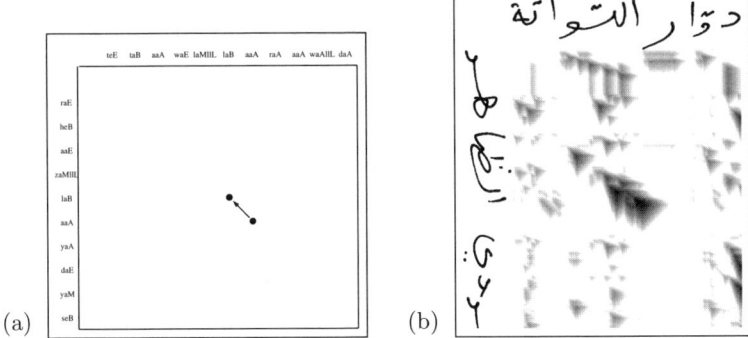

Fig. 1. Lexical (a) and feature (b) distance matrices for query ae07_014 vs. reference ae07_002

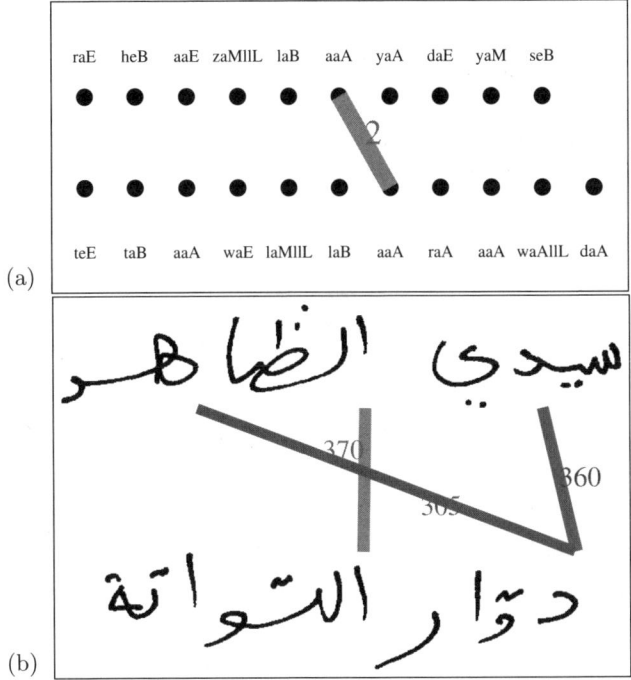

Fig. 2. Lexical (a) and feature (b) match graphs for query ae07_014 vs. reference ae07_002

trigram matching at the end of both the words. Both are also found in the feature graph, in Fig. 4(b), among the top-3 matches. However, the strongest edge, of strength 925, corresponds to the trigram, and the next strongest edge, of strength 545, corresponds to the 4-gram. The third edge, of strength 250, is spurious. We note that, because of both signal noise and variability in the character-widths, the

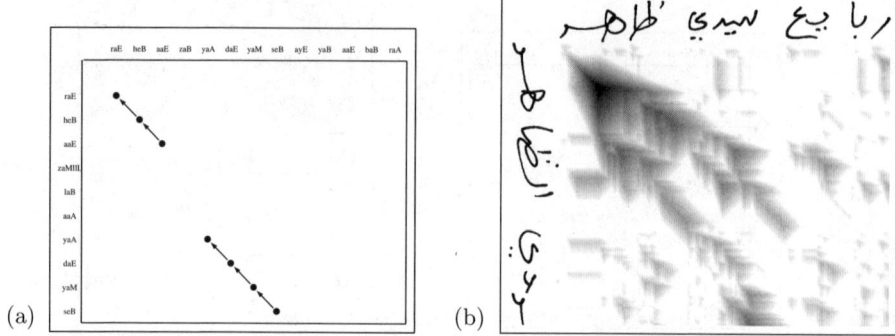

Fig. 3. Lexical (a) and feature (b) distance matrices for query ae07_014 vs. reference ae07_045

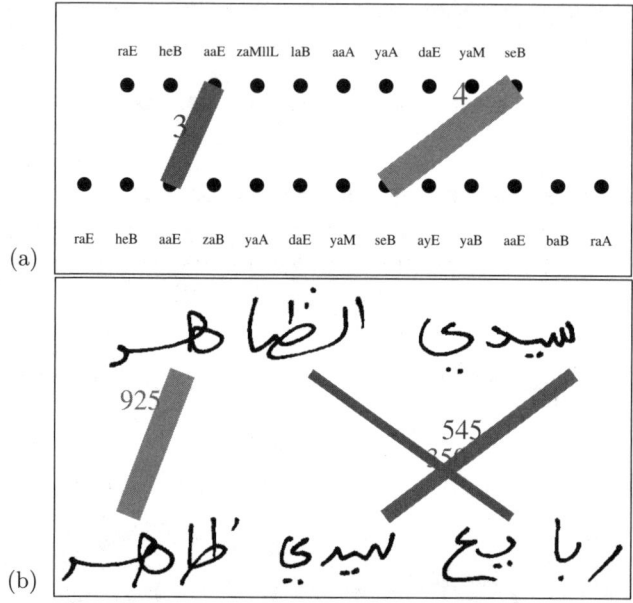

Fig. 4. Lexical (a) and feature (b) match graphs for query ae07_014 vs. reference ae07_045

strength of a correctly matched edge in the feature graph only weakly correlates with the strength of its corresponding edge in the lexical graph.

Even though the feature set used in our examples is not particularly well-adapted to Arabic, the feature matching process correctly selects the lexical matches in many cases. However, many spurious matches occur as well. Our second-level matching process, described in [10], is shown to be robust against a large number of spurious matches, but at the expense of increased computation time. Therefore, we plan to explore a post-processing approach to eliminate some bad matches. The basic idea here is to use non-sequential features to screen the 2-D regions identified by every feature match. Hull [15] employs a similar idea in another context, to select candidates for whole-word recognition, even when they are printed in different fonts. Consider, for example, the feature graph in Fig. 4(b) showing the top-3 matches. The image region in the query word corresponding to the weakest edge, which has the strength of 250, has a flat stroke with a diacritic mark above it while that corresponding to the reference word has diacritic marks below the stroke. It should be possible to reject this match based on 2-D features that summarize the dominant directions at each black pixel in different sub-regions of the two images.

3 Chinese Character Recognition

Almost any method can recognize neat handwritten Chinese with better than 85% accuracy, and newsprint at over 95%. Making allowance for the usual 2:1 reject/error trade-off, this implies that we must concentrate on 35% of the handwritten material and 15% of the print. These figures are based on the standardized character forms used in the People's Republic of China, which are somewhat more difficult to recognize than the characters used in Taiwan, Japan, and Korea because the simplifications fifty years ago removed many "redundant" strokes.

Printed Chinese characters are usually fixed-pitch, without ascenders or descenders, and all the characters fit into the same size, horizontally aligned, bounding boxes. Whether the reading order is left-to-right or top-to-bottom is easily determined. Segmentation is, however, a major source of error in handwriting. Rushed writers connect and even overlap characters, do not adhere to a clear baseline, and cannot squeeze complex characters into bounding boxes that are ample for simpler characters.

Both handwriting and print exhibit pairs (occasionally even triples) of characters with almost identical shapes but different meanings. (Some researchers deliberately exclude such confusion pairs from reported error statistics.) Human readers resolve such ambiguities through broad context. A far more restricted set of language constraints is also used in Chinese OCR. Dictionary (lexicon) look-up cannot be applied in the same way as in Western languages, but the extreme skew of the distribution of unigrams and of two- and three-character sequences can be readily exploited. We note, in particular, that the number of Chinese family and given names, where mistakes cannot be tolerated, is less than in most Western nations. Foreign names may be transliterated or printed in their native script.

We discussed a new approach to segmentation-free character recognition in the section on Arabic. Here, we present style-constrained field classification, which is the only recourse when there is insufficient linguistic context. When we cannot read a letter, we look for easier-to-recognize instances of the same shape. Other instances of an unknown character may be easier to classify because there is less (or different) noise, or they are segmented better, or because there is more language context. Adaptive algorithms that benefit from typeface and writer

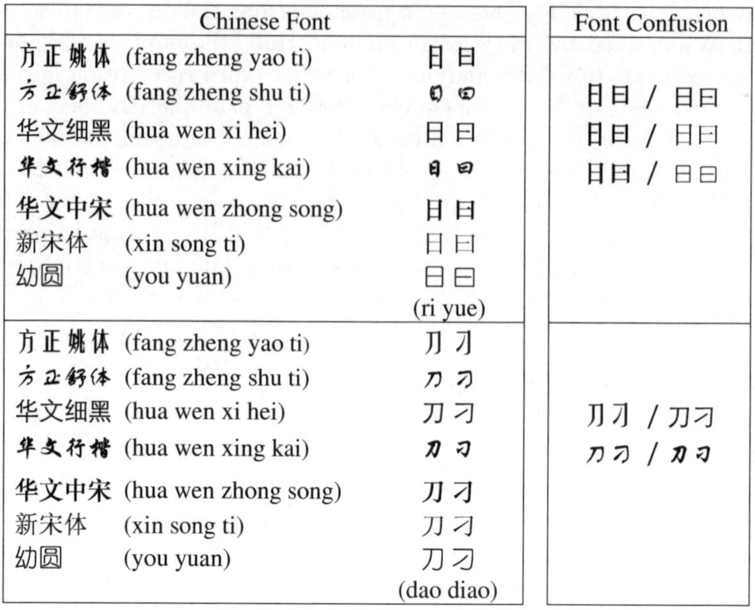

Chinese Font			Font Confusion
方正姚体 (fang zheng yao ti)	日	日	
方正舒体 (fang zheng shu ti)	ㄖ	ㄖ	日日 / 日日
华文细黑 (hua wen xi hei)	日	日	日日 / 日日
华文行楷 (hua wen xing kai)	日	日	日日 / 日日
华文中宋 (hua wen zhong song)	日	日	
新宋体 (xin song ti)	日	日	
幼圆 (you yuan)	日	日	
(ri yue)			
方正姚体 (fang zheng yao ti)	刀	刁	
方正舒体 (fang zheng shu ti)	刀	刁	刀刁 / 刀刁
华文细黑 (hua wen xi hei)	刀	刁	刀刁 / 刀刁
华文行楷 (hua wen xing kai)	刀	刁	
华文中宋 (hua wen zhong song)	刀	刁	
新宋体 (xin song ti)	刀	刁	
幼圆 (you yuan)	刀	刁	
(dao diao)			

Fig. 5. Two Han confusion pairs (ri/yue and dao/diao) in seven fonts. The left column and its transliterations are the font names. On the right, are a few of the 7x6/2=21 possible different-font confusion pairs, on which a conventional singlet classifier is likely to make errors.

intra-class consistency of this kind have been known for decades [16,17,18,19], but have been incorporated into commercial systems only recently [20]. The scope of adaptation is typically a page: it is assumed that each page is written by a single person, or printed in a limited set of typefaces. A set of reliable prototypes is collected in a first pass, and the remaining problematic characters are recognized in one or more subsequent passes.

Fig. 5 shows some easily confused characters where adaptation can help. (We use printed examples for ease of interpretation by readers who cannot read Chinese. The handwritten version of these characters are, of course, even more ambiguous.) However, adaptation works well only with long fields, where there are several samples of each class. In Chinese, much longer fields are needed than in alphabetic languages.

We have recently demonstrated a much less intuitive aspect of local shape consistency that we call inter-class style. The underlying idea is simply that knowing how an individual writes a **g** or a **p** may help us predict how she may write a **q**. In fact, the shape of every class provides some information about every other class. In a statistical framework, we say that the features of one class are style-conditionally dependent on the features of another class. Abandoning the customary independence assumption leads to a more complex mathematical framework. Nevertheless, the optimal maximum a posteriori (MAP) classifier can be formulated neatly [21,22,23]. In the last three years, we have demonstrated

	Font1/ Font2	Font2/ Font1
Singlets:	日/日	日/日
	刁/刀	刁/刀
Pairs:	子日/日子	子日/日子
	刁钻/刀钻	刁钻/刀钻

Fig. 6. Scenarios faced by a singlet classifier (above) and by a pair classifier (below), on two pairs of similar characters. When it is known that both characters are from the same style (font or writer), the confusions are more easily resolved by a style-constrained classifier with additional information from another character in the same style.

significant gains in accuracy through style-constrained field classification on both printed and hand-printed digits. Fig. 6 suggests why pairs of Chinese characters are easier to classify than individual characters.

We note that printers, copiers, scanners, and cameras also introduce usable style constraints. Human readers resort to field classification when necessary. Like humans, machines must also be enabled to do field classification, but only when needed as it is expensive. The number of field classes increases exponentially with field length. Whereas with numerals we used field lengths up to five, for Chinese we propose to apply style constraints only to selected pairs and triples.

For the sake of completeness, we note that font recognition is an inefficient form of style-constrained classification. It generally requires separate features for font and class identification, becomes confused when fonts share some shapes, wastes statistical evidence on identifying the font when only class labels are wanted, and cannot accommodate font miscegenation.

4   Interaction

All OCR systems benefit from some human help, typically at the beginning or end of the process. Scanning is almost always checked, because even current scanners occasionally bungle digitization. At the beginning, the operator may label some unusual characters, select a language model, or provide general format information. He or she may also occasionally assist page segmentation. After OCR has taken place, low-confidence labels are verified or corrected. When there are too many errors, the entire page may be keyed-in instead of corrected.

Current OCR systems do not make the most efficient use of the operator, perhaps because such work is often outsourced and off-shored. However, for urgent and critical applications, the operator may well be the end-user. Workers with other primary missions are not likely to tolerate the repetitive routine of data entry personnel. The interaction therefore must take place wherever and whenever it is most effective and, above all, it should not be wasted. The software should attempt every task. The operator must, however, have the opportunity of correcting the result whenever necessary. Whether a particular error should be corrected requires the kind of judgment that, at present, machines lack.

We have made the case for a personal, mobile, multilingual support system at SDIUT05 [5], on interactive table interpretation at DAS06 [24], and on large-scale document entry at DIAL06 [24]. We have argued that every operator action should result in some change in the configuration of the system that decreases the likelihood of the same situation occurring again. In other words, the system must improve with use.

5   Discussion

The ideas we have described in this paper arise from an underlying philosophy that in-house training sets for most offline handwriting recognition tasks are never large enough and never representative enough. To escape from this constraint, the system must be capable of seamlessly augmenting its operation as it works on samples of actual (real-time, real-world) documents of interest. Symbolic Indirect Correlation and Style-Constrained Classification are both designed with this goal in mind.

SIC employs flexible matching based on subsequences of any length, although these are typically chosen to be longer than a single character, grapheme, or phoneme. Common distortions in handwriting, camera- and tablet-based OCR (stretching, contraction), and speech (time-warping) can be accommodated. A general paradigm, the basic notion of SIC is independent of medium, feature set, and vocabulary. Perhaps SIC's biggest advantage is that no training is necessary - all that is required is a labeled reference set, as in the case of Nearest Neighbor classification - thus allowing for unsupervised adaptation. Domain-dependent recognition lexicons can be created "on-the-fly."

SCC exploits the observation that in many applications, including, most notably, single-author offline handwriting recognition, patterns occur in isogenous (same-source) groups (fields). Other examples of isogenous fields include text files printed using the same font, successive issues of a given newspaper or magazine, and documents created using the same printer, photocopier, or fax machine, or acquired using the same scanner or camera. For handwriting, an author's distinctive style can include slant, formation of ascenders and descenders, inter-character and inter-word spacing, ligatures, etc. A common source results in common traits which SCC can take advantage of to improve recognition accuracy.

We conclude by offering a scenario where SIC and SCC might be applied profitably. Imagine that a military or law enforcement operation uncovers a cache of high-value documents authored by a small number of writers, and the inaccessibility of the language, or the complexities of the content, make it desirable to digitize the information contained therein. Existing techniques are confounded. It would take far too long and be much too expensive to label manually the large quantities of training data required by traditional handwriting recognition techniques; perhaps time is of the utmost urgency. SIC and SCC seem ideally suited to such situations: use SIC when segmentation is found to be difficult (i.e., Arabic), and SCC when style can blur class differences (i.e., Chinese).

Both SIC and SCC are promising new approaches that can be applied to the handwriting recognition problem. The groundwork has been laid, but future work is needed to address feature selection, adaptation strategies, computational efficiency, and user interfaces and interaction.

Acknowledgments

Daniel Lopresti acknowledges support from the National Science Foundation under Award #0430338 and a DARPA IPTO seedling grant administered by BBN Technologies. George Nagy acknowledges support from the National Science Foundation under Award #0414854.

References

1. Casey, R.G., Nagy, G.: Recognition of Printed Chinese Characters. IEEE Transactions on Electronic Computers 15, 91–100 (1966)
2. Casey, R.G., Nagy, G.: Chinese Character Recognition: A Twenty-five-year Perspective. In: Proc. International Conference on Pattern Recognition, Rome, Italy, pp. 1023–1026 (1988)
3. Kanai, J., Liu, Y., Nagy, G.: An OCR-oriented Overview of Ideographic Writing Systems. In: Bunke, H., Wang, P.S.P. (eds.) Handbook of Character Recognition and Document Image Analysis, pp. 285–304. World Scientific, Singapore (1997)
4. Lorigo, L.M., Govindaraju, V.: Offline Arabic Handwriting Recognition: A Survey. IEEE Transactions on Pattern Analysis and Machine Intelligence 28, 712–724 (2006)
5. Lopresti, D., Nagy, G.: Mobile Interactive Support System for Time-Critical Document Exploitation. In: Proc. Symposium on Document Image Understanding Technology, College Park, MD, pp. 111–119 (2005)
6. Nagy, G., Seth, S.C., Mehta, S.K., Lin, Y.: Indirect Symbolic Correlation Approach to Unsegmented Text Recognition. In: Proc. Conference on Computer Vision and Pattern Recognition Workshop on Document Image Analysis and Retrieval (DIAR 2003), Madison, WI, pp. 22–32 (2003)
7. Nagy, G., Lopresti, D., Krishnamoorthy, M., Lin, Y., Seth, S., Mehta, S.: A Nonparametric classifier for unsegmented text. In: Proc. IS&T-SPIE International Symposium on Document Recognition and Retrieval, San Jose, pp. 102–108 (2004)
8. Joshi, A., Nagy, G.: Online Handwriting Recognition Using Time-Order of Lexical and Signal Co-Occurrences. In: Proc. 12th Biennial Conference of the International Graphonomics Society, Salerno, Italy, pp. 201–205 (2005)
9. Lopresti, D., Joshi, A., Nagy, G.: Match Graph Generation for Symbolic Indirect Correlation. In: Proc. IS&T-SPIE International Symposium on Document Recognition and Retrieval, San Jose, CA, vol. 6067-06 (2006)
10. Joshi, A., Nagy, G., Lopresti, D., Seth, S.: A Maximum-Likelihood Approach to Symbolic Indirect Correlation. In: Proc. International Conference on Pattern Recognition, Hong Kong, China, pp. 99–103 (2006)
11. Joshi, A.: Symbolic Indirect Correlation Classifier. Rensselaer Polytechnic Institute, ECSE Department, Troy, NY, Ph.D. Thesis (2006)

12. Märgner, V., Pechwitz, M.: IFN/ENIT-database: Database of Handwritten Arabic Words. Available online at (2007), http://www.ifnenit.com/index.htm
13. El-Hajj, R., Likforman-Sulem, L., Mokbel, C.: Arabic Handwriting Recognition Using Baseline Dependant Features and Hidden Markov Modeling. In: Proc. Int. Conference on Document Analysis and Recognition ICDAR, pp. 893–897 (2005)
14. Smith, T.F., Waterman, M.S.: Identification of Common Molecular Sequences. Journal of Molecular Biology 147, 195–197 (1981)
15. Hull, J.J.: Incorporating Language Syntax in Visual Text Recognition with a Statistical Model. IEEE Transactions on Pattern Analysis and Machine Intelligence 18, 1251–1256 (1996)
16. Nagy, G., Shelton, G.L.: Self-Corrective Character Recognition System. IEEE Transactions on Information Theory 12, 215–222 (1966)
17. Baird, H.S., Nagy, G.: A Self-correcting 100-font Classifier. In: Proc. IS&T/SPIE International Symposium on Document Recognition and Retrieval, San Jose, CA, pp. 106–115 (1994)
18. Xu, Y., Nagy, G.: Prototype Extraction and Adaptive OCR. IEEE Transactions on Pattern Analysis and Machine Intelligence 21, 1280–1296 (1999)
19. Ho, T.K., Nagy, G.: OCR with No Shape Training. In: Proc. International Conference on Pattern Recognition, Barcelona, Spain, pp. 27–30 (2000)
20. Marosi, I., Tóth, L.: OCR Voting Methods for Recognizing Low Contrast Printed Documents. In: Proc. 2nd IEEE International Conference on Document Image Analysis for Libraries (DIAL 2006), Lyon, France, pp. 108–115.
21. Veeramachaneni, S., Nagy, G.: Adaptive Classifiers for Multisource OCR. International Journal of Document Analysis and Recognition 6, 154–166 (2004)
22. Veeramachaneni, S., Nagy, G.: Style Context with Second Order Statistics. IEEE Transactions on Pattern Analysis and Machine Intelligence 27, 14–22 (2005)
23. Sarkar, P., Nagy, G.: Style consistent classification of isogenous patterns. IEEE Transactions on Pattern Analysis and Machine Intelligence 27, 88–98 (2005)
24. Embley, D.W., Lopresti, D., Nagy, G.: Notes on Contemporary Table Recognition. In: Proc. 7th International Workshop on Document Analysis Systems (DAS 2006), Nelson, New Zealand, pp. 164–175 (2006)
25. Nagy, G., Lopresti, D.: Interactive Document Processing and Digital Libraries. In: Proc. 2nd IEEE International Conference on Document Image Analysis for Libraries (DIAL 2006), Lyon, France, pp. 2–11 (2006)

Multi-lingual Offline Handwriting Recognition Using Hidden Markov Models: A Script-Independent Approach

Prem Natarajan, Shirin Saleem, Rohit Prasad, Ehry MacRostie,
and Krishna Subramanian

BBN Technologies, 10 Moulton Street,
Cambridge, MA 02138, USA
{pnataraj,ssaleem,rprasad,emacrost,ksubrama}@bbn.com

Abstract. This paper introduces a script-independent methodology for multi-lingual offline handwriting recognition (OHR) based on the use of Hidden Markov Models (HMM). The OHR methodology extends our script-independent approach for OCR of machine-printed text images. The feature extraction, training, and recognition components of the system are all designed to be script independent. The HMM training and recognition components are based on our Byblos continuous speech recognition system. The HMM parameters are estimated automatically from the training data, without the need for laborious hand-written rules. The system does not require pre-segmentation of the data, neither at the word level nor at the character level. Thus, the system can handle languages with cursive handwritten scripts in a straightforward manner. The script independence of the system is demonstrated with experimental results in three scripts that exhibit significant differences in glyph characteristics: English, Chinese, and Arabic. Results from an initial set of experiments are presented to demonstrate the viability of the proposed methodology.

1 Introduction

Most offline handwriting recognition (OHR) systems are designed for a particular script or language. In this paper, we introduce an approach to OHR that, in principle and by design, is script-independent and can be used for the vast majority of the world's languages. In particular, the core feature extraction, training, and recognition components remain the same for all languages; only the data-specific components, such as the dictionary and the language model, depend on the specific language. Except for the pre-processing and feature extraction components, which are specific to OCR and OHR, the training and recognition components are taken without significant modification from our continuous speech recognition (CSR) system, called the BBN Byblos CSR system. Hence, we call our OHR system, the BBN Byblos OHR system.

The basic modeling paradigm we employ is that of Hidden Markov Models (HMM) [1]. HMMs are capable of modeling the variability of a feature vector as a function of one independent variable. In speech [2], there is one natural independent variable: time. In OHR and OCR, there are two independent variables since text images are two-dimensional (2-D), so 1-D HMMs cannot be used directly. We structure the OHR problem as a combination of two 1-D pattern recognition tasks. In the first task, called line

D.S. Doermann and S. Jaeger (Eds.): SACH 2006, LNCS 4768, pp. 231–250, 2008.
© Springer-Verlag Berlin Heidelberg 2008

finding, we locate the individual lines of text on a page, then, recognize the text content of each line.

Even the OHR problem at the level of a single line is, in truth, 2-D as well; however, we convert it into a 1-D problem by extracting a feature vector that is a function of only one dimension (usually horizontal position). The feature vector is extracted from narrow vertical strips along each line of text [32]. The fact that the feature vector we extract does not depend on the script being recognized gives one reason that our approach is script-independent. The other reason is that the HMM modeling approach itself does not change with the script being recognized. In particular, given no separate character segmentation component, neither in training nor in recognition, the same system can recognize scripts where the characters are separate or connected. To demonstrate the script-independence of our approach, we present OHR results in three different scripts: Arabic, Chinese, and English. Arabic and English presents the challenge of dealing with a cursive script, and Chinese presents the challenge of dealing with a large number of characters.

A number of research efforts have used HMMs in offline printed and handwriting recognition [3-31]. All these efforts attempt the recognition of only a single language or script. From a methodological perspective, our approach differs each principally in the emphasis we place on script independence.

In Section 2, we present the theoretical framework of the HMM paradigm. Section 3 gives a description of the BBN Byblos OHR system. Sections 2 and 3 closely follow the related Sections in [32] and are summarized here for the convenience of the reader. In Section 4, we present experimental recognition results on English, Chinese and Arabic, and we conclude with a summary in Section 5.

2 Theoretical Framework

2.1 Problem Formulation

We represent a line of text from a scanned image by a sequence of feature vectors X. The aim is to find the sequence of characters that maximizes $P(C|X)$, the probability of a sequence of characters C, given the feature vector sequence X. Using Bayes' rule, $P(C|X)$ may be written as:

$$P(C|X) = P(X|C) \cdot P(C)/P(X) \tag{1}$$

We call $P(X|C)$ the feature model and $P(C)$ the language model (or grammar). $P(X|C)$ models the feature vector sequence X, given a sequence of characters C, and is approximated as the product of the component probabilities, $P(X_i|c_i)$, where X_i is the sequence of feature vectors that corresponds to character c_i. The feature model for each character is given by a specific HMM.

$P(C)$, the language model, is the prior probability of a sequence of characters C; it basically provides a soft constraint on allowable character sequences. The language model used in the Byblos OCR system is an n-gram Markov model, which computes $P(C)$ by multiplying the probabilities of consecutive groups of n characters or words. $P(X)$ in (1) is the a priori probability of the data and does not depend on C; therefore, we can maximize $P(C|X)$ by maximizing the product $P(X|C) P(C)$.

2.2 Hidden Markov Models

A hidden Markov model (HMM) [1] is essentially a Markov chain with one significant difference: in a Markov chain a state associate with a unique, deterministic output value, whereas in an HMM each state associates with a probability distribution over all possible output values. (We use the word "output" because Markov models are generally thought of as generative models that produce the observed data as output.) Figure 1 shows a simple 4-state HMM, with transitions and their probabilities, and the output probability distribution associated with each of the four states. These probability distributions are defined over the feature vector x, which is a high-dimensional vector. The model shown in Figure 1 is known as a left-to-right model, because it flows from left to right as one traverses the model in producing the output sequence.

Given a sequence of feature vectors extracted from a line of text, the OHR or OCR problem is to find the sequence of states or characters that "generated" the observed sequence of feature vectors. However, because of the probabilistic nature of the output generated by a state, almost any sequence of states could, in principle, generate the observed output. Because it is not possible to uniquely map a sequence of feature vectors to a sequence of states/characters, the sequence of states that actually generated the vectors is hidden from the observer – hence the term hidden Markov model. Nevertheless, we can compute the probability that the observed sequence of feature vectors could have been generated by a particular sequence of states. Of particular interest is the sequence of states that has the highest probability of having generated the observed feature-vector sequence. By using the Markov property of the HMM, we can find that optimal state sequence efficiently using the Viterbi algorithm [32] or other search algorithms [33, 34]. The resulting sequence of characters becomes the output of the recognition component.

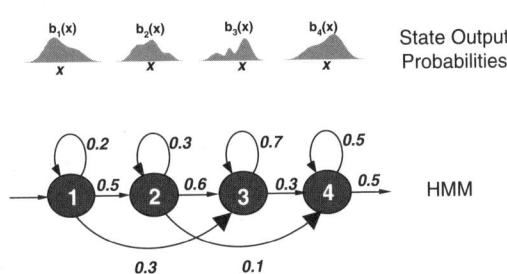

Fig. 1. An example of a 4-state, left-to-right, hidden Markov model (HMM) of the type used in the Byblos OCR system. It includes one-state skips and self loops.

3 Byblos OHR System

The Byblos OHR system evolved from the Byblos OCR system. Therefore, in the following, we first provide a brief review of the Byblos OCR system. This review is followed by a discussion of some features unique to the OHR task. For a more detailed description of the OCR system, the reader is referred to [32].

3.1 Review of Byblos OCR System

The Byblos OCR system is a statistical, HMM-based recognition system that uses the Byblos HMM engine [32, 36-39], which was originally developed for speech recognition at BBN. At present, the OCR system handles single columns of text containing one or more paragraphs. A separate page, layout analysis module segments each input image into single column text zones. Figure 2 shows a block diagram of the system. As indicated in the diagram, the OCR system can be sub-divided into two basic functional components: training and recognition. Both training and recognition have the same pre-processing and feature extraction stages.

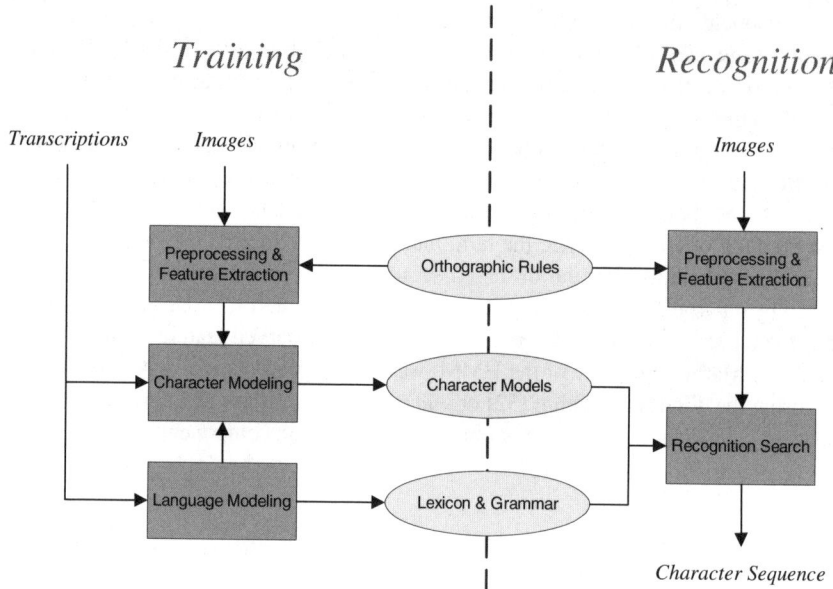

Fig. 2. Block diagram of the BBN OCR system

3.1.1 Pre-processing

The pre-processing stage has two functions: skew removal and line finding. We assume that the image has been skewed, owing to a rotation of the text during scanning. The details of our de-skewing algorithm are presented in [32]. After de-skewing, the image segment into lines of text using either an HMM-based or a connected-component based lgorithm. The choice of the particular line finding algorithm is based on the characteristics of the data. Details of the HMM line finding procedure are presented in [38]. In the result of the line finding program, each line of text is bounded at the top by one baseline and at the bottom by another.

3.1.2 Feature Extraction

For each line of text (as determined by the line finding process), features are computed from a sequence of overlapped windows. For each window, also called a frame, several features are computed. The feature extraction program typically computes a total of 81 features per frame. We use Linear Discriminant Analysis (LDA) [35] to reduce the number of features per frame from 81 to, typically, 15. The decision to use 15 LDA features was made empirically after conducting a set of experiments and choosing the number of features that resulted in the minimum character error rate. The resulting vector of 15 LDA features is a compact numerical representation of the data in the frame and is the feature vector used in our recognition experiments. For a detailed description of the feature extraction procedure, refer to [32].

3.1.3 Training

The OCR system models each character with a multi-state, left-to-right HMM; the model for a word is the concatenation of the models for the characters in the word. Each state has an associated output probability distribution over the features, as shown in Figure 1. Each output probability distribution is modeled as a weighted sum of Gaussians, called a Gaussian mixture. A Gaussian mixture is completely given parameters by the means and variances of the component Gaussians, along with the weight of each Gaussian in the mixture. The number of states and the allowable transitions system parameters that can b e set includes for our experiments we have used 14-state, left-to-right HMMs.

Training – the process of estimating the parameters (transition probabilities and feature probability distributions) of each of the character HMMs – uses what has been known, alternately, as the Baum-Welch [36], forward-backward, or expectation-maximization (EM) algorithm [37, 38]. It iteratively aligns the feature vectors with the character models to obtain maximum likelihood estimates of HMM parameters. The algorithm guarantees a convergence of a local maximum of the likelihood function. The feature probability distributions in our system are characterized by the means, variances, and weights of the Gaussian mixtures.

Depending on the amount of available training data, it may not be possible to achieve robust estimates of all the HMM parameters for all the characters. That is one reason we use LDA to reduce the size of our feature vector. Another method used to reduce the total number of parameters in the system involves sharing some Gaussians across different character models. In particular, three such methods are available in our Byblos system: the Tied Mixture (TM) mode, the Character Tied Mixture (CTM) mode, and the State Tied Mixture Mode (STM) [44-46]. In the TM mode, we train only one set of Gaussians (referred to as a codebook of Gaussians or just a codebook) shared between all states of all character models. The individuality of each state output probability distribution is characterized solely by the specific component mixture weights. In the CTM mode, we train one codebook of Gaussians for each character model; the Gaussians in a character codebook are thus shared among the states of the model for that character, but no sharing happens across characters. The CTM mode offers a greater number of free parameters and, with it, the possibility of better performance, subject to the availability of sufficient data for training all the parameters. For purposes of clarity, the STM mode is explained in Section 4.1.2 (English Experimental Results).

The training process is performed as follows: assume that, for each line of text, we are given the corresponding ground truth, which simply contains the sequence of characters on that line. Note that no information is given about the location of each character on the line; that is, no pre-segmentation is necessary. The training algorithm automatically and iteratively aligns the sequence of feature vectors along the line of text with the sequence of character models. This is why this method does not differ given connected characters or not, and why it can handle languages with connected script, as well as other scripts where the characters are not connected. It also explains why touching characters, from a fax or other degradations, do not require any special handling with this method.

3.1.4 Recognition

After pre-processing a line of text and performing feature extraction, as described above, the recognition process consists of a search for the sequence of character models with the highest probability of having generated the observed sequence of feature vectors, given the trained character models, a possible word lexicon, and a statistical language model of the possible character or word sequences. The recognition search is a two-pass [34, 35] (a forward pass and a backward pass) beam search for the most likely sequence of characters. The width of the search beam can be set as a system parameter. Typically, lowering the beam width increases the speed but degrades the accuracy of recognition. The forward pass provides an approximate but efficient procedure for generating a small list of character sequences that are possible candidates for being the most likely sequence. The backward pass gives a more detailed search for the most likely character sequence within this small list. Even though we typically use the same set of character HMMs in the forward and backward passes, the search program itself does not impose any such constraint, i.e., if needed we can use two different sets of character HMMs, one in the forward and the other in the backward pass.

The use of a word lexicon during recognition is optional, and its use generally results in a lower error rate. The lexicon is estimated from a suitably large text corpus. The language model, which provides the probability of any character or word sequence, is also estimated from the same corpus. Note that the text corpus here does not require the presence of corresponding images; only the sequence of words in the text is needed.

3.2 Slant Correction

Handwritten text exhibits many differences from machine-printed text, all of which make the OHR task much more difficult than machine-printed text recognition. Critical differences include slanted writing, relative differences in the sizes of various characters, non-linear baseline even within a single word, and trailing strokes that hang above or below neighboring characters. These differences need to be either normalized, or modeled effectively to achieve reasonably high recognition accuracy.

The OHR effort reported in this paper was initiated recently, and the system is currently under development. Recognizing the importance of slant normalization in handwriting recognition, our first modification of the OCR pre-processing component incorporate a slant correction algorithm that works on each connected component within a page of text. Typically, a connected component comprises a word or a fraction of a word. Other enhancements to the pre-processing (various types of normalization) and feature extraction (new features for handwriting) procedures will be designed and implemented as the work progresses. We conclude this section with a brief description of our slant correction algorithm.

The goal of the slant correction step is to eliminate any slant in each word and to make the vertical strokes perpendicular to the baseline. To normalize the slant, we estimate, then apply a non-linear, 2-D transform to each connected component (CC) within an input (black-white) text image.

The estimation of the non-linear transform is based upon the approach presented in [47]. We apply the slant correction procedure iteratively until the estimated slant crests below a certain threshold. A section of the original image and the slant corrected images for each of four successive iterations of the correction procedure are shown in Table 1.

Table 1. Example for Slant Correction

Original Image	*Griffiths*
Iteration 1	*Griffiths*
Iteration 2	*Griffiths*
Iteration 3	*Griffiths*
Iteration 4	*Griffiths*

While repeated application of the transform progressively reduces the slant of text, a closer inspection of the image indicates that it leaves the perimeter of the text progressively jagged. Table 2 shows a section of the original image and slant correctedimage after four applications of the non-linear transform. An area of future work involves improving the slant correction procedure to reduce the manifestation of such jagged perimeters.

Table 2. (a) Section of original image, (b) Image after slant correction

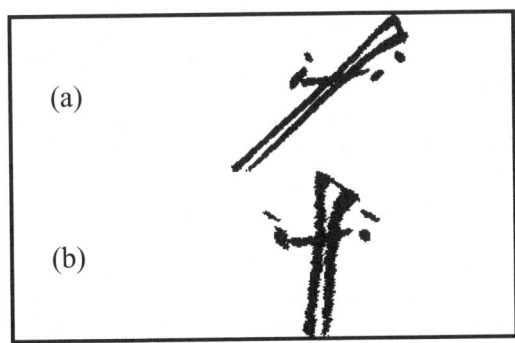

4 Experimental Results

In this section we present the results of some early exploratory experiments, in which we have applied our Byblos Offline Handwriting Recognition (OHR) system to text handwritten in English and in Chinese. These experiments have a goal of establishing the viability of the proposed approach for recognizing handwritten text. System performance is measured using the word error rate (WER) or the character error rate (CER), defined as:

$$WER\ (CER) = \frac{\text{deletions} + \text{insertions} + \text{substitutions}}{\text{total number of words (characters) in reference}} \tag{2}$$

where the reference is the manually generated ground truth.

In the following, we present in separate sub-sections, the data sets, experimental procedure, and results for English, Chinese and Arabic OHR.

4.1 English OHR

4.1.1 Corpus

For our English OHR experiments, we used the IAM database [48]. The IAM English database consists of unconstrained handwritten English sentences from the LOB corpus [49]. The database was collected by distributing forms with printed text to writers, and having them write the text on the forms in their own handwriting. A total of 1,539 images from 657 different writers, scanned at a resolution of 300 dpi were used in our experiments. We split the corpus into three sets: a training set, a development set, and a reserved test set. In dividing the corpus into the three sets, we ensured that no writer's handwriting appears both in test and in training (i.e., a writer-independent test condition). Further, to ensure fair language models, all handwritten samples of a form are assigned entirely to a single set (training, development, or test). In other words, a particular passage of text is either in training or in (development) test, but never in both. Table 3 contains samples from the IAM database. The samples illustrate the tremendous diversity in writing styles contained within the IAM database.

Table 4 lists the characteristics of the training, development, and test sets used in our experiments. The IAM database includes annotations of the bounding boxes for each word. For the experiments reported in this paper, we used the word bounding box information to determine the top and bottom of the lines of text within each image.

4.1.2 English Results

We ran a series of six training and recognition experiments on the IAM database in order to exercise different capabilities within our OHR system and to characterize their impact on the error rate.

In the first experiment we used only the machine-printed versions of the forms. We trained a set of individual English character HMMs using the machine-printed training data. Training was performed using 14-state context-independent HMMs. For any given character, the characters to its left and right defined its context. For example, in the word "cat," character "a" is said to be in the context of "c" and "t", whereas in the word "halibut", the same character "a" is in the context of an "h" and an "l". In machine-printed text, the shape of a character is typically unaffected by its context, and it is, therefore, appropriate to model each character with a single, context-independent HMM. In a context-independent configuration, a single HMM is shared across all contexts of a character. We used a CTM configuration with a separate codebook of 256 Gaussians for each character HMM.

Table 3. Sample images from the IAM database

Table 4. Characteristics of training, dev, and test sets for English experiments

Characteristic	Train	Development	Test
Number of Images	1239	150	150
Number of Lines	10726	1316	1311
Total Number of Words	95512	11632	11308
Unique Number of Words	10217	3135	3093
Number of Writers	506	108	97

Recognition was performed using the trained character HMMs and a character tri-gram language model (LM). We did not use a word lexicon during recognition or during post-processing. We obtained a word error rate (WER) of 0.9% on the machine-printed test set. The fact that all the forms in the IAM database were rendered in a single font contributed to the low WER.

In our second experiment, we trained a set of context-independent character HMMs using the IAM handwritten training data set. The HMM and language model configura-tion remained the same as in our first experiment. The trained models when tested against the handwritten test data yielded a WER of 68.50%, with an associated CER of 40.10%. We then performed a third experiment in which we replaced the character tri-gram language model with a word tri-gram language model. With a word LM, the WER dropped to 52.80% and the CER dropped to 33.80%.

Unlike machine-printed data, handwritten text exhibits a certain amount of context dependency. In other words, the shape of a particular character glyph can vary based on the character that precedes it and the one that follows it. Therefore, we ran a fourth ex-periment in which we trained context-dependent character HMMs. In the context-dependent configuration, a separate HMM models each different contextual instance of a character, where a character's context is defined by the characters appearing to its left and right. Using context-dependent HMMs and a word LM, we obtained a WER of 49.30% and a CER of 31.00%.

In our fifth experiment, we used a separate set of Gaussians for each state of all the context-dependent HMMs associated with a particular character. For example, we esti-mated a set of 128 Gaussians for the first state of all HMMs associated with the character "a", and a separate set of 128 Gaussians for the second state of all HMMs for "a", and so forth. This configuration, referred to as the state tied mixture (STM) configuration, pro-vides a better model for the structural evolution of a character glyph in the direction of writing. With the STM model, we obtained a WER of 46.1% and a CER of 28.1%.

After exercising the various modeling capabilities of our system, we ran a final ex-periment in which we repeated the fifth experiment using slant-corrected versions of the training and test images, instead of the raw versions from the database. Testing on the slant-corrected test images using context-dependent HMMs in a 128 Gaussian STM configuration, we obtained a WER of 40.1% and a CER of 23.3%. The results of the six experiments are summarized in Table 5.

We used a 10K word vocabulary derived from the IAM training transcriptions alone. The out-of-vocabulary (OOV) rate on the test set for the 10K IAM vocabulary was 10.01%. We also ran an experiment using a 30K word vocabulary that included words from our Broadcast News speech corpus. The OOV rate using the 30K vocabulary was 4.49%, but the WER and % Correct did not change significantly. The only other work on this database using a HMM-based approach with statistical language models is [28]. We cannot directly compare our results with that in [28] because of differences in the training and test sets. Nevertheless, using the results reported in [28] as a generic bench-mark, our English OHR performance is clearly state-of-the-art.

Table 5. Summary of English recognition results

Data Type	HMM Configuration	Language Model	CER - %	WER - %
Machine print	Context-independent, CTM	Char 3-gram	0.2	0.9
Handwriting	Context-independent, CTM	Char 3-gram	40.1	68.5
Handwriting	Context-independent, CTM	Word 3-gram	33.8	52.8
Handwriting	Context-dependent, CTM	Word 3-gram	31.0	49.3
Handwriting	Context-dependent, STM	Word 3-gram	28.1	46.1
Handwriting	Context-dependent, STM Slant corrected images	Word 3-gram	23.3	40.1

4.2   Chinese OHR

4.2.1   Chinese Handwriting Databases

We used two different corpora for our experiments in Chinese: the ETL9B corpus and the BBN Chinese Handwriting (BBN-CH) database.

The ETL9B database is published by the Japanese Technical Committee for Optical Character Recognition. The database was first released in 1993 and many researchers have reported recognition performance on that database. ETL9B contains 200 instances each of 71 Hiragana and 2,965 Kanji characters for a total of 3,036 unique characters. Following the split in [29], we used the first 20 instances of each character as the development set, the last 20 instances of each character as our test set, and the remaining 160 instances as our training set.

The second Chinese corpus that we used comes from the BBN Chinese Handwriting (BBN-CH) database that was collected at BBN by distributing randomly selected pages from a machine-printed corpus, consisting of scanned pages from books and newspapers to six different authors. The authors were instructed to replicate the printed pages in their own handwriting. Each author on average contributed about 17 pages of handwritten data. The data was scanned at a resolution of 300 dpi and manually transcribed using the source printed text as the reference.

Data from five authors was reserved for training. The amount of handwritten training data available is limited, so the models were bootstrapped with data from the machine printed corpus.

The test set consists of a few pages from the five data sets in training, as well as data from the remaining author's work not used for training. In the experimental results section, we report the results for writer-dependent and writer-independent test conditions. Table 6 summarizes the characteristics of the database used for the experiments.

Table 6. Characteristics of the training and test sets for the BBN CH Database

Characteristic	Train-HW	Train-MP	Test-HW
Number of images	77	352	(8)+20
Number of lines	1106	11399	(101)+311
Total Number of characters	24220	348147	(2134)+6966
Number of unique characters	1641	4457	(601)+977
Number of writers	5	-	(5)+1

4.2.2 Results on ETL Database

To assess the viability of our OHR approach for Chinese handwriting recognition, we ran one experiment using images from the ETL9B database. To collect the ETL9B database, writers were instructed to write a single character on distributed sheets with clearly marked squares. Each character is scanned into a 64x63 black-white bitmap image. The images are all clean (we could not find any extraneous noise in the character images), and a visual review indicates that writers were careful in maintaining a high degree of legibility. A review of the relevant literature [29-31] indicates that a common practice is to assume prior knowledge that each image contains only a single character. Many authors [29-31] have reported on the ELT9B database, and the reported recognition rates for a single system are greater than 96%. These recognition rates, which are unusually high in the context of an unconstrained handwriting recognition task, seem to stem from the characters in the database being carefully written and clearly segmented. The images are clean, and many reported techniques leverage characteristics specific to the database.

We configured our Byblos OHR system with a 14-state HMM for each of the 3,036 characters. No slant correction occurred, and we computed script-independent features directly from the raw images in the corpus. Given the nature of the corpus, a unigram language model with a uniform probability distribution was used. We trained on 160 instances of each of the characters and tested on 20 instances of each character. Our first experiment, with no modification to the machine-printed training and recognition procedure, yielded a recognition accuracy of 83%. While our recognition accuracy on this dataset rests significantly lower than that reported in the literature, our initial goal aimed simply to establish the viability of our approach. Given the unique nature of the ETL9B database, we are unsure whether improvements obtained on this database would continue with a more generic, unconstrained handwriting situation. As a result, having established viability, we did not perform any additional experiments or optimizations on this database.

4.2.3 Results on BBN-CH Database

We ran two training experiments using the BBN-CH database. In the first experiment we trained models using the 77-page, five writer handwritten data set, and in the second we trained models using the five writer handwritten data set along with the 352-page machine-printed training data set. In the second experiment, we trained separate HMMs for machine-printed and handwritten versions of each character.

Table 7. Chinese Recognition Results on the BBN-CH Database

Training Data	Test Data	CER – %	Correct – %
77-page Handwritten Set	Writers-in-training	46.7	55.6
	Fair Writer	66.7	37.7
77-Page Handwritten Set with Jack-knifing	Writers-in-training	N/A	N/A
	Fair Writer (average with six runs)	65.9	37.1
352-page Machine-printed plus 77-page Handwritten Set	Writers-in-training	44.1	57.5
	Fair Writer	62.4	39.8

The test set for all experiments consists of pages written by one writer not included in the training set, as well as a few pages written by writers who are represented in the training set (but the test pages themselves were not included in the training set).

As can be seen from the results in Table 7, the writer-independent error rate on this set is 62.4% - surprisingly high given the much lower WER observed for English. We validated the writer-independent error rate by running a series of six jack-knifing experiments in each of which we set aside data from one writer for testing (a different writer each time) and used the data from the remaining writers for training. The jack-knifing experiment yielded a CER of 65.9% for the writer-independent condition. After an initial analysis of the results, we hypothesized that the lack of adequate training data primarily caused the high writer-independent (and, for that matter, the writer-in-training) error rate. Adding machine-printed data, which on the average exhibits strikingly different characteristics than handwritten data, helped improve performance which is a good indicator that we have inadequate handwritten training data.

To explore the correlation of CER with training data, we further categorized the handwritten training characters into five categories based on their frequency of occurrence in the training set. Table 8 shows the five categories along with the associated CER and correct percentages. As seen from Table 8 data, the correlation between the frequency of the character in training and the associated error rate is striking – as the number of training instances increases, the CER decreases. For 50 training samples or more, CER reduces dramatically.

Table 8. Number of characters, % CER (on writer-independent test set), and % Correct (on writer-independent test set) in each category

Category	Number of Training Samples	CER – %	Correct – %
1	> 100	28.5	75.48
2	50 – 99	48.4	55.18
3	10 – 49	73.9	28.83
4	5 – 9	96.9	3.92
5	1 – 4	99.6	0.45

4.3 Arabic OHR

4.3.1 Corpus

For our Arabic OHR experiments, we used the IFN/ENIT corpus [50]. This corpus was collected by distributing forms with pre-selected text of Tunisian city names and postal codes to multiple writers and having them write the text on the forms. A total of 26,459 images consisting of 937 unique city names from 411 different writers are available for training and testing. These images have been distributed into four sets by the creators of the corpus: set *a*, set *b*, set *c*, and, set *d*. For our experiments, we used sets *a, b,* and, *c* for training/development, and set *d* for test purposes. This split is exactly the same as reported in the ICDAR 2005 Arabic handwriting recognition competition [51]. As shown in Table 9, we reserved 1741 images from 30 writers in the training set for additional test/development purposes. Table 10 contains samples from the IFN/ENIT database. These samples illustrate the broad diversity in writing styles contained within the database.

Table 9. Characteristics of training, development, and test sets selected from IFN/ENIT corpus

Characteristic	Train	Development	Test
Dataset	*a, b*, and, *c*	*a, b*, and, *c*	*D*
Number of Images	17983	1741	6735
Number of Unique City Names	937	492	850
Number of Writers	277	30	104

Table 10. Sample images from the IFN/ENIT database

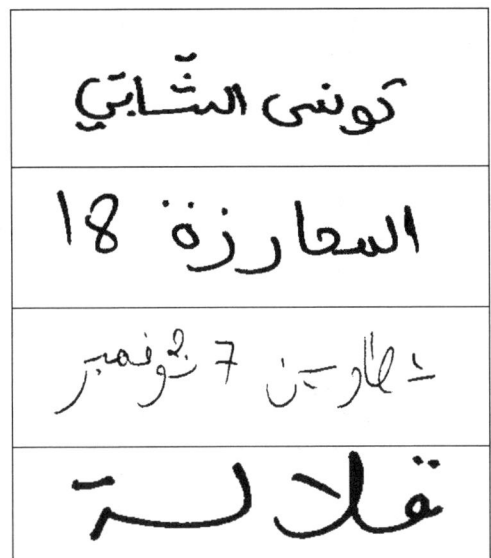

4.3.2 Arabic Results

We ran multiple recognition experiments on the reserved (fair) development test set to determine the best configuration with which to decode the test set, set *d*.

The first recognition experiment used 14-state context-independent character HMMs and a character tri-gram LM, both trained on the IFN/ENIT corpus. For training the character HMMs, we used a CTM configuration with a separate codebook of 256 Gaussians for each character in the training set. With this configuration, the recognition accuracy on the city names in the development set was 40.7%.

In our second experiment, we replaced the character tri-gram LM with a *compound word LM*, where words constituting a city name joined into a single, distinct token. With the compound word LM, we obtained a recognition accuracy of 88.2%, almost a factor of two better than using a character tri-gram LM.

Next, we performed a third experiment in which we trained context-dependent character HMMs. Using context-dependent HMMs and the compound word LM, we obtained a recognition accuracy of 88.6%, a 0.4% absolute improvement to using context-independent character HMMs. The improvement in recognition accuracy with context-dependent HMMs compared to context-independent HMMs appears significantly smaller than the improvement obtained on English OHR. For Arabic this occured because both our OCR and OHR systems use the contextual form of characters to train character HMMs. The contextual form in Arabic already captures the change in a character glyph due to the neighboring characters, therefore, it is not surprising that using context-dependent HMMs yields only a small improvement.

In our fourth experiment, we applied slant correction to the training data and re-trained the context-dependent character HMMs. Testing on the slant-corrected test images using context-dependent HMMs and compound word LM resulted in a recognition accuracy of 89.0% on city names in the development set.

Next, we trained context-dependent character HMMs with a STM configuration. We used a separate set of 128 Gaussians to model the output distribution at each state for all contexts of a particular character. The recognition accuracy on city names in the development set improved to 89.4%.

In our sixth and final experiment, we used the recognition results from above to adapt the character HMMs for each writer (unsupervised adaptation). We used Maximum Likelihood Linear Regression (MLLR) [52] with a maximum of eight transformations to dapt the means of the Gaussians associated with each character HMM. The adapted models resulted in a recognition accuracy of 89.8%, a 0.4% absolute improvement compared to un-adapted recognition.

After exercising the various modeling capabilities of our system on the development set, we used the best configuration to recognize the images in test set, set d. The recognition accuracy on set d with *unsupervised* writer-adapted context-dependent STM character HMMs trained on slant-corrected images and compound word LM was 89.4%.

Our HMM models on set d performed better than the best reported result in the ICDAR 2005 Arabic handwriting competition [51]. To assess the performance of the different model configurations on set d, we repeated all the recognition experiments on set d. The recognition accuracy with all six configurations on development and test sets is summarized in Table 11.

Table 11. Summary of recogniton experiments on IFN/ENIT Arabic handwriting corpus

Character HMM Configuration	Language Model	Accuracy - %	
		Dev Set	Set d
Context-independent, CTM	Character	40.7	41.1
Context-independent, CTM	Compound word	88.2	87.1
Context-dependent, CTM	Compound word	88.6	88.2
Context-dependent, CTM, Slant corrected images	Compound word	89.0	88.8
Context-dependent, STM, Slant corrected images	Compound word	89.4	89.0
Context-dependent, STM, Slant corrected, unsupervised writer adaptation	Compound word	89.8	89.4

5 Summary and Future Work

In this paper we have introduced a script-independent methodology for multi-lingual offline handwriting recognition based on Hidden Markov Models (HMM) used to model characters. This methodology extends our approach to the OCR of machine-printed text. While HMMs offer an inherently language-independent framework, it is the combination of that framework with a script-independent feature extraction procedure that enabled the development of a truly script-independent OHR/OCR system. The framework allows us to incorporate other constraints, such as a language model, into the recognition process to improve overall system performance.

At this early stage in the development of our OHR technology, the use of slant normalization and context-dependent HMMs are the two salient differences between our OCR and OHR systems. The experimental results on English and Arabic handwritten corpora demonstrate the fundamental strength of our HMM approach in enabling script-independent offline handwriting recognition.

To our best knowledge, the best previous results on the English IAM database were reported in a recent June 2006 paper [28]. While the training and test sets used by the authors of [28] no doubt differ from ours, our work yielded better results than those reported in [28], indicating that, at the very least, our OHR approach delivers state-of-the-art performance in English.

The recognition accuracy obtained by our system on the Arabic IFN/ENIT database can directly compare to results reported in ICDAR 2005 competition on Arabic offline handwriting [51]. The best result, with a fair training and test condition, reported in [51] is 88.95%, which is slightly worse than the accuracy of 89.4% obtained by our Arabic OHR system.

In the case of Chinese, we demonstrated the viability of our approach using the ETL9B data set. Furthermore, the results on the unconstrained handwritten images in the BBN-CH corpus indicate that, given adequate data, reasonable recognition accuracy on clean data can be obtained.

Notwithstanding the recognition performance reported in this paper, it is clear that, for the vast majority of real-world data, offline handwriting recognition continues to remain an open research problem. Nevertheless, we believe that the approach outlined in this paper offers a powerful framework for tackling that problem. Potential areas of future work include the development of more robust and discriminative features, including baseline-dependent features, better normalization techniques, and the development of better language modeling techniques.

Acknowledgments. The authors are grateful to the creators of the IAM, ETL, and IFN/ENIT corpora and for making them available to the document research community.

References

1. Rabiner, l.: A Tutorial on Hidden Markov Models and Selected Applications in Speech Recognition. Proc. IEEE 77, 257–286 (1989)
2. Makhoul, J., Schwartz, R.: State of the Art in Continuous Speech Recognition. Proc. Natl. Acad. Sci. USA 92, 9956–9963 (1995)
3. Kundu, A., Bahl, P.: Recognition of Handwritten Script: a Hidden Markov Model Based Approach. Pattern Recognition 22, 283–297 (1989)
4. Levin, E., Pieraccini, R.: Dynamic Planar Warping for Optical Character Recognition. In: IEEE Int. Conf. Acoustics, Speech, Signal Processing, San Francisco, CA, vol. III, pp. 149–152 (1992)

5. Vlontzos, J.A., Kung, S.Y.: Hidden Markov Models for Character Recognition. IEEE Trans. Image Processing 1, 539–543 (1992)
6. Agazzi, O.E., Kuo, S.: Hidden Markov Model Based Optical Character Recognition in the Presence of Deterministic Transformations. Pattern Recognition 26, 1813–1826 (1993)
7. Chen, M.Y., Kundu, A., Srihari, S.N.: Handwritten Word Recognition Using Continuous Density Variable Duration Hidden Markov Model. In: Int. Conf. Acoustics, Speech, Signal Processing, Minneapolis, MN, vol. 5, pp. 105–108 (1993)
8. Bose, C.B., Kuo, S.S.: Connected and Degraded Text Recognition Using Hidden Markov Model. Pattern Recognition 27, 1345–1363 (1994)
9. Rocha, J., Pavlidis, T.: Character Recognition without Segmentation. IEEE Trans. Pattern Analysis and Machine Intelligence 17, 903–909 (1995)
10. Bunke, H., Roth, M., Schukat-Talamazzini, E.G.: Off-line Cursive Handwriting Recog- nition Using Hidden Markov Models. Pattern Recognition 28, 1399–1413 (1995)
11. Oh, C., Kim, W.S.: Off-line Recognition of Handwritten Korean and Alphanumeric Characters Using Hidden Markov Models. In: Proc. Int. Conf. Document Analysis and Recognition, Montreal, Canada, vol. 2, pp. 815–818 (1995)
12. Anigbogu, J.C., Belaid, A.: Hidden Markov Models in Text Recognition. Int. J. Pattern Recognition and Artificial Intelligence 9, 925–958 (1995)
13. Casey, R.G., Lecolinet, E.: A Survey of Methods and Strategies in Character Segmenta- tion. IEEE Trans. Pattern Analysis and Machine Intelligence 18, 690–706 (1996)
14. Kim, W.S., Park, R.H.: Off-line Recognition of Handwritten Korean and Alphanumeric Characters Using Hidden Markov Models. Pattern Recognition 29, 845–858 (1996)
15. Park, H.S., Lee, S.W.: Off-line Recognition of Large-set Handwritten Characters with Multiple Hidden Markov Models. Pattern Recognition 29, 231–244 (1996)
16. Allam, M.: Segmentation Versus Segmentation-free for Recognizing Arabic Text. In: Proc. SPIE, vol. 2422, pp. 228–235 (1995)
17. Ben Amara, N., Belaid, A.: Printed PAW Recognition Based on Planar Hidden Markov Models. In: 13th Int. Conf. Pattern Recognition, Vienna, Austria, vol. II, pp. 220–224 (1996)
18. Yarman-Vural, F.T., Atici, A.: A Heuristic Algorithm for Optical Character Recognition of Arabic Script. In: Proc. SPIE. Part 2, vol. 2727, pp. 725–736 (1996)
19. Kaltenmeier, A., Caesar, T., Gloger, J.M., Mandler, E.: Sophisticated Topology of Hidden Markov Models for Cursive Script Recognition. In: Proc. Int. Conf. Document Analysis and Recognition, Tsukuba City, Japan, pp. 139–142 (1993)
20. Cho, W., Lee, S.W., Kim, J.H.: Modeling and Recognition of Cursive Words with Hidden Markov Models. Pattern Recognition 28, 1941–1953 (1995)
21. Mohamed, M., Gader, P.: Handwritten Word Recognition using Segmentation-Free Hid- den Markov Modeling and Segmentation-based Dynamic Programming Techniques. IEEE Trans. Pattern Analysis and Machine Intelligence 18, 548–554 (1996)
22. Elms, A.J., Illingworth, J.: Modelling Polyfont Printed Characters with HMMs and a Shift Invariant Hamming Distance. In: Proc. Int. Conf. Document Analysis and Recognition, Montreal, Canada, pp. 504–507 (1995)
23. Aas, K., Eikvil, L.: Text Page Recognition using Grey-level Features and Hidden Markov Models. Pattern Recognition 29, 977–985 (1996)
24. Kornai, A.: Experimental HMM-based Postal OCR System. In: Proc. Int. Conf. Acoustics, Speech, Signal Processing, Munich, Germany, vol. 4, pp. 3177–3180 (1997)
25. Al-Badr, B., Mahmoud, S.: Survey and Bibliography of Arabic Optical Text Recognition. Signal Processing 41, 49–77 (1995)

26. Starner, T., Makhoul, J., Schwartz, R., Chou, G.: On-line Cursive Handwriting Recognition Using Speech Recognition Methods. In: IEEE Int. Conf. Acoustics, Speech, Signal Processing, Adelaide, Australia, vol. V, pp. 125–128 (1994)

27. Park, H., Lee, S.: A Truly 2-D Hidden Markov Model. Pattern Recognition 31(12), 1849–1864 (1998)

28. Vinciarelli, A., Bengio, S., Bunke, H.: Offline Recognition of Unconstrained Handwritten Texts Using HMMs and Statistical Language Models. IEEE Transactions on Pattern Analysis and Machine Intelligence 26(6), 709–720 (2004)

29. Liu, C.-L., Marukawa, K.: Global Shape Normalization for Handwritten Chinese Character Recognition: A New Method. In: Proceedings of the 9th International Workshop on Frontiers in Handwriting Recognition (IWFHR-9) (2004)

30. Wu, T., Ma, S.: Feature Extraction by Hierarchical Overlapped Elastic Meshing for Handwritten Chinese Character Recognition. In: Proceedings of the Seventh International Conference on Document Analysis and Recognition (ICDAR) (2003)

31. Tang, Y.Y., Tu, L., Liu, J., Lee, S., Lin, W., Shyu, I.: Offline Recognition of Chinese Handwriting by Multifeature and Multilevel Classification. IEEE. Trans. On Pattern Analysis and Machine Intelligence 20(5) (May 1998)

32. Natarajan, P., Lu, Z., Bazzi, I., Schwartz, R., Makhoul, J.: Multilingual Machine Printed OCR. International Journal of Pattern Recognition and Artificial Intelligence 15(1), 43–63 (2001)

33. Forney, G.D.: The Viterbi Algorithm. Proc. IEEE 61, 268–278 (1973)

34. Austin, S., Schwartz, R., Placeway, P.: The Forward-Backward Search Algorithm. In: IEEE Int. Conf. Acoustics, Speech, Signal Processing, Toronto, Canada, vol. V, pp. 697–700 (1991)

35. Schwartz, R., Nguyen, L., Makhoul, J.: Multiple-Pass Search Strategies. In: Lee, C.-H., Soong, F.K., Paliwal, K.K. (eds.) Automatic Speech and Speaker Recognition: Advanced Topics, pp. 429–456. Kluwer Academic Publishers, Dordrecht (1996)

36. Nguyen, L., Anastasakos, T., Kubala, F., LaPre, C., Makhoul, J., Schwartz, R., Yuan, N., Zavaliagkos, G., Zhao, Y.: The 1994 BBN/BYBLOS Speech Recognition System. In: Proc. ARPA Spoken Language Systems Technology Workshop, Austin, TX, pp. 77–81. Morgan Kaufmann Publishers, San Francisco (1995)

37. Makhoul, J., Schwartz, R., LaPre, C., Bazzi, I.: A Script-Independent Methodology for Optical Character Recognition. Pattern Recognition 31(9), 1285–1294 (1998)

38. Lu, Z., Schwartz, R., Raphael, C.: Script-Independent, HMM-based Text Line Finding for OCR. In: Int. Conf. Pattern Recognition, Barcelona, Spain, vol. 4, pp. 551–554 (September 2000)

39. Makhoul, J., Schwartz, R.: Language-Independent and Segmentation-Free Optical Character Recognition. U.S. Patent No. 5933525, (August 3, 1999)

40. Fukunaga, K.: Introduction to Statistical Pattern Recognition, ch. 10, 2nd edn. Academic Press, New York (1990)

41. Baum, L.E.: An inequality and Associated Maximization Technique in Statistical Estimation for Probabilistic Functions of Markov Processes. Inequalities 3, 1–8 (1972)

42. Dempster, A.P., Laird, N.M., Rubin, D.B.: Maximum-likelihood from Incomplete Data via the EM Algorithm. J. Royal Statist. Soc. Ser. B (methodological) 39, 1–38 (1977)

43. Redner, R.A., Walker, H.F.: Mixture Densities, Maximum Likelihood and the EM Algorithm. SIAM Review 26, 195–239 (1984)

44. Bellegarda., J., Nahamoo, D.: Tied Mixture Continuous Parameter Models for Large Vocabulary Isolated Speech Recognition. In: IEEE Int. Conf. Acoustics, Speech, Signal Processing, Glasgow, Scotland, vol. 1, pp. 13–16 (1989)

45. Huang., X.D., Jack, M.A.: Semi-continuous Hidden Markov Models for Speech Recognition. Computer Speech and Language 3 (1989)
46. Lu, Z., Schwartz, R., Natarajan, P., Bazzi, I., Makhoul, J.: Advances in the BBN BYBLOS OCR System. In: Proc. Of Intl. Conf. Doc. Analysis and Recognition, Bangalore, India, pp. 337–340 (1999)
47. Tay, Y.H., Lallican, P.M., Khalid, M., Viard-Gaudin, C., Knerr, S.: An Offline Cursive Handwritten Word Recognition System. In: Proceedings of IEEE Region 10 Conference (2001)
48. Marti, U., Bunke, H.: A Full English Sentence Database for Off-line Handwriting Recognition. In: Proc. of the 5th Int. Conf. on Document Analysis and Recognition, ICDAR 1999, Bangalore, pp. 705–708 (1999)
49. Johansson, S., Leech, G.N., Goodluck, H.: Manual of Information to Accompany the Lancaster-Oslo/Bergen Corpus of British English, for Use with Digital Computers. Department of English, University of Oslo, Norway (1978)
50. Pechwitz, M., Maddouri, S.S., Märgner, V., Ellouze, N., Amiri, H.: IFN/ENIT-Database of Handwritten Arabic Words. In: 7th Colloque International Francophone sur l'Ecrit et le Document, CIFED 2002, Hammamet, Tunis, October 21-23 (2002)
51. Märgner, V., Pechwitz, M., El Abed, H.: ICDAR 2005 Arabic Handwriting Recognition Competition. In: 8th International Conference on Document Analysis and Recognition, ICDAR 2005, Seoul, Korea, August 29-Sepember 01 (2005)
52. Legetter, C.J., Woodland, P.C.: Maximum Likelihood Linear Regression for Speaker Adaptation of Continuous Density Hidden Markov Models. Computer Speech and Language 9, 171–185 (1995)

Handwritten Character Recognition of Popular South Indian Scripts

Umapada Pal[1], Nabin Sharma[1], Tetsushi Wakabayashi[2], and Fumitaka Kimura[2]

[1] Computer Vision and Pattern Recognition Unit, Indian Statistical Institute, Kolkata-108, India
umapada@isical.ac.in
[2] Graduate School of Engineering, Mie University, Kurimamachiya-cho, TSU, Japan

Abstract. India is a multi-lingual, multi-script country. Considerably less work has been done towards handwritten character recognition of Indian languages than for other languages. In this paper we propose a quadratic classifier based scheme for the recognition of off-line handwritten characters of three popular south Indian scripts: Kannada, Telugu, and Tamil. The features used here are mainly obtained from the directional information. For feature computation, the bounding box of a character is segmented into blocks, and the directional features are computed in each block. These blocks are then down-sampled by a Gaussian filter, and the features obtained from the down-sampled blocks are fed to a modified quadratic classifier for recognition. Here, we used two sets of features. We used 64-dimensional features for high speed recognition and 400-dimensional features for high accuracy recognition. A five-fold cross validation technique was used for result computation, and we obtained 90.34%, 90.90%, and 96.73% accuracy rates from Kannada, Telugu, and Tamil characters, respectively, from 400 dimensional features.

1 Introduction

Recognition of handwritten characters has been a popular research area for many years because of its various application potentials, such as postal automation, bank cheque processing, automatic data entry, etc. Many pieces of work exist for handwritten recognition of Roman, Japanese, Chinese, Korean, and Arabic scripts, and various approaches have been proposed by the researchers for handwritten character recognition [1, 2, 5, 12, 28]. Although many scripts and languages exist in India (there are more than 19 official languages and 11 scripts), not much research has been done for the recognition of handwritten Indian characters. In this paper, we propose a system for the recognition of off-line handwritten characters of three popular south Indian scripts: Kannada, Telugu, and Tamil.

Much work has solved Indian printed characters, at present, OCR systems are commercially available for some printed Indian scripts [3, 21, 24, 27]. Although several pieces of research exist on Indian printed characters, only a few attempts have been made towards the recognition of Indian off-line handwritten characters. Among off-line Indian handwritten work, maximum research has been done for Bangla. Roy, et al. [29] proposed a quadratic classifier based method for Bangla character recognition. Bhowmik, et al. [18] proposed a Multi Layer Perceptron (MLP) based scheme for the recognition of Bangla handwritten characters. Basu, et al. [19] proposed an MLP-based scheme for the

D.S. Doermann and S. Jaeger (Eds.): SACH 2006, LNCS 4768, pp. 251–264, 2008.
© Springer-Verlag Berlin Heidelberg 2008

recognition of Bangla characters, and the feature set used for recognition included 24 shadow features, 16 centroid features, and 36 longest-run features. Rahman, et al. [20] proposed a multistage approach for handwritten Bangla character recognition, and the major features used for the multistage approach include matra/shirorekha, upper part of the character, disjoint section of the character, vertical line and double vertical lines. Some systems have also been developed for unconstrained Bangla handwritten word recognition for Indian postal recognition [13,31].

For handwritten Devnagari characters the first research report was published in 1977 [30], but not much research work has been done since that. At present, researchers have begun to work on handwritten Devnagari numerals and characters, and few a research reports have been published recently. Hanmandlu and Murthy [6] proposed a Fuzzy model based recognition of handwritten Hindi (Hindi language is written in Devnagari script) numerals. Bajaj, et al. [7] employed three different kinds of features, namely, density features, moment features, and descriptive component features, for classification of Devnagari numerals. Bhattacharaya, et al. [9] proposed a Multi-Layer Perceptron (MLP) neural network based classification approach for the recognition of Devnagari handwritten numerals. They considered multi-resolution features based on wavelet transform in their proposed system. Kumar and Singh [8] proposed a Zernike moments based approach for Devnagari character recognition. Recently, Sharma, et al. [11] proposed a Devnagari character recognition method based on 64 dimensional chain code features.

For Telugu script, a few pieces of work considered the recognition of machine-printed text [21, 22]. Some pieces of work on on-line recognition of Telugu script are also available in the literature [23]. But, to the best of our knowledge, no work considered the recognition of off-line handwritten Telugu characters.

Like Telugu script, Kannada also has only few pieces of work for the recognition of its text [25]. Some literature is also available on on-line recognition of Kannada script [4]. But, to the best of our knowledge, only one work has looked at the recognition of off-line handwritten Kannada characters, and that work is reported by us [26].

Compared to Bangla and Devnagari script, pieces of research work on Tamil script are considerably fewer. Shanthi and Duraiswamy [15] discussed some pre-processing steps performed prior to the recognition of Tamil handwritten character recognition. Chinnuswamy and Krishnamoorthy [16] used a linguistic approach for hand printed Tamil character recognition. Hewavitharana and Fernando [17] used a two-stage classification approach for Tamil character recognition. In the first stage a given character is classified into one of the three groups: core, ascending, and descending characters. The second stage uses a statistical classifier for final recognition.

In this paper, we concentrate on the recognition of off-line handwritten characters of three popular South Indian scripts: Kannada, Telugu, and Tamil. The features for the classifier are obtained from the directional information [12] of the characters contour points. A Modified Quadratic Discriminant Function (MQDF) [12] recognizes the characters. In the proposed scheme, at first, the bounding box of a character segments into blocks, and directional features are computed in each of these blocks. Next, these blocks are down sampled by a Gaussian filter. Finally, the features obtained from the down sampled blocks are to the classifier for recognition.

The paper is organized as follows. In Section 2, we discuss the properties of the South Indian scripts considered here. Section 3 deals with data collection. The feature extraction procedure is presented in Section 4. Section 5 details the classifier used for the recognition.

The experimental results are shown in Section 6. Finally, the paper's conclusion is given in Section 7.

2   Properties of Kannada, Telugu and Tamil Languages

Most of the Indian scripts originated from *Brahmi* script through various transformations. The writing style of Kannada, Telugu and Tamil scripts reads from left to right, and have no concept of upper/lower case. A brief overview of these scripts and their character are discussed below.

Kannada is the official language of the Southern Indian state, Karnataka. Kannada, a Dravidian language, is spoken by about 44 million people in the Indian states of Karnataka, Andhra Pradesh, Tamil Nadu, and Maharashtra. The Kannada alphabets deveoped from the Kadamba and Cālukya scripts, descendents of Brahmi used between the 5th and 7th centuries AD. The modern Kannada script contains 14 vowels and 34 consonants, called *basic characters*. In Indian scripts, generally a vowel following a consonant takes a modified shape. These modified shapes are called *modifiers or matra*. A consonant/vowel following a consonant sometimes takes a compound orthographic shape, which we call *compound character*. As a result, almost 250 characters exist in most Indian scripts. In this paper, we will consider only the basic characters of Kannada, Telugu, and Tamil scripts. A sample of Kannada handwritten samples of basic characters is shown in Figure 1.

Telugu is a popular script in India, being a Dravidian language spoken by about 75 million people in the Southern Indian state, Andhra Pradesh, and its neighboring states. Telugu is also spoken in Bahrain, Fiji, Malaysia, Mauritius, Singapore, and the UAE. The alphabet of the modern Telugu script consists of 48 basic characters (14 vowels and 34 consonants). Figure 2 shows a set of handwritten basic characters of Telugu script. From the figure, it may be noted that Telugu script shares many similarities with Kannada script.

Tamil is one of the oldest languages in the world. The Tamil script derives from the *Grantha* script, a descendant of the ancient *Brahmi* script of India. Apart from India, it is also one of the official languages in Singapore, Malaysia, and Sri Lanka. Almost 62 million people in India speak Tamil. It has the oldest literature amongst the Dravidian languages. The Government of India recognized Tamil as a classical language in 2004, and it is the first language to get such recognition. Tamil alphabets can be divided into a set of vowels, consonants, composite letters, and special letters. Tamil is written horizontally from left to right, and the basic set of alphabets consists of 12 vowels, 23 consonants (18 basic consonants and 5 *Grantha* letters) and one special character. Grantha letters are used to write consonants borrowed from Sanskrit, and also some words of English origin. A set of Tamil basic characters is shown in Figure 3.

The challenging part of Indian handwritten character recognition comes from the distinction between the similar shaped characters. Sometimes, a minuscule part distinguishes between two characters or numerals. These small distinguishing parts increase the recognition complexity. Given the writing styles of different individuals, the same characters may take different shapes, and two or more different characters may take a similar

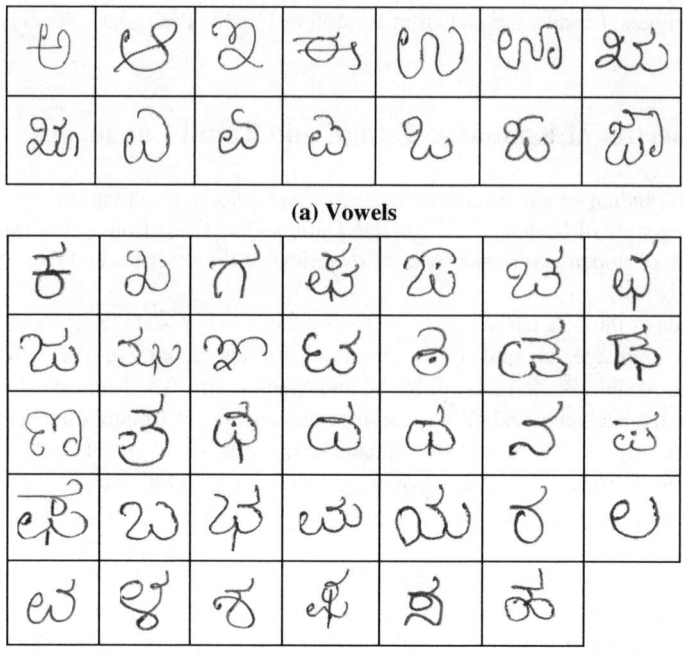

(a) Vowels

(b) Consonants

Fig. 1. Handwritten samples of Kannada basic characters

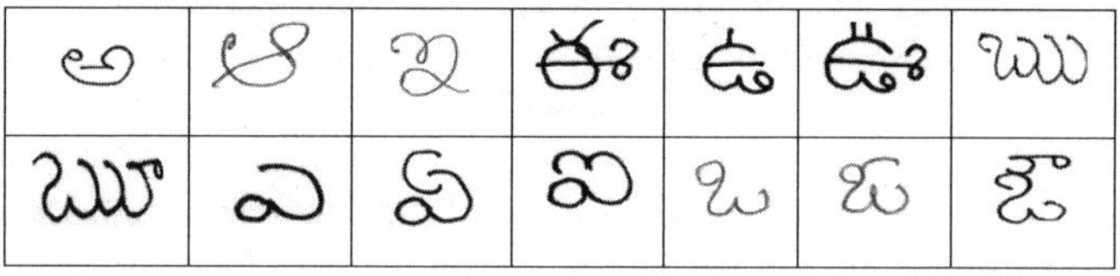

(a) Vowels

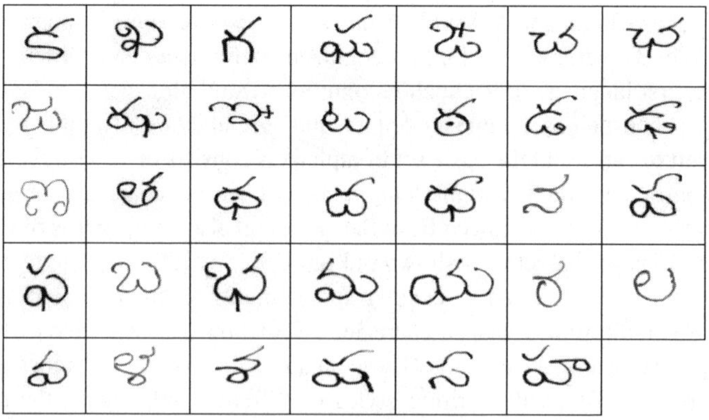

(b) Consonants

Fig. 2. Handwritten samples of Telugu basic characters

shape. These factors also increase the complexity of handwritten character recognition. Some examples of similar shape characters in Kannada, Telugu, and Tamil scripts are given in Figure 4.

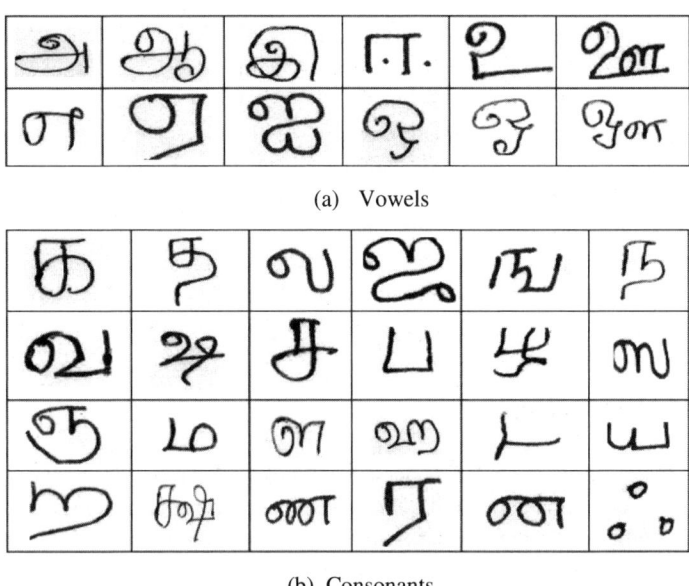

(a) Vowels

(b) Consonants

Fig. 3. Handwritten samples of Tamil basic characters

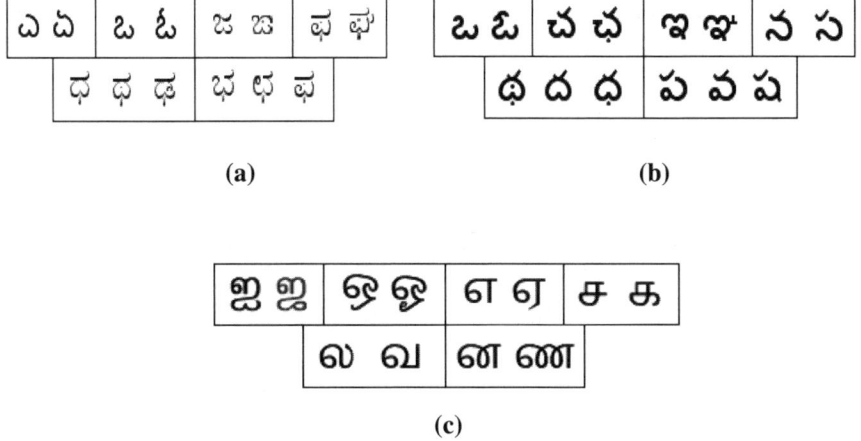

(a)   (b)

(c)

Fig. 4. Similar shaped characters in (a) Kannada, (b) Telugu, and (c) Tamil

3 Data Collection

Data for the experiment was collected from different individuals of various professions. Data for different scripts has been collected from different Indian States, where these scripts are the official language. For example, the Kannada data set has been collected from Karnataka State of India because Kannada is the official language of Karnataka. Similarly, the Telugu and Tamil data sets were collected from Andhra Pradesh and Tamil Nadu, respectively.

To our best knowledge, no standard database exists for research work of Indian handwritten characters. Currently, we are developing a database for Kannada, Telugu, and Tamil scripts. We considered 10,779, 10,872, and 10,216 data samples of Kannada, Telugu, and Tamil script, respectively, for our experiment.

A flatbed scanner was used for digitization, with images in gray tone at 300 dpi and stored as Tagged Image File (TIF) format. We used the Otsu method [10] to convert gray tone images into two-tone (0 and 1) images.

4 Feature Extraction

We computed two feature sets for recognition purposes. We use a 64-dimensional feature for high-speed recognition and a 400-dimensional feature for high accuracy recognition. A comparative study on the recognition accuracy of these two different feature sets is presented in the result and discussion parts of the paper.

64-dimensional Feature Extraction:

Given a two-tone image, we first find the contour points of the image by the following algorithm. For all object points in the image, consider a 3 x 3 window surrounding the object point. If any of the four neighboring points (as shown in Figure 5(a)) is a background point, then this object point (P) is considered as a contour point. Otherwise, it is a non-contour point.

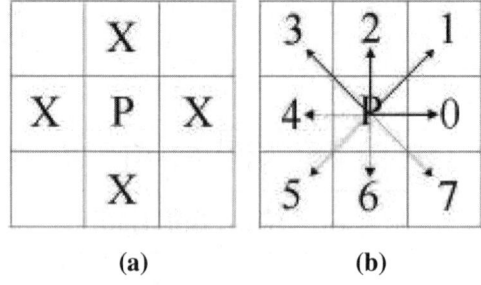

(a)   (b)

Fig. 5. (a) A point P and its four neighbors marked by 'X', (b) For a point P the direction codes used for its eight neighboring points

The bounding box (minimum rectangle containing the character) of an input character is then divided into 7 x 7 blocks (as shown in Figure 6(c)). In each of these blocks, the direction chain code for each contour point is noted, and the frequency of the direction codes is computed. We use a chain code of four directions only [directions 0 (horizontal), 1 (45 degree slanted), 2 (vertical) and 3 (135 degree slanted)]. See Figure 5(b) for an illustration of the four chain code directions considered here. We assume the chain code of direction 0 and 4, 1 and 5, 2 and 6, 3 and 7, are the same. Thus, in each block we obtain an array of four integer values, representing the frequencies, and those frequency values become a feature. The histogram of the values of these four direction codes in each block of a Tamil character is shown in Figure 6(e). Thus, for 7 x 7 blocks, we get 7 x 7 x 4 =196 features. To reduce the feature dimension, after the histogram calculation in 7 x 7 blocks, the blocks are down sampled into 4x4 blocks by a Gaussian filter. As a result, we have 4 x 4 x 4 = 64 features for recognition. The histogram of the values of all the chain code directions obtained after down sampling is shown in Figure 6(f). The features are normalized before feeding them to the classifier for recognition.

400-dimensional Feature Extraction:

The gray-scale local-orientation histogram of the component is used for 400 dimensional feature extractions. To obtain 400-dimensional features, we apply the following steps.

Step 1: Size normalization of the input binary image is done. Here, we normalize the image into 126 x 126 pixels.
Step 2: The input binary image is then converted into a gray-scale image, by applying a 2×2 mean filtering 5 times.
Step 3: The gray-scale image is normalized so that the mean gray scale becomes zero with a maximum value of 1.
Step 4: Normalized image is then segmented into 9×9 blocks.
Step 5: A Roberts filter is then applied on the image to obtain the gradient image. The arc tangent of the gradient (direction of gradient) is quantized into 16 directions, and the strength of the gradient is accumulated for each of the quantized direction. By strength of Gradient ($f(x, y)$) we mean

$$f(x, y) = \sqrt{(\Delta u)^2 + (\Delta v)^2} \text{ and}$$

by direction of gradient ($\theta(x, y)$) we mean $\theta(x, y) = \tan^{-1} \dfrac{\Delta v}{\Delta u}$, where

$\Delta u = g(x+1, y+1) - g(x, y)$, and $\Delta v = g(x+1, y) - g(x, y+1)$, and $g(x, y)$ is a gray scale at (x, y) point.
Step 6: Histograms of the values of 16 quantized directions are computed in each 9 x 9 blocks.
Step 7: 9×9 blocks are down sampled into 5×5 by a Gaussian filter. Thus, we obtain a 5×5×16 = 400 dimensional feature.

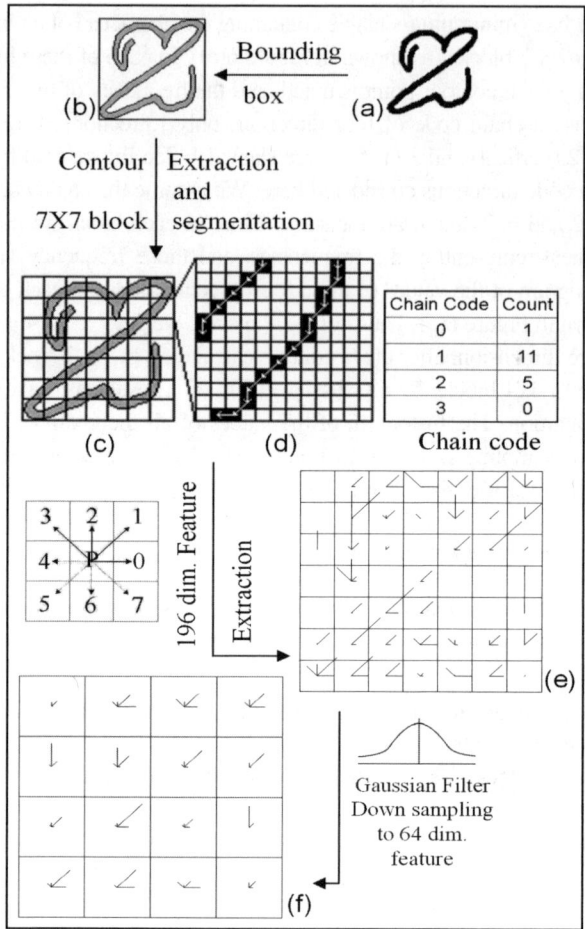

Fig. 6. Example of 64-dimensional feature extraction. (a) Tamil character. (b) Contour extracted image shown in its bounding box. (c) Contour extracted image segmented into 7 x 7 blocks. (d) Contour of the character in a block (zoomed version) and its chain code count. (e) Block-wise chain code histogram of contour points. (f) Histogram of chain code direction of contour points after down sampling into 4 x 4 blocks from 7 x 7 blocks.

5 Recognition Classifier

Recognition of characters in quadratic classifier [12] occurs by using the following discriminate function:

$$g(X) = (N + N_0 + n - 1)\ln[1 + \frac{1}{N_0\sigma^2}[\|X - M\|^2$$

$$- \sum_{i=1}^{k} \frac{\lambda_i}{\lambda_i + \frac{N_0}{N}\sigma^2}\{\Phi_i^T(X - M)\}^2]] + \sum_{i=1}^{k}\ln(\lambda_i + \frac{N_0}{N}\sigma^2)$$

where X is the feature vector of an input character; M is a mean vector of samples; $\mathbf{\Phi}_i^T$ is the ith eigenvector of the sample covariance matrix; λ_i is the ith eigenvalue of the sample covariance matrix; k is the number of eigenvalues considered here, n is the feature size; σ^2 is the initial estimation of a variance; N is the number of learning samples; and N_o is a confidence constant for σ, and N_o is considered as $N/4$ ($3N/7$), $N/9$ (N), and $N/9$ ($N/4$) for a 64 400-dimensional feature in Kannada, Telugu, and Tamil scripts, respectively. We do not use all the eigenvalues and their respective eigenvectors for the classification. For 64 400-dimensional feature, we sort the eigenvector in descending order, and we consider first 20 (40), 60 (60), and 60 (50) eigenvalues, respectively, for Kannada, Telugu, and Tamil, and their respective eigenvectors for classification. The number of eigenvalues considered here is chosen from the experiment.

6   Results and Discussion

We have used a 5-fold cross validation scheme for recognition result calculation. Here the database of each script divides into five subsets, and are done on each subset using the other four subsets for learning. The recognition rates for all the five test subsets of a database averaged to obtain the accuracy. As mentioned earlier, we considered 10,779, 10,872, and 10,216 data samples of Kannada, Telugu, and Tamil script, respectively, for our experiment.

6.1   Global Recognition Results

From experiments we note the overall character recognition accuracies of the proposed scheme for Kannada, Telugu, and Tamil scripts are 85.27%, 88.33% and 95.19%, respectively, when a 64-dimensional feature vector is considered. We obtained 90.34%, 90.90%, and 96.73% for Kannada, Telugu, and Tamil script, respectively, when a 400-dimensional

Table 1. Recognition accuracy of different top choices (with 0% rejection)

Script / Top Choices	Kannada		Telugu		Tamil	
	64 Dim	400 Dim	64 Dim	400 Dim	64 Dim	400 Dim
1	85.27%	90.34%	88.33%	90.90%	95.19%	96.73%
2	93.97%	96.50%	95.49%	96.58%	97.75%	98.79%
3	96.59%	98.11%	96.94%	97.76%	98.39%	99.16%
4	97.74%	98.58%	97.69%	98.29%	98.79%	99.43%
5	98.38%	98.96%	98.17%	98.62%	98.99%	99.55%

feature vector was considered. Zero-percent rejection rate was considered for this accuracy calculation. We also computed a recognition accuracy of different top choices of both 64- and 400-dimensional feature vectors. The detail character recognition results obtained for the three scripts using 64- and 400-dimensional feature vectors with different top choices are given in Table 1. From the table, the note a 7% accuracy increase in 64-dimension feature vector when we first considered the two top choices in Kannada and Telugu scripts, this happened mostly because of confusion between the similar shaped character pairs.

6.2 Results on Individual Characters

We computed the accuracy of the individual characters of the three scripts and the accuracies of some of the characters based on 400-dimension feature vector are given in Table 2. We obtained highest accuracy for the characters ౭(98.66%), ౙ(100%), ౦ ౦ (100.00%) in Kannada, Telugu, and Tamil scripts, respectively. From the experiment, we also note the characters for which the lowest accuracy occurred in each of the scripts. We observed the lowest accuracy obtained in Kannada, Telugu, and Tamil scripts for character ౬ (60.27 %), ౮ (63.83%), and ౯ (86.47%), respectively. The lower accuracy of these characters happened mostly because of shape similarity with other characters of their respective scripts.

Table 2. Accuracies of some characters in Kannada, Telugu, and Tamil scripts (using a 400-dimensional feature with 0% rejection)

Kannada		Telugu		Tamil	
Character	**Accuracy**	**Character**	**Accuracy**	**Character**	**Accuracy**
౭	98.66%	ౙ	100.00%	౦ ౦	100.00%
ౝ	98.21%	౫	99.10%	౬	99.65%
౮	97.77%	౯	98.69%	౰	99.64%
౱	97.75%	౳	98.23%	౴.	99.64%
౵	97.35%	౶	97.81%	౷	99.64%

6.3 Confusing Pair Computation

We also note the main confusing character pairs of different scripts, and we observe that main reason of such confusion comes from shape similarity. From Table 3, note that for the 400-dimensional feature, 36.69% samples of the Kannada character ౬ were mis-recognized as the Kannada character ⟨image⟩, or vice–versa. In Telugu (Tamil) the main confusing character pair was ⟨image⟩ and ⟨image⟩, (⟨image⟩ and ⟨image⟩), and they confused in 26.16% (10.33%) cases. Table 3 gives the details of some confusing pairs of characters in the different scripts.

6.4 Error Versus Rejection Rate

We also analyzed error verses rejection rate of the classifier. In Kannada, we note that 8.70% errors occurred when the rejection rate was 2.05%. Only 4.90% error occurred when 10.14% data were rejected. 8.05% errors occurred when the rejection rate was 2.06% and 4.53% errors occurred when 10.17% samples were rejected in Telugu script. In Tamil, we note that 2.26% errors occurred when the rejection rate was 2.04%. Only 0.45% error occurred when 10.19% data were rejected. A rejection criterion of the

Table 3. Some confusion character pairs in the three scripts

Kannada		Telugu		Tamil	
Character pair	% of confusion	Character pair	% of confusion	Character pair	% of confusion
⟨image⟩ ⟨image⟩	36.69	⟨image⟩ ⟨image⟩	26.16	⟨image⟩ ⟨image⟩	10.33
⟨image⟩ ⟨image⟩	25.89	⟨image⟩ ⟨image⟩	16.77	⟨image⟩ ⟨image⟩	7.77
⟨image⟩ ⟨image⟩	18.56	⟨image⟩ ⟨image⟩	12.77	⟨image⟩ ⟨image⟩	3.31
⟨image⟩ ⟨image⟩	14.17	⟨image⟩ ⟨image⟩	8.79	⟨image⟩ ⟨image⟩	1.57

Table 4. Rejection versus error rate (using 400 dimension feature)

Kannada		Telugu		Tamil	
Rejection rate	Error rate	Rejection rate	Error rate	Rejection rate	Error rate
0.00	9.66	0.00	9.10	0.00	3.27
2.05	8.70	2.06	8.05	2.04	2.26
5.11	7.18	5.08	6.62	5.07	1.20
7.11	6.08	7.10	5.67	7.14	0.67
10.14	4.90	10.17	4.53	10.19	0.45

proposed system is mainly based on the difference of 1st and 2nd value of the discriminant function g(X). Table 4 presents the detail results of error versus rejection rate.

6.5 Erroneous Results

To understand why our system generates erroneous results, samples of erroneous characters are shown in Table 5. From the table it can be noted that given their shape similarity, such mis-recognition occurs (in the table, input handwritten samples are shown in the first row and the printed samples of their recognized class are shown in the respective columns of second row). Actual classes to which input samples belong are shown in respective columns of the third row of the table.

Table 5. Some erroneous samples

Script	Kannada		Telugu		Tamil	
Input Samples (Handwritten)	ಕ	೩	ఞ	೦	ඔ	ಜ
Recognized as (Printed sample)	ಛ	೨೩	ఢ	ఠ	௫	ಜ
Actual Class (Printed sample)	ಛ	ಓ	ఢ	ఠ	௫	ಜ

6.6 Comparison of Results

Given no other work on Telugu off-line handwritten characters, we cannot compare our results for Telugu script.

To our best knowledge, one work exists on Kannada off-line handwritten character recognition, and this work is reported by us [26]. We obtained 85.71% accuracy from that work, and we obtained 90.34% accuracy from this work.

A few pieces of work exist on Tamil handwritten characters, and we compared the results of our proposed method with some of these work. The results are shown in Table 6. Chinuswamy, et al. [16] tested their system on 36 classes of Tamil characters and obtained an accuracy of 60%. Hewavitharana, et al. [17] tested their system on 800 Tamil

Table 6. Comparison of results

Method	No. of class	Data Size	Accuracy
Chinnuswamy et.al. [16]	36	Not-known	60%
Hewavitharana et.al. [17]	26	800	79.9%
Proposed method	36	10216	96.73%

characters and obtained 79.9% accuracy. Instead of 36 classes, they considered only 26 classes. Here, we consider 36 classes of Tamil characters and obtained 96.73% accuracy. So, our proposed method shows 16.83% better result than Hewavitharana et al. [17].

7 Conclusion

In this paper, we proposed a quadratic classifier based scheme for the recognition of three popular south Indian scripts: Kannada, Telugu and Tamil. The features used for recognition are obtained from the directional information of the image. The recognition results obtained are encouraging. The authors hope this work will help the researchers in future work for the recognition of other Indian script characters.

Acknowledgement. The authors like to thank S. Murali, PES college of Engineering, Karnataka; R. S. Hegadi and K. Mallikarjun, Gulbarga University, Karnataka; N. Naushad, University of Mysore, Karnataka; A Wahi and Pradeep Kumar, Bannari Amman Institute of Technology, Tamil Nadu; K. Kulkarni, B. V. Bhoomaradi College of Engg. and Tech., Karnataka, for their sincere help towards data collection.

References

1. Plamondon, R., Srihari, S.N.: On-Line and Off-line Handwritten Recognition: A Comprehensive Survey. IEEE Trans on PAMI 22, 62–84 (2000)
2. Lorigo, L., Govindaraju, V.: Arabic Handwritten Word Recognition: A Survey. IEEE Trans on PAMI 28, 712–724 (2006)
3. Pal, U., Chaudhuri, B.B.: Indian Script Character Recognition: A Survey. Pattern Recognition 37, 1887–1899 (2004)
4. Kunte, R.S.R., Samuel, R.D.S.: On-line Character Recognition for Handwritten Kannada Characters using Wavelet Features and Neural Classifier. IETE Journal of Research 46, 387–392 (2000)
5. Liu, C.-L., Nakashima, K., Sako, H., Fujisawa, H.: Handwritten Digit Recognition: Benchmarking of State-of-the-Art Techniques. Pattern Recognition 36, 2271–2285 (2003)
6. Hanmandlu, M., Murthy, O.V.R.: Fuzzy Model Based Recognition of Handwritten Hindi Numerals. In: Intl.Conf. on Cognition and Recognition, pp. 490–496 (2005)
7. Bajaj, R., Dey, L., Chaudhury, S.: Devnagari Nnumeral Recognition by Combining Decision of Multiple Connectionist Classifiers. Sadhana 27, 59–72 (2002)
8. Kumar, S., Singh, C.: A Study of Zernike Moments and its use in Devnagari Handwritten Character Recognition. In: Intl. Conf. on Cognition and Recognition, pp. 514–520 (2005)
9. Bhattacharya, U., Parui, S.K., Shaw, B., Bhattacharya, K.: Neural Combination of ANN and HMM for Handwritten Devnagari Numeral Recognition. In: Proc. 10th IWFHR, pp. 613–618 (2006)
10. Otsu, N.: A Threshold Selection Method from Grey Level Histogram. IEEE Trans on SMC 9, 62–66 (1979)
11. Sharma, N., Pal, U., Kimura, F., Pal, S.: Recognition of Offline Handwritten Devnagari Characters using Quadratic Classifier. In: Kalra, P.K., Peleg, S. (eds.) ICVGIP 2006. LNCS, vol. 4338, pp. 805–816. Springer, Heidelberg (2006)

12. Kimura, F., Takashina, K., Tsuruoka, S., Miyake, Y.: Modified Quadratic Discriminant Function and the Application to Chinese Character Recognition. IEEE Trans. on PAMI 9, 149–153 (1987)
13. Roy, K., Pal, U., Chaushuri, B.B.: A System for Joining and Recognition of Broken Bangla Characters for Indian Postal Automation. In: Proc. of 4th Indian Conf. on Computer Vision Graphics and Image Processing, pp. 641–646 (2004)
14. Pal, U., Chaudhuri, B.B.: Automatic Recognition of Unconstrained Off-line Bangla Handwritten Characters. In: Tan, T., Shi, Y., Gao, W. (eds.) ICMI 2000. LNCS, vol. 1948, pp. 371–378. Springer, Heidelberg (2000)
15. Shanthi, N., Duraiswamy, K.: Preprocessing Algorithms for Recognition of Tamil Handwritten Characters. In: 3rd Int. CALIBER (2005)
16. Chinnuswamy, P., Krishnamoorthy, S.G.: Recognition of Hand Printed Tamil Characters. Pattern Recognition 12, 141–152 (1980)
17. Hewavitharana, S., Fernand, H.C.: A Two Stage Classification Approach to Tamil Handwriting Recognition. In: Tamil Internet, California, USA (2002)
18. Bhowmick, T.K., Bhattacharya, U., Parui, S.K.: Recognition of Bangla Handwritten Characters Using an MLP Classifier Based on Stroke Features. In: Pal, N.R., et al. (eds.) ICONIP 2004. LNCS, vol. 3316, pp. 814–819. Springer, Heidelberg (2004)
19. Basu, S., et al.: Handwritten Bangla Alphabet Recognition Using an MLP Based Classifier. In: Proc. of 2nd NCCPB Dhaka (2005)
20. Rahman, A.F.R., Rahman, R., Fairhurst, M.C.: Recognition of Handwritten Bengali Characters: a Novel Multistage Approach. Pattern Recognition 35, 997–1006 (2002)
21. Negi, A., Bhagvati, C., Krishna, B.: An OCR System for Telugu. In: Proc. ICDAR, pp. 1110–1114 (2001)
22. Sukhaswami, M.B., Seetharamulu, P., Pujari, A.K.: Recognition of Telugu Characters Using Neural Networks. Int. J. Neural Syst. 6, 7–357 (1995)
23. Swethalakshmi, H., Jayaram, A., Chakraborty, V.S., Sekhar, C.C.: Online Handwritten Character Recognition of Devanagari and Telugu Characters using Support Vector Machines. In: Proc. 10th IWFHR, pp. 367–372 (2006)
24. Aparna, K.G., Ramakrishnan, A.G.: A Complete Tamil Optical Character Recognition System. In: Proc. in the 5th Intl. workshop on Document Analysis and Systems, pp. 53–57 (2002)
25. Kumar, B., Vijay, Ramakrishnan, A.G.: Machine Recognition of Printed Kannada Text. In: 5th Int. Workshop on DAS, pp. 37–48 (2000)
26. Pal., U., Sharma, N., Kimura, F., Pal, S.: Offline Handwritten Kannada Character Recognition. Proc. International Conference on Signal and Image Processing 1, 174–177 (2006)
27. Pal, U.: Automatic Script Identification: A Survey. Vivek 16, 26–35 (2006)
28. Kim, H.Y., Kim, J.H.: Hierarchical Random Graph Representation of Handwritten Characters and Its Application to Hangul Recognition. Pattern Recognition 34, 187–201 (2001)
29. Roy, K., Pal, U., Kimura, F.: Bangla Handwritten Character Recognition. International Journal of Tomography & Statistics 5, 27–36 (2007)
30. Sethi, I.K., Chatterjee, B.: Machine Recognition of Constrained Hand Printed Devnagari. Pattern Recognition 9, 69–75 (1977)
31. Pal, U., Roy, K., Kimura, F.: A Lexicon Driven Method for Unconstrained Bangla Handwritten Word Recognition. In: Proc. 10th IWFHR, pp. 601–606 (2006)

Ensemble Methods to Improve the Performance of an English Handwritten Text Line Recognizer

Roman Bertolami and Horst Bunke

Institute of Computer Science and Applied Mathematics
University of Bern, Neubrückstrasse 10, CH-3012 Bern, Switzerland
{bertolam,bunke}@iam.unibe.ch

Abstract. This paper describes recent work on ensemble methods for offline handwritten text line recognition. We discuss techniques to build ensembles of recognizers by systematically altering the training data or the system architecture. To combine the results of the ensemble members, we propose to apply ROVER, a voting based framework commonly used in continuous speech recognition. Additionally, we extend this framework with a statistical combination method. The experimental evaluation shows that the proposed ensemble methods have the potential to improve the recognition accuracy compared to a single recognizer.

1 Introduction

The performance of computers in the recognition of machine printed text has reached levels comparable to that of humans. However, the recognition of offline handwritten text is still an open field with rather low recognition rates and many challenges. Early research activities in offline handwriting recognition have been restricted to isolated characters or numeral recognition. Next, the recognition of cursively written words and digit sequences has been considered, motivated by automatic check [1,2] and postal address reading [3,4].

Research on general handwritten text recognition, as considered in this paper, started much later. As of today, this problem is considered widely unexplored, particularly if no constraints are imposed on the writer. There are large differences in individual writing style as well as in writing instruments. The underlying lexicon often contains a large amount of different word classes to be distinguished. Furthermore, the correct number of words in a text line is unknown in advance, which often leads to segmentation errors. For these reasons, a high recognition accuracy is difficult to achieve. In the literature, recognition rates between 50% and 80% are reported, depending on the experimental setup [5,6,7,8].

From the application oriented point of view, the automatic reading of general handwritten text is interesting for tasks such as the transcription of handwritten archives and the automatic reading of forms, handwritten faxes, personal notes, and annotations on documents. However, often the current methodology does not achieve recognition rates good enough for these applications.

D.S. Doermann and S. Jaeger (Eds.): SACH 2006, LNCS 4768, pp. 265–277, 2008.

A possible strategy to improve the accuracy of pattern classifiers involves the use of ensemble methods, which has been shown to be effective for different classification problems [9,10,11]. By combining the results of multiple classifiers, the recognition accuracy often improves compared to a single classifier. In other words, given that the errors made by the individual classifiers are different, we can expect that, by proper combination of multiple classifiers, errors made by the individual classifiers can be avoided.

In handwriting recognition, several ensemble methods have been presented for character [12], numeral [13,14,15], and word [16,17] recognition. An automatic self-configuration scheme to combine multiple character recognition systems has been proposed in [12]. For this method, genetic algorithms are used. In numeral recognition, the application of statistical combination methods has been reported in [13]. The behavior knowledge space methods were especially able to successfully combine classifiers. A feature selection approach, based on a hierarchical algorithm, was used in [14] to build ensembles of digit recognizers. In [15], a framework to combine numeral string recognizers was proposed that uses a graph-based approach for combination. An evaluation of several decision combination strategies for handwritten word recognition has been reported in [16]. Borda count methods, fuzzy integrals, and multilayer perceptrons have been compared. In [17], various ensemble methods, including Bagging, Boosting, and feature subspace methods have been applied to handwritten word recognition.

The investigation of ensemble methods for unconstrained offline handwritten text line recognition began only recently [18,19,20,21,22]. The combination of multiple text line recognition systems requires additional synchronisation effort because the number of words in the output returned by the individual recognizers might differ. This paper surveys ensemble methods recently applied to offline handwritten text line recognition. Different possibilities to generate multiple recognizers as well as different methods to combine the results of multiple text line recognizers are discussed.

The rest of the paper is organized as follows. The next section introduces the underlying handwritten text line recognizer. Section 3 describes the ensemble creation methods, whereas the combination approaches are discussed in Sect. 4. Experimental evaluation is presented in Sect. 5 and conclusions are drawn in the last section of the paper.

2   Hidden Markov Model Based Recognizer

Most ensemble creation methods require a base recognizer to generate multiple diverse recognizers. The offline handwritten text line recognition system we use as the base recognizer is an enhanced version of the recognition system introduced in [23]. Improvements happen at the language model integration level, as well as in the modeling of the characters. The system can be divided into three major parts: preprocessing, hidden Markov model (HMM) based recognition, and postprocessing.

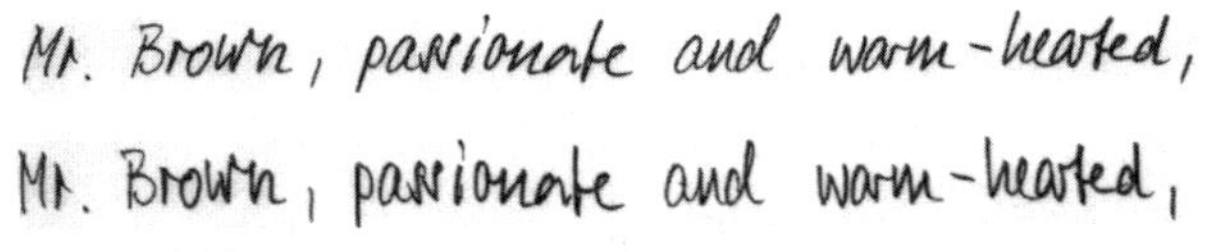

Mr. Brown, passionate and warm-hearted,

Mr. Brown, passionate and warm-hearted,

Fig. 1. Preprocessing of an image of handwritten text. The first line shows the original image, whereas the normalized image is shown on the second line.

To reduce the impact of different writing styles, a handwritten text line image is normalized with respect to skew, slant, and baseline position in the preprocessing phase. An example of this normalization appears in Fig. 1. After these normalization steps, a handwritten text line is converted into a sequence of feature vectors. For this purpose, a sliding window of one pixel is used. The window is moved from left to right, one pixel at each step and nine geometrical features are extracted at each position of the sliding window.

In the HMM based recognition phase, each character is modeled with a linear HMM. The number of states is chosen individually for each character [8], and twelve Gaussian mixture components model the output distribution in each state. The Baum-Welch algorithm is used for the training of the HMMs, whereas the recognition is performed by the Viterbi algorithm. A statistical language model supports the Viterbi decoding step. The integration of this language model is optimized on a validation set, as described in [8].

In the postprocessing phase, a confidence measure is computed for each recognized word w. This confidence measure indicates the degree of confidence the recognizer has for its decision. It can be used either to reject certain parts of the input or as a local weight when combining outputs of multiple recognizers. An overview of different confidence measures for handwritten text line recognition is given in [24].

3   Ensemble Creation

To build a multiple classifier system, two main issues must be addressed. First, an ensemble creation strategy must be defined to generate multiple classifiers. The second issue is to find an appropriate combination method that enables us to fuse the results of the individual classifiers and to compute the final result. In this section, the ensemble creation issue is addressed, and combination methods are discussed in the next section.

Diversity among the individual ensemble members presents a key requirement to obtain good results with multiple classifier methods [21,25,26]. The goal of multiple classifier systems aims to correct the errors of one ensemble member with the output of other ensemble members. To achieve this goal, we need a certain diversity among the ensemble members. Intuitively speaking, the members should make no coincident errors. Several diversity measures have been proposed in the literature for multi-class problems. Surveys can be found in [11,27].

Basically, two different strategies can create multiple classifiers. In the first, the training data alters, and, in the second, the architecture of the recognizers varies.

Many different methods have been proposed to achieve multiple classifiers by supplying the classifier with different training data. The best known among these methods are k-fold cross validation [28], Bagging [29], and Boosting [30]. In k-fold cross validation, the data set divides into k subsets. Individual classifiers are obtained by reserving one of the k subsets. Under the Bagging method, the ensemble contains classifiers trained on bootstrap replicas of the training set. Given a training set S of size N, the Bagging method builds n new training sets $S_1, \ldots, S_n$ each of size N, by randomly choosing elements of the original training set. Boosting applies an iterative approach to creating an ensemble. Training samples misrecognized by the current classifier are 'boosted' in importance, so the next recognizer has a higher likelihood to classify them correctly. The feature subspace method described in Sect. 3.1 is based on altering the training data as well. The individual recognizers use randomly chosen subsets of all available features for training and testing.

Many fewer investigations have been conducted on using different classifier architectures, or varying part of the classifiers. Typically such variations are problem specific and so not generally applicable as different training sets. In [31], the number of hidden neurons varies to produce multiple artificial neural networks. For handwritten text line recognition, we developed an approach that varies the language model integration to get multiple recognition result as described in Sect. 3.2.

3.1   Random Feature Subspace

In the random feature subspace method [32], the individual recognizers use only a subset of all available features for training and testing. These subsets are chosen randomly with a fixed size d. The only constraint is that the same subset must not be used twice.

For the handwriting recognition system we use, only nine features are available, which is a rather low number. The dimension of the subsets d is set to six. This number has been found to be optimal for a similar experiment in the field of handwritten word recognition [17].

3.2   Language Model Integration Variation

One possible architecture modification to create multiple recognition results alters the integration of the statistical language model [19]. It has been shown that those parts of a recognized word sequence sensitive to changes in the underlying language model are often recognized incorrectly [24,33]. For these parts, we seek alternative interpretations to improve the recognition rate.

For an HMM based recognition system with an integrated language model, such as the one used in our experiments, the most likely word sequence $\hat{W} = (w_1, \ldots, w_m)$ for a given observation sequence X is computed as follows:

$$\hat{W} = \underset{W}{\operatorname{argmax}} \left\{ \log p(X|W) + \alpha \, \log p(W) + m\beta \right\} \tag{1}$$

Barry and Eric have enthusiasm.

α	β	Recognition result
0	-100	Barry arm inch we enthusiasm
0	150	B my arm inch we m run rush :
30	-100	Barry and include enthusiasm
30	150	Barry and Eric have enthusiasm .
60	-100	Barry and include enthusiasm
60	150	Barry and in have enthusiasm .

Fig. 2. Multiple recognition results derived from specific integration of a language model

According to Eq. 1, the likelihood of the optical model $p(X|W)$, which is the result of the HMM decoding, combines with the likelihood $p(W)$ obtained from the language model. Because HMM decoding and language model merely produce approximations of probabilities, we use two additional parameters α and β to control the integration of the language model. The parameter α, called *Grammar Scale Factor* (GSF), weights the impact of the statistical language model. The term *Word Insertion Penalty* (WIP) is used for parameter β, which controls the segmentation rate of the recognizer. A higher value of β results in more individual words to be output by the recognizer.

By varying the parameters α and β, various recognition results can be produced from the same image of a handwritten text. To obtain n recognition results, we choose n different parameter pairs (α_i, β_i), where $i = 1, \ldots, n$.

An example of recognizers based on different integration of a language model appears in Fig. 2. Multiple transcriptions are produced for the handwritten text *"Barry and Eric have enthusiasm."* This example provides a good illustration of the impact of the two parameters α and β. We observe that if we increase parameter α, the influence of the language model is increased and nonsense word sequences, for example *"B my arm inch we m run rush :"*, are eliminated. Furthermore, we see the influence of parameter β on the segmentation of W_i. The average amount of words (including punctuation marks) increases if β is increased.

3.3 Ensemble Member Selection

Instead of using all recognizers produced by an ensemble generation method in one large ensemble, we apply an ensemble member selection strategy. The goal is to use only those recognizers that add a benefit to the ensemble, a method also known as overproduce-and-select [11].

On a validation set, we apply a greedy forward search to find the optimized ensemble [20]. First, the individual recognizer that performs best is selected as the first ensemble member. Then, we tentatively add each other available recognizers and measure the performance of the resulting new ensembles. The best performing ensemble continues, and, iteratively, we add the best remaining individual recognizer to the ensemble. We continue until the last available recognizer has been added. Then, we can determine the best performing ensemble among all generated ensembles. Thus, with this greedy search, we can not only find good performing ensembles but also optimize the ensemble size n.

4   Combination

Once having generated an ensemble of recognizers, an appropriate procedure must be defined to combine the outputs of the members to derive the final result of the ensemble.

Many methods for classifier combination have been proposed in the literature [10,11,34]. They depend on the type of output produced by the individual classifiers. If the output is only the best-ranked class, then majority voting can be applied. More sophisticated combination schemes look at dependencies between classifiers in the so-called Behavior-Knowledge Space (BKS) [13]. If the classifiers' output is a ranked list of classes, Borda count or related methods may apply [35]. In the most general case, a classifier outputs a confidence value for each class. The recognizer used in this paper outputs a confidence measure for each recognized word in a text line (see Sect. 2 for details).

The combination of handwritten text line recognizers differs from most other classifier combination problems due to the large number of classes, and because the output of the recognizers are sequences of classes rather than simply a single class. Given the large number of classes, standard statistical decision strategies as BKS are not usually feasible because not enough training data is available to estimate the required probabilities appropriately. Additionally, all classifier combination rules discussed above do not directly apply if each recognizer of the ensemble outputs a sequence of class names rather than a single class. Because of segmentation errors it cannot be assumed that the sequences produced by the different recognizers have the same length. Therefore, a synchronization mechanism is needed. It has been proposed to use dynamic programming techniques to align the individual outputs of the recognizers. However, this topic is still under research, and only a few solutions have been reported in the handwriting recognition literature [15,18,36].

4.1   ROVER Combination

The *Recognizer Output Voting Error Reduction* (ROVER) framework was developed in the domain of speech recognition and first used to combine multiple continuous speech recognizers [37]. The ROVER framework can be divided into two modules, alignment and voting.

In the alignment module, we find an alignment of n word sequences. For computational reasons, an incremental alignment algorithm is used. At the beginning, the first two sequences align with a standard string matching algorithm [38] resulting in a *Word Transition Network* (WTN). The third word sequence then

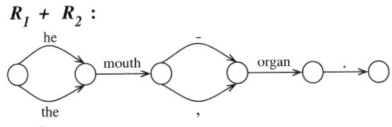

R_1: he mouth - organ.
R_2: the mouth, organ.
R_3: the truth - or go.

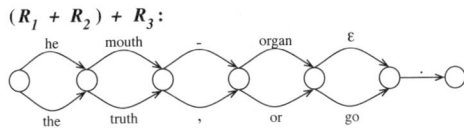

Fig. 3. Example of an iterative alignment of multiple recognition results

aligns with this WTN, resulting in a new WTN, which then aligns with the fourth word sequence, and so on. We refer to [37] for further details.

The iterative alignment procedure does not guarantee an optimal solution with minimal edit costs, as the alignment is affected by the order in which the word sequences are considered. In practice, however, the sub-optimal alignment produced by the algorithm often provides an adequate solution for the trade-off between computational complexity and alignment accuracy.

An example of multiple sequence alignment using ROVER is shown in Fig. 3. Given the image of the handwritten text, 'the mouth-organ', the recognizers R_1, R_2, and R_3 produce three different results. In the first step, the results of R_1 and R_2 align in a single WTN. Subsequently, the result of R_3 aligns with this WTN.

The voting module combines the different word sequences after they are aligned in a WTN. The goal is to identify the best scoring word sequence in the WTN and extract it as the final result.

The decisions are made individually for each segment of the WTN. Thus, neither adjacent segment has any effect on the current segment. Each decision depends only on the size n of the ensemble, on the number of occurrences m_w of a word w in the current segment, and on the confidence measure c_w of word w. The confidence measure c_w is defined as the maximum confidence measure among all occurrences of w at the current position in the WTN. For each possible word class w, we calculate the score s_w as follows:

$$s_w = \lambda \frac{m_w}{n} + (1 - \lambda)c_w \tag{2}$$

As a final result for the current segment, we then select the word class w with the highest score s_w.

To apply Eq. 2, we have to determine the value of λ experimentally. Parameter λ weights the impact of the number of occurrences against the confidence measure c_w. Additionally, we determine the confidence measure c_ϵ for null transition arcs, because no confidence score associates with a null transition ϵ. For this purpose, we probe various values of λ and c_ϵ on a validation set.

4.2   Statistical Decision

Various statistical decision strategies for combining the results of multiple classifiers have been proposed in the literature [10,13,39]. However, if the number of classes is large, most methods are not feasible because not enough training data is available to estimate the required probabilities sufficiently. In contrast, the statistical decision method described below can handle an arbitrarily large number of classes. It considers not the class label itself, but which recognizers output a particular class label. The decision method extends the ROVER combination scheme. It uses the same alignment module, but applies a strategy other than voting to find the final decision.

Having completed the alignment, we apply the statistical decision method to each segment of the WTN. A feature vector X_w is constructed for each word class w that occurs in the considered segment. The feature vector indicates whether word w is output by a specific recognizer:

$$X_w = (x_{w,C_1}, \ldots, x_{w,C_n}) \tag{3}$$

where

$$x_{w,C_i} = \begin{cases} 1 \text{ if classifier } C_i \text{ outputs } w \\ 0 \text{ else} \end{cases} \tag{4}$$

The feature vector X_w is used as input to a Multi-Layer Perceptron (MLP). The MLP consists of l input neurons, one hidden layer, and two output neurons. One output neuron represents the score for w being correct, whereas the other output neuron represents the score for w being incorrect under input X_w. The score for correctness estimates the probability $p(w$ is correct $|X_w)$.

The final word class $\hat{w}$ is then calculated by

$$\hat{w} = \underset{w}{argmax}\, p(w \text{ is correct}|X_w). \tag{5}$$

Note that, in contrast to the ROVER combination scheme, the statistical decision method does not require the recognizers to output confidence values. Thus, it applies more generally.

An example of the statistical decision method is given in Fig. 4. The scanned image of the handwritten text *'leave in the autumn'* appears in (a). In this example, three different recognizers R_1, R_2, R_3 are used. The outputs of these recognizers align in a WTN, as shown in (b). Next, a binary feature vector is built for each word that occurs in a segment according to Eq. 4. The resulting feature vectors are listed in (c). For each of these vectors, the MLP calculates the score for a correct decision (d). The final combination result, shown in (e), is then derived according to Eq. 5.

a) Input image of handwritten text:

leave in the autumn

(b) WTN including the aligned recognition results of R_1, R_2, R_3:

	Segment 1	Segment 2	Segment 3	Segment 4
R_1:	leave	is	the	autumn
R_2:	leave	in	that	autumn
R_3:	leave	is	that	august

(c) Input feature vectors:

Segment 1: $X_{leave} = (1, 1, 1)$
Segment 2: $X_{is} = (1, 0, 1)$ $X_{in} = (0, 1, 0)$
Segment 3: $X_{the} = (1, 0, 0)$ $X_{that} = (0, 1, 1)$
Segment 4: $X_{autumn} = (1, 1, 0)$ $X_{august} = (0, 0, 1)$

(d) Estimated probabilities for the correctness of a decision:

Segment 1: $p(correct|X_{leave}) = 0.9$
Segment 2: $p(correct|X_{is}) = 0.5$ $p(correct|X_{in}) = 0.7$
Segment 3: $p(correct|X_{the}) = 0.7$ $p(correct|X_{that}) = 0.3$
Segment 4: $p(correct|X_{autumn}) = 0.6$ $p(correct|X_{august}) = 0.2$

(e) Combination result:

leave in the autumn

Fig. 4. Example of the statistical decision procedure

5   Experimental Evaluation

In this section we present the experimental evaluation of the proposed ensemble methods. Two main experiments have been conducted. In the first experiment, ensembles derived from specific integration of a language model as described in Sect. 3.2 are evaluated. In the second experiment, the feature subspace method of Sect. 3.1 and the statistical decision method described in Sect. 4.2 are tested. The experimental setup of the two experiments differs slightly, thus the results cannot be compared directly.

All experiments reported in this paper make use of the HMM based recognition system described in Sect. 2. A bigram language model supports the HMM decoding. A writer-independent task has been considered, which implies that no information about the writers who contributed to the test set is available during the training and validation phase. The text lines we used for training, validation, and testing originate from the IAM[1] database [40].

The experimental setup used in the second experiment differs from the one of the first experiment in three aspects. First, it employs a larger test set containing 2,781 text lines by 161 writers (compared to 1,863 text lines from 128 writers). Secondly, more text trains the statistical language model. Thirdly, the lexicon

---

[1] The IAM database is publicly available for download at
http://www.iam.unibe.ch/~fki/iamDB

Table 1. Results on the test set. The columns show the different ensemble creation methods whereas the rows represent different combination strategies.

	Experiment 1 LM Integration	Experiment 2 Feature Subspace
Reference System	67.35%	64.48%
ROVER Combination	68.03%	65.29%
Statistical Decision	-	65.35%

used in the first experiment is closed over the test set and contains the 12,502 words given by the union of training, test, and validation set. In the second experiment, the 20,000 most frequent words that occur in the corpora used to train the language model are employed and no closing over the test set is done. Thus, words may appear in the test set that do not occur among the 20,000 most frequent words included in the lexicon. This scenario is more realistic than a closed test set because the texts in the test set are usually unknown in advance.

In the first experiment, we generate the recognizers by specific integration of a statistical language model. Next, we select the best performing ensemble on a validation set with the greedy forward search. Using the ROVER combination scheme, we achieve a statistical significant improvement in the recognition accuracy. The base recognition system attains a word level accuracy of 67.35%, whereas the ensemble method achieves 68.03%.

In the experiments using the feature subspace recognizer, not only ROVER is used to combine the recognizers' results but also the statistical decision approach described in Sect. 4.2. The single base recognizer achieves a word recognition accuracy of 64.48%. The ensemble combined with the ROVER algorithm attains an accuracy of 65.29%. The use of the novel statistical decision method slightly improves this accuracy to 65.35%. Compared to the base recognizer, the improvements are statistically significant, whereas the difference between ROVER and the statistical decision methods is not statistically significant.

Under both experimental setups, we improved the recognition performance by the use of ensemble methods. The results of the two experiments are summarised in Tab. 1.

6   Conclusions

In this paper we described recent work on multiple classifier methods for offline handwritten text line recognition. We discussed the individual handwriting recognizer, ensemble creation methods, and result combination schemes.

The handwritten text line recognizers described in this paper use hidden Markov models. After the normalization of the image, a sliding window method extracts nine geometrical features at each position. The character models use a mixture of twelve Gaussians and an individual number of states. A statistical language model supports the recognition step.

Different ensemble generation methods, based on either altering the training set or the system architecture, can build ensembles of handwritten text line recognizers. We examined the use of the random feature subspace methods, as well as the variation of the integration of the statistical language model in the recognition step, to achieve multiple recognizers. To select the final ensemble members, we applied a greedy forward search.

The combination of multiple text line recognizers requires a synchronization process because the output word sequences of the individual ensemble members might have different lengths. We applied the ROVER framework developed in the field of speech recognition. This framework consists of two modules, alignment and voting. Furthermore, we developed an extension to this framework by applying a statistical decision procedure instead of voting.

Experimental evaluation conducted on large sets of text lines from the IAM database shows that the proposed ensemble methods have the potential to perform statistically significantly better than a single recognizer.

Acknowledgment

This research was supported by the Swiss National Science Foundation (Nr. 200020-19124/1).

References

1. Impedovo, S., Wang, P., Bunke, H. (eds.): Automatic Bankcheck Processing. World Scientific, Singapore (1997)
2. Gorski, N., Anisimov, V., Augustin, E., Baret, O., Maximov, S.: Industrial bank check processing: the A2iA CheckReaderTM. International Journal on Document Analysis and Recognition 3(4), 1433–2833 (2001)
3. Mahadevan, U., Srihari, S.: Parsing and recognition of city, state, and zip codes in handwritten addresses. In: Proc. 5th International Conference on Document Analysis and Recognition, Bangalore, India, pp. 325–328 (1999)
4. Brakensiek, A., Rigoll, G.: Handwritten address recognition using hidden Markov models. In: Dengel, A., Junker, M., Weisbecker, A. (eds.) Reading and Learning, pp. 103–122. Springer, Heidelberg (2004)
5. Kim, G., Govindaraju, V., Srihari, S.: Architecture for handwritten text recognition systems. In: Lee, S.-W. (ed.) Advances in Handwriting Recognition, pp. 163–172. World Scientific Publ. Co., Singapore (1999)
6. Senior, A., Robinson, A.: An off-line cursive handwriting recognition system. IEEE Transactions on Pattern Analysis and Machine Intelligence 20(3), 309–321 (1998)
7. Vinciarelli, A., Bengio, S., Bunke, H.: Offline recognition of unconstrained handwritten texts using HMMs and statistical language models. IEEE Transactions on Pattern Analysis and Machine Intelligence 26(6), 709–720 (2004)
8. Zimmermann, M., Chappelier, J.C., Bunke, H.: Offline grammar-based recognition of handwritten sentences. IEEE Transactions on Pattern Analysis and Machine Intelligence 28(5), 818–821 (2006)
9. Dasarathy, B.V.: Decision Fusion. IEEE Computer Society Press, Los Alamitos, USA (1994)

10. Oza, N., Polikar, R., Kittler, J., Roli, F. (eds.): MCS 2005. LNCS, vol. 3541. Springer, Heidelberg (2005)
11. Kuncheva, L.I.: Combining Pattern Classifiers: Methods and Algorithms. John Wiley & Sons Inc., Chichester (2004)
12. Sirlantzkis, K., Fairhurst, M., Hoque, M.: Genetic algorithms for multi-classifier system configuration: A case study in character recognition. In: Kittler, J., Roli, F. (eds.) MCS 2001. LNCS, vol. 2096, pp. 99–108. Springer, Heidelberg (2001)
13. Huang, Y.S., Suen, C.: A method of combining multiple experts for the recognition of unconstrained handwritten numerals. IEEE Transactions on Pattern Analysis and Machine Intelligence 17(1), 90–94 (1995)
14. Oliveira, L.S., Morita, M., Sabourin, R.: Feature selection for ensembles applied to handwriting recognition. International Journal on Document Analysis and Recognition 8(4), 262–279 (2006)
15. Ye, X., Cheriet, M., Suen, C.Y.: StrCombo: combination of string recognizers. Pattern Recognition Letters 23, 381–394 (2002)
16. Gader, P., Mohamed, M., Keller, J.: Fusion of handwritten word classifiers. Pattern Recognition Letters 17, 577–584 (1996)
17. Günter, S., Bunke, H.: Ensembles of classifiers for handwritten word recognition. International Journal on Document Analysis and Recognition 5(4), 224–232 (2003)
18. Marti, U.-V., Bunke, H.: Use of positional information in sequence alignment for multiple classifier combination. In: Kittler, J., Roli, F. (eds.) MCS 2001. LNCS, vol. 2096, pp. 388–398. Springer, Heidelberg (2001)
19. Bertolami, R., Bunke, H.: Multiple handwritten text recognition systems derived from specific integration of a language model. In: Proc. 8th International Conference on Document Analysis and Recognition, Seoul, Korea, vol. 1, pp. 521–524 (2005)
20. Bertolami, R., Bunke, H.: Ensemble methods for handwritten text line recognition systems. In: Proc. International Conference on Systems, Man and Cybernetics, Hawaii, USA, pp. 2334–2339 (2005)
21. Bertolami, R., Bunke, H.: Diversity analysis for ensembles of word sequence recognisers. In: Yeung, D.-Y., et al. (eds.) SSPR 2006 and SPR 2006. LNCS, vol. 4109, pp. 667–686. Springer, Heidelberg (2006)
22. Bertolami, R., Bunke, H.: Multiple classifier methods for offline handwritten text line recognition. In: Haindl, M., Kittler, J., Roli, F. (eds.) MCS 2007. LNCS, vol. 4472, pp. 72–81. Springer, Heidelberg (2007)
23. Marti, U.V., Bunke, H.: Using a statistical language model to improve the performance of an HMM-based cursive handwriting recognition system. International Journal of Pattern Recognition and Artificial Intelligence 15, 65–90 (2001)
24. Bertolami, R., Zimmermann, M., Bunke, H.: Rejection strategies for offline handwritten text line recognition. Pattern Recognition Letters 27(16), 2005–2012 (2006)
25. Dietterich, T.: Ensemble methods in machine learning. In: 1st International Workshop on Multiple Classifier Systems, Cagliari, Italy, pp. 1–15 (2000)
26. Brown, G., Wyatt, J., Harris, R., Yao, X.: Diversity creation methods: A survey and categorisation. Information Fusion 6, 5–20 (2005)
27. Windeatt, T.: Diversity measures for multiple classifier system analysis and design. Information Fusion 6(1), 21–36 (2004)
28. Kohavi, R.: A study of cross-validation and bootstrap for accuracy estimation and model selection. In: Proc. International Joint Conference on Artificial Intelligence, pp. 1137–1145 (1995)
29. Breiman, L.: Bagging predictors. Machine Learning 24(2), 123–140 (1996)

30. Freund, Y., Schapire, R.E.: A decision-theoretic generalization of on-line learning and an application to boosting. In: Proc. European Conference on Computational Learning Theory, pp. 23–37 (1995)
31. Partridge, D., Yates, W.B.: Engineering multiversion neural-net systems. Neural Computation 8(4), 869–893 (1996)
32. Ho, T.K.: The random space method for constructing decision forests. IEEE Transactions on Pattern Analysis and Machine Intelligence 20(8), 832–844 (1998)
33. Zeppenfeld, T., Finke, M., Ries, K., Westphal, M., Waibel, A.: Recognition of conversational telephone speech using the janus speech engine. In: Proc. International Conference on Acoustics, Speech, and Signal Processing, Munich, Germany, pp. 1815–1818 (1997)
34. Rahmann, A., Fairhurst, M.: Multiple expert classification: A new methodology for parallel decision fusion. International Journal on Document Analysis and Recognition 3(1), 40–55 (2000)
35. Ho, T.K., Hull, J.J., Srihari, S.N.: Decision combination in multiple classifier systems. IEEE Transactions on Pattern Analysis and Machine Intelligence 16(1), 66–75 (1994)
36. Wang, W., Brakensiek, A., Rigoll, G.: Combination of multiple classifiers for handwritten word recognition. In: Proc. 8th International Workshop on Frontiers in Handwriting Recognition, Niagara-on-the-Lake, Canada, pp. 117–122 (2002)
37. Fiscus, J.: A post-processing system to yield reduced word error rates: Recognizer output voting error reduction. In: Proc. IEEE Workshop on Automatic Speech Recognition and Understanding, Santa Barbara, pp. 347–352 (1997)
38. Wagner, R., Fischer, M.: The string-to-string correction problem. Journal of the ACM 21(1), 168–173 (1974)
39. Xu, L., Krzyzak, A., Suen, C.Y.: Methods of combining multiple classifiers and their applications to handwriting recognition. IEEE Transactions on Systems, Man, and Cybernetics 22(3), 418–435 (1992)
40. Marti, U.V., Bunke, H.: The IAM-database: an English sentence database for offline handwriting recognition. International Journal on Document Analysis and Recognition 5, 39–46 (2002)

Author Index

AbdulKader, Ahmad   70

Ball, Gregory R.   57
Belaïd, Abdel   36
Bertolami, Roman   265
Bunke, Horst   265

Chang, Fu   161
Cheriet, Mohamed   1
Choisy, Christophe   36

Ding, Xiaoqing   196

El Abed, Haikal   82

Fujisawa, Hiromichi   129

Ge, Yong   152
Guo, Feng-Jun   152

Izadi, Sara   22

Kimura, Fumitaka   251
Kitadai, Akihito   170

Liu, Cheng-Lin   104
Liu, Hailong   196
Lopresti, Daniel   218

MacRostie, Ehry   231
Märgner, Volker   82

Nagy, George   218
Nakagawa, Masaki   170
Natarajan, Prem   231

Oda, Hideto   170
Onuma, Motoki   170

Pal, Umapada   251
Prasad, Rohit   231

Sadri, Javad   22
Saleem, Shirin   231
Seth, Sharad   218
Sharma, Nabin   251
Solimanpour, Farshid   22
Srihari, Sargur N.   57
Srinivasan, Harish   57
Subramanian, Krishna   231
Suen, Ching Y.   22

Tokuno, Junko   170

Wakabayashi, Tetsushi   251

Zhang, Xiaoli   218
Zhang, Yun   152
Zhen, Li-Xin   152
Zhu, Bilan   170

Printing: Mercedes-Druck, Berlin
Binding: Stein+Lehmann, Berlin

Lecture Notes in Computer Science

Sublibrary 6: Image Processing, Computer Vision, Pattern Recognition, and Graphics

For information about Vols. 1– 1679
please contact your bookseller or Springer

Vol. 4958: V.E. Brimkov, R.P. Barneva, H.A. Hauptman (Eds.), Combinatorial Image Analysis. XVI, 446 pages. 2008.

Vol. 4931: G. Sommer, R. Klette (Eds.), Robot Vision. XI, 468 pages. 2008.

Vol. 4901: D. Zhang (Ed.), Medical Biometrics. XII, 324 pages. 2007.

Vol. 4844: Y. Yagi, S.B. Kang, I.S. Kweon, H. Zha (Eds.), Computer Vision – ACCV 2007, Part II. XXVIII, 915 pages. 2007.

Vol. 4843: Y. Yagi, S.B. Kang, I.S. Kweon, H. Zha (Eds.), Computer Vision – ACCV 2007, Part I. XXVIII, 969 pages. 2007.

Vol. 4842: G. Bebis, R. Boyle, B. Parvin, D. Koracin, N. Paragios, S.-M. Tanveer, T. Ju, Z. Liu, S. Coquillart, C. Cruz-Neira, T. Müller, T. Malzbender (Eds.), Advances in Visual Computing, Part II. XXXIII, 827 pages. 2007.

Vol. 4841: G. Bebis, R. Boyle, B. Parvin, D. Koracin, N. Paragios, S.-M. Tanveer, T. Ju, Z. Liu, S. Coquillart, C. Cruz-Neira, T. Müller, T. Malzbender (Eds.), Advances in Visual Computing, Part I. XXXIII, 831 pages. 2007.

Vol. 4815: A. Ghosh, R.K. De, S.K. Pal (Eds.), Pattern Recognition and Machine Intelligence. XIX, 677 pages. 2007.

Vol. 4814: A. Elgammal, B. Rosenhahn, R. Klette (Eds.), Human Motion – Understanding, Modeling, Capture and Animation. X, 329 pages. 2007.

Vol. 4792: N. Ayache, S. Ourselin, A. Maeder (Eds.), Medical Image Computing and Computer-Assisted Intervention – MICCAI 2007, Part II. XLVI, 988 pages. 2007.

Vol. 4791: N. Ayache, S. Ourselin, A. Maeder (Eds.), Medical Image Computing and Computer-Assisted Intervention – MICCAI 2007, Part I. XLVI, 1012 pages. 2007.

Vol. 4781: G. Qiu, C. Leung, X.-Y. Xue, R. Laurini (Eds.), Advances in Visual Information Systems. XIII, 582 pages. 2007.

Vol. 4778: S.K. Zhou, W. Zhao, X. Tang, S. Gong (Eds.), Analysis and Modeling of Faces and Gestures. X, 305 pages. 2007.

Vol. 4768: D. Doermann, S. Jaeger (Eds.), Arabic and Chinese Handwriting Recognition. VIII, 279 pages. 2008.

Vol. 4756: L. Rueda, D. Mery, J. Kittler (Eds.), Progress in Pattern Recognition, Image Analysis and Applications. XXI, 989 pages. 2007.

Vol. 4738: A. Paiva, R. Prada, R.W. Picard (Eds.), Affective Computing and Intelligent Interaction. XVIII, 781 pages. 2007.

Vol. 4729: F. Mele, G. Ramella, S. Santillo, F. Ventriglia (Eds.), Advances in Brain, Vision, and Artificial Intelligence. XVI, 618 pages. 2007.

Vol. 4713: F.A. Hamprecht, C. Schnörr, B. Jähne (Eds.), Pattern Recognition. XIII, 560 pages. 2007.

Vol. 4679: A.L. Yuille, S.-C. Zhu, D. Cremers, Y. Wang (Eds.), Energy Minimization Methods in Computer Vision and Pattern Recognition. XII, 494 pages. 2007.

Vol. 4678: J. Blanc-Talon, W. Philips, D. Popescu, P. Scheunders (Eds.), Advanced Concepts for Intelligent Vision Systems. XXIII, 1100 pages. 2007.

Vol. 4673: W.G. Kropatsch, M. Kampel, A. Hanbury (Eds.), Computer Analysis of Images and Patterns. XX, 1006 pages. 2007.

Vol. 4642: S.-W. Lee, S.Z. Li (Eds.), Advances in Biometrics. XX, 1216 pages. 2007.

Vol. 4633: M. Kamel, A. Campilho (Eds.), Image Analysis and Recognition. XII, 1312 pages. 2007.

Vol. 4584: N. Karssemeijer, B. Lelieveldt (Eds.), Information Processing in Medical Imaging. XX, 777 pages. 2007.

Vol. 4569: A. Butz, B. Fisher, A. Krüger, P. Olivier, S. Owada (Eds.), Smart Graphics. IX, 237 pages. 2007.

Vol. 4538: F. Escolano, M. Vento (Eds.), Graph-Based Representations in Pattern Recognition. XII, 416 pages. 2007.

Vol. 4522: B.K. Ersbøll, K.S. Pedersen (Eds.), Image Analysis. XVIII, 989 pages. 2007.

Vol. 4485: F. Sgallari, A. Murli, N. Paragios (Eds.), Scale Space and Variational Methods in Computer Vision. XV, 931 pages. 2007.

Vol. 4478: J. Martí, J.M. Benedí, A.M. Mendonça, J. Serrat (Eds.), Pattern Recognition and Image Analysis, Part II. XXVII, 657 pages. 2007.

Vol. 4477: J. Martí, J.M. Benedí, A.M. Mendonça, J. Serrat (Eds.), Pattern Recognition and Image Analysis, Part I. XXVII, 625 pages. 2007.

Vol. 4472: M. Haindl, J. Kittler, F. Roli (Eds.), Multiple Classifier Systems. XI, 524 pages. 2007.

Vol. 4466: F.B. Sachse, G. Seemann (Eds.), Functional Imaging and Modeling of the Heart. XV, 486 pages. 2007.

Vol. 4418: A. Gagalowicz, W. Philips (Eds.), Computer Vision/Computer Graphics Collaboration Techniques. XV, 620 pages. 2007.

Vol. 4417: A. Kerren, A. Ebert, J. Meyer (Eds.), Human-Centered Visualization Environments. XIX, 403 pages. 2007.

Vol. 4391: Y. Stylianou, M. Faundez-Zanuy, A. Esposito (Eds.), Progress in Nonlinear Speech Processing. XII, 269 pages. 2007.

Vol. 4370: P.P. Lévy, B. Le Grand, F. Poulet, M. Soto, L. Darago, L. Toubiana, J.-F. Vibert (Eds.), Pixelization Paradigm. XV, 279 pages. 2007.

Vol. 4358: R. Vidal, A. Heyden, Y. Ma (Eds.), Dynamical Vision. IX, 329 pages. 2007.

Vol. 4338: P.K. Kalra, S. Peleg (Eds.), Computer Vision, Graphics and Image Processing. XV, 965 pages. 2006.

Vol. 4319: L.-W. Chang, W.-N. Lie (Eds.), Advances in Image and Video Technology. XXVI, 1347 pages. 2006.

Vol. 4292: G. Bebis, R. Boyle, B. Parvin, D. Koracin, P. Remagnino, A. Nefian, G. Meenakshisundaram, V. Pascucci, J. Zara, J. Molineros, H. Theisel, T. Malzbender (Eds.), Advances in Visual Computing, Part II. XXXII, 906 pages. 2006.

Vol. 4291: G. Bebis, R. Boyle, B. Parvin, D. Koracin, P. Remagnino, A. Nefian, G. Meenakshisundaram, V. Pascucci, J. Zara, J. Molineros, H. Theisel, T. Malzbender (Eds.), Advances in Visual Computing, Part I. XXXI, 916 pages. 2006.

Vol. 4245: A. Kuba, L.G. Nyúl, K. Palágyi (Eds.), Discrete Geometry for Computer Imagery. XIII, 688 pages. 2006.

Vol. 4241: R.R. Beichel, M. Sonka (Eds.), Computer Vision Approaches to Medical Image Analysis. XI, 262 pages. 2006.

Vol. 4225: J.F. Martínez-Trinidad, J.A. Carrasco Ochoa, J. Kittler (Eds.), Progress in Pattern Recognition, Image Analysis and Applications. XIX, 995 pages. 2006.

Vol. 4191: R. Larsen, M. Nielsen, J. Sporring (Eds.), Medical Image Computing and Computer-Assisted Intervention – MICCAI 2006, Part II. XXXVIII, 981 pages. 2006.

Vol. 4190: R. Larsen, M. Nielsen, J. Sporring (Eds.), Medical Image Computing and Computer-Assisted Intervention – MICCAI 2006, Part I. XXXVVIII, 949 pages. 2006.

Vol. 4179: J. Blanc-Talon, W. Philips, D. Popescu, P. Scheunders (Eds.), Advanced Concepts for Intelligent Vision Systems. XXIV, 1224 pages. 2006.

Vol. 4174: K. Franke, K.-R. Müller, B. Nickolay, R. Schäfer (Eds.), Pattern Recognition. XX, 773 pages. 2006.

Vol. 4170: J. Ponce, M. Hebert, C. Schmid, A. Zisserman (Eds.), Toward Category-Level Object Recognition. XI, 618 pages. 2006.

Vol. 4153: N. Zheng, X. Jiang, X. Lan (Eds.), Advances in Machine Vision, Image Processing, and Pattern Analysis. XIII, 506 pages. 2006.

Vol. 4142: A. Campilho, M. Kamel (Eds.), Image Analysis and Recognition, Part II. XXVII, 923 pages. 2006.

Vol. 4141: A. Campilho, M. Kamel (Eds.), Image Analysis and Recognition, Part I. XXVIII, 939 pages. 2006.

Vol. 4122: R. Stiefelhagen, J.S. Garofolo (Eds.), Multimodal Technologies for Perception of Humans. XII, 360 pages. 2007.

Vol. 4109: D.-Y. Yeung, J.T. Kwok, A. Fred, F. Roli, D. de Ridder (Eds.), Structural, Syntactic, and Statistical Pattern Recognition. XXI, 939 pages. 2006.

Vol. 4091: G.-Z. Yang, T. Jiang, D. Shen, L. Gu, J. Yang (Eds.), Medical Imaging and Augmented Reality. XIII, 399 pages. 2006.

Vol. 4073: A. Butz, B. Fisher, A. Krüger, P. Olivier (Eds.), Smart Graphics. XI, 263 pages. 2006.

Vol. 4069: F.J. Perales, R.B. Fisher (Eds.), Articulated Motion and Deformable Objects. XV, 526 pages. 2006.

Vol. 4057: J.P.W. Pluim, B. Likar, F.A. Gerritsen (Eds.), Biomedical Image Registration. XII, 324 pages. 2006.

Vol. 4046: S.M. Astley, M. Brady, C. Rose, R. Zwiggelaar (Eds.), Digital Mammography. XVI, 654 pages. 2006.

Vol. 4040: R. Reulke, U. Eckardt, B. Flach, U. Knauer, K. Polthier (Eds.), Combinatorial Image Analysis. XII, 482 pages. 2006.

Vol. 4035: T. Nishita, Q. Peng, H.-P. Seidel (Eds.), Advances in Computer Graphics. XX, 771 pages. 2006.

Vol. 3979: T.S. Huang, N. Sebe, M. Lew, V. Pavlović, M. Kölsch, A. Galata, B. Kisačanin (Eds.), Computer Vision in Human-Computer Interaction. XII, 121 pages. 2006.

Vol. 3954: A. Leonardis, H. Bischof, A. Pinz (Eds.), Computer Vision – ECCV 2006, Part IV. XVII, 613 pages. 2006.

Vol. 3953: A. Leonardis, H. Bischof, A. Pinz (Eds.), Computer Vision – ECCV 2006, Part III. XVII, 649 pages. 2006.

Vol. 3952: A. Leonardis, H. Bischof, A. Pinz (Eds.), Computer Vision – ECCV 2006, Part II. XVII, 661 pages. 2006.

Vol. 3951: A. Leonardis, H. Bischof, A. Pinz (Eds.), Computer Vision – ECCV 2006, Part I. XXXV, 639 pages. 2006.

Vol. 3948: H.I. Christensen, H.-H. Nagel (Eds.), Cognitive Vision Systems. VIII, 367 pages. 2006.

Vol. 3926: W. Liu, J. Lladós (Eds.), Graphics Recognition. XII, 428 pages. 2006.

Vol. 3872: H. Bunke, A.L. Spitz (Eds.), Document Analysis Systems VII. XIII, 630 pages. 2006.

Vol. 3852: P.J. Narayanan, S.K. Nayar, H.-Y. Shum (Eds.), Computer Vision – ACCV 2006, Part II. XXXI, 977 pages. 2006.

Vol. 3851: P.J. Narayanan, S.K. Nayar, H.-Y. Shum (Eds.), Computer Vision – ACCV 2006, Part I. XXXI, 973 pages. 2006.

Vol. 3832: D. Zhang, A.K. Jain (Eds.), Advances in Biometrics. XX, 796 pages. 2005.

Vol. 3736: S. Bres, R. Laurini (Eds.), Visual Information and Information Systems. XI, 291 pages. 2006.

Vol. 3667: W.J. MacLean (Ed.), Spatial Coherence for Visual Motion Analysis. IX, 141 pages. 2006.

Vol. 3417: B. Jähne, R. Mester, E. Barth, H. Scharr (Eds.), Complex Motion. X, 235 pages. 2007.

Vol. 2396: T.M. Caelli, A. Amin, R.P.W. Duin, M.S. Kamel, D. de Ridder (Eds.), Structural, Syntactic, and Statistical Pattern Recognition. XVI, 863 pages. 2002.